Progressive New York

Progressive New York

Change and Reform in the Empire State,
1900–1920:
A Reader

Edited by

BRUCE W. DEARSTYNE

Cover credit: Women strike pickets, New York. Bain News Service, Library of Congress, Prints and Photographs Division

Published by State University of New York Press, Albany

© 2024 State University of New York

All rights reserved

Printed in the United States of America

No part of this book may be used or reproduced in any manner whatsoever without written permission. No part of this book may be stored in a retrieval system or transmitted in any form or by any means including electronic, electrostatic, magnetic tape, mechanical, photocopying, recording, or otherwise without the prior permission in writing of the publisher.

For information, contact State University of New York Press, Albany, NY
www.sunypress.edu

Library of Congress Cataloging-in-Publication Data

Name: Dearstyne, Bruce W., 1944– compiler.
Title: Progressive New York : change and reform in the Empire State, 1900–1920: a reader / Bruce W. Dearstyne.
Description: Albany : State University of New York Press, [2024]. | Includes bibliographical references and index.
Identifiers: LCCN 2023039241 | ISBN 9781438497372 (hardcover : alk. paper) | ISBN 9781438497396 (ebook) | ISBN 9781438497389 (pbk. : alk. paper)
Subjects: LCSH: New York (N.Y.)—History—1898-1951—Sources. | New York (N.Y.)—Social conditions—20th century—Sources.
Classification: LCC F128.5 .D44 2024 | DDC 974.7/04—dc23/eng/20231106
LC record available at https://lccn.loc.gov/2023039241

10 9 8 7 6 5 4 3 2 1

Contents

Acknowledgments	xv
Introduction	1

Chapter 1. Gauging the Tenor of the Times | 19

Extreme Wealth on Display	20
From *The Reign of Gilt* (1905) by David Graham Phillips	20
From "Drift" to "Mastery"	23
From *Drift and Mastery* (1914) by Walter Lippmann	24
Making Systematic, Incremental Progress	26
From *The New Democracy* (1912) by Walter E. Weyl	26
The Rising Standard of Living	30
From *The City Worker's World in America* (1917) by Mary K. Simkhovitch	31
The "Social Gospel" Fuels Progressivism	34
From *Christianity and the Social Crisis* (1907) by Walter Rauschenbusch	34
A Skeptical View of Modern Trends	39
From "A Layman's Views of an Art Exhibition," *Outlook* (1913) by Theodore Roosevelt	40

A Plea for Rural Values 43
    From *The Country Life Movement in the United States* (1915)
    by Liberty Hyde Bailey 44

The Anarchist's Plea 48
    From *What I Believe* (1908) by Emma Goldman 49

Chapter 2. Building Grand Enterprises | 55

A Grand Expo in Buffalo 56
    From *Official Catalogue and Guide Book to the Pan-American Exposition* (1901) 57

A New Cross-State Canal 61
    From *The Thousand-Ton Barge Improvement* (1903) by
    Canal Improvement State Committee 61

New York City Opens Its Subway 64
    From "Our Subway Open, 150,000 Try It," *New York Times*
    (October 28, 1904) 64

An Outstanding New Venue for Baseball 69
    From "Ebbets Field Has No Rival in Baseball," *New York Tribune*
    (April 6, 1913) 70

Pioneering in Aviation 72
    From "Flight Down the Hudson River from Albany to
    New York City," *The Curtiss Aviation Book* (1912)
    by Glenn Hammond Curtiss 72

A Grand New Train Station 76
    From "New Grand Central Terminal Opens Its Doors,"
    New York Times (February 2, 1913) 76

Technology and Innovation 79
    From *Book of the Kodak Exhibition* (1912) by Eastman Kodak
    Company 79

Chapter 3. Reforming Politics and Government | 83

Politics, Government, and "Honest Graft"	84
From *Plunkett of Tammany Hall* (1905) by George Washington Plunkett and William L. Riordon	85
"Muckrakers" Help Propel Progressivism	87
From "Concerning Three Articles in this Number of McClure's and a Coincidence That May Set Us Thinking," *McClure's* (1903) by S. S. McClure	88
Newspapers Expose Political Corruption	89
From *New York Evening Post* (January 18, 1910)	90
The "Treason of the Senate"	93
From "The Treason of the Senate: New York's Misrepresentatives," *Cosmopolitan Magazine* (March 1906) by David Graham Phillips	93
Direct Primaries	95
From "Message to the Legislature" (January 6, 1909) in *Public Papers of Charles E. Hughes, Governor* by Governor Charles Evans Hughes	96
A Day of Reform Triumph	99
From "Message to the Legislature" (December 8, 1913) in *Public Papers of Martin H. Glynn, Governor* by Governor Martin H. Glynn	100
From "All Glynn Bills to Pass This Week," *New York Times* (December 10, 1913)	101
New York's Progressive Party Presents an Aspirational Agenda	102
From *State Platform, National Progressive Party of the State of New York Adopted by the State Convention, Syracuse, N.Y. Sept. 5, 1912* (1912) by National Progressive Party of the State of New York	103

viii | Contents

Veering Away from Progressivism ... 108
    From *Revolutionary Radicalism* (1920) by the Joint Legislative
    Committee Investigating Seditious Activities ... 109

Chapter 4. Improving People's Lives | 117

Educating Young New Yorkers ... 118
    From *American Education* (1909) by Andrew S. Draper ... 119

Revealing How Poor New Yorkers Live ... 121
    From *How the Other Half Lives: Studies Among the Tenements
    of New York* (1901) by Jacob Riis ... 122

The Benefits of Tenement House Reform ... 124
    From *The Tenement House Problem* (1908) edited by
    Robert W. DeForest and Lawrence Veiller ... 125

Charitable Assistance for New York's Poor ... 128
    From *Twenty-Sixth Annual Report for the Year Ending
    September 30, 1908* (1908) by the Charity Organization Society
    of the City of New York ... 129

Helping People Take Care of Themselves ... 132
    From *For You: It is Hard to Get Money, It is Harder to Spend
    it Right, Health is Wealth* (1910) by Charity Organization
    Society of New York and New York City Tenement House
    Department ... 133

Settlement Houses and Visiting Nurses Ease City Life ... 136
    From *The House on Henry Street* (1915) by Lillian D. Wald ... 137

Restricting Alcoholic Beverages ... 140
    From "New York" in *Proceedings of the Nineteenth National
    Convention of the Anti-Saloon League of America* (1919)
    by William H. Anderson ... 140

Censorship Impacts Lives ... 143
    From *Anthony Comstock: Roundsman of the Lord* (1927)
    by Haywood Broun and Margaret Leech ... 143

Strengthening Public Health 146
From *Thirty Sixth Annual Report of the State Department of Health for the Year Ending December 31, 1915* (1915)
by New York State Department of Health 147

Protecting Rural New York 151
From *Powers and Territory of the New York State Troopers* (1918)
by Committee for State Police 151

Chapter 5. Strengthening Women's Status | 157

Women Struggle for Equality in the Workplace 158
From *A Woman of Fifty* (1924) by Rheta Childe Dorr 159

Women Already Influence Public Policy; They Should Be Able to Vote 162
From "The Legislative Influence of Unenfranchised Women" (1914) by Mary Ritter Beard 162

Making the Case for Woman Suffrage 165
From "What Woman Suffrage Stands For" (1917) booklet by New York State Woman Suffrage Party 166

From "Twelve Reasons Why Women Should Vote" (1917) booklet by New York State Woman Suffrage Party 166

From "Modern Representative Government" (1917) booklet by New York State Woman Suffrage Party 167

From "Suffrage as a War Measure" (1917) booklet by New York State Woman Suffrage Party 168

Securing the Right to Vote 169
From *Woman Suffrage and Politics: The Inner Story of the Suffrage Movement* (1923), by Carrie Chapman Catt and Nettie Rogers Schuler 170

Women Can Vote, What Comes Next? 174
From "Now We Can Begin," *The Liberator* (1920) by Crystal Eastman 174

x | Contents

Public Support Encourages Women's Labor Activism	178
From "The Working Girls and Women of Rochester," *The Common Good: An Independent Magazine of Civic and Social Rochester* (1913) by Edwin and Catherine Rumball	179
Advocating for "Voluntary Womanhood"	180
From *Woman and the New Race* (1921) by Margaret Sanger	181

Chapter 6. Welcoming Newcomers | 187

Immigrants Encounter New York	188
From *The Rise of David Levinsky* (1917) by Abraham Cahan	189
Adjusting to American Ways	191
From "The Making of an American," *Outlook* (1903) by David Blaustein	192
Aiding Immigrants	195
From "Solving the Immigration Problem," *Outlook* (1904) by Gino Carlo Speranza	196
Explaining the Immigrant Experience	201
From *An American in the Making: The Life Story of an Immigrant* (1917) by Marcus Eli Ravage	201
Documenting Immigrants' Challenges in New York	205
From *Report of the Commission on Immigration of the State of New York* (1909)	206
Asserting That Some Newcomers Are a Threat	211
From *The Passing of the Great Race* (1916) by Madison Grant	212
Defining New York's "Cultural Pluralism"	214
From "Democracy Versus the Melting Pot," *The Nation* (1915) by Horace M. Kallen	215

Chapter 7. Reckoning with Race | 221

Probing Black New Yorkers' Burdens	222
From *Half a Man: The Status of the Negro in New York* (1911) by Mary White Ovington	223

Contents | xi

An Outburst of Cultural Achievement 226
    From *The New Negro: An Interpretation* (1925) by Allain Locke 227

Harlem Becomes a Center of Black Culture 230
    From "Harlem: The Cultural Center," in Alain Locke, ed.,
    The New Negro (1925) by James Weldon Johnson 230

New York's Racial Ambivalence 234
    From "The Paradox of Color" in Alain Locke, ed., *The New
    Negro* (1925) by Walter White 235

Black Women Cope with Racism 238
    From "The Double Task: The Struggle of Negro Women for Sex
    and Race Emancipation," *Survey Graphic: Harlem Number 1*
    (1925) by Elise Johnson McDougald 238

The Push for Racial Justice 244
    From *The Crisis: A Record of the Darker Races* (1910 and 1911)
    by W. E. B. DuBois 245

Chapter 8. Regulating Business | 253

Regulation of Insurance Companies 254
    From *Report of the Joint Committee of the Senate and Assembly
    of the State of New York Appointed to Investigate the Affairs of
    Life Insurance Companies* (1906) 255

A New Governor Sets a Progressive Tone 258
    From "Inaugural Address" (1907) by Charles Evans Hughes 259

Asserting State Authority over Public Utilities 261
    From "Governor Hughes," *Outlook* (1908) by Burton J. Hendrick 262

Lenient State Regulation 266
    From "The Work of the Public Service Commission, Second
    District..." (1908) by Frank W. Stevens 266

Reigning In the New York-Led "Money Trust" 269
    From *Report of the Committee Appointed Pursuant to House
    Resolutions 429 and 504 to Investigate the Concentration of
    Control of Money and Credit* (1913) 270

xii | Contents

Chapter 9. Helping Workers | 277

Industrial Morality and Social Progress 278
    From *Modern Industry in Relation to the Family, Health,*
    Education, Morality (1914) by Florence Kelley 279

Ending Child Labor 282
    "The City's Child Labor," *New York Tribune*, January 2, 1903 . . . 283

    "Little Wage Earners," *New York Tribune*, February 13, 1903 . . . 284

From Tragedy to Action 284
    From speech by Rose Schneiderman in *The Survey* (1911) 285

A Progressive Industrial Code 286
    From *Preliminary Report of the Factory Investigating Commission*
    (1912) 287

Special Protection for Women Workers 291
    From *Women in the Bookbinding Trade* (1913)
    by Mary Van Kleeck 291

Workers' Compensation for On-the-Job Injuries 295
    From *Report to the Legislature . . . by the Commission Appointed*
    Under Chapter 518 of the Laws of 1909 to Inquire Into the
    Question of Employers' Liability (1910) 296

Documenting the Harmful Effects of Long Working Hours 298
    From *Fatigue and Efficiency: A Study in Industry* (1912)
    by Josephine Goldmark 299

Workers Take Direct Action 301
    From "The Spirit of the Girl Strikers," *Outlook* (1910)
    by Miriam Finn Scott 302

Unions Advance Labor 305
    From *Organized Labor: Its Struggles, Its Enemies and Its Fool*
    Friends (1904) by Samuel Gompers 305

Strong Unions Get Results through Collective Bargaining — 308
From "Editorial: Manufacturers Plunged Cloak Industry Into War," *The Ladies' Garment Worker* (1916) — 308

Chapter 10. Appealing to History | 313

The "New History" Makes History More Relevant — 314
From "The New History" in *Proceedings of the American Philosophical Society* (1911) by James Harvey Robinson — 315

Putting History to Work for Progressivism — 318
From *An Economic Interpretation of the Constitution of the United States* (1913) by Charles A. Beard — 319

Public Pageants Boost New York History — 320
From *The Hudson-Fulton Celebration, 1909* (1910) by Herman Hagaman Hall — 321

Students Need to Study History — 323
From *No Mummified History in New York Schools* (1912) by Andrew S. Draper — 324

Making American History More Engaging and Relevant — 326
From *Syllabus for the Secondary Schools* (1910) by the State Education Department — 327

History Should Aid Students' Social Development — 330
From *The School and Society* (1915) by John Dewey — 331

A New Departure for Higher Education — 333
From *A Proposal for an Independent School of Social Science for Men and Women* (1919) by New School for Social Research — 334

Writing a First Draft of History — 336
From *The Story of an Epochmaking Movement* (1926) by Maud Nathan — 337

Selected Bibliography — 343

Index — 349

Acknowledgments

I am very grateful to everyone at SUNY Press for their dedication and work that makes books like this possible. Senior acquisitions editor Richard Carlin deserves special thanks for suggesting the topic of the book and advising me on its development. Jenn Bennett-Genthner, manuscript editorial manager, shepherded it through the production process. Michelle Alamillo, promotions manager, and Michael Campochiaro, senior marketing manager, led in marketing and promoting the book. Everyone at SUNY Press made the whole process easy. Thank you all!

Cyra Nealon, my sister-in-law, and Mary Foglia, my niece, read the draft of the book and identified changes and corrections that significantly improved the final product. Mary also suggested a number of items for inclusion in the book. I am very grateful to them for all their work.

Several other people also made suggestions for documents for the book. I very much appreciate their recommendations even though I wasn't able to include everything they suggested. Thank you, Sherri Cash, associate professor, Utica University; Susan Goodier, assistant professor, SUNY Oneonta; Edward Knoblauch, who teaches New York history at SUNY Adirondack and other colleges; Susan Lewis, professor emerita, SUNY New Paltz; and Shannon Risk, associate professor, Niagara University.

I am also grateful for the comments and suggestions from three anonymous readers who reviewed the draft of the manuscript. Their recommendations were very helpful as I made the final revisions of the draft.

My family has been a constant source of support as I worked on this book and previous ones. My four grandchildren are always a source of joy and inspiration. I hope this book will deepen their appreciation of the history of their state and of history generally. Thank you for everything, Stella Roberts, Maddie Roberts, Jack Gregory, and Abbie Gregory.

Finally, I dedicate this book to my wife, Susan V. Dearstyne. She read and commented on it in draft, made many helpful recommendations, and also indexed it. Her patience, wisdom, insights, and encouragement have sustained my life and work for five decades. She has been essential to all my books including this one. Without Susan's constant help and support, I could not have undertaken and completed the book.

Introduction

The Advent of Progressivism

The progressive era—circa 1900 to 1920—was a time of ferment and change in New York (and the rest of the nation). *Progressives* and *progressive reformers*, as the terms are used in this book, mean people and groups that were dissatisfied with, and determined to improve, the status quo.

The term is meant to be broad, encompassing a wide range of people. Progressives came from all sectors of society. They included poor people, middle class, and the wealthy. Some inherited wealth and social status, bur more were self-made people who excelled on their own. Some worked as individuals, but many united with other like-minded people in groups or organizations. The progressives in this book included, but went far beyond, the members or candidates of the short-lived political Progressive Party of 1912. Some were politicians, but the majority were social reformers, advocates, journalists, academics, novelists, ministers, inventors, champions of various causes, or ordinary citizens moved to take some action.

They are also much different from "progressives" today, who favor dramatic expansion of government programs and government intervention in the economy and society. The progressives in this book were less interventionist, more tentative and experimental in their approaches, more modest in their expectations. The progressive reform impulse was felt by individuals, groups, and both of New York's mainline political parties.

The progressive era was a time for public reckoning with social and economic issues that had accumulated and intensified in the late nineteenth century. New York (and the nation) expanded in population, cities grew to overshadow rural areas, and complex industries rose to dominate the economy. Americans felt buffeted by the social and economic disruptions caused by industrialization, urbanization, and immigration. These developments produced a sense of "dislocation and bewilderment." Many people were apprehensive, swept along by large, impersonal forces beyond their control. They were living in a "distended society." They were searching for patterns, order, ways to make sense out of and assert some measure of control over the changes swirling around them.[1]

Progressives stepped forward to lead that "search for order." They realized there was no turning back to simpler, less complex times. Progressives repudiated the self-centered, hyper-individualist, laissez-faire doctrine of the Gilded Age, a period of flashy materialism and corrupt politics in the final decades of the nineteenth century.

Instead, they insisted, people needed to move forward. The progressives experienced, and urged others to undertake, a sort of moral awakening and enlightenment that sharpened their motivation to work for the betterment of society. They exhorted their fellow citizens to support reform. Progressives liked American capitalism, representative government, and constitutional law. But they wanted to rein in the excesses of these institutions and make them more responsive to the public interest. They mostly rejected radical solutions, including socialism and anarchism. They sought more moderate political reform and government intervention in social and economic affairs on behalf of the powerless and underempowered, such as children, women, factory workers, and the poor and disadvantaged.

The progressives shifted public thinking away from old values such as "frugality, promptness, foresight, [and] efficiency" and espoused new values such as "continuity and regularity, functionality and rationality, administration and management" in order to manage twentieth-century problems. This, in turn, meant "the need for a government of continuous involvement" with an accent on executive power and administrative applications. "Throughout the pattern ran the central theme of modern reform: functional specialization, continuity, adjustment. And behind it rested the assumptions of a bureaucratic order: a society of ceaselessly interacting voluntary groups assisted in their course by a powerful, responsive government."[2]

Progressives wanted change but were determined to work within the system rather than radically change or overthrow it. They were persistent but seldom confrontational. They were steady, pragmatic gradualists. Inclined to compromise when necessary, progressives sometimes were content to try things out on a small scale or in prototype before pushing for expansion. "Progressives managed to fashion slow and steady reforms as an alternative to calls for revolution. Progressive reformers quickly learned that in order to succeed they would have to compromise—to find a way to put personal property rights, personal liberty, and economic growth on more equal footing with communitarian ideals and the protection of the weak and vulnerable, and to work within existing systems to bring change."[3] They were clearly distinct from socialists, who favored more social programs, and fearful of anarchists, who wanted to overthrown the existing order and begin afresh.

They often appealed to New York and US history for incentives and justification. In their interpretation, that history demonstrated the constant need for change and adjustment in order to keep institutions fresh and relevant. Progressives saw themselves as being part of that tradition. In that sense, they sometimes explained, history was on their side.

President (and former New York governor) Theodore Roosevelt, in a 1906 speech, commended the progressive spirit. "In so far as this movement of agitation throughout the country takes the form of a fierce discontent with evil, of a firm determination to punish the authors of evil, whether in industry or politics, the feeling is to be heartily welcomed as a sign of healthy life."[4]

The Progressive Wave in New York

New York, the nation's largest, most diverse, and most vibrant state, was at the forefront of the new progressive wave. According to census counts, its population rose from 7,268,012 in 1900 to 10,385,227 in 1920. Within the state, New York City rose from 3,437,202 to 5,620,048 two decades later. Much of the growth was due to immigration. Approximately 35 percent of the city's population in 1920 was foreign-born. Other cities grew at a rapid pace in this twenty-year time period. Buffalo jumped from 353,387 to 573,076; Rochester from 162,608 to 290,720. At the same time, the ethnic composition of the cities shifted and diversified with the arrival of more immigrants from southern and eastern Europe and more Blacks migrating from the south. Steelmaking, railroads, and newer industries like photography and electric machinery kept the economy growing. Growth was powered by large commercial banks. The New York Stock Exchange, established in 1792, expanded and moved to a new building with a huge trading floor in 1903. "Wall Street" became the most powerful banking conglomerate in the nation.

New York statesman Elihu Root described "the new conditions incident to the extraordinary industrial development" in a 1912 address.[5] Individuals were caught up in vast, complex enterprises, Root explained. "In place of the old individual independence of life, in which every intelligent and healthy citizen was competent to take care of himself and his family, we have come to a high degree of interdependence, in which the greater part of our people have to rely for all the necessities of life upon the systematized co-operation of a vast number of other men working through complicated industrial and commercial machinery."

Conditions "are continuously and progressively demanding the readjustment of the relations between great bodies of men and the establishment of new legal rights and obligations not contemplated when existing laws were passed or existing limitations upon the powers of government were prescribed in our Constitution."

People had been used to living on farms or working in small shops. But now they were employed by industrial companies—"great aggregations of capital in enormous industrial establishments working through vast agencies of commerce and employing great masses of men in movements of production and transportation and trade so great in the mass that each individual concerned in them is quite helpless by himself."

This, in turn, necessitated the intervention of government with new powers to rebalance the rights of individuals with the power of the new organizations, Root concluded. "The relations between the employer and the employed, between owners of aggregated capital and the units of organized labor, between the small producer, the small trader, the consumer and the great transporting and manufacturing and distributing agencies, all present new questions for the solution of which the old reliance upon the free action of individual wills appears quite inadequate."

New York's rapid growth and diversity made it the state where many of the critical issues of the era first manifested themselves and, therefore, the first state to deal with them. Other states watched New York and followed its lead. That makes New York's story all the more important, because New York was in a sense a prototype for what much of the nation would try out. New Yorkers also helped shape national policies. A New Yorker was nominated for president or vice president by one of the two major political parties in every election from 1900 to 1920. Two New Yorkers ran against each other for president in 1904. Former governor

Theodore Roosevelt applied some of the emerging progressive policies he had developed as governor to the national government during his presidency (1901–1909).

But New York's progressive story was inconsistent, discursive rather than linear, and sometimes contradictory. Even the concept of progressivism in New York was "a fuzzy term" that "eschewed commitment to a specific political line, in favor of situating its users on the cutting edge of history." New Yorkers who labeled themselves "progressive" "distanced themselves from dogmatism; there were no hard-and-fast theoretical or programmatic positions to defend or proclaim; the label conveyed open-mindedness and an up-to-dateness." They agreed, though, on some things. "The bulk of the reformers shared an antipathy for the competitive economy and its enabler ideology, laissez-faire government. They agreed that the free-for-all, socially heedless marketplace in goods and labor must be regulated, and the state brought in to mitigate the myriad social problems spawned by the chaotic economic order." [6]

Charles Evans Hughes, New York's great progressive Republican governor, in his 1907 inaugural address, endorsed forward-looking legislative action and "sympathy with every aspiration for the betterment of conditions and a sincere and patient effort to understand every need and to ascertain in the hard light of experience the means best adapted to meet it."[7]

Early in the progressive era, some reformers tried to apply intensified and expanded versions of strategies that they had used in the closing years of the old century. But these strategies often proved not up to the task of wrestling with the issues of the day. For instance, the New York Consumers' League, founded in 1891, focused mostly on publicity about the need for good working conditions, and they certified garment factories that provided these conditions. Such establishments were eligible for a special label that they could sew into their clothing. That helped, but the league soon turned to lobbying for government action. Leaders of the Charities Aid Association, which encouraged and coordinated voluntary contributions and assistance for the poor, began pushing for government programs. The Woman's Christian Temperance Union pushed for voluntary abstinence from alcohol but, when that effort flagged, switched to an emphasis on government prohibition. It was soon joined by powerful lobbying and politically influential organizations such as the Anti-Saloon League.

New York became a leader in government labor reform, business regulation, and social welfare programs. It was the first state to establish a comprehensive labor department (1901), health department (1901) and modern public health system that it coordinated, education department (1904), and public utilities' regulation office (1907). It enacted a model tenement house law (1901). New York was the first to outlaw night work by women in factories (1899; reenacted 1903), proscribe child labor (1903), enact workers' compensation (1910), pass a comprehensive workplace safety and fire code (1912–1914), and regulate carrying of concealed weapons (1911). New York enacted civil rights laws in 1895 and 1913. It began offering college scholarships to qualified students in 1913. This was the state where the National Association for the Advancement of Colored People (NAACP) and the American Civil Liberties Union (ACLU) were established, in 1909 and 1920 respectively.

On the other hand, along with these advancements, progressives sometimes had their own agendas, which sometimes seemed class-specific, narrow, indifferent to the needs of some groups, or even racist. Sometimes they brought and imposed middle-class values and perspectives on problems affecting less-well-off New Yorkers without fully understanding their needs and goals. There was de facto racial segregation in New York's large cities, and people of color generally were disadvantaged in seeking jobs and forging careers. Political power and, therefore, state and municipal services were inequitably distributed. New York had a civil rights law, as noted above, but it pertained only to public accommodations (such as hotels) and was lightly enforced. New York progressives by and large did not seem much concerned with these inequities, though they did take play leading roles in establishing the NAACP in New York City in 1909 and the Committee on Urban Conditions Among Negroes (soon renamed the National Urban League) in 1910.

Attitudes toward working women could seem condescending, vacillating between pushing for hovering government protection and assertions that women workers should be left on their own. They passed laws to restrict women's working hours without consulting working women themselves. New York City was a haven for Jews fleeing persecution in Europe, but antisemitism lurked just beneath the surface in the state. It was manifested in discrimination against Jews in higher education, public accommodations, and jobs. A few progressives condoned or even supported the notion of white race supremacy, a particularly insidious theme in New York and US history in the early twentieth century. Some of the most enlightened progressive reformers came to favor limiting immigration, favoring northern and eastern Europe over other areas, and generally being exclusionary rather than welcoming and inclusive. Some progressives endorsed excessive censorship and anti-vice initiatives. Many progressives supported prohibition to curb excessive drinking, ignoring predictions, which proved accurate, that people would resent and resist this curtailment of their liberties.

New York progressives made slow headway against some of these inequities and inconsistencies, but they ignored or minimized others. They had flaws and shortcomings. Yet, viewed in they context of their times, they were well-meaning, generous, and mostly enlightened and forward-looking.

By the end of the period, circa 1920, the progressive movement was losing momentum in New York. That was partly because it had achieved many of its goals of reform, partly because of the weariness produced by World War I, and partly because the public had become fatigued by exhortations to improve and change. In the 1920 election, New York voters turned out progressive Democratic governor Alfred E. Smith (elected in 1918) and selected instead conservative Republican Nathan Miller. The politicians who took charge in Albany halted political reform, yearning for a return to what Republican Warren Harding, elected president in 1920, called "normalcy." They turned on socialists, "radicals," and others who rocked the boat. New York more or less settled into a pattern of calm, complacency, and drift. Progressivism had run its course, though conservative Republicans kept most of what had been achieved over the past couple of decades. Progressivism would reemerge in a renewed and different form in the 1930s in President Franklin D. Roosevelt's "New Deal." FDR had been a young New York progressive, first elected to the New York state senate in 1910. A number of other New York progressives went on to serve with Roosevelt in Washington.

Themes in New York Progressivism

Several themes played out in the story of New York's progressive history.

THE POLITICAL PARTIES CHANGED COURSE

New York had two dominant parties, Republicans and Democrats. There was a socialist party that garnered little support, a progressive party that lasted only one year (1912), and occasionally other minor third parties of temporary duration. Republicans and Democrats, emerging from a late nineteenth-century tradition of domination by top political leaders, sometimes resisted and sometimes embraced progressive reform. They were moved by progressives' ideas and proposals, media pressure, political scandal, opportunism (taking stands to score electoral victories), and new leadership.

In 1900, Democrats ran New York City, but Republicans dominated most of the rest of New York State. In Albany, in part because of the way the state legislature was apportioned, Republicans predominated in state government. Both parties were conservative, wedded to the status quo, controlled by political "bosses," and in league with business interests. Over the next couple of decades, both parties underwent transformations.

Republicans changed course in 1906. Press exposure and legislative investigations of mismanagement and exploitation by gas and insurance companies in 1905 had exposed their close ties to the Republicans. Reluctantly, they nominated reformer Charles Evans Hughes, who had served as counsel to the investigations, for governor in 1906. He won and pushed the legislature to enact a broad progressive agenda. The results were mixed: they expanded regulation of insurance companies and passed laws to regulate railroads and other public utilities but balked at enacting a meaningful direct primary law and other political reforms. In 1910, Hughes left to take a Supreme Court appointment, and a bribery scandal discredited top Republican legislative leaders. Democrats elected a governor and legislative majority that fall.

The Democrats, heeding the call of progressive reformers and reacting to the changing needs of their largely urban base, swung toward reform in 1911. Over the next few years, they enacted a broad progressive agenda, including the direct primary and labor regulations. But in 1913, the Democrats impeached and removed from office their own governor, William Sulzer, for misuse of campaign funds. Disillusioned voters elected a Republican governor and legislative majority in 1914. That party turned conservative and obstructionist. Progressive legislation halted. The Democrats made a partial comeback in 1918, electing Alfred E. Smith governor, but in turn he was defeated in 1920.

WOMEN OFTEN TOOK THE LEAD

Men were usually the public leaders, and got most of the credit, for progressive reforms. The governors, state legislators, and judges were all men. So also were the business leaders and most of the ministers and leaders of volunteer and civic organizations. Women could not even vote in New York until 1917.

But women led many of New York's most important progressive reforms, sometimes out front, more often behind-the-scenes. The leaders were mostly middle class and college-educated. When faced with the deplorable economic and social conditions of cities, they were galvanized into action. They were articulate and prolific speakers, writers, and organizers. They spent much of their time getting media attention to conditions they sought to remedy and converting men to the cause. They were persistent and adept at moving public opinion.

A cadre of leaders including Susan B. Anthony, Harriot Stanton Blatch, Carrie Chapman Catt, Margaret Fuller, and Rosalie Gardner Jones led the campaign for women's suffrage and women's rights generally. Black women's rights champions such as Hester Jeffrey of Rochester and Mary Burnett Talbert of Buffalo were vital to the movement.

Florence Kelley, a leader with exceptional energy and brilliance, began her career in Chicago as a labor reformer and settlement house supporter and moved to New York City in 1899. There she became the director of the Consumers' League, which pushed for shorter hours , better pay, and better working conditions for workers. She led the campaign to outlaw child labor in New York and nationally and pushed for protection of women factory workers. She was one of the founders of the NAACP and a long-time civil rights advocate. Kelley served as mentor to several other women leaders and built a network of activists and advocates for labor and other reform legislation.

Lillian Wald founded a pioneering settlement house in New York City and was an innovator in providing community health care. She was the founder of what is now the Visiting Nurse Service of New York State. Like many of her colleagues, she was also a supporter of other causes, including women's suffrage and banning child labor.

Crystal Eastman investigated working conditions, documented the impact of industrial accidents, raised public awareness about the needs of injured workers, and helped lead the development of New York's pioneering workers compensation law. She also campaigned for women's rights, served as a journalist and editor, campaigned against militarism, and joined the socialist cause.

PEOPLE IN NEW YORK CITY'S PROGRESSIVE COMMUNITY REINFORCED EACH OTHER

Most of New York's progressive activists were in New York City. They created an array of leagues, committees, and commissions to tackle particular issues. "Analysts researched them, discovered their causes, designed solutions, wrote reports. Then they mobilized public support, lobbying for legislation, bringing court cases, and waging political battles to win the backing of municipal or state governments. Many were single-issue entities, focused on specific efforts—to curtail child labor, regulate women's work, establish social insurance, alleviate poverty, reorganize public and private health care, or restructure the city's school system."[8] Their network was facilitated by physical proximity. They could easily meet each other in person and cooperated with each other. Some began as single-issue reformers but branched out into other areas through their association with people they met in the reform community. "They developed interlocking, overlapping memberships. They jointly held conferences, created journals, developed funding institutions. Collectively they created one of the nation's most advanced social policy complexes."[9] This "advanced social policy complex" directly or indirectly generated many of the ideas that found their way into reform initiatives and legislation. It also led to many national initiatives, most notably those reforms that took root in New York but later spread to other states and Washington.

Many Reforms Started in New York City and Spread to the Rest of the State (and Sometimes to the Rest of the Nation)

Members of New York City's progressive community often were the initiators of reform initiatives and proposals. Their ideas took root there but soon spread to the rest of New York State, particularly the larger cities, which faced urban problems and issues like New York City's, though on a much smaller and less intense scale. Several key proposals which had emanated from the New York City progressives were enacted into state law in Albany.

Reformers Innovated and Improvised

In part because New York was the first to enter the arena of change-driven reform, many progressive initiatives, precedents, and models from the federal government and other states were unavailable. The New Yorkers articulated new concepts of government's responsibility and authority and invented new types of agencies to deliver public policy.

For instance, the federal government had a limited workers' compensation law, but New York was the first state to pass one, in 1910, and it was more comprehensive than the federal program. New York's law was invalidated by the courts in 1911, but by the time it was repassed in 1913 (after a state constitutional amendment to sanction it), several other states had used New York's 1910 law as a partial model for their own new compensation laws. New York's Public Service Commissions law (1907) bestowed much more extensive public utility regulatory authority than any other state or the federal government (even the Interstate Commerce Commission had more limited authority).

News Media, "Muckrakers" and Analytical Reports Paved the Way

Much of the change in New York was propelled by heightened public discussion of issues and demands for change. Some of this was due to exposés in the New York newspapers and periodicals (mostly published in New York City). These reform-minded journalists and writers were sometimes called "muckrakers," a pejorative term coined by President Theodore Roosevelt in the 1906 speech referenced above. T.R. emphasized the benefits of investigative reporting but thought some writers went too far, always looking downward toward "the muck" of scandal. The term stuck and came to refer to progressive-era exposés generally.

For instance, newspaper stories about unsanitary working conditions and contaminated baked goods in bakeries led to New York's first progressive regulation, an 1895 law governing bakers' working hours and conditions. The *New York Times, New York World, New York Journal-American*, and other papers pioneered in investigative journalism and competed to expose business wrongdoing and political corruption. The New York child labor committee sent the press its reports on exploitation of children in factories; the newspapers carried them in front-page stories. Newspaper reports on mismanagement and corruption in gas and insurance companies headquartered in New York City brought legislative investigations that resulted in breakthrough new regulations. News reports on bribery in the legislature in 1910 led to the defeat of the Republican ticket in the fall elections.

Popular magazines and journals such as *McClure's, The American Magazine, Colliers, Cosmopolitan, Everybody's, Leslie's,* and *Outlook*—almost all published in New York City—disclosed corrupt linkages among business, labor, and government and aroused a public demand for change.

Longer reports were another important catalyst for legislation. Several were compiled by the legislature, state agencies, or commissions appointed by the governor. The state printing budget was generous, and copies of long state reports went to individual legislators (where their findings and recommendations helped shape new legislation) and to newspapers (which distilled them into laypersons' terms).

For example, commissions set up by Governor Theodore Roosevelt (1899–1901) produced reports that led to regulation of tenement houses (1901), a new cross-state canal (1903), and a state education department (1904). Legislative investigations and reports on the gas and insurance industries in 1905 precipitated new regulatory measures in 1906. Governor Charles Evans Hughes persuaded the legislature to appoint a committee to investigate factory accidents in 1909, and the committee's report was the basis for New York's first workers' compensation law in 1910. Reports and recommendations of a legislative factory investigating commission produced sweeping new factory safety and sanitation regulations between 1912 and 1914. New York's forward-looking public health program emerged from the report of a 1913 gubernatorial commission.

STATE GOVERNMENT MOVED FROM THE MARGINS TO CENTER STAGE

Progressive reformers continued voluntary organizations and encouraged philanthropic programs to deal with social issues. But, as noted above, one of their new departures was to call on government (particularly state government) to step in to regulate businesses, impose limits on people's freedoms in the name of the common good, and intervene to help the disadvantaged. Government rules for social and economic affairs are common today, but in the 1900–1920 period they were something new and untried. New York vastly increased business regulation. It enacted detailed building and sanitary codes and safety requirements for factories. It banned child labor and regulated women's working hours. A 1911 law banned unlicensed carrying of concealed weapons. A 1917 act created New York's first state police. Other laws enabled local governments to license and regulate peddlers, barbers, and contractors.

Yet the story of progress was mixed. State government, a modest affair in 1900, had grown into a sprawling maze by 1920. The legislature created new departments and agencies that partially overlapped with existing ones. A panel appointed by Governor Alfred E. Smith in 1919 found there were 189 departments and commissions. Some of the department heads were elected. Others were appointed by governors, but senate approval was required both to appoint and remove them. The appointees' terms did not correspond with governors' terms, leaving governors with commissioners whom they had not appointed and could not replace. There was no budget system. Agencies got their appropriations directly from the legislature and so lobbied key legislators and in turn were beholden to them. The agencies issued reports but to the legislature, not the governor (though of course he read them, and they were available to the public). Strong governors asserted a measure of consistency and control over this maze, but consolidation of scattered agencies into a manageable number of cabinet-level departments reporting to the governor and a unified state budget proposed by Governor Smith had to wait until the 1920s.

New York Courts Generally Backed the Progressives

In some states, progressives were deterred or thwarted by their state's conservative courts, which struck down progressive regulations as unconstitutional. The US Supreme Court was also very conservative. These courts often ruled that the reference to the right of "due process of law" in the Fourteenth Amendment to the US Constitution meant government regulations could not curtail individuals' or businesses' rights to do what they wished.

But New York's highest court, the Court of Appeals, took a much more liberal view. In those days, most constitutional law cases were settled in state rather than federal courts, and appeals to the Supreme Court were rare, so the state's highest court's rulings were definitive.

The Court of Appeals generally ruled that the courts should support the legislature unless an enactment was clearly in violation of the New York state or federal constitutions. In contrast to the Supreme Court, it held that the Fourteenth Amendment, passed in 1868, was intended to protect the rights of formerly enslaved Blacks in the south, not businesses.

For instance, in 1904 the court validated the 1895 bakeshop law, referenced above. "The courts are frequently confronted with the temptation to substitute their judgment for that of the legislature," but whether the legislation is wise "is not for us to consider," said the court. Judges "are bound to assume that the law making body acted with a desire to promote the public good" and should be "inclined to so construe the statute as to validate it."[10] The Supreme Court reversed that decision the next year, but the New York's Court of Appeals kept to its principles in deciding cases.

In another 1904 decision, involving New York's authority to require smallpox vaccinations in the schools, the court ruled that "when the sole object and general tendency of the legislation is to promote the public health, there is no invasion of the Constitution even if the enforcement of the law interferes to some extent with liberty or property." The vaccination requirement was valid.[11] That, in turn, encouraged other public health initiatives.

In 1907, the court struck down a law forbidding night work by women in factories. But the legislature soon passed a different version of the law, basing it on protection of women's health. When that law was appealed in the courts in 1915, women's rights advocates presented extensive evidence that night work was harmful to women. This time, the court validated the law. The legislature had concluded that night work was injurious and therefore "the interest of public health and welfare" justified the law said the decision.[12]

Reckoning with New York's Progressive Era

A century and more after the close of the progressive era, how should we assess the degree of success and impact of the changes and reforms brought about by New York's progressive community?

We need to understand and evaluate the people and ideas from that era mostly by the standards of their time and avoid imposing our own values a century after their work. The people in this book were essentially late nineteenth-century people evolving and trying to invent new ways for the new twentieth century. The documents in the book reveal an earnest questioning of the old and a quest for new ways of looking at and doing things. The New York progressives believed they were in the vanguard of changes that would improve the common good. They made government the central engine of change in an unprecedented way that evolved later into the New Deal and some of the comprehensive programs of modern-day government. They brought a new mindset to issues. They endorsed the notion of trying new things; if they worked, they would try to keep and even expand them, but if not, they would modify or abandon them. The progressives in this book were incrementalists, but persistent ones.

They had their limitations and flaws, like leaders of change everywhere. They seemingly made little headway against such historic dilemmas as race and income inequality. But more than a century later, New York (and the nation) have still not resolved them.

But the progressives did accomplish a great deal, as the documents in this book make clear. Moreover, they provided new ways of framing issues and crystallized options in ways that are still helpful today. The theoretical approaches and hands-on solutions they proposed were useful policy frameworks. The New York progressives developed insights and strategies that continue to influence and civic-minded people today. The documents in the book provide an opportunity for them to speak to us in their own words.

Plan of the Book

The book presents a profile of progressive New York in ten chapters. The topics are distinct, but they also overlap.

> Chapter 1, *Gauging the Tenor of the Times*, conveys some of the vibrance, excitement, and sense of change in the period.
> Chapter 2, *Building Grand Enterprises*, shows New Yorkers at their most dynamic, building grand things on a large scale.
> Chapter 3, *Reforming Politics and Government*, documents the campaign to make politicians and government more responsive to the public interest.
> Chapter 4, *Improving People's Lives*, provides examples of the progressive era's mission to make things better for people.
> Chapter 5, *Strengthening Women's Status*, presents documents on women's struggle for equality.
> Chapter 6, *Welcoming Newcomers*, goes into the issues of immigration and cultural pluralism.
> Chapter 7, *Reckoning with Race*, includes documents of the experience of Black people in New York.
> Chapter 8, *Regulating Business*, shows efforts to expand state oversight of its industries.

> Chapter 9, *Helping Workers*, describes efforts to improve working conditions and safety.
>
> Chapter 10, *Appealing to History,* includes example of how progressives' interpretations of history enhanced their reform message.

There is a vast amount of documentation from New York's progressive era. This book is, necessarily, very selective. The documents in the book are all contemporary—that is, they were written at the time and so constitute a first-hand account of what was happening. They were selected by considering a number of criteria:

- The document was prepared by a person or group that was clearly in touch with the intellectual, social, and political currents of the time. It is representative or indicative of what many people seemed to be thinking or saying at the time.

- It was recognized at the time for its clarity, coherence, informational value, insights, and persuasiveness. It has an analysis of events and also suggestions for how critical issues were being or might be addressed.

- People read and heeded it as evidenced by references to it in the news media and other documents and by the actions people took based on the document.

- It provides evidence of New York's complexity, diversity, and historical distinctiveness.

- It describes an issue of importance in New York that later affected the rest of the country, making New York a pioneer in addressing it.

> For each chapter, I have begun with a short introduction to the topic.
>
> For each of the documents, I have included a short introduction in *italics*.
>
> I have tried to include the most meaningful parts of each document. I have indicated omissions by using ellipses (. . .). In a few cases, I have broken long paragraphs into shorter ones for easier reading, or consolidated short ones into longer ones.

At the end of each chapter, there is a list of sources, including a full citation and URL where the full document I used can be found. This is helpful for anyone wanting to read more from the document. Most of the references are to HathiTrust (https://www.hathitrust.org). But I suggest beginning any search with the Online Books Page (https://onlinebooks.library.upenn.edu/lists.html), which often has links not only to HathiTrust but also to other online versions of the documents. You can also use it to search for any author, title, or subject.

The readings in the bibliography provide additional sources.

The documents are quoted directly from the originals and reflect the vocabulary and societal and cultural sentiments and expressions of the time period. Some of the terms may seem outdated, insensitive, or even insulting today. The writers sometimes include terms such as *Negro* and *colored*, which were commonly used in those days to refer to Black Americans. Their references to minorities can sometimes seem condescending or uncaring. Discussions of racial issues may seem to us a century later to be, unintentionally, racist themselves. Some of the writings on the Jewish immigration experience in New York in the era sound almost anti-Semitic today. The ways the writers used terms and the ways they expressed themselves can indicate both the extent of their beneficial ambitions and the limits of their vision and interests.

But a book of documents like this one is designed to meet the writers where they were, in their own time, and let them express viewpoints and sentiments in their own words. This approach, hopefully, imparts a sense of directness, connection, and authenticity. It is designed to convey people's insights without being overly judgmental.

Notes

1. Robert H. Wiebe, *The Search for Order, 1877–1920* (New York: Hill & Wang, 1967), 11–43.
2. Wiebe, *The Search for Order*, 164–95.
3. Robert D. Putnam, *The Upswing: How America Came Together a Century Ago and How We Can Do It Again* (New York: Simon and Schuster, 2020), 336.
4. Michael McGerr, *A Fierce Discontent: The Rise and Fall of the Progressive Movement in America, 1870–1920* (New York: Free Press, 2003), 176.
5. Bruce W. Dearstyne, *The Crucible of Public Policy: New York Courts in the Progressive Era* (Albany: State University of New York Press, 2022), 3–4. Root

served as secretary of war (1899–1904), secretary of state (1905–1909), and US senator from New York (1905–1915).

6. Mike Wallace, *Greater Gotham: A History of New York City from 1898 to 1919* (New York: Oxford University Press, 2017), 506–7.

7. Robert F. Wesser, *Charles Evans Hughes: Politics and Reform in New York, 1905–1910* (Ithaca: Cornell University Press, 1967), 109.

8. Wallace, *Greater Gotham*, 508.

9. Wallace, *Greater Gotham*, 508.

10. New York State Court of Appeals, *People v. Lochner*, 175 NY 145, 158 (1904).

11. New York State Court of Appeals, *Matter of Viemeister*, 179 N.Y.235, 238 (1904).

12. New York State Court of Appeals, *People v. Charles Schweinler Press*, 214 NY 395, 401.

1

Gauging the Tenor of the Times

Figures 1a and 1b. New York City's Fifth Avenue (left) represented New York's wealth and achievements in the new century. But residents of Mulberry Street (right), many of them immigrants and first-generation New Yorkers, experienced urban overcrowding and marginal economic conditions. *Sources:* Library of Congress Prints & Photographs Collection; Detroit Publishing Company, Library of Congress Prints & Photographs Collection.

The progressive era was a time of questioning the validity of the inherited status quo, criticizing concentrated wealth and opulent lifestyles, highlighting disparities in opportunity and income, and envisioning and planning for a better collective future. There were lots of new voices, people with new ideas and new proposals—novelty was in the air. The intellectual excitement blossomed in New York City, but it was also manifested throughout the state. The documents in this chapter are examples of the ferment of the time. They reveal (1) the idea that the status quo can and should be improved; (2) the power of the media and books to present evidence and dramatize and frame issues in new ways; (3) the notion that it is up to all New Yorkers to reexamine their attitudes and views and become advocates for change; and (4) the idea that progress is possible but not inevitable and we need to fashion our collective future deliberately.

Extreme Wealth on Display

David Graham Phillips (1867–1911) was a famed New York novelist and "muckraking" journalist. His novels, which often explored the tensions of personal relations and modern life, were bestsellers in their day. Phillips also wrote articles in popular magazines and a number of nonfiction books exposing and ridiculing the lives of New York City's wealthy elite.

In his novels, the wealthy people had usually either inherited their money ("Old Money") or made it more recently ("New Money") through sharp business practices in banking or railroads. They enjoyed flaunting their wealth, spending large sums ostentatiously on opulent homes, lavish furnishings, and excessive parties and entertainment. Phillips's work accentuated the progressive era's concern about the gap between New York's very rich and its middle and lower classes.

His 1905 book The Reign of Gilt *described the "plutocracy" and "money maniacs" who flaunted their wealth. Chapter 3, "Plutocracy at Home," reproduced in part below, profiles the Fifth Avenue home of "Mr. Multi-Millionaire."*

∽

FROM *THE REIGN OF GILT* (1905) BY DAVID GRAHAM PHILLIPS

Let us glance at our typical Mr. Multi-Millionaire's town house. It is a palace of white marble, on Fifth avenue, near Fifty-ninth street—the view across the Park from the upper windows is superb. This palace was the inaugural of the family's recent fashionable career. It is the struggle to live up to it that is making them famous in New York.

The palace was to have cost our family a million, including the site. Up to the present time it has cost them two and a half millions, and that does not include the one hundred and seventy-five thousand dollar set of tapestries for the dining-room which is on its way from Europe. The site cost half a million; the house three-quarters of a million; the rest went for furniture, and the house still looks bare to the family. "A wretched barn," madame calls it. There are one hundred and fifty thousand dollars in paintings and statuary in the entrance-hall, fifty thousand dollars in paintings, statuary, and such matters in the rest of the house. Two hundred thousand dollars could easily be spent without overcrowding. The furniture, thinly scattered in the long and lofty salon, cost two hundred and fifty thousand dollars—it is amazing how fast the money disappears once one goes in for old furniture.

As you look round these show rooms the vast entrance-hall, the enormous dining-room, the great library, the salon which is used as ballroom, the comparatively small and exquisitely furnished reception-rooms—you are struck by the absence of individual taste. You are in a true palace—the dwelling-place, but in no sense the home, of people of great wealth, but of no marked aesthetic development. They have the money, and to a certain extent the faculty of appreciation. But others have supplied the active, the creative brains.

You go up the grand stairway, and at the turn pause to look down at the magnificent rug which almost covers the floor of the entrance-hall, up at the splendid painting which adorns the ceiling. The owner tells you that each cost twenty-five thousand dollars.

And then he takes you into the wife's living-rooms. She is out of town.

Madame lives in five great rooms—a sitting-room, a dressing-room, a bedroom, a room where her clothes in use—quantities of dresses, hats, wraps, boots, shoes, slippers, drawers full of the finest underclothing—are kept, and a bathroom. She is very crowded, she will tell you. For instance, where is her secretary to sit and work when she wishes to use her sitting-room for a private talk with her son or daughter, or some intimate friend?

You look round these rooms and again you note the absence of individual taste. Madame is always on the wing; she has no time to impress herself on her immediate surroundings. But a very capable artist has been at work and has not neglected the opportunities which his freedom in the matter of money opened to him. He has created several marvelous color schemes through harmonious shadings in rugs, upholstery, the brocade coverings of the walls, the curtains, the woodwork and the ceilings. You are not surprised that a hundred thousand dollars went in making suitable surroundings for a lady of fashion and fortune. You know that there are several dozen suites more expensive than this within gun-shot, and scores almost as expensive within a radius of half a mile. . . .

Each member of the family has his or her own sitting-room and there receives callers from within or without the family—except that the daughter receives men callers in the smallest of the three reception-rooms on the ground floor. Each has his or her own personal attendants; each lives his or her separate social life. They rarely meet at breakfast—it is more comfortable to breakfast in one's sitting-room; they rarely meet at luncheon–luncheon is the favorite time for going to one's intimates; they rarely meet at dinner—one or more are sure to be dining out or the mother is giving a dinner for married people. . . .

For the man-servant is the beginning of fashion, and its height can be measured—as certainly as in any other way—by the number of men-servants and the splendor of their liveries.

Of course, our family of pacemakers have an "adequate" supply of secretaries, tutors, governesses, valets, maids; and the housekeeper has her staff, the chef his, the butler his, the head coachman his, the captain of the yacht his. Then there are caretakers, gardeners and farmers, the racing-stable staff, various and numerous occasional employees. . . .

Our multi-millionaire did not make his fortune; he inherited it. But he has been very shrewd in managing it, for all his extravagance. Though he is cautious about expenses in one way, he shows by the allowances he makes to the various members of his family that he believes in carrying out to the uttermost the idea that his family must live in state. His wife has a million in her own name, but he makes her an allowance of three hundred and fifty thousand dollars a year to maintain herself and their households. The grown son has had an allowance of twenty-five thousand dollars a year, and when he marries it will be trebled—perhaps quadrupled. This is large for persons of their modest fortune, but many fathers of smaller means are doing as much for their children, and our multi-millionaire will not see his children suffer. His grown daughter has an allowance of fifteen thousand dollars—more than she needs, as she has only to buy her clothes and pay her small expenses out of it. The boy in college has five thousand dollars a year; he is always in debt, but his mother helps him. The youngest child has ten dollars a week—her clothes are bought for her, and she can always get money from her father or mother when she wishes to make handsome presents. . . .

It is amazing how many great and beautiful palaces of a kind such as is occupied by our multi-millionaire are being added yearly to New York's fashionable quarter. And there is not a single palace in New York that is comfortable. No way has yet been devised for making them otherwise than chilly and draughty. The human animal is too small for such huge surroundings; and there are not enough competent servants or even competent available housekeepers to make the domestic machinery run smoothly.

The new millionaires slip into New York, into their new palaces, attracting little attention. Men with a scant million or two are coming all the time unobserved. If it were not necessity that drove them here, many of them would doubtless become angry at their insignificance and would go where less money gives distinction. But the rapid concentration of the directing forces of the business of the country in Manhattan Island compels them to yield to the entreaties of their wives and daughters and remain.

From "Drift" to "Mastery"

Many people in the progressive era were disoriented by the massive changes wrought by industrialization, urbanization, and the transportation revolution of automobiles and airplanes. A number of leading writers in New York explained that people needed to step beyond old ways of thinking and find new, "scientific" approaches to contemporary issues.

Walter Lippmann (1889–1974) was a progressive writer, reporter, and political commentator who spent much of his life in New York and was one of the founders of the New York–based progressive/liberal journal The New Republic *in 1914. He captured this concept of new thinking in his influential 1914 book* Drift and Mastery. *The book criticized "drift"—simplistic, outdated solutions to complex modern social and economic problems. It called for adaptation to new conditions and application of scientific methods and well-conceived initiatives, which would result in "mastery" of current problems.*

Chapter 14, entitled "Mastery," excerpted below, discusses conservative resistance to new ideas and the imperative to adopt new methods. Mastery is defined as "the substitution of conscious intention for unconscious striving." That definition summarizes one of the subthemes of progressivism.

Lippman followed up Drift and Mastery *with several other thoughtful books and was soon recognized as the leading social and political commentator of his era.*

∽

From *Drift and Mastery* (1914) by Walter Lippmann

Tradition will not work in the complexity of modern life. For if you ask Americans to remain true to the traditions of all their Fathers, there would be a pretty confusion if they followed your advice. There is great confusion, as it is, due in large measure to the persistency which men follow tradition in a world unsuited to it. They modify a bit, however they apply "the rule of reason" to their old loyalties, and so a little adjustment is possible.

But there can be no real cohesion for America in following scrupulously the inherited ideals of our people. . . . The only possible cohesion now is a loyalty that looks forward. America is preeminently the country where there is practical substance in Nietzsche's advice that we should live not for our fatherland but for our children's land. To do this men have to substitute purpose for tradition; and that is, I believe, the profoundest change that has ever taken place in human history. We can no longer treat life as something that has trickled down to us. We have to deal with it deliberately, devise its social organization, alter its tools, formulate its methods, educate and control it. In endless ways we put intention where custom has reigned. We break up routines, make decisions, choose our ends, select means.

The massive part of man's life has always been, and still is, subconscious. The influence of his intelligence seems insignificant in comparison with attachments and desires, brute forces, and natural catastrophes. Our life is managed from behind the scenes: we are actors in dramas that we cannot interpret. Of almost no decisive event can we say: this was our own choosing. We happen upon careers, necessity pushing, blind inclination pulling. If we stop to think we are amazed that we should be what we are. And so we have come to call mysterious everything that counts, and the more mysterious the better some of us pretend to think it is.

We drift into our work, we fall in love, and our lives seem like the intermittent flicker of an obstinate lamp. War panics, and financial panics, revivals, fads sweep us before them. Men go to war not knowing why, hurl themselves at cannon as if they were bags of flour, seek impossible goals, submit to senseless wrongs, for mankind lives to-day only in the intervals of a fitful sleep. . . .

That, I think, is the beginning of what we call reflection: a desire to realize the drama in which we are acting, to be awake during our own lifetime. When we cultivate reflection by watching ourselves and the world outside, the thing we call science begins. We draw the hidden into the light of consciousness, record it, compare phases of it, note its history, experiment, reflect on error, and we find that our conscious life is no longer a trivial iridescence, but a progressively powerful way of domesticating the brute.

This is what mastery means: the substitution of conscious intention for unconscious striving. Civilization, it seems to me, is just this constant effort to introduce plan where there has been clash, and purpose into the jungles of disordered growth. But to shape the world nearer to the heart's desire requires a knowledge of the heart's desire and of the world. You cannot throw yourself blindly against unknown facts and trust to luck that the result will be satisfactory.

Yet from the way many business men, minor artists, and modern philosophers talk you would think that the best world can be created by the mere conflict of economic egotisms, the mere eruption of fantasy, and the mere surge of blind instinct. There is today a widespread attempt to show the futility of ideas. Now in so far as this movement represents a critical insight into the emotional basis of ideas, it is a fundamental contribution to human power. But when it seeks to fall back upon the unconscious, when the return to nature is the ideal of a deliberate vegetable, this movement is like the effort of the animal that tried to eat itself: the tail could be managed and the hind legs, but the head was an insurmountable difficulty.

You can have misleading ideas, but you cannot escape ideas. To give up theory, to cease formulating your desire is not to reach back, as some people imagine, to profounder sources of inspiration. It is to put yourself at the mercy of stray ideas, of ancient impositions or trumped-up fads. Accident becomes the master, the accident largely of your own training, and you become the plaything of whatever happens to have accumulated at the bottom of your mind, or to find itself sanctified in the newspaper you read and the suburb that suited your income.

There have been fine things produced in the world without intention. Most of our happiness has come to us, I imagine, by the fortunate meeting of events. But happiness has always been a precarious incident, elusive and shifting in an unaccountable world. In love, especially, men rejoice and suffer through what are to them mysterious ways. Yet when it is suggested that the intelligence must invade our unconscious life, men shrink from it as from dangerous and clumsy meddling. It is dangerous and clumsy now, but it is the path we shall have to follow. We have to penetrate the dreaming brute in ourselves, and make him answerable to our waking life.

It is a long and difficult process, one for which we are just beginning to find a method. But there is no other way that offers any hope. To shove our impulses underground by the taboo is to force them to virulent and uncontrolled expression. To follow impulse wherever it leads means the satisfaction of one impulse at the expense of all the others. The glutton and the rake can satisfy only their gluttonous and rakish impulses, and that isn't enough for happiness. What civilized men aim at is neither whim nor taboo, but a frank recognition of desire, disciplined by a knowledge of what is possible, and ordered by the conscious purpose of their lives.

Making Systematic, Incremental Progress

Walter E. Weyl (1873–1919) was a journalist and economist who wrote widely on public policy. His 1912 book The New Democracy *outlined a path for future progress based on middle-class values, compromise, gradual and incremental change and reforms, and rejection of the excesses of unbridled capitalism as well as radical notions of upheaval. What he called the "social surplus"—economic abundance generated by American enterprise—would keep change and reform gradual and modest. Weyl's vision was one of continuing, steady, incremental progress guided by widely accepted principles and wise government policies. Weyl was widely cited and quoted during the progressive era. He joined Walter Lippmann and Herbert Croly to establish the progressive journal* The New Republic *in New York in 1914.*

∽

From *The New Democracy* (1912) by Walter E. Weyl

Three primary factors determine in the main the methods of the American democracy. The first of these factors is the complex of traditions, descended to us from the pioneer period. The second is our growing social surplus. The third is the wide diversity among the groups striving for democracy. Because of our American traditions, our democrats are more likely to proceed in a tentative, experimental, and rather illogical way; to sail forward by tacking; to break as little and as gradually as possible with our ingrained individualism.

Americans are not abstract, uncompromising thinkers. They are not like the men of the French Revolution, who would have dared to abolish the universe and recreate it on the morrow. We shall probably seek our salvation, to the limited extent still possible, outside of the state, and we shall doubtless "try out" governmental novelties in a few Western commonwealths [states] (our political experiment stations) before applying them in the grand manner to the whole nation. Because of our traditions, we are likely to make changes by indirection and to preserve the form while altering the substance.

Our wealth, actual and potential, reinforces these tendencies. We live in a civilization where political animosities are not exacerbated by the actual hunger of the main bodies of contestants. The struggle is not less intense (just as prize fighting is not less intense because gloves have taken the place of bare knuckles), but the improved, and above all the improvable, economic status of the masses, tends to make their action more confident, compromising, and pacific. Our economic development, by giving some little wealth to so large a majority, binds over all parties to keep the peace. It exacts hostages to social order. It removes the incitement to the worst forms of social recklessness. Without recklessness, because not without hope, with a status to be bettered and with political rights with which to better it, the people, growing in power and discontent, can move forward gradually and quietly against the intrenchments of the plutocracy. . . .

The vastness of the wealth to be conserved makes even our revolutionaries somewhat conservative, for there is small wisdom in laying waste a city in which the victors must forevermore dwell. The victorious socialists of Milwaukee, but recently dreaded as iconoclasts, turn out to be constructive, conciliatory, Chesterfieldian, and enormously effective. Our most possessing classes are equally afraid of violence, not because it is likely to be successful, but because of the damage which would be inflicted before the bull could be driven from the china shop. They are therefore willing (as they are also able) to insure against the utter recklessness of misery by allaying the worst evils of poverty; just as the democratic masses are willing (and able) to refrain from recklessness because of the counter-recklessness which it would provoke, and because of the injury to their ultimate possessions which it would inflict.

In America we can for the time being lay this specter of violence. What might happen if certain nation-debasing tendencies, now at work, were to overcome counteracting forces, what might happen if misery and oppression grew with the growth of wealth, is another question. For the day it is easier to vote and easier to get your vote counted than it is to fight, and curative forces are leading away from the sharp antagonism which would involve an appeal to naked force. Today, when our soldiers under arms represent less than one per thousand of the population, when our militia are loosely and not undemocratically organized, our broader democratic movements will in all probability neither rely upon force nor be resisted by force. Not only is it probable (though not certain) that democratic progress will be unaccompanied by a clash of armed men but the process is also more likely, because of our accumulated wealth, to be a social upbuilding from within rather than a demolition with a subsequent "reconstruction."

It is common today to see a vast railway station completely rebuilt, while, simultaneously, the traffic is carried on. So necessary is continuity when enormous interests are involved, that change, destruction, rebuilding do not interfere with the ordinary conduct of the business. Our social revolution must be consummated with a minimum of shock to delicate industrial, political and social machinery. . . .

We grow into democracy or are educated into democracy through uncontested victories, through sheer technical progresses, improved political and industrial education, through an increased capacity for combined activity, through an enlarged social consciousness, through a widened social outlook. The mere expansion of the trade-union movement in England, Germany, and America; the growth of the socialist party in Germany; the spread of the cooperative movement in Belgium; the popularization of education in the United States; the development in America of a spirit of insurgency against respectable evils, are all steps toward the attainment of democracy, independently of the actual use of such movements in eventual social conflicts.

In a certain sense, these conflicts themselves constitute less a class struggle than a national adjustment. In this adjustment the mutual attractions and repulsions of social groups play their part, but so great is the potential overweight of the democratic mass—once a strong solidarity is achieved—that victory depends not on the people's ability to fight, but on their capacity to unite. What hampers the democracy is not the actual, visible power of an intrenched plutocracy, but the lack of an intellectual perception to unite divergent classes; the lack of an emotional appeal to overcome the divisive forces within the majority itself. The democracy is halted by its fear that it cannot run its own business; by its very own conservatism. It is this inherent, though curable, timorousness, this social paralysis, as well as a tendency to split up into its constituent groups, rather than any outside constraining force, which in the past has delayed our democratic progress and has confined us to the ruts of a traditional thinking and voting. The internal adjustment of the democracy is a process of uniting groups, by no means agreed in the details of what constitutes progress. We have "semi-democrats," with "leanings" or tendencies toward certain democratic reforms, but opposed to others.

For this reason (and it is an outstanding reason) we are forced to content ourselves with half-reforms, especially when the half-successes are the earnest of further successes. Men opposed to the regulation of corporations will support ballot reform and direct primaries, and men who would bitterly fight a progressive income tax will support a corporation law. All these "semi-democrats" are utilized by the advancing democratic movement. Democracy hitches on behind even when the wagon does not go the whole way. The democracy proceeds along a middle path, which is the line of least resistance. It uses broad phrases, vague enough to attract by different hopes men who are dissatisfied with only the details of our national economy, as well as those who wish a basic change in business and politics. The democracy, seeking ever to appeal to a majority, recasts its doctrines to attain that majority. It does not favor confiscation because its own majority has property.

But it *does* attack "swollen" fortunes (which belong to the minority), as it attacks the monopoly. There is, of course, no clear boundary line to confiscation, and it is a matter of degree and opinion where taxation, reasonable regulation, or fair payment end and confiscation begins. Our courts have been wholly unable to give any logical and universally applicable definition of confiscation. This leads to the "special privilege" which increases them, the unequal, or evaded, taxation which conserves them, and the business secrecy and business oligarchy which make them perpetual. The democracy does not permit the issue to become one between the propertied and the unpropertied, but distinguishes between property and privilege, between earned, and unearned, increment; between, legitimate investment and promoters' profits. By taking this line of least resistance, the democracy finds allies where a more uncompromising group would find enemies.

Men who are dependent on an industry, workmen and stockholders alike, do not necessarily desire an autocratic rule within the industry. The policyholders of the great insurance companies—the real investors—are benefited, not injured, by an effective governmental control. In the same spirit the democracy stops short, at least temporarily, of doing more than the immediately necessary. The government regulates interstate railroad traffic and other businesses affected with a public interest, and, as the need becomes apparent, control by the nation becomes more complete. But the democracy is not so impracticable as to wish to regulate the tillage of the independent farmer, the hours of labor of the doctor or lawyer, the capitalization and profits of the corner grocery store. The goal of the democracy is a maximum of control with a minimum of regulation. In other words, the democracy, not being slavishly bound to logic, would rather be successful than thorough. It does not tear up root and branch, but merely weeds out roughly, for social, like natural, evolution permits the survival of harmless rudiments. Just as the vestige of a prehuman tail survives in the human coccyx, so we have, and always will have, a social coccyx, a social vermiform appendix, and other reminders of a lower past. America will always be a jumble of old and new, of "Yankee notions" in government and business and the political junk of the seventeenth and eighteenth centuries.

The Rising Standard of Living

Many New York progressives agreed with Walter Weyl's sentiments (in his 1912 book The New Democracy, *excerpted above): the rising "social surplus" in the nation was the key to the future.*

But others went further: these resources needed to be applied to raising everyone's standard of living. Progressive social worker Mary K. Simkhovitch (1867-1954) articulated this in her 1917 book The City Worker's World in America. *After years working for private New York charitable aid organizations, in 1902 she took the lead in organizing Greenwich House, a leading-edge settlement house in New York City. She served as its director from its founding until 1946. Greenwich House served immigrants and other New York City residents with a range of recreational, educational, and health programs. Over the years, Simkhovitch also taught social work courses at Columbia University, served as chairperson of New York City's 1907 Committee on Congestion, and became an energetic advocate for women's suffrage, public schools, public housing, childcare centers, and social welfare programs.*

Along with all this tireless work, she also articulated in her writings one of the underlying themes of progressivism: raising working people's standard of living should be an essential public policy goal. Everyone should be able to enjoy "a mode of life that is satisfactory to the community" is the way she put it in The City Worker's World in America, *excerpted below.*

∼

FROM *THE CITY WORKER'S WORLD IN AMERICA* (1917)
BY MARY K. SIMKHOVITCH

There are two essentials upon which everyone who sincerely desires a dynamic, progressive, democratic state insists: wages that will admit of such a standard of life that the worker can contribute his best to the whole, and a mode of life that is satisfactory to the community, apart from the consideration of wages. What decides the wage most largely is, of course, supply and demand, modified indeed by custom, by publicity, by combination.

But the newly aroused public opinion is especially active in the improvement of living conditions that make for a higher standard of life for all, irrespective of wages, the consideration of fixing which the public is still loath to undertake.

The reasons for this contemporary emphasis on these social reform measures, as they may be called, are of the deepest interest. They are two-fold. First the obvious increase in genuine social concern. The passion that has hitherto so largely gone into commerce and all forms of material enterprise is beginning to manifest itself in other fields. The last decade has witnessed not only a revival of spiritual forces but really a new epoch in American life, partly due to the world-wide awakening to the consciousness of our common lot, but more specifically to our own economic development. The extraordinary growth of our industries and the resultant power of capital have brought into sharp relief the different lots of rich and poor. Early American days witnessed a practically undifferentiated economic status. We are not unaware of the pomp of colonial officials or of the extreme poverty with which it often co-existed, yet for all this there was an open field for all competitors, as our natural resources were virgin and undeveloped. This common struggle produced a kind of rough equality, or at least a potential equality. Such differences as existed—and they were marked—were rather those of intellectual or official, than economic, status. Thus the New England minister had a position of authority and power that money could not give, but with the use of our natural resources and the development of capital that became so marked after recovery from the Civil War, values changed.

Power no longer was obtained through exercise of religious authority, nor through the social pressure of a great name nor through the prestige gained by a university education. Power came through wealth, which in its turn may provide education or luxury and thus become the readiest way to the enjoyment of life. With the disappearance of much that was fine, much that was false in the older conceptions disappeared also. The smallness of certain aristocratic pretensions was swept away. With the growth of wealth and the sense of power, a sort of expansion, extravagance and waste took place that can, according to one's point of view, be classed as vulgar, or as vastly hopeful, if one can discern in it a new kind of soil from which new virtues may spring.

What California does for its fruits and flowers, wealth has done for the new life that is now expanding before our eyes. We are dissatisfied with the picayune. Nothing but the biggest and most perfect fruits will answer. If we must have the best steam yachts and the largest number of automobiles, if we must have country seats and grand opera, we must also have the finest hospitals, the best schools, the purest water supplies, the cleanest streets, the least tuberculosis in the world. Nothing is too good for us. Shall the old world get ahead of us in our social improvements any more than in our threshing machines? If we can buy old masters we are beginning to want to paint them! The thirst to excel is with us and this eagerness to try our power has extended to the field of raising the standard of living among the masses.

The process of raising the standard is of course complex. In the first place our extraordinary prosperity is due to the working of our national resources. A virgin continent open to all precluded the possibility of the rise of poverty during a limited period, until the growth of capital and its consolidation gave an economic advantage to a group. It was not till the disappearance of free, or easily acquired land, that the pressure began to be felt. Second, as a byproduct of our prosperity, and especially through the growth of transportation facilities, a larger range of commodities for popular consumption has appeared on the market and these have become a part of the staple wants of the community. A variety in diet has been one of the most important results. Third, the pressure of trade unions has helped to raise the standard.

The United States as a matter of fact has been able to continue its policy of protection only because of the claim that such a policy resulted in a better standard of life for the American workingman. We have then a common conviction, extending through all classes, that the American standard must be maintained. Here and there may exist a belief that the working class should labor for the benefit of the advantaged classes from whom alone the flower of life is to be expected, but this belief is so foreign to the American consciousness that it dare not come to open expression. Its dangerous and anti-democratic character will not allow this doctrine, secretly cherished by many, to live in the open. The democratic point of view is still the only decent one for Americans openly to avow and it is still, we may believe, the dominant theory of social belief and practice, notwithstanding the great changes that have taken place with the growth of privilege.

The essential soundness of American ideals is indicated in the growth of social legislation during the past decade. This legislation has not been the unaided work of the classes directly affected by it. On the contrary, strenuous and successful as has been the work of the unions in putting through legislation for the benefit of the working classes, equally valuable help has come from totally other sources, where class interest has not been the prime motive.

The value of social legislation depends upon two elements, its regard for facts and its correlation with the public opinion of the period. Too often legislation has been secured that became a dead letter at once, owing to its being unenforceable through lack of public support. The massing of careful evidence in support of the need of legislation is of prime importance. We see, then, that the development of the social conscience, determined to raise the standard of living and to guard the ground gained with as watchful eye as ever government guarded its new colonial possessions, is due to a complex of causes and to the contagion of conviction that is possible only in the modern world of a free interchange of opinions. . . .

To sum up, we have attempted to show that the American public is intent upon maintaining the American standard of living, both through motives of democratic conviction, and through desire to excel. We have seen that, due to the existence of the struggle between employer and employed, the consideration of the maintenance of a high wages standard has been relatively neglected in favor of a policy of socialization which will indirectly secure to workers social and economic benefits. We have also shown that this process of improvement of living conditions through legislation and various educational and public health measures can never accomplish the purpose for which this process is intended without due attention to the maintenance of wages, and therefore to the protection and support of an intelligent organization of the working class.

And we have endeavored to give some practical point to these conclusions by showing that the latest and most accurate and scientific study of workingmen's budgets indicate that from $1000 to $1200 is the income that the city family must secure in order to maintain the American standard of living. The untold thousands who fall below this line indicate the magnitude of the problem that still waits for solution.

The "Social Gospel" Fuels Progressivism

The closing years of the nineteenth century witnessed a movement within mainline Protestant churches to apply Christian ethics to social and economic problems such as economic inequality, poverty, and slums. Called the "social gospel," it was advanced by several theologians and church leaders and made its way into Sunday sermons across New York and the nation.

But it was Walter Rauschenbusch (1861–1918), who led a church in New York City and then became a theology professor in Rochester, who crystallized and popularized the concept. His 1907 book Christianity and the Social Crisis *highlighted the gap between the masses of people and vested interests representing the rich and powerful. America had produced a fundamentally unjust social and economic system. To rectify things, churches and their members must work for a more equitable distribution of resources and act on behalf of disadvantaged people.* Christianity and the Social Crisis *captured the imagination of mainline Christians. It was a bestseller, going through six reprints in two years, and it propelled the social gospel out of the shadows of religious scholarship into the arena of public discourse, boosting the progressive movement. He elaborated on some of these concepts in his book* A Theology for the Social Gospel *(1917) and other writings.*

∽

From *Christianity and the Social Crisis* (1907)
by Walter Rauschenbusch

Western civilization is passing through a social revolution unparalleled in history for scope and power. Its coming was inevitable. The religious, political, and intellectual revolutions of the past five centuries, which together created the modern world, necessarily had to culminate in an economic and social revolution such as is now upon us.

By universal consent, this social crisis is the overshadowing problem of our generation. The industrial and commercial life of the advanced nations are in the throes of it. In politics all issues and methods are undergoing upheaval and re-alignment as the social movement advances. In the world of thought, all the young and serious minds are absorbed in the solution of the social problems. Even literature and art point like compass-needles to this magnetic pole of all our thought.

The social revolution has been slow in reaching our country. We have been exempt, not because we had solved the problems, but because we had not yet confronted them. We have now arrived, and all the characteristic conditions of American life will henceforth combine to make the social struggle here more intense than anywhere else. The vastness and the free sweep of our concentrated wealth on the one side, the independence, intelligence, moral vigor, and political power of the common people on the other side, promise a long-drawn grapple of contesting forces which may well make the heart of every American patriot sink within him.

It is realized by friend and foe that religion can play, and must play, a momentous part in this irrepressible conflict. The Church, the organized expression of the religious life of the past, is one of the most potent institutions and forces in Western civilization. Its favor and moral influence are wooed by all parties. It cannot help throwing its immense weight on one side or the other. If it tries not to act, it thereby acts; and in any case its choice will be decisive for its own future.

Apart from the organized Church, the religious spirit is a factor of incalculable power in the making of history. In the idealistic spirits that lead and in the masses that follow, the religious spirit always intensifies thought, enlarges hope, unfetters daring, evokes the willingness to sacrifice, and gives coherence in the fight. Under the warm breath of religious faith, all social institutions become plastic. The religious spirit removes mountains and tramples on impossibilities. Unless the economic and intellectual factors are strongly reenforced by religious enthusiasm, the whole social movement may prove abortive, and the New Era may die before it comes to birth. It follows that the relation between Christianity and the social crisis is one of the most pressing questions for all intelligent men who realize the power of religion, and most of all for the religious leaders of the people who give direction to the forces of religion.

The question has, in fact, been discussed frequently and earnestly, but it is plain to any thoughtful observer that the common mind of the Christian Church in America has not begun to arrive at any solid convictions or any permanent basis of action. The conscience of Christendom is halting and groping, perplexed by contradicting voices, still poorly informed on essential questions, justly reluctant to part with the treasured maxims of the past, and yet conscious of the imperious call of the future. . . .

The spiritual force of Christianity should be turned against the materialism and mammonism of our industrial and social order.

If a man sacrifices his human dignity and self-respect to increase his income, or stunts his intellectual growth and his human affections to swell his bank account, he is to that extent serving mammon and denying God. Likewise if he uses up and injures the life of his fellow-men to make money for himself, he serves mammon and denies God. But our industrial order does both. It makes property the end, and man the means to produce it.

Man is treated as a thing to produce more things. Men are hired as hands and not as men. They are paid only enough to maintain their working capacity and not enough to develop their manhood. When their working force is exhausted, they are flung aside without consideration of their human needs.

Jesus asked, "Is not a man more than a sheep?" Our industry says "No." It is careful of its livestock and machinery, and careless of its human working force. It keeps its electrical engines immaculate in burnished cleanliness and lets its human dynamos sicken in dirt. In the 15th Assembly District in New York City, between 10th and 11th avenues, 1321 families in 1896 had three bath tubs between them. Our industrial establishments are institutions for the creation of dividends, and not for the fostering of human life. In all our public life the question of profit is put first. Pastor Stöcker, in a speech on child and female labor in the German Reichstag, said: "We have put the question the wrong way. We have asked: How much child and female labor does industry need in order to flourish, to pay dividends, and to sell goods abroad? Whereas we ought to have asked: How ought industry to be organized in order to protect and foster the family, the human individual, and the Christian life?" That simple reversal of the question marks the difference between the Christian conception of life and property and the mammonistic.

"Life is more than food and raiment." More, too, than the apparatus which makes food and raiment. What is all the machinery of our industrial organization worth if it does not make human life healthful and happy?

But is it doing that? Men are first of all men, folks, members of our human family. To view them first of all as labor force is civilized barbarism. It is the attitude of the exploiter. Yet unconsciously we have all been taught to take that attitude and talk of men as if they were horse-powers or volts. Our commercialism has tainted our sense of fundamental human verities and values. We measure our national prosperity by pig-iron and steel instead of by the welfare of the people. In city affairs the property owners have more influence than the family owners. For instance, the pall of coal smoke hanging over our industrial cities is injurious to the eyes; it predisposes to diseases of the respiratory organs; it depresses the joy of living; it multiplies the labor of housewives in cleaning and washing. But it continues because it would impose expense on business to install smoke consumers or pay skilled stokers. If an agitation is begun to abolish the smoke nuisance, the telling argument is not that it inflicts injury on the mass of human life, but that the smoke "hurts business," and that it really "pays" to consume the wasted carbon. In political life one can constantly see the cause of human life pleading long and vainly for redress, like the widow before the unjust judge. Then suddenly comes the bass voice of Property, and all men stand with hat in hand.

Our scientific political economy has long been an oracle of the false god. It has taught us to approach economic questions from the point of view of goods and not of man. It tells us how wealth is produced and divided and consumed by man, and not how man's life and development can best be fostered by material wealth. It is significant that the discussion of "Consumption" of wealth has been most neglected in political economy; yet that is humanly the most important of all. Theology must become christocentric; political economy must become anthropocentric. Man is Christianized when he puts God before self; political economy will be Christianized when it puts man before wealth. Socialistic political economy does that. It is materialistic in its theory of human life and history, but it is humane in its aims, and to that extent is closer to Christianity than the orthodox science has been. . . .

Summary of the Argument

We undertook in this chapter to suggest in what ways the moral forces latent in Christian society could be mobilized for the progressive regeneration of social life, and in what directions chiefly these forces should be exerted. . . . The fundamental contribution of every man is the change of his own personality. We must repent of the sins of existing society, cast off the spell of the lies protecting our social wrongs, have faith in a higher social order, and realize in ourselves a new type of Christian manhood which seeks to overcome the evil in the present world, not by withdrawing from the world, but by revolutionizing it.

If this new type of religious character multiplies among the young men and women, they will change the world when they come to hold the controlling positions of society in their maturer years. They will give a new force to righteous and enlightened public opinion, and will apply the religious sense of duty and service to the common daily life with anew motive and directness.

The ministry, in particular, must apply the teaching functions of the pulpit to the pressing questions of public morality. It must collectively learn not to speak without adequate information; not to charge individuals with guilt in which all society shares; not to be partial, and yet to be on the side of the lost; not to yield to political partisanship, but to deal with moral questions before they become political issues and with those questions of public welfare which never do become political issues. They must lift the social questions to a religious level by faith and spiritual insight. The larger the number of ministers who attempt these untrodden ways, the safer and saner will those be who follow. By interpreting one social class to the other, they can create a disposition to make concessions and help in securing a peaceful settlement of social issues.

The force of the religious spirit should be bent toward asserting the supremacy of life over property. Property exists to maintain and develop life. It is unchristian to regard human life as a mere instrument for the production of wealth.

The religious sentiment can protect good customs and institutions against the inroads of ruthless greed, and extend their scope. It can create humane customs which the law is impotent to create. It can create the convictions and customs which are later embodied in good legislation.

Our complex society rests largely on the stewardship of delegated powers. The opportunities to profit by the betrayal of trust increase with the wealth and complexity of civilization. The most fundamental evils in past history and present conditions were due to converting stewardship into ownership. The keener moral insight created by Christianity should lend its help in scrutinizing all claims to property and power in order to detect latent public rights and to recall the recreant stewards to their duty. . . .

The splendid ideal of a fraternal organization of society cannot be realized by idealists only. It must be supported by the self-interest of a powerful class. The working class, which is now engaged in its upward movement, is struggling to secure better conditions of life, an assured status for its class organizations, and ultimately the ownership of the means of production. Its success in the last great aim would mean the closing of the gap which now divides industrial society and the establishment of industry on the principle of solidarity and the method of cooperation. Christianity should enter into a working alliance with this rising class, and by its mediation secure the victory of these principles by a gradual equalization of social opportunity and power.

A Skeptical View of Modern Trends

Changes in New York during the progressive era delighted some New Yorkers but confounded and upset others. Theodore Roosevelt (1858–1919), who served as New York governor (1899–1901), vice president in (1901), and then president (1901–1909), led progressive reform in government in those years. But after his presidency (and a failed run for the office again as the nominee of the short-lived Progressive Party), he was skeptical of and unsettled by changes in other sectors of public life. T. R. considered himself an expert on modern social trends and culture, and many Americans admired him and valued his opinions.

He attended a New York art show known as the International Exhibition of Modern Art, organized by the Association of American Painters and Sculptors, in 1913. Some of the art was conventional, but some was considered risqué at the time, particularly Marcel Duchamp's Nude Descending a Staircase. *Critics' reactions varied, some praising the leading-edge, daring art, others panning it as too abstract or offensive.*

Roosevelt wrote a review for the popular magazine Outlook, *where he served as an editor and essayist. Taking a balanced view, he praised some items, cited others for at least not being boring or conventional, but exhibited a clear distaste for others created by what he called "extremists" and "the lunatic fringe." His ambivalence reflected the reactions of many New Yorkers to the changes swirling around them.*

∼

From "A Layman's Views of an Art Exhibition," *Outlook* (1913) by Theodore Roosevelt

The recent "International Exhibition of Modern Art" in New York was really noteworthy. Messrs. Davies, Kuhn, Gregg, and their fellow members of the Association of American Painters and Sculptors have done a work of very real value in securing such an exhibition of the works of both foreign and native painters and sculptors. Primarily their purpose was to give the public a chance to see what has recently been going on abroad. No similar collection of the works of European "moderns" has ever been exhibited in this country. The exhibitors are quite right as to the need of showing to our people in this manner the art forces which of late have been at work in Europe, forces which cannot be ignored.

This does not mean that I in the least accept the view that these men take of the European extremists whose pictures are here exhibited. It is true, as the champions of these extremists say, that there can be no life without change, no development without change, and that to be afraid of what is different or unfamiliar is to be afraid of life. It is no less true, however, that change may mean death and not life, and retrogression instead of development. Probably we err in treating most of these pictures seriously. It is likely that many of them represent in the painters the astute appreciation of the powers to make folly lucrative which the late P. T. Barnum showed with his faked mermaid. There are thousands of people who will pay small sums to look at a faked mermaid; and now and then one of this kind with enough money will buy a Cubist picture, or a picture of a misshapen nude woman, repellent from every standpoint.

In some ways it is the work of the American painters and sculptors which is of most interest in this collection, and a glance at this work must convince any one of the real good that is coming out of the new movements, fantastic though many of the developments of these new movements are. There was one note entirely absent from the exhibition, and that was the note of the commonplace. There was not a touch of simpering, self-satisfied conventionality anywhere in the exhibition. Any sculptor or painter who had in him something to express and the power of expressing it found the field open to him. He did not have to be afraid because his work was not along ordinary lines. There was no stunting or dwarfing, no requirement that a man whose gift lay in new directions should measure up or down to stereotyped and fossilized standards.

For all of this there can be only hearty praise. But this does not in the least mean that the extremists whose paintings and pictures were represented are entitled to any praise, save, perhaps, that they have helped to break fetters. Probably in any reform movement, any progressive movement, in any field of life, the penalty for avoiding the commonplace is a liability to extravagance. It is vitally necessary to move forward and to shake off the dead hand, often the fossilized dead hand, of the reactionaries; and yet we have to face the fact that there is apt to be a lunatic fringe among the votaries of any forward movement.

In this recent art exhibition the lunatic fringe was fully in evidence, especially in the rooms devoted to the Cubists and the Futurists, or Near-Impressionists. I am not entirely certain which of the two latter terms should be used in connection with some of the various pictures and representations of plastic art—and, frankly, it is not of the least consequence.

The Cubists are entitled to the serious attention of all who find enjoyment in the colored puzzle pictures of the Sunday newspapers. Of course there is no reason for choosing the cube as a symbol, except that it is probably less fitted than any other mathematical expression for any but the most formal decorative art. There is no reason why people should not call themselves Cubists, or Octagonists, or Parallelopipedonists, or Knights of the Isosceles Triangle, or Brothers of the Cosine, if they so desire; as expressing anything serious and permanent, one term is as fatuous as another.

Take the picture which for some reason is called "A naked man going down stairs." There is in my bath-room a really good Navajo rug which, on any proper interpretation of the Cubist theory, is a far more satisfactory and decorative picture. Now if, for some inscrutable reason, it suited somebody to call this rug a picture of, say, "A well-dressed man going up a ladder," the name would fit the facts just about as well as in the case of the Cubist picture of the "naked man going down stairs." From the standpoint of terminology, each name would have whatever merit inheres in a rather cheap straining after effect; and from the standpoint of decorative value, of sincerity, and of artistic merit, the Navajo rug is infinitely ahead of the picture.

As for many of the human figures in the pictures of the Futurists, they show that the school would be better entitled to the name of the "Pastists." I was interested to find that a man of scientific attainments who had likewise looked at the pictures had been struck, as I was, by their resemblance to the later work of the paleolithic artists of the French and Spanish caves. There are interesting samples of the strivings for the representation of the human form among artists of many different countries and times, all in the same stage of paleolithic culture, to be found in a recent number of the "Revue d'Ethnographie." The paleolithic artist was able to portray the bison, the mammoth, the reindeer, and the horse with spirit and success, while he still stumbled painfully in the effort to portray man.

This stumbling effort in his case represented progress, and he was entitled to great credit for it. Forty thousand years later, when entered into artificially and deliberately, it represents only a smirking pose of retrogression, and is not praiseworthy. So with much of the sculpture. A family group of precisely the merit that inheres in a structure made of the wooden blocks in a nursery is not entitled to be reproduced in marble. Admirers speak of the kneeling female figure by Lehmbruck—I use "female" advisedly, for although obviously mammalian it is not especially human—as "full of lyric grace," as "tremendously sincere," and "of a jewel-like preciousness." I am not competent to say whether these words themselves represent sincerity or merely a conventional jargon; it is just as easy to be conventional about the fantastic as about the commonplace. In any event one might as well speak of the "lyric grace" of a praying mantis, which adopts much the same attitude; and why a deformed pelvis should be called "sincere," or a tibia of giraffe-like lengths "precious," is a question of pathological rather than artistic significance.

This figure and the absurd portrait head of some young lady have the merit that inheres in extravagant caricature. It is a merit, but it is not a high merit. It entitles these pieces to stand in sculpture where nonsense rhymes stand in literature and the sketches of Aubrey Beardsley in pictorial art. These modern sculptured caricatures in no way approach the gargoyles of Gothic cathedrals, probably because the modern artists are too self-conscious and make themselves ridiculous by pretentiousness. The makers of the gargoyles knew very well that the gargoyles did not represent what was most important in the Gothic cathedrals. They stood for just a little point of grotesque reaction against, and relief from, the tremendous elemental vastness and grandeur of the Houses of God. They were imps, sinister and comic, grim and yet futile, and they fitted admirably into the framework of the theology that found its expression in the towering and wonderful piles which they ornamented.

Very little of the work of the extremists among the European "moderns" seems to be good in and for itself; nevertheless it has certainly helped any number of American artists to do work that is original and serious; and this not only in painting but in sculpture. I wish the exhibition had contained some of the work of the late Marcius Symonds; very few people knew or cared for it while he lived; but not since Turner has there been another man on whose canvas glowed so much of that unearthly "light that never was on land or sea." But the exhibition contained so much of extraordinary merit that it is ungrateful even to mention an omission. To name the pictures one would like to possess—and the bronzes and tanagras and plasters—would mean to make a catalogue of indefinite length. One of the most striking pictures was the "Terminal Yards"—the seeing eye was there, and the cunning hand. I should like to mention all the pictures of the President of the association, Arthur B. Davies. As first-class decorative work of an entirely new type, the very unexpected pictures of Sheriff Bob Chandler have a merit all their own. The "Arizona Desert," the "Canadian Night," the group of girls on the roof of a New York tenement-house, the studies in the Bronx Zoo, the "Heracles," the studies for the Utah monument, the little group called "Gossip," which has something of the quality of the famous Fifteenth Idyl of Theocritus, the "Pelf," with its grim suggestiveness—these, and a hundred others, are worthy of study, each of them; I am naming at random those which at the moment I happen to recall. I am not speaking of the acknowledged masters, of Whistler, Puvis de Chavannes, Monet; nor of John's children; nor of Cezanne's old woman with a rosary; nor of Redon's marvelous color pieces—a worthy critic should speak of these. All I am trying to do is to point out why a layman is grateful to those who arranged this exhibition.

A Plea for Rural Values

Horticulturalist and botanist Liberty Hyde Bailey (1858–1954) spent most of his career teaching at Cornell University, where he established the College of Agriculture (now the College of Agriculture and Life Sciences) in 1904. He wrote many books and essays on farm and country life, agriculture, and crops, including fruit gardening and plant breeding, which led to improved farming practices. In 1908, he served as chairman of President Theodore Roosevelt's National Commission on Country Life. Its 1909 report called for rebuilding a great agricultural civilization in the nation.

Bailey became a champion of country life and agriculture in New York State and nationally. At a time of rapid urbanization and industrialization and the declining role of agriculture in the state's economy, Bailey espoused the steadfastness, hard work, and rural values of country people. The state's and nation's intensifying "industrial civilization" should use rural cultural values as a model. Bailey brought a touch of nostalgia to the surging progressive era.

∼

FROM *THE COUNTRY LIFE MOVEMENT IN THE UNITED STATES* (1915) BY LIBERTY HYDE BAILEY

Some Interrelations of the City and Country

Everyone knows that city populations are increasing more rapidly than country populations. By some persons, this of itself is considered to be a cause for much alarm. But the relative size of the populations is not so disturbing as the economic and social relations existing between these two phases of civilization.

Some contrasts of town folk and country folk

We know that farming is the primitive and underlying business of mankind. As human desires have arisen, other occupations have developed to satisfy the increasing needs and aspirations, the products of the earth have been assembled and changed by manufacture into a thousand forms, and these departures have resulted in more refined products, a more resourceful civilization, and a more sensitive people.

Complex developments have been taken out of and away from agriculture, and have left it with the simple and undifferentiated products and the elemental contact with nature. The farmer is largely a residuary force in society; this explains his conservatism.

If we have very highly developed persons in the city, we have very rugged persons in the country. If the sense of brotherhood is highly evolved in the city, individualism is strongly expressed in the country. If the world movement appeals to men in the city, local attachments have great power with men in the country. If commercial consolidation and organization are characteristic of the city, the economic separateness of the man or family is highly marked in the country. The more marked progress of the city is due to its greater number of leaders and to its consolidated interests; country people are personally as progressive as city people of equal intellectual groups, but they have not been able to attract as much attention or perhaps to make as much headway.

COMPARISONS OF TOWN AND COUNTRY AFFAIRS

Civilization oscillates between two poles. At the one extreme is the so-called laboring class, and at the other are the syndicated and corporate and monopolized interests. Both these elements or phases tend to go to extremes. Many efforts are being made to weld them into some sort of share-earning or commonness of interest, but without very great results. Between these two poles is the great agricultural class, which is the natural balance force or the middle-wheel of society. These people are steady, conservative, abiding by the law, and are to a greater extent than we recognize a controlling element in our social structure.

The man on the farm has the opportunity to found a dynasty. City properties may come and go, rented houses may be removed, stocks and bonds may rise and fall, but the land still remains; and a man can remain on the land and subsist with it so long as he knows how to handle it properly. It is largely, therefore, a question of education as to how long any family can establish itself on a piece of land.

In the accelerating mobility of our civilization it is increasingly important that we have many anchoring places; and these anchoring places are the farms.

These two phases of society produce marked results in ways of doing business. The great centers invite combinations, and, because society has not kept pace with guiding and correcting measures, immense abuses have arisen and the few have tended to fatten on the many. There are two general modes of correcting, or at least of modifying, these abuses, by doing what we can to make men personally honest and responsible, and by evening up society so that all men may have something like a natural opportunity.

THE TWO MINDS

There is a town mind and a country mind. I do not pretend to know what may be the psychological processes, but it is clear that the mode of approach to the problem of life is very different as between the real urbanite and the real ruralite [sic]. This factor is not sufficiently taken into account by city men who would remove to real farms and make a living there. It is the cause of most of the failure of well-intentioned social workers to accomplish much for country people.

All this is singularly reflected in our literature, and most of all, perhaps, in guide-books. These books, made to meet the demand, illustrate how completely the open country has been in eclipse. There is little rural country discoverable in these books, unless it is mere "sights" or "places," nothing of the people, of the lands, of the products, of the markets, of the country dorfs [towns], of the way of life; but there is surfeit of cathedrals, of history of cities, of seats of famous personages, of bridges and streets, of galleries and works of art. We begin to see evidences of travel out into the farming regions, part of it, no doubt, merely a desire for new experiences and diversion, and we shall now look for guide-books that recognize the background on which the cities rest. But all this will call for a new intention in travel.

WILL THE AMERICAN FARMER HOLD HIS OWN?

What future lies before the American farmer? Will he hold something like a position of independence and individualism, or will he become submerged in the social order, and form only an underlying stratum? What ultimate hope is there for a farmer as a member of society?

It is strange that the producer of the raw material has thus far in the history of the world taken a subordinate place to the trader in this material and to the fabricator of it. The trader and fabricator live in centers that we call cities. One type of mind assembles; the other type remains more or less scattered. So there have arisen in human society two divergent streams, the collective and cooperative, and the isolated and individualistic.

The fundamental weakness in our civilization is the fact that the city and the country represent antagonistic forces. Sympathetically, they have been and are opposed. The city lives on the country. It always tends to destroy its province.

The city sits like a parasite, running out its roots into the open country and draining it of its substance. The city takes everything to itself—materials, money, men—and gives back only what it does not want; it does not reconstruct or even maintain its contributory country. Many country places are already sucked dry.

The future state of the farmer, or real countryman, will depend directly on the kind of balance or relationship that exists between urban and rural forces; and in the end, the state of the city will rest on the same basis. Whatever the city does for the country, it does also for itself.

Mankind has not yet worked out this organic relation of town and country. City and country are gradually coming together fraternally, but this is due more to acquaintanceship than to any underlying cooperation between them as equal forces in society. Until such an organic relationship exists, civilization cannot be perfected or sustained, however high it may rise in its various parts. . . .

WHAT IS TO BE THE OUTCOME OF OUR INDUSTRIAL CIVILIZATION?

We know that the whole basis of civilization is changing. Industry of every kind is taking the place of the older order. Its most significant note is that it brings the people of the world together in consultation and in trade. We are escaping our localism, and we look on all problems in their relation to all mankind. Brotherhood has become a real power in the world.

But what does industry in itself, including all forms of land-culture, offer as an ultimate goal to civilized man? What are to be the man's ideals toward which he should lead his thoughts? I am not one of those who consider a sordid and commercial end to be the necessary result of industrialism. We must develop the ideals in an industrial civilization, that they may lead us into the highest personal endeavor; and everywhere it should be possible for a man to make the most of himself. There must be something in every business beyond the financial gain if it is to make any final contribution to civilization. Finding this ultimate, industrial society will grow into perfect flower.

So far as agriculture is concerned, I see two points of high endeavor within the business, lying beyond the making of a good living, and toward which the coming countryman may set his imagination.

1. THE MAKING OF A NEW SOCIETY

A new social order must be evolved in the open country, and every farmer of the new time must lend a strong hand to produce it. We have been training our youth merely to be better farmers; this, of course, is the first thing to do, but the man is only half trained when this is done. What to do with the school, the church, the rural organizations, the combinations of trade, the highways, the architecture, the library, the beauty of the landscape, the country store, the rousing of a fine community helpfulness to take the place of the old selfish individualism, and a hundred other activities, is enough to fire the imagination and to strengthen the arm of any young man or woman.

The farmer is to contribute his share to the evolution of an industrial democracy. . . .

We have scarcely begun even the physical conquest of the earth. It is not yet all explored. The earth is an island, and it is only two years ago that we got to one end of it. There are mountains to pierce, sea-shores to reclaim, vast stretches of submerged land to drain, millions of acres to irrigate and many more millions to utilize by dry-farming, rivers to canalize, the whole open country to organize and subdue by means of local engineering work, and a thousand other great pieces of construction to accomplish, all calling for the finest spirit of conquest and all contributing to the training of men and women. There is no necessity that the race become flabby.

The Anarchist's Plea

For a few New Yorkers, even the most hopeful and advanced policies of mainline progressives were not enough. Some were socialists, advocating government ownership of some industries. But a small minority were anarchists who deemed capitalism exploitative, government oppressive and mostly a means to protect private property, marriage a form of subjugation of women, and religion a form of superstition.

Anarchism went way beyond progressivism and found little support in New York or the rest of the country. In fact, the progressives sometimes used it as something of a foil to contrast their own, moderate views with extremist radicalism. Yet some of the anarchists' views—for example, on free speech—later found their way, with modifications, into mainstream political discourse.

Emma Goldman (1869–1940) was the best-known leader in New York's anarchist community. She spoke and wrote widely on the issues of the day, including government censorship, women's rights, birth control, and militarism.

The essay excerpted below, which appeared in the New York World *newspaper on July 19, 1908, was Goldman's attempt to explain her views. Goldman, an eloquent articulator of the anarchist creed, was deported from the United States in 1918 mainly because of her opposition to American participation in World War I.*

∼

FROM "WHAT I BELIEVE" (1908) BY EMMA GOLDMAN

Anarchists are by no means passive spectators in the theatre of social development; on the contrary, they have some very positive notions as regards aims and methods. That I may make myself as clear as possible without using too much space, permit me to adopt the topical mode of treatment of "What I Believe."

I. As to Property

"Property" means dominion over things and the denial to others of the use of those things. So long as production was not equal to the normal demand, institutional property may have had some *raison d'être*. One has only to consult economics, however, to know that the productivity of labor within the last few decades has increased so tremendously as to exceed normal demand a hundred-fold and to make property not only a hindrance to human well-being, but an obstacle, a deadly barrier, to all progress. It is the private dominion over things that condemns millions of people to be mere nonentities, living corpses without originality or power of initiative, human machines of flesh and blood, who pile up mountains of wealth for others and pay for it with a gray, dull, and wretched existence for themselves. I believe that there can be no real wealth, social wealth, so long as it rests on human lives—young lives, old lives, and lives in the making.

It is conceded by all radical thinkers that the fundamental cause of this terrible state of affairs is (1) that man must sell his labor; (2) that his inclination and judgment are subordinated to the will of a master.

Anarchism is the only philosophy that can and will do away with this humiliating and degrading situation. It differs from all other theories inasmuch as it points out that man's development, his physical well-being, his latent qualities and innate disposition alone must determine the character and conditions of his work. Similarly will one's physical and mental appreciations and his soul cravings decide how much he shall consume.

To make this a reality will, I believe, be possible only in a society based on voluntary cooperation of productive groups, communities, and societies loosely federated together, eventually developing into a free communism, actuated by a solidarity of interests. There can be no freedom in the large sense of the word, no harmonious development, so long as mercenary and commercial considerations play an important part in the determination of personal conduct.

II. As to Government

I believe government, organized authority, or the State, is necessary only to maintain or protect property and monopoly. It has proven efficient in that function only. As a promoter of individual liberty, human well-being, and social harmony, which alone constitute real order, government stands condemned by all the great men of the world.

I therefore believe, with my fellow-Anarchists, that statutory regulations, legislative enactments, constitutional provisions, are invasive. They never yet induced man to do anything he could and would not do by virtue of his intellect or temperament, nor prevented anything that man was impelled to do by the same dictates. Millet's pictorial description of "The Man with the Hoe," Meunier's masterpieces of the miners that have aided in lifting labor from its degrading position, Gorky's descriptions of the underworld, Ibsen's psychological analysis of human life, could never have been induced by government any more than the spirit which impels a man to save a drowning child or a crippled woman from a burning building has ever been called into operation by statutory regulations or the policeman's club. I believe, indeed, I know, that whatever is fine and beautiful in the human spirit expresses and asserts itself in spite of government, and not because of it.

The Anarchists are therefore justified in assuming that Anarchism—the absence of government—will insure the widest and greatest scope for unhampered human development, the cornerstone of true social progress and harmony.

As to the stereotyped argument that government acts as a check on crime and vice, even the makers of law no longer believe it. This country spends millions of dollars for the maintenance of her "criminals" behind prison bars, yet crime is on the increase. Surely this state of affairs is not owing to an insufficiency of laws! Ninety per cent of all crimes are property crimes, which have their root in our economic iniquities. So long as these latter continue to exist we might convert every lamppost into a gibbet without having the least effect on the crime in our midst. Crimes resulting from heredity can certainly never be cured by law. Surely we are learning even today that such crimes can effectively be treated only by the best modern medical methods at our command and, above all, by the spirit of a deeper sense of fellowship, kindness and understanding. . . .

IV. As to Free Speech and Press

Many good people imagine that the principles of free speech or press can be exercised properly and with safety within the limits of constitutional guarantees. That is the only excuse, it seems to me, for the terrible apathy and indifference to the onslaught upon free speech and press that we have witnessed in this country within the last few months.

I believe that free speech and press mean that I may say and write what I please. This right, when regulated by constitutional provisions, legislative enactment, almighty decisions of the Postmaster General or the policeman's club, becomes a farce. I am well aware that I will be warned of consequences if we remove the chains from speech and press. I believe, however, that the cure of consequences resulting from the unlimited exercise of expression is to allow more expression.

Mental shackles have never yet stemmed the tide of progress, whereas premature social explosions have only too often been brought about through a wave of repression. Will our governors never learn that countries like England, Holland, Norway, Sweden, and Denmark, with the largest freedom of expression, have been freest from "consequences"? Whereas Russia, Spain, Italy, France, and, alas, even America, have raised these "consequences" to the most pressing political factor. Ours is supposed to be a country ruled by the majority, yet every policeman who is not vested with power by the majority can break up a meeting, drag the lecturer off the platform, and club the audience out of the hall in true Russian fashion. The Postmaster General, who is not an elective officer, has the power to suppress publications and confiscate mail. From his decision there is no more appeal than from that of the Russian Czar. Truly, I believe we need a new Declaration of Independence. Is there no modern Jefferson or Adams?

V. As to the Church

At the recent convention of the political remnants of a once revolutionary idea it was voted that religion and vote getting have nothing to do with each other. Why should they? So long as man is willing to delegate to the devil the care of his soul, he might, with the same consistency, delegate to the politician the care of his rights. That religion is a private affair has long been settled by the Bis-Marxian [sic] Socialists of Germany. Our American Marxians, poor of blood and originality, must need go to Germany for their wisdom. That wisdom has served as a capital whip to lash the several millions of people into the well-disciplined army of Socialism. It might do the same here. For goodness' sake, let's not offend respectability, let's not hurt the religious feelings of the people.

Religion is a superstition that originated in man's mental inability to solve natural phenomena. The Church is an organized institution that has always been a stumbling block to progress. Organized churchism has stripped religion of its naïveté and primitiveness. It has turned religion into a nightmare that oppresses the human soul and holds the mind in bondage. "The Dominion of Darkness," as the last true Christian, Leo Tolstoi, calls the Church, has been a foe of human development and free thought, and as such it has no place in the life of a truly free people.

VI. As to Marriage and Love

I believe these are probably the most tabooed subjects in this country. It is almost impossible to talk about them without scandalizing the cherished propriety of a lot of good folk. No wonder so much ignorance prevails relative to these questions. Nothing short of an open, frank, and intelligent discussion will purify the air from the hysterical, sentimental rubbish that is shrouding these vital subjects, vital to individual as well as social well-being.

Marriage and love are not synonymous; on the contrary, they are often antagonistic to each other. I am aware of the fact that some marriages are actuated by love, but the narrow, material confines of marriage, as it is, speedily crush the tender flower of affection. Marriage is an institution which furnishes the State and Church with a tremendous revenue and the means of prying into that phase of life which refined people have long considered their own, their very own most sacred affair. Love is that most powerful factor of human relationship which from time immemorial has defied all man-made laws and broken through the iron bars of conventions in Church and morality. Marriage is often an economic arrangement purely, furnishing the woman with a life-long life insurance policy, and the man with a perpetuator of his kind or a pretty toy. That is, marriage, or the training thereto, prepares the woman for the life of a parasite, a dependent, helpless servant, while it furnishes the man the right of a chattel mortgage over a human life.

How can such a condition of affairs have anything in common with love, with the element that would forego all the wealth of money and power and live in its own world of untrammeled human expression? But this is not the age of romanticism, of Romeo and Juliet, Faust and Marguerite, of moonlight ecstasies, of flowers and songs. Ours is a practical age. Our first consideration is an income. So much the worse for us if we have reached the era when the soul's highest flights are to be checked. No race can develop without the love element.

But if two people are to worship at the shrine of love, what is to become of the golden calf, marriage? "It is the only security for the woman, for the child, the family, the State." But it is no security to love; and without love no true home can or does exist. Without love no child should be born; without love no true woman can be related to a man. The fear that love is not sufficient material safety for the child is out of date. I believe when woman signs her own emancipation, her first declaration of independence will consist in admiring and loving a man for the qualities of his heart and mind and not for the quantities in his pocket. The second declaration will be that she has the right to follow that love without let or hindrance from the outside world. The third and most important declaration will be the absolute right to free motherhood.

In such a mother and an equally free father rests the safety of the child. They have the strength, the sturdiness, the harmony to create an atmosphere wherein alone the human plant can grow into an exquisite flower.

Sources

Bailey, Liberty Hyde, *The Country Life Movement in the United States* (New York: Macmillan, 1915), 14–21, 55–60. Available at HathiTrust, https://babel.hathitrust.org/cgi/pt?id=uc2.ark:/13960/t3mw2bg7q&view=page&seq=9.

Goldman, Emma, *What I Believe* (New York: Mother Earth Publishing Association, 1908), 4–7, 10–13, reprinted from *New York World*, July 19, 1908. Available at HathiTrust, https://babel.hathitrust.org/cgi/pt?id=mdp.39015081787973&view=page&seq=13.

Lippmann, Walter, *Drift and Mastery: An Attempt to Diagnose the Current Unrest* (New York: M. Kennerley, 1914), 265–272. Available at HathiTrust, https://babel.hathitrust.org/cgi/pt?id=nyp.33433069249328&view=page&seq=9.

Phillips, David Graham, *The Reign of Gilt* (New York: James Pott & Company, 1905), 32–48. Available at Project Gutenberg, https://www.gutenberg.org/ebooks/64402.

Rauschenbusch, Walter, *Christianity and the Social Crisis* (New York: Macmillan, 1908), xi–xii, 369–372. Available at HathiTrust, https://babel.hathitrust.org/cgi/pt?id=chi.10089293&view=page&seq=9.

Roosevelt, Theodore, "A Layman's Views of an Art Exhibition," *Outlook* 103 (March 29, 1913), 718–720. Available at HathiTrust, https://babel.hathitrust.org/cgi/pt?id=msu.31293006865137&view=page&seq=1.

Simkhovitch, Mary K., *The City Worker's World in America* (New York: Macmillan, 1917), 43–47, 59. Available at HathiTrust. https://catalog.hathitrust.org/Record/000954359.

Weyl, Walter E., *The New Democracy* (New York: Macmillan, 1912) 255–256, 276–282. Available at HathiTrust, https://babel.hathitrust.org/cgi/pt?id=coo1.ark:/13960/t00z7qx1c&view=page&seq=9.

2

Building Grand Enterprises

Figure 2. The Electric Tower at the 1901 Pan American Exposition in Buffalo symbolized technological enterprise and prowess in the new century. Source: Library of Congress Prints & Photographs Collection.

New York always does things on a grand scale, and the progressive era was no exception. New Yorkers in the new century excelled in developing new technology, organizing big new business enterprises, and building things that were large and extravagant. New York state government built a grand new cross-state canal in 1918 to replace the outdated Erie Canal. It opened a new block-long State Education Building in 1912 that featured thirty-six marble columns in front, meant to be an imposing structure projecting the power of the State Education Department, established eight years earlier. Following the renovation and expansion of a historic building, Court of Appeals Hall opened in 1917 for the state's highest court.

Buffalo, with state encouragement, hosted a flashy Pan-American Exposition in 1901. New York City opened its state-of-the-art subway in 1904.

The New York Central Railroad, the state's largest company, built one of the nation's largest freight yards in Buffalo in the early years of the century and the nation's most prominent passenger station in New York City in 1913. Eastman Kodak, established in 1888, by the early twentieth century was the nation's leading camera manufacturer. The Computing-Tabulating-Recording Company, established in Endicott in 1911, led the way in data processing machines and expanded and changed its name to International Business Machines (IBM) in 1924. The Curtiss Aeroplane and Motor Corporation in Buffalo was the nation's largest aircraft company in the World War I years. The General Electric Company, founded in 1892 with headquarters in Schenectady, by the turn of the century was the national leader in manufacture of dynamos, electric engines, electrical fixtures, and other machines powered by what would be one of the leading technologies and drivers of change in the twentieth century.

New Yorkers had a knack for publicizing their achievements as symbols of their state's grandeur and leadership.

A Grand Expo in Buffalo

Buffalo civic and business leaders worked tirelessly to promote their city in the new century. They were determined that their city would not fall into the shadows of Toronto in nearby Canada or New York City at the other end of the state. They touted Buffalo's cultural attractions and its leadership in trade, industry, and commerce. Looking for a high-visibility public venue, they organized an international exposition that ran May 1 to November 1, 1901.

The "Pan-American Exposition" featured exhibits on trade, manufacturing, mining, and agriculture. There were buildings devoted to the arts, music, and entertainment. Visitors could see exhibits on Africa, Egypt, Hawaii, Germany, and Japan and a recreation of a canal in Venice, complete with boats and gondoliers. A "Trained Wild Animal Show" and a building where visitors were treated to "A Trip to the Moon" rounded out the entertainment venues. The expo celebrated electric power generation at nearby Niagara Falls, and its buildings were illuminated at night. A New York State Building emphasized the state's leadership and attractions.

President William McKinley visited the fair and was shot by an anarchist; he died some days later, marring the festivities. But nearly eight million people visited during its six-month tenure.

Afterward, the buildings and exhibits were dismantled, except for the New York State Building, which was turned over to the Buffalo Historical Society (now Buffalo History Museum). The building has been used to preserve and promote Western New York history ever since.

Buffalo promoters published several "guidebooks" with colorful, exciting descriptions of the Exposition building and attractions.

∼

FROM *OFFICIAL CATALOGUE AND GUIDE BOOK TO THE PAN-AMERICAN EXPOSITION* (1901)

The Exposition

Situated as Buffalo is, the center from which radiate trunk lines to every point of the compass, it may safely be said to enjoy railway facilities possessed by no other city in the world. In the heart of the commercial continent, accessible by rail from all parts of the country, and in direct communication with the system of Great Lakes. Attractive in topography and ornate in every description of architecture, the Queen City of the Lakes invites the world to come into her midst and be her guest from May first to November first, 1901.

The Rainbow City, thirty minutes' ride from the heart of Buffalo, under splendid domes, attractive minarets, towers and pavilions aglow with numberless pleasing hues and tints, and within the classic outlines of its buildings, visitors will be regaled with views showing the progress of the few years past, ornamented and enlarged by attractive exhibits from all parts of the Western Hemisphere. Second in size only to the [Chicago] World's Fair and far more attractive and unique in many particulars beyond that display in 1893, and thoroughly original in its most distinctive features, the Pan-American Exposition opens its gates feeling confident that no visitor will be disappointed.

General Plan of Grounds

The general plan of the Exposition grounds can be compared to that of an inverted "T" with the cross arm as the Esplanade extending east and west, and the vertical stem extending north, terminating in the Propylaea or entrance to the railway station. The Court of Fountains is in the center of the vertical stem and starting from its four corners is the beginning of the main group of large buildings. From the railway station and passing through the Plaza, the visitors enter the court; to the westward are the Electricity, the Machinery and Transportation buildings, separated by the Sunken Gardens which are filled with the choicest of flowers and cooling fountains, the water taking the form of beautiful flowers, &c. To the eastward are the buildings for Agriculture, and Manufactures and Liberal Arts, also separated by Sunken Gardens. Standing in a broad basin to the northward of the Court is the Electric Tower, rising to a height of 391 feet, adorned with many costly groups of sculpture upon its salient points, and from a niche in its southern face gushes a cascade 70 feet high and 30 feet wide. Connecting with this basin, a canal bordered by beautiful trees and crossed by arched bridges, runs westward, to the north of the Electricity building and eastward to the north of the Agriculture building and then turns and flows southward terminating in the Mirror Lake, filled with grottoes and effects of marvelous beauty and interest.

Facing the Esplanade on the north is the Cascade Fountain, and at either end are the Esplanade fountains, surrounded as they are with statuary of every description. The Esplanade is designed so as to be capable of holding 250,000 people, and from its southern end, entrance is effected from the Fore Court over the Triumphal Bridge, surmounted on its four corners by four massive towers two hundred feet high.

Exposition Color Scheme

In all previous expositions, the main feature has been the architectural work and not color. But this one represents both, and is after the plan designed and directed by C. Y. Turner, representing the fierce struggle of "man to overcome the elements."

As one enters the grounds, on the left will be seen buildings which represent "elements," and on the right those representing man and his affairs, or that which man has gained after long years of struggling to overcome the elements.

The struggles are represented by heavy deep coloring of red, blue, green and gold, graduating gently but firmly in tints, until the electric tower is reached, where it again commences in a deep green as near the color of Lake Erie as it was possible to get it. The tower itself is a cream white with sculpture work of the four corners, and is tinted with blue, green and gold, getting fainter until the top is reached, terminating in the figure representing all that man has accomplished over the elements.

Illumination

The illumination is the most brilliant and elaborate ever contemplated. An Electric Tower soaring to a lofty height, and surmounted by a splendid statue of the Goddess of Light, is the centerpiece of this great dominating feature of the Exposition. It is studded with incandescent lamps and powerful searchlights, one of which, at a great height, sends its gleams for many miles around, embracing in its grand circle the Falls of Niagara and the Canadian Frontier.

Every great building is outlined with a myriad of lights, and the staff glows with effulgent splendor. The Court of Fountains is brilliantly and fantastically illuminated. Colored lights from concealed electric bulbs are absorbed by the flowers in the gardens of the courts. A cascade gushes from a niche in the tower, from which scores of searchlights play their iridescent colors upon the scene.

Architectural Features

The style of architecture, a free treatment of the Spanish Renaissance, is a compliment to the Latin-American countries, who are prominent exhibitors. Column and entablature have been used for decorative, rather than for architectural effect, and the exterior of every building presents great richness of design, by the generous use of colonnades, balconies, loggias, towers and minarets, commanding broad views of the grounds. Grand original sculptured groups, designed by leading American artists, guard entrances and bridges, lacking only life to complete the ideality of their purpose.

Instead of glaring white, there is color everywhere, and color used on color to gain the desired effect. Beautiful decorations in color are so profuse that it makes one shudder to reflect that all this was improvised for the fleeting purpose of a season's passing show.

The largest architectural synthesis of the Exposition surrounds the Court of Fountains. Here are grouped on the east and west the Manufactures and Liberal Arts and the Machinery and Transportation buildings, with the Agriculture and Electricity buildings opposite, while between the Court and the Plaza rises the Electric Tower to a height of 391 feet, upon which are displayed electrical phenomena hitherto unattempted.

At the base of the tower two colonnades, 75 feet high, sweep to the southward and form a semi-circular space opening toward the Court of Fountains, and on the top of its domed cupola a superb figure, the Goddess of Light, is poised, overlooking and dominating the entire Exposition.

But even here the art spirit dominates, and the entire exterior of the tower is richly ornamented with plastic design and sculpture, and the ordinary visitor will certainly find himself more inclined to study the wonderful freedom and beauty of the decorations than to go seriously into the evidence they give of the progress of electrical science. In the center of this Court lies the Aquatic Basin, covering two acres. This has been treated with a view to bringing out special designs in jets of water, which take the form of magnificent sculptures in large numbers. . . .

The Grand Canal

The Grand Canal, over a mile in length, extends around the central group of large buildings. Winding lagoons connecting with the canal branch off in all directions. The Mirror Lakes in the southern portion of the canal, form a picturesque feature. The outer bank of the canal and the banks of the lagoons are sodded and set with trees and flowers, producing vistas of unusual interest and beauty. Electric launches, gondolas and other small craft ply from place to place. The ride is a refreshing one, with charming views at every turn. Romantic bridges span the waterway at convenient points, and statuary placed everywhere adds to the picturesque effect.

A New Cross-State Canal

By the dawn of the twentieth century, New York's famed Erie Canal, completed in 1825, had fallen into obsolescence. It could not accommodate the large freight-carrying barges coming into vogue in the new century. Railroads had siphoned off most of its freight and passenger traffic. Maintenance and repairs were expensive. Following an 1898 scandal involving shoddy work and corrupt overcharging by contractors on a major canal repair and enlargement project, Governor Theodore Roosevelt appointed a committee to advise on New York's future canal policy. That committee in 1900 recommended replacing the Erie Canal with a massive new canal capable of handling thousand-ton freight barges. That would bring an upsurge of commerce to New York, particularly Buffalo and New York City.

Commercial interests in those two cities formed a Canal Improvement State Committee, which led a successful campaign for legislative approval in 1903. The committee made another push that fall for voter approval of a $101 million bond issue (over $35 billion in today's dollars), the largest bond issue by any state up to that time. The massive lobbying campaign featured a series of advocacy documents, one of which is excerpted below. It was enough to overcome the opposition of rural groups and cities distant from the canal that did not expect to benefit from it and the half-hearted opposition of railroads, which by that time no longer saw canals as serious rivals. Voters approved the new canal by a sizeable margin.

Work on the new Barge Canal began in 1904, and the new waterway opened in 1918. It was one of the largest public improvement projects ever undertaken by any state.

∽

FROM *THE THOUSAND-TON BARGE IMPROVEMENT* (1903)
BY THE CANAL IMPROVEMENT STATE COMMITTEE

Canal Case Summed Up

For a period of nearly twenty years past, the business interests of the State have been patiently and persistently working for a proper improvement of the State's waterways. This agitation was begun and continued for the reason that year after year the port of New York has been steadily losing its proper share of export and import traffic of the country, and the growth in manufacturing and industrial enterprises in the State has not kept pace with sister States in proportion to our natural advantages. In order that the best plan of improvement might be secured, having in view the present needs of the State and with careful consideration of the future, most competent commissions were appointed by Governors [Frank] Black and [Theodore] Roosevelt carefully to investigate this proposition. In addition, most careful surveys and estimates were made, and information was collected by the State authorities through the office of the State Engineer. As a result of the conclusion reached by these various eminent authorities, the business interests of the State have decided that the commercial, manufacturing, industrial and agricultural supremacy of the State will best be preserved and maintained through the construction of the 1,000-ton barge canal.

These twenty years of agitation have served to bring forth certain phases of opposition to the proposition, and it is proper that the various arguments against canal improvement should be carefully considered.

One of the most common statements made by the enemies of the canals is that the demand for the improvement of the canals can be traced to certain terminal, dock, and elevator interests in the cities of New York and Buffalo. The facts are that while perhaps not the sole owners, the railroads centering at Buffalo and New York practically control the terminal, elevator, dock, and lighterage [transfer of cargo between ships] interests of those ports, and certainly they would not be likely to be clamoring for canal improvement. The opposition leave out of sight the fact that there is not a single commercial organization in the cities of New York and Buffalo that does not demand the enlargement and improvement of the Erie Canal as provided for under the 1,000-ton barge canal plan, and the further fact that the preponderating business interests of both cities emphatically agree in urging the adoption of the proposed plan for the improvement of the waterways of the State.

The statement is sometimes made that there is no condition or emergency in the development of the great commercial centers of New York and Buffalo which would justify the incurring by the State of an indebtedness for the construction of the 1,000-ton barge canal; practically saying that the rate of increase in the population and wealth of the cities of New York and Buffalo justifies the conclusion that the cities of New York and Buffalo have sufficiently prospered and do not require any further aid through the improvement of the waterways of the State.

Admitting that the cities of New York and Buffalo have developed and prospered under the construction and operation of the Erie Canal, which was a most efficient transportation route until within the last thirty years, the fact yet remains that the former commerce of the City of New York has not only shown a relative decrease as compared with competing cities of this country during the last twenty years, but has actually fallen off in export as well as in import trade in the last few years. Proofs as to the correctness of this assertion can be found by consulting the reports of the Chamber of Commerce of New York, the reports of the Commerce Commission appointed by Governor Black to examine into the commerce of New York, the cause of its decline and the means for its revival, and the report of the Committee on Canals of New York State appointed by Governor Roosevelt, and we do not believe that the concurrent testimony of these bodies, consisting of most competent men who have given very careful attention to the subject, can be lightly disregarded.

This testimony goes to show conclusively that the commerce of the State of New York is now at the mercy and under the control of the railroad combinations, which, through discrimination, divert traffic to other ports and to other States as may best suit their convenience or their business interest; that the Erie Canal is at the present time in a nearly useless condition, in which it cannot furnish the service required to compete with the railroads and exercise its former vocation of a regulator of transportation rates, whereas the roads have steadily and enormously increased their efficiency. . . .

The statement is sometimes made that there is the highest degree of probability that the estimates of cost of construction of the 1,000-ton barge canal are too low. This statement invariably emanates from men who are not engineers and who have had no experience in the construction of great public works, but who make this wild and random statement simply for the purpose of misleading others. Such assertion is entirely unsupported by the opinion of any engineer of standing, and those who make it have certainly not consulted any expert opinion in the matter of the estimates of the cost of construction. . . .

It has been stated that the work of canal improvement will bring an excessive influx of foreign labor into this State to the detriment of its existing labor interests. If this argument were a sound one, no public improvement of any kind should ever be undertaken, because it would be likely to furnish a very large amount of work to be done by someone. It is certain that the proposed improvement of the Erie Canal will bring employment and good wages to a very large number of our people in this State, not only in the construction of the work itself, but in the enterprises which the canal improvement will create throughout the State at large.

New York City Opens Its Subway

New York City's rapid growth introduced the need for better public transportation, well beyond horses and carriages and the surface and elevated passenger lines constructed in the late nineteenth century. An 1894 referendum authorized a subway to be built with city funds. That would be a pioneering effort. The first practical subway in the United States had opened in Boston in 1897. Other American cities would not build them until later in the new century.

Advocates explained that a subway would relieve urban congestion by permitting dissemination of the population and also serve New York City's business interests and its growing tourism traffic. After delays, a contract was awarded to the Rapid Transit Subway Construction Company and work began in 1900. Construction involved digging up streets and building tunnels in one of the most densely populated cities in the world. But the work proceeded more or less on schedule. The first segment opened on October 27, 1904, with speeches by political leaders and the subway's builders and celebration by New Yorkers. Thousands tried it out the first day. It was a milestone in New York City's history.

The entire initial system was in operation by 1908. Over the years, the subway expanded and modernized and has played a major role in moving New Yorkers around and supporting growth of the city. It is one of the city's proudest and most iconic features.

∼

From "Our Subway Open, 150,000 Try It," *New York Times*, October 28, 1904

Mayor McClellan Runs the First Official Train

Big Crowds Ride At Night

Average of 25,000 an Hour From 7 PM Till Past Midnight

For the first time in his life, Father Knickerbocker [a popular personification for New York City] went underground yesterday, went underground he and his children, to the number of 150,000, amid the tooting of whistles and the firing of salutes, for a first ride in a subway which for years had been scoffed at as an impossibility. New York's dream of rapid transit became a reality at exactly 2:35 o'clock yesterday afternoon, when the running of trains with passengers began.

With a silver controller Mayor [George B.] McClellan [Jr.] started the first train, the official train, which bore John B. McDonald, the contractor who dug the subway; William Barclay Parsons, Chief Engineer of the Rapid Transit Commission, and most of the other men who made the subway a possibility and a reality.

The Mayor liked his job as motorman so well that he stayed at the controller until the train reached Broadway and One Hundred and Third Street, when he yielded the place to the company's motor conductor.

Official Train on Time

The official train made its run exactly on time, arriving at One Hundred and Forty-fifth Street in exactly twenty six minutes, and all along the way crowds of excited New Yorkers were collected around the little entrances talking about the unheard trains that they knew were dashing by below, and waiting eagerly for the first passengers to emerge from the underground passageways at their feet.

Before this was done there had been simple ceremonies at the City Hall, while a multitude waited outside, kept in check with a strong force of police. After the first train came others in quick succession, almost treading on its heels, so that the first train had hardly turned back to make the run down to City Hall before another train passed it.

Those who rode on these trains were the 15,000 invited guests and their friends. The general public would not be admitted until 7 o'clock, and its curiosity was vastly whetted all the afternoon by the unfamiliar appearance of crowds emerging from the earth.

Of this sight New York seemed never to tire, and no matter how often it was seen there was always the shock of the unaccustomed about it. All the afternoon the crowds hung around the curious-looking little stations, waiting for heads and shoulders to appear at their feet and grow into bodies. Much as the Subway has been talked about, New York was not prepared for this scene and did not seem able to grow used to it.

Even on the first or official train, however, there were a great many who did not make the round trip from City Hall Park to One Hundred and Forty-fifth Street and back again, but got off at their own station on the return trip in the most natural and matter-of-fact way, as if they had been doing it all their lives, and so within half an hour from the start the waiting crowds at the stations were getting that half-shocking sense of the unfamiliar as the heads and shoulders came up from underground.

Carnival Night in Town

The result was that at night a vast crowd stormed the terminal entrances and taxed the best efforts of New York's police, who had been on duty all day to shepherd them. It was carnival night in New York. Every noise-making instrument known to election night was in operation, and a great mass of people surrounded the celebration at Times Square. The crowd was, as on election night, a good-natured crowd, it disposed to snarl or say, "Awww, who're yer shovin'."

Long before noon, the City Hall Park was surrounded with crowds, there to wait patiently for hours to gaze at the flag-decked building and at the end to see nothing but some silk hats moving rapidly toward an unimpressive looking steam-siren-shaped affair which was the entrance to the City Hall station. Through them, at least until they became too densely packed, circulated hacksters [sic] with every cry from "Popcorn!" to "Git a programme, git a programme!"

At 2 o'clock there was a wild shriek of whistles, because everybody who had a whistle to blow had in mind the Mayor's request, and thought that the City Hall ceremonies were over. They were not, because some of the speakers could not resist the temptation to talk a little longer than the programme called for. The tactful Mayor, in anticipation of some such event, held his speech down to the minimum, but even at that it was 2:26 o'clock before the silk-hatted procession emerged from the City Hall to the snapping of cameras and vitascope machines, and amid whistles from persons with messenger-boy lungs.

The crowd that banked Broadway and swarmed on Mail Street and stretched back to the Brooklyn Bridge did not have much to pay it for its pains. It was too far away to see much but the few silk hats and some running messenger boys and lookers-on. Then the official party disappeared down the steps, and nine minutes later the running of regular trains for passengers through the Subway began.

It was astonishing how little noise there was on that first train; but then, it was an official train. Somebody with a shrill tin whistle furnished most of the noise. And there was something strangely natural about the whole thing, picturesquely unnatural as it was in this town of trolleys and elevated trains. In that first train there was the usual elevated jam, the regulation number of strapholders. It seemed singularly homelike and familiar, despite the olive-green woodwork, the queer and unfamiliar air, the darkness alongside, and the sudden shooting into beautiful white stations like nothing that the elevated ever had.

But on the later trains all that was made up for. They were well filled but not crowded. Yet even on one of these was noted that familiar sight, a young man with his bare head lounged luxuriously back on the seat, his hat beside him and his eyes closed. Homelike? Why, in two days it will seem to New York as if it had never ridden anywhere but in the subway.

Several Cases of Firsts

There are a few firsts to be noted in writing the history of this great change in New York transportation. The first man to give up his seat to a woman in New York's subway was F. B. Shipley of Philadelphia. He was on the official train, and the lady was good looking, but he said that made no difference, in Philadelphia everybody was polite.

The first man to ask for a transfer refused to give his name. It was on the return trip of the official train. He wanted to get off at Spring Street and he asked "can I get a transfer?"

There were other firsts, no doubt, and they will fight over it in later years as now men dispute who was the first man to answer Lincoln's call to arms, and who was the first man to enter Richmond in 1865. This was a historic event, and nobody seemed to doubt it, except the youth with the closed eyes and his hat by his side.

Everybody was busy all the way up explaining to everybody else "where we were." The big signs on the white-walled stations left nobody in any real doubt, but the explaining crank was as busy as was the portly man who was buttonholing everybody with "As I said to McDonald ten years ago, says I."

Rapid Transit was assured. The evidence of that was convincing as was the evidence that Harlem knows it and realizes that a great event for Harlem has happened. For when the first train whizzed through the tunnel and out into the open air above Manhattan Street, it broke up a ball game. It was a hotly contested game, too, and one of the players had just made a home run; yet as the olive green train shot past, the players dropped bat, ball and the business of the hour, the spectators forgot that there was such a thing as baseball, and the whole crowd surged up to the fence waving bats and handkerchiefs and yelling like mad at this beginning of fraternity between Harlem and City Hall Park.

An Old Story Even Now

It was astonishing, though, how easily the passengers fell into the habit of regarding the Subway as a regular thing. While the crowds above were still eagerly watching the entrances to see men emerge, were still enthralled by the strangeness of it all, the men on the trains were quietly getting out at their regular stations and going home, having finished what will be to them the daily routine for the rest of their lives. It is hard to surprise New York permanently.

On every hand there were evidences that the novelty was gone soon and the time is not many hours distant when few, save the "oldest inhabitant," would be prepared to admit that they had more than a vague reminiscence of the days before the Subway began to run.

It was forty-one minutes after the start from One Hundred and Forty-fifth Street when, headed by Mr. Orr, the leaders of the Subway emerged from the little station at City Hall park and walked rapidly across the pavement. The Mayor was smoking a cigar which looked guiltily short, as if he had lighted it on the train, and he was stepping briskly toward his office, with sharp salutes to those of his acquaintances who shouted recognition to him on the way. He dashed up the steps as if he had just left some hard work up there and had just remembered about it.

The official or afternoon end was over and everybody concerned in it was returning to work. It was typical again of New York.

Then at night began the real introduction of New York to the Subway, and at two places there was a genuine election-night jam: the two terminals, the Brooklyn Bridge Station and the One Hundred and Forty-fifth Street Station. At the latter, the reserves had to be called out. But for the intervening stations the way New York received the great change was beautifully Knickerbockerish. Everybody took it with the utmost calmness. The early trains were very little crowded after the rush from the two terminals had been taken care of.

Then the trains began gradually to fill up, until people were standing, but it was a full hour after the Subway was opened before people were elbowing each other and there was the usual indecent crush of elevated and trolley lines.

The crowds varied from hour to hour. At first, the down-town trains were sparsely filled and the up-town trains crowded. The explanation was simple; the good folk of Brooklyn and Jersey had come over early to try the subway and get home to bed. Later on the down-town trains began to bear the preponderance; the up-town New Yorkers were trying the new experiment, and the Brooklynites and Jerseyites had gone home.

And it was amusing to note the difference. The up-bound Brooklynites and Jerseyites and Richmondites had boarded the trains with the stolid air of an African chief suddenly admitted into civilization and unwilling to admit that anything surprised him. The Manhattanites boarded the trains with the sneaking air of men who were ashamed to admit that they were doing something new, and attempting to cover up the disgraceful fact. They tried to cover it up with gibes and jokes.

An Outstanding New Venue for Baseball

By the end of the nineteenth century, baseball had become a very popular sport in New York State as well as elsewhere in the nation. There were organized amateur or semiprofessional teams in many cities in the state. Thousands of people attended games. Big cities had professional teams. The New York Giants traced their origins to 1883, the Yankees to 1903. Brooklyn, an independent city until it merged with New York City in 1898, had its own team, organized in 1883, which had gone by various names, and in the early twentieth century was called the Superbas.

Charles Ebbets, team owner, believed that an outstanding team deserved an exceptional field. In 1913, he opened Ebbets Field, at the time one of the most modern and largest in the nation. It was the pride of Brooklyn. The Superbas debuted in their new home on April 5, 1913, beating their crosstown rivals, the Yankees, in an exhibition game before a cheering crowd of about thirty thousand people.

The Superbas soon changed their name to the Dodgers, which became one of the most famous baseball teams in history. The Dodgers were beloved in Brooklyn but also a source of pride in the rest of the city. Ebbets Field was one of the best-known baseball venues in the nation. The spacious new stadium was filled to capacity for home games for many years. But interest began to wane and attendance fell off in the 1950s. The Dodgers left Brooklyn and moved to Los Angeles in 1958, and Ebbets Field was torn down two years later to make way for apartments.

∼

From "Ebbets Field Has No Rival in Baseball," *New York Tribune* (April 6, 1913)

New Home of Brooklyn Superbas Combines Every Idea of Comfort for Patrons

Crowding is Eliminated

Great Grandstand Can Be Filled and Emptied Through Myriad Styles With No Stairs to Climb

Ebbets Field is the last word in the way of a baseball park. Charles H. Ebbets, owner and president of the Brooklyn club, has spared neither money nor constant care to add to the comfort and convenience of the "fans" and players. Nothing has been overlooked. From the grandstand to playing field, every modern improvement has been made and the home of the Brooklyn Superbas who, according to one of their most ardent rooters, "are first in well-wishers, first in enthusiasm, and only seventh in the National League pennant race," stands out as the most complete field in the country today.

Erected at a cost of $750,000, the park includes everything that could be thought out by the fertile mind of a master in baseball. The grandstand is the pride of Mr. Ebbets and he has good reason to be proud, as he practically designed it himself. The entrance to the stand is more like that of some vast theater than of a ballpark and the "fans" have never seen anything like it. The main gate is located at the corner of Cedar Place and Sullivan Street, named after General Sullivan of Revolutionary War fame.

The lobby of the entrance is more than eighty feet in diameter and is resplendent with its marble and glazed brick walls, its glass plate windows in the ticket booths and brass railings. There are a dozen ticket windows placed about the rotunda, and enormous crowd can be handled with little trouble. Since all stairs have been done away with, and inclined runways installed in place, the "fans" will have no trouble in finding their seats quickly.

The holders of unreserved seats will enter through the stile, which will be marked, and, ascending the short incline, will come out in the center of the stand, from which they make take the best seats procurable. The holders of box seats and seats in the reserve section will proceed through the proper stile under and through the front of the stand and to their proper seats.

There will be no unnecessary intermingling of the fans. Those who old tickets on the upper tiers will ascend the runways at the rear of the stands and so up to their seats. The bleacherites [sic] will find ticket booths at convenient points. Only one point is lacking to add to the comfort of all. There is not a single knothole in the whole blooming fence for what with the great still girders and solid concrete, the small boy will have to draw his own conclusions from the volume of noise that will arise from the inner battlements.

The park is centrally located and easily accessible to all. For the benefit of the New York "fans" who will make the trip, be it noted that the fastest and shortest way of reaching the park is by taking the Brighton Beach "L" train to Consumers' Park station and walking across the block to Cedar Place, arriving right at the entrance to the rotunda.

The admissions rates will be as follows: general admission, 75 cents; reserved seats (lower tier) first nine rows, first nine rows on Saturdays and holidays (four rows on other days), $1; box seats, $ 1.50; exchange rates from upper to lower tier, 25 cents. Upper tier admission $1, box seats $1.50. Pavilion general admission 50 cents, north end pavilion 25 cents.

The games will start at 3:30 in the afternoon. . . .

Among the conveniences which may be found at the new park are a ladies' suite, which is located on the lower tier of the main grandstand, consisting of a parlor, private retiring room with maid, telephone and writing desk; a checkroom where all articles may be checked free of charge, incoming telephone messages received and umbrellas loaned at the nominal charge of 10 cents.

Brooklyn owes the fact that she can boast of the finest ball park in the country to Charles H. Ebbets, after whom the park is named. [After construction delays] now all is ready and Brooklyn has one of the most magnificent monuments to the great national game.

Pioneering in Aviation

The Wright Brothers are history's best-known aviation pioneers, but Glenn Curtiss (1878–1930) from Hammondsport, New York, was a major leader in aircraft development. Curtiss developed wing flaps, known as ailerons (and still in use today), control and landing systems, and leading-edge motors. Curtiss was the first to make a preannounced, publicly witnessed airplane flight sanctioned by a professional association, in 1908. The Wrights claimed patent infringement and Curtiss fought them in court from 1910 to 1917, when the federal government forced a compromise.

Curtiss made the first Albany-to-New York City air flight on May 29, 1910. He flew to win a prize offered by the New York World *newspaper to the first person who made such a flight, stopping no more than once. It was a publicity stunt for the* World, *but Curtiss welcomed the challenge in part because he needed the prize money to fight the Wrights in court.*

The daring flight made Curtiss famous. He later started his own airplane manufacturing company, pioneered in naval aviation, and built planes for military use in World War I. His company in Buffalo was at that time the largest airplane manufacturing factory in the nation.

∽

From "Flight Down the Hudson River from Albany to New York City," *The Curtiss Aviation Book* (1912) by Glenn Hammond Curtiss

[I] shall always remember Albany as the starting place of my first long cross-country flight. My machine was brought over from Hammondsport and set up; the Aero Club [a professional association that would certify the event] sent up its official representatives, Mr. Augustus Post and Mr. Jacob L. Ten Eyck, and the newspapers of New York City sent a horde of reporters. A special train was engaged to start from Albany as soon as I got under way, carrying the newspapermen and the Aero Club representatives, as well as several invited guests. It was the purpose to have this train keep even with me along the entire trip of one hundred and fifty-two miles, but as it turned out, it had some trouble in living up to the schedule.

The aeroplane, christened the "Hudson Flier," was set up on Rensselaer Island [adjacent to Albany]. It was now up to the weatherman to furnish conditions I considered suitable. This proved a hard task, and for three days I got up at daybreak, when there is normally the least wind, ready to make an early start. On these days the newspapermen and officials, not to mention crowds of curious spectators, rubbed the sleep out of their eyes before the sun got up and went out to Rensselaer Island. But the wind was there ahead of us and it blew all day long. The weather bureau promised repeatedly, "fair weather, with light winds," but couldn't live up to promises. I put in some of the time in going over every nut, bolt, and turnbuckle on the machine with shellac. Nothing was overlooked; everything was made secure. I had confidence in the machine. I knew I could land on the water if it became necessary, as I had affixed two light pontoons to the lower plane, one on either end, and a hydro-surface under the front wheel of the landing-gear. This would keep me afloat some time should I come down in the river. . . .

[After a series of weather-related delays,] Sunday [May 29] proved to be the day. The delay had got somewhat on my nerves and I had determined to make a start if there was half a chance. The morning was calm and bright—a perfect summer day. News from down the river was all favourable. I determined it was now or never. I sent Mrs. Curtiss to the special train [to New York City, parallel to the aircraft's route] and informed the *World* representative and the Aero Club officials that I was ready to go. Shortly after eight o'clock the motor was turned over and I was off!

It was plain sailing after I got up and away from Rensselaer Island. The air was calm and I felt an immense sense of relief. The motor sounded like music and the machine handled perfectly. I was soon over the river and when I looked down I could see deep down beneath the surface. This is one of the peculiar things about flying over the water. When high up a person is able to see farther beneath the surface.

I kept a close lookout for the special train, which could not get under way as quickly as I had, and pretty soon I caught sight of it whirling along on the tracks next to the river bank. I veered over toward the train and flew along even with the locomotive for miles. I could see the people with their heads out the windows, some of them waving their hats or hands, while the ladies shook their handkerchiefs or veils frantically. It was no effort at all to keep up with the train, which was making fifty miles an hour. It was like a real race and I enjoyed the contest more than anything else during the flight. At times I would gain as the train swung around a short curve and thus lost ground, while I continued on in an air line.

All along the river, wherever there was a village or town, and even along the roads and in boats on the river, I caught glimpses of crowds or groups of people with their faces turned skyward, their attitudes betokening the amazement which could not be read in their faces at that distance. Boatmen on the river swung their caps in mute greeting, while now and then a river tug with a long line of scows in tow, sent greetings in a blast of white steam, indicating there was the sound of a whistle behind. But I heard nothing but the steady, even roar of the motor in perfect rhythm, and the whirr of the propeller. Not even the noise of the speeding special train only a few hundred feet below reached me, although I could see every turn of the great drive-wheels on the engine.

On we sped, the train and the aeroplane, representing a century of the history of transportation, keeping abreast until Hudson had been past. Here the aeroplane began to gain, and as the train took a wide sweeping curve away from the bank of the river, I increased the lead perceptibly, and soon lost sight of the special.

It seemed but a few minutes until the great bridge spanning the Hudson at Poughkeepsie, came into view. It was a welcome landmark, for I knew that I had covered more than half the journey from Albany to New York, and that I must stop to replenish the gasoline. I might have gone on and taken a chance on having enough fuel, but this was not the time for taking chances. There was too much at stake.

I steered straight for the center of the Poughkeepsie bridge, and passed a hundred and fifty feet above it. The entire population of Poughkeepsie had turned out, apparently, and resembled swarms of busy ants, running here and there, waving their hats and hands. I kept close watch for the place where I had planned to turn off the river course and make a landing. A small pier jutting out into the river was the mark I had chosen beforehand and it soon came into view. I made a wide circle and turned inland, over a clump of trees, and landed on the spot I had chosen on my way up to Albany. But the gasoline and oil which I had expected to find waiting for me, were not there. I saw no one for a time but soon a number of men came running across the fields and a number of automobiles turned off the road and raced toward the aeroplane. I asked for some gasoline and an automobile hurried away to bring it. . . . The gasoline having arrived, and the tank being refilled, the special train got under way; once more I rose into the air, and the final lap of the journey was on.

Out over the trees to the river I set my course, and when I was about midstream, turned south. At the start I climbed high above the river, and then dropped down close to the water. I wanted to feel out the air currents, believing that I would be more likely to find steady air conditions near the water. I was mistaken in this, however, and soon got up several hundred feet and maintained about an even altitude of from five hundred to seven hundred feet. Everything went along smoothly until I came within sight of West Point. Here the wind was nasty and shook me up considerably. Gusts shot out from the rifts between the mountains and made extremely rough riding. The worst spot was encountered between Storm King and Dunderberg, where the river is narrow and the mountains rise abruptly from the water's edge to more than a thousand feet on either side. Here I ran into a downward suction that dropped me in what seemed an interminable fall straight down, but which as a matter of fact was not more than a hundred feet or perhaps less. It was one of Willard 's famous "holes in the air." The atmosphere seemed to tumble about like water rushing through a narrow gorge. At another point, a little farther along, and after I had dropped down close to the water, one blast tipped a wing dangerously high, and I almost touched the water. I thought for an instant that my trip was about to end, and made a quick mental calculations as to the length of time it would take a boat to reach me after I should drop into the water. . . .

Soon I caught sight of some of the skyscrapers that make the skyline of New York City the most wonderful in the world. First I saw the tall frame of the Metropolitan Tower, and then the lofty Singer building. These landmarks looked mighty good to me, for I knew that, given a few more minutes' time flight, I would finish the flight. . . .

From the extreme northern limits of New York to Governor's Island, at the southern limit, was the most inspiring part of the trip. News of the approach of the aeroplane had spread throughout the city, and I could see crowds everywhere. New York can turn out a million people probably quicker than any other place on earth, and it certainly looked as though half of the population was along Riverside Drive or on top of the thousands of apartment houses that stretch for miles along the river. Every craft on the river turned on its siren and faint sounds of the clamour reached me even above the roar of my motor. It seemed but a moment until the Statue of Liberty came into view. I turned westward, circled the Lady with the Torch and alighted safely on the parade ground on Governor's Island.

General Frederick Grant, commanding the Department of the East, was one of the first officers who came up to extend congratulations and to compliment me on the success of the undertaking. From that moment I had little chance for anything except the luncheons and dinners to which

I was invited. First came the luncheon at the Astor House given by the *New York World*, and then the big banquet at the Hotel Astor, presided over by Mayor [William J.] Gaynor and attended by many prominent men interested in aviation. The speeches were all highly laudatory, of course, and there were many predictions by the orators that the Hudson river would become a highway for aerial craft, as it had for steam craft when Fulton first steered the old *Clermont* [the first viable steamship] from New York to Albany [in 1807].

A Grand New Train Station

New Yorkers in the progressive era built several large-scale structures that reflected their pride and confidence in their state's future. New York City residents saw their city, the nation's commercial and cultural capital, as deserving of a majestic train station commensurate with the city's preeminence. The existing union station, built in 1871, had outgrown the city's needs. Other big cities were building their own impressive terminals. The advent of electric locomotives, a major technological breakthrough around the turn of the century, meant that train tracks could be placed underground, the smoke and fire risk from coal-fired locomotives eliminated. It was time for something new to transport people into and out of the nation's leading city.

The New York Central Railroad, the state's largest company, which owned the station, was in an expansive mode in the new century. It decided to build a magnificent new station to replace the obsolete one. The new station was designed by a team of architects noted for architectural innovation and excellence. The interior of the station was huge, but the structure also had several underground stories. The Central also owned and developed the surrounding area, including a stately new hotel, office buildings, and other facilities. Construction began in 1903, and the new terminal opened to great fanfare a decade later. It was one of the largest and most famous structures built in New York in the progressive era, and it is still in operation today.

∽

From "New Grand Central Terminal Opens Its Doors,"
New York Times (February 2, 1913)

With the surrounding buildings, it covers an area of 30 blocks, can accommodate 100,000,000 people a year.

The new Grand Central Terminal was thrown wide [open] to the public at midnight last night. Out of all the excavation and the scaffolding, to the accompaniment of whistles and blasting and the chorus of the riveting machine, the new station has risen amid the wreckage of the old. Already the suburban concourse has been in use for several months, the finishing touches have been made on the rest of the structure and, beginning today, the newest gateway to New York will be ready for the traveling public. Through the gateway in the coming 12 months close to 24,000,000 persons will pass on their way to and from the biggest city in the western world. The schedule called for the dispatching of the first train load of them at 12:25 this morning.

Many of the hurrying thousands who pass through on this first day will see only the beauty and convenience of the world's newest railway terminal. But to those who will have heard or read of the plans, the fact about the new terminal that will seem the most outstanding and most significant is that the new Grand Central is more than a gateway, more than a terminal. The terminal proper, the great head house and all its accompanying buildings, are simply the heart and the cause of a group of buildings that has been described as a "terminal city."

The old Grand Central was considered the Marvel of its day, but when it became outgrown and the directors of the New York Central and the New York, New Haven and Hartford began to consider the ways and means for buildings as successor, then they took a task larger than the mirror replacement of the old station by a newer and larger one. They undertook to fashion anew that entire section of the city where the old station stood, to build or cause to be built thirty blocks of buildings in Manhattan, all guided by one hand that would supervise their purpose and direct the general harmony of architecture.

This was made possible by the realization that the railroad could put its "air rights" to some good purpose. For decades, it owned the land where the tracks us their way down to the very heart of the huge, gaping, dirty, unsightly trainyards that helped so largely to make the idea of smoke and noise inseparable from the 19th century conception of a big railway station. With the coming of the electric motor, the old steam locomotive was banished, and from that banishment the builders of the new terminal developed the idea of roofing over the tracks and the train's and building above them as though the road had also suddenly come into possession of scores of vacant lots.

This possibility, this idea, was fraught with tremendous importance to the city of New York. Its development meant reclamation work in the busiest and most compressed part of the continent, commensurate with the reclamation work carried on in the great arid structures of the Far West. It meant the restoration to the city of streets that for years been given over to the purses of the railroad. Park Avenue from 45th Street to 56th Street and the cross streets that formally stopped abruptly at either side of the yawning train yards are now appearing as streets, some of them already in use.

The two levels of tracks reaching from the outskirts of the city to 42nd Street have been depressed below the surface of the streets, great girders have been swung across to support the restored thoroughfares, and over all the buildings of the terminal city are rising one by one, a real estate development of monumental proportions. It was started ten years ago. It will not be completed for many years to come. The opening of the terminal simply means the opening of the most significant structure of all, the keynote building of the group. All this terminal city, this assemblage of buildings of such varied purposes, was made possible by the installation of the electric motor. The scheme could not have been carried out, it could not even have been conceived, in the day of the dirt, smoke and noise of the old steam locomotive. The rock bottom fact of the entire enterprise is the electric motor, powerful, swift, silent and clean.

Reclamation of Millions

The reclamation work by the New York Central is reclamation work in one of the costliest stretches of ground on the continent. Its end is the recovery of city blocks where land of every block is worth between $2,000,000 and $3,000,000. It is the restoration of land in a part of America where according to estimates which experts have made, the very area taken up by one of the road's Pullman cars is worth $30,000. It means the recovery and use of a great stretch of land that would cost an almost inconceivable fortune to buy.

The entire scheme involves the use of some thirty city blocks. Part of this the railway already owned. Part of it had to be specially bought but the idea of using air rights reduced by an immense sum the costs of the terminal. From a business standpoint, it was just as though the space to be excavated for the tracks of the terminal were in a part of the country where land cost little or nothing instead of one of the busiest and most intense parts of Manhattan.

Technology and Innovation

New Yorkers were adept at inventing new products that capitalized on emerging technology. In 1888, Rochester's George Eastman (1854–1932) developed the first practical, inexpensive, easy-to-use camera. Eastman's "Kodak" brand cameras became bestsellers and soon millions of people were snapping away to take lasting images of family members, landscapes, buildings, and other things that struck their fancy. Thousands of commercial photo studios opened to do more formal portraits. Photography became a major industry. Kodak outdistanced competitors through its design and services. In the early years, people could just send the camera back to the Kodak office in Rochester and they would develop the film, reload the camera, and send the camera and the finished prints back to the sender. Later Kodak, always a trendsetter, sold cameras, film, and materials for home-development of photos.

Kodak also pioneered robust advertising and promotion, including sponsoring public exhibitions like the one described in the document below, where people could show off what they had produced with their Kodak cameras.

∽

FROM *BOOK OF THE KODAK EXHIBITION* (1912)
BY EASTMAN KODAK COMPANY

The Kodak Exhibition is not intended as an art exhibit, but rather as an exposition of how photography touches every human interest. We could, had we so desired, have made up a collection of pictures that would have appealed, from their massing of lights and shades, from their subtlety of line and lighting, to those who love art for art's sake alone. But for the most part Kodakery appeals because it enables people without a technical knowledge of photography and without special training along artistic lines to make pictures of the things that they themselves are interested in.

With a few exceptions, the names in this catalogue are not the names of those who are known in the art world for their photographic creations. The pictures were made for the sake of preserving the thing photographed—not with the thought that it would be a picture deserving of salon honors.

Yet these pictures are artistic because they have the greatest attribute of art—simplicity. They compel interest because they are pictures of things worthwhile in travel, sport, adventure and in the home.

The photography of today touches vitally every field of human endeavor, every recreation, and, most of all it is welcomed as the keeper of that most cherished of all stories, the story of the home.

And so, although these pictures are not common-place, they should be looked upon, not as an art exhibit, but as a portrayal of what the Kodak has done for others and what it can do for you.

Photography today has come to be recognized as a fine art, witness the admission of photographs to the Paris Salon; but after all it is in its picture stories of the things that interest us that its chief charm lies. In the recording not only of the unusual and the picturing of our travels, but even more in its portrayal of the every-day, common places at home—in these is the true witchery of Kodakery. . . .

The Kodak Idea

Simplicity is the key note of the Kodak idea in picture making—not merely simplicity in the camera itself, but likewise simplicity in the after processes.

Back in 1888, the Kodak, crude as compared with the Kodaks of to-day, first made amateur photography popular. It made the actual taking of the picture a simple matter, but the loading, the unloading, the developing and the printing were processes requiring skill—and a darkroom. Hence our famous offer: "You press the button; we do the rest."

Today the dark-room has been eliminated from Kodak photography. Simplicity is not confined to the picture taking, but extends as well to the picture making. The Kodak loads and unloads in daylight; the films are developed in any light in the Kodak Film Tank for a certain length of time, in solutions of certain strength and temperature, and developed as well by the novice who will follow the simple directions as they can be developed by the expert. Skill and individual judgment in developing are not necessary. Indeed, it has been fully demonstrated that the Tank can more than equal the work of the most expert workmen when they use the old dark-room methods. The experience is in the Tank.

Likewise Velox paper [used in home dark-rooms at that time] offers a simple medium for print making, and may be had in a variety of grades and surfaces to suit all tastes and all negatives.

In our work of simplifying photography, quality and dependability have not been overlooked. Kodak films, for instance, ask no odds of glass plates in speed or quality. In the true rendering of color values they are not merely highly orthochromatic [made for film development by people in home darkrooms]; they are properly orthochromatic—are practical. And they give the greatest possible latitude—that is, they of themselves, within any reasonable limits, correct errors of over and under exposure, a matter of the utmost importance to the beginner.

Simplicity, quality, dependability, upon these the Kodak success has been built. These qualities have made it a simple matter for everybody to take and make good pictures.

"Kodak"

Is our registered and common-law trade mark and cannot be rightfully applied except to goods of our manufacture. When a dealer tries to sell you a camera or films or other goods not of our manufacture under the Kodak name, you can be sure that he has an inferior article that he is trying to market on the Kodak reputation.

If it isn't an Eastman, it isn't a Kodak.

Sources

Canal Improvement State Committee, *The Thousand Ton Barge Improvement* (New York: Canal Improvement State Committee, 1903), 152–153, 159–160. Available at HathiTrust, https://babel.hathitrust.org/cgi/pt?id=uiug.30112106975813&view=page&seq=9.

Curtiss, Glenn Hammond, "Flight Down the Hudson River from Albany to New York City," *The Curtiss Aviation Book* (New York: Frederick A. Stokes, 1912), 94–105. Available at HathiTrust, https://babel.hathitrust.org/cgi/pt?id=mdp.39015023083408&view=page&seq=11.

Eastman Kodak Company, *Book of the Kodak Exhibition* (Rochester: Eastman Kodak Company, 1912), 32–34. Available at Internet Archive, https://archive.org/details/bookofkodakexhib00unse/page/n1/mode/2up.

"Ebbets Field Has No Rival in Baseball," *New York Tribune*, April 6, 1913.

"New Grand Central Terminal Opens Its Doors," *New York Times*, February 2, 1913.

Official Catalogue and Guide Book to the Pan-American Exposition, Buffalo, N. Y., May 1–November 1, 1901 (Buffalo: Charles Ahrhart, 1901), 11, 13–14, 15–17. Available at HathiTrust, https://babel.hathitrust.org/cgi/pt?id=njp.32101072896291&view=page&seq=5.

"Our Subway Open, 150,000 Try It," *New York Times*, October 28, 1904.

3

Reforming Politics and Government

Figure 3. Florence Kelley was a tireless champion of responsive government, women's rights, and improved working conditions. *Source:* Library of Congress Prints & Photographs Collection.

One of the themes of the progressive era in New York, other states, and at the national level was a concerted movement to make government more responsive to public needs. Voluntary associations and nongovernment organizations could accomplish a good deal, but, given the magnitude and complexity of the issues that New York faced, unprecedented government intervention and action were deemed essential. That meant curbing the power of political "bosses," ensuring that public policy was more independent of politics, and making government more responsible to the people. It meant setting and setting and resetting the agenda for government action. It meant some experimentation and improvisation to try out new things and modify them if needed. All of this required progressives to build public understanding and support as they advanced

The two major political parties, tradition-bound and conservative in 1900, both embraced and enacted some progressive proposals, often through compromise forged in the arena of politics. They became more attuned to the popular will and shifted toward initiating change. The state primary system (which diluted political bosses' hold on the parties) and direct election of US senators in 1913 through amendment to the Constitution (replacing the system under which legislatures had selected them) brought more popular control of the political process. The documents in this section articulate these dynamic themes.

Politics, Government, and "Honest Graft"

Tammany Hall, the powerful New York City Democratic organization, dominated city politics and the state's Democratic party in the early twentieth century. It mostly opposed and blocked reform initiatives. One Tammany stalwart, state senator George W. Plunkett (1842–1924), discussed the organization's tactics with reporters in a series of impromptu talks. Newsman William L. Riordon wrote down what Plunkett said and later published his musings verbatim, including his colloquialisms and slang terms, in a book entitled Plunkett of Tammany Hall *(1905).*

Plunkett endorsed what he called "honest graft," for example, buying land that he knew would be used for municipal projects and selling it to the city at a profit. He defended other questionable practices, such as using political office to steer contracts to allies. He dismissed reformers as "mornin' glories" whose impact was minimal.

The book is something of a classic statement of the rationale for the sort of early twentieth-century "machine politics" that progressive reformers were determined to replace with politics and government more responsive to popular will and popular needs. Within a few years of Plunkett's talks, though, Tammany and the Democrats, recognizing a shift in public sentiment, changed the party's image and took the lead in several progressive reforms.

∽

From *Plunkett of Tammany Hall* (1905)
by George Washington Plunkett and William L. Riordon

Everybody is talkin' these days about Tammany men growin' rich on graft, but nobody thinks of drawin' the distinction between honest graft and dishonest graft. There's all the difference in the world between the two. Yes, many of our men have grown rich in politics. I have myself. I've made a big fortune out of the game, and I'm gettin' richer every day, but I've not gone in for dishonest graft—blackmailin' gamblers, saloonkeepers, disorderly people, etc.—and neither has any of the men who have made big fortunes in politics. There's an honest graft, and I'm an example of how it works. I might sum up the whole thing by sayin': "I seen my opportunities and I took 'em."

Just let me explain by examples. My party's in power in the city, and it's goin' to undertake a lot of public improvements. Well, I'm tipped off, say, that they're going to lay out a new park at a certain place. I see my opportunity and I take it. I go to that place and I buy up all the land I can in the neighborhood. Then the board of this or that makes its plan public, and there is a rush to get my land, which nobody cared particular for before. Ain't it perfectly honest to charge a good price and make a profit on my investment and foresight? Of course, it is. Well, that's honest graft.

Or supposin' it's a new bridge they're goin' to build. I get tipped off and I buy as much property as I can that has to be taken for approaches. I sell at my own price later on and drop some more money in the bank. Wouldn't you? It's just like lookin' ahead in Wall Street or in the coffee or cotton market. It's honest graft, and I'm lookin' for it every day in the year. I will tell you frankly that I've got a good lot of it, too.

I'll tell you of one case. They were goin' to fix up a big park, no matter where. I got on to it, and went lookin' about for land in that neighborhood. I could get nothin' at a bargain but a big piece of swamp, but I took it fast enough and held on to it. What turned out was just what I counted on. They couldn't make the park complete without Plunkitt's swamp, and they had to pay a good price for it. Anything dishonest in that?

Up in the watershed I made some money, too. I bought up several bits of land there some years ago and made a pretty good guess that they would be bought up for water purposes later by the city. Somehow, I always guessed about right, and shouldn't I enjoy the profit of my foresight? It was rather amusin' when the condemnation commissioners came along and found piece after piece of the land in the name of George Plunkitt of the Fifteenth Assembly District, New York City. They wondered how I knew just what to buy. The answer is—I seen my opportunity and I took it. I haven't confined myself to land; anything that pays is in my line.

For instance, the city is repavin' a street and has several hundred thousand old granite blocks to sell. I am on hand to buy, and I know just what they are worth. How? Never mind that. I had a sort of monopoly of this business for a while, but once a newspaper tried to do me. It got some outside men to come over from Brooklyn and New Jersey to bid against me.

Was I done? Not much. I went to each of the men and said: "How many of these 250,000 stones do you want?" One said 20,000, and another wanted 15,000, and another wanted 10,000. I said: "All right, let me bid for the lot, and I'll give each of you all you want for nothin'." They agreed, of course. Then the auctioneer yelled: "How much am I bid for these 250,000 fine pavin' stones?" "Two dollars and fifty cents," says I. "Two dollars and fifty cents!" screamed the auctioneer. "Oh, that's a joke! Give me a real bid." He found the bid was real enough. My rivals stood silent. I got the lot for $2.50 and gave them their share. That's how the attempt to do Plunkitt ended, and that's how all such attempts end.

I've told you how I got rich by honest graft. Now, let me tell you that most politicians who are accused of robbin' the city get rich the same way. They didn't steal a dollar from the city treasury. They just seen their opportunities and took them. That is why, when a reform administration comes in and spends a half million dollars in tryin' to find the public robberies they talked about in the campaign, they don't find them.

The books are always all right. The money in the city treasury is all right. Everything is all right. All they can show is that the Tammany heads of departments looked after their friends, within the law, and gave them what opportunities they could to make honest graft. Now, let me tell you that's never goin' to hurt Tammany with the people. Every good man looks after his friends, and any man who doesn't isn't likely to be popular. If I have a good thing to hand out in private life, I give it to a friend—Why shouldn't I do the same in public life?

Another kind of honest graft. Tammany has raised a good many salaries. There was an awful howl by the reformers, but don't you know that Tammany gains ten votes for every one it lost by salary raisin'? The Wall Street banker thinks it shameful to raise a department clerk's salary from $1500 to $1800 a year, but every man who draws a salary himself says: "That's all right. I wish it was me." And he feels very much like votin' the Tammany ticket on election day, just out of sympathy.

Tammany was beat in 1901 [mayoral election in New York City] because the people were deceived into believin' that it worked dishonest graft. They didn't draw a distinction between dishonest and honest graft, but they saw that some Tammany men grew rich, and supposed they had been robbin' the city treasury or levyin' blackmail on disorderly houses, or workin' in with the gamblers and lawbreakers.

As a matter of policy, if nothing else, why should the Tammany leaders go into such dirty business, when there is so much honest graft lyin' around when they are in power? Did you ever consider that? Now, in conclusion, I want to say that I don't own a dishonest dollar. If my worst enemy was given the job of writin' my epitaph when I'm gone, he couldn't do more than write: "George W. Plunkitt. He Seen His Opportunities, and He Took 'Em."

"Muckrakers" Help Propel Progressivism

Early in the twentieth century, a number of popular New York–based magazines that had been devoted mostly to fiction and some news coverage began adding new features—articles exposing political corruption, graft, and other things that needed correcting. President Theodore Roosevelt, in a 1905 speech, used the term muckraker *to characterize these investigative journalists who, in his view, seemed to go beyond just reporting what they had found and went on to sensationalize it. The pejorative term stuck. And yet these "muckrakers" were essential in rousing public indignation about some of the social, political, and economic conditions that T. R., and his progressive counterparts in the states, including Governor Charles Evans Hughes in New York, 1907–1910, built on to enact key reforms.*

Samuel S. (S. S.) McClure (1857–1949) was a leader in this hard-hitting style of investigating journalism. He founded and ran McClure's Magazine *in New York City from 1903 to 1911. It carried numerous stories of wrongdoing in business and government by some of the leading writers of* the day, including Ida Tarbell, Lincoln Steffens, and Ray Stannard Baker. These were accompanied by other feature articles and short stories that soon made McClure's one of the most popular magazines in the nation.

McClure's set the standard, and other magazines, almost all New York–based, aspired to match it with their own blend of exposés and fiction. The list included The American Magazine, Collier's, Cosmopolitan (the next document presents an example), Everybody's Magazine, Hampton's, and Munsey's. It was a golden age of thoughtful investigative articles in popular journals. But, like other aspects of the progressive era, it began to wane after 1920.

McClure himself set the tone for the muckraking style in a 1903 editorial, reproduced below. He sounded one of the major themes of the movement: journalists could expose wrongdoing, but it would be up to the public at large to demand and force change and reform.

∽

From "Concerning Three Articles in this Number of McClure's and a Coincidence That May Set Us Thinking," *McClure's* (1903) by S. S. McClure

How many of those who had read through this number of the magazine noticed that it contained three articles on one subject? We did not plan it so; it is a coincidence that the January McClure's is such an arraignment of American character as should make every one of his stop and think. How many noticed that?

The leading article, "The Shame of Minneapolis," might have been called "The American Contempt of Law." That title could well have served for the current chapter of Miss Tarbell's History of Standard Oil. And it would have fitted perfectly Mr. Baker's "The Right to Work." All together, these articles come pretty near showing how universal is this dangerous trait of ours. Miss Tarbell has our capitalists conspiring among themselves, deliberately, shrewdly, upon legal advice, to break the law so far as it restrained them and to misuse it to restrain others who were in their way. Mr. Baker shows labor, the ancient enemy of capital, and the chief complainant of the trusts' unlawful acts, itself committing and excusing crimes. And in "The Shame of Minneapolis" we see the administration of a city employing criminals to commit crimes for the profit of elected officials, while the citizens—Americans of good stock and more than average culture, and honest, healthy Scandinavia—stood by complacent and not alarmed.

Capitalists, workingmen, politicians—all breaking the law, or letting it be broken. Who is left to uphold it? The lawyer? Some of the best lawyers in this country are hired not to go to court to defend cases but to advise corporations and business firms how they can get around the law without too great a risk of punishment. The judges? Too many of them so respect the law that for some "error" or quibble they restore to office and liberty men convicted on evidence overwhelming convincing to common sense. The churches? We know of one, an ancient and wealthy establishment which had to be compelled by a Tammany hold-over health office to put its tenements in sanitary condition. The colleges? They do not understand.

There is no one left; none but all of us. Capital is learning (with indignation at labor's unlawful acts) that its rival's contempt of law is a menace to property. Labor has shrieked the belief that the legal power of capital is a menace to the worker. Last November, when a strike was threatened by the yard-men on all the roads entering Chicago, the men got together and settled by raising wages and raising freight rates too. We are all doing our worst and making the public pay. The public is the people. We forget that we are all the people; that while each of us in his group can shove off on the rest of us the bill of today, the debt is only postponed; the rest are passing it back to us. We have to pay in the end, every one of us. And in the end the sum total of the debt will be our liberty.

Newspapers Expose Political Corruption

During the progressive era, several New York newspapers, including the New York Evening Post, New York Journal, New York Times, *and the* New York World, *took the lead in exposing political favoritism, corruption, and the connections between business and politics. Sometimes the stories were embellished or exaggerated to sell more copies of the newspaper. But most times they were based on effective investigative journalism, editorial objectivity, and integrity. The news exposés had an impact similar to what the muckraking journals were doing: rousing public opinion to action.*

The New York Evening Post *set the tone for careful, responsible investigative journalism. Established in New York by Alexander Hamilton, the* Evening Post's *editors had included several luminaries, including famed poet and human rights advocate William Cullen Bryant. The* Evening

Post *already had a reputation for reform-leaning journalism when Oswald Garrison Villard (1872–1949) took over as publisher in 1897. The grandson of famed abolitionist William Lloyd Garrison, Villard was a champion of women's rights, anti-imperialism, and uplift for Blacks. He always had an ear out for news that would feed into the progressive thrust.*

In January 1910, he got wind of an important story. A Republican senator, Benn Conger, had accused another senator, the just-elected majority leader Jotham Allds, of accepting a bribe to kill regulatory legislation when they had both been in the Assembly years earlier. Villard investigated, got the facts, and broke the story on the front page of the Evening Post *on January 18. He followed up with more revelations, and other New York papers joined in and followed suit. The result was a senate investigation that discredited not only Allds but also other Republican legislative leaders. The public was outraged by the revelations. The exposé kicked off by the* Evening Post *contributed to Republican loss of control of the legislature in the fall 1910 election.*

∼

From *New York Evening Post* (January 18, 1910)

Allds is Accused

Charges of Bribery by Senator Conger

Asserts Personal Knowledge of Corruption

The curtain at Albany, behind which has long performed the swiftest maneuverings of the Black Horse Cavalry[1] has been drawn up long enough to reveal an interesting story of bribe-taking involving Jotham P. Allds, the newly-elected leader of the Republican Party in the State Senate, chosen to succeed the late John Raines. The accuser is Senator Benn Conger, perhaps the most prominent business-man in Tompkins County, also a Republican Senator; and a party and organization associate of the man he accuses.

Senator Conger declares that when he and Allds were both Assemblymen, a few years ago, Allds took money in consideration of his aid in preventing the passage of a bill amending the Highway Law which Conger and his associates knew would severely injure the bridge business in which they were engaged, an opinion in which they were not mistaken, as has appeared since the bill became a law. It was a "holdup bill," Conger asserts, intended to injure a legitimate business, and he and his associates "gave up" like many other able business men, to protect themselves, their employees, and their interests. For some years, this worked; then in 1906, the bill became a law.

What makes this revelation all the more astounding is that Senator Conger is no "silked stockinged reformer" or anti-organization Republican. He had never been known as a "kicker" or bolter until the question of Allds' leadership came up after John Raines' death. Conger has been a practical, machine-made legislator, voting straight against Governor Hughes' proposed reforms. He has nursed his wrath quietly until now; perhaps if Allds had not been put forward as Speaker, the charge might never have come out. This was more than Senator Conger could stand as his charge, printed for the first time in the *Evening Post*, shows. Perhaps never before has so specific a charge of personal corruption been made against a man in as high a political position in New York State as Senator Allds. . . .

Senator Conger's Exact Charge

As made yesterday to the *Evening Post*"—Senator Allds "retained" to "stop a bill."

In order to verify the story of Senator Conger's charges against Senator Allds, a report of an alleged conversation relating to the selection of the President Pro Tem of the Senate, in possession of the *Evening Post*, was submitted to Senator Conger in Albany yesterday. He said: "The report you show me is in some respects erroneous and rather than permit a mistaken account to be published, I will explain my refusal to vote for Senator Allds for President Pro Tem of the Senate. . . . I had personal knowledge that when leader of the Assembly he received money for aiding in the defeat of legislation before that body."

Question: "What was the history of that bill?"

Answer: "It was an amendment to the Highway Law. It was first introduced in 1900 and referred to the Committee on Internal Affairs in the Assembly, of which I was a member. I believed that the bill was not in the best interests of the State, and that the people behind the bill were not sincere in their interest to pass it. I knew that if it passed it would ruin the business in New York State of several companies in which I was interested and that there had been no demand on the part of town boards for its passage. In 1900, the bill was held in committee for those reasons."

"The bridge interests, however, thus became exposed to attack. In 1901, the bill was again introduced and the threat was made that it would be passed unless certain persons were 'retained.' Leader Allds as one of those 'retained.'"

Question: "Who were the others besides Allds?"

Answer: "Some are dead, others are out of public affairs, and I will not name them."

Question: "How do you come to have personal knowledge of the transaction?"

Answer: "My company was one of the victims of the hold-up. I will be ready to state the fact, the exact truth, before any regularly constituted committee of the Senate."

Denial by Allds

Statement of Conger is "Absolutely Untrue"

Will Call for an Investigation by the Legislature

Says that any assertion as to money paid for holding up measures in Albany "Must Have Been a Hasty, Angry Remark." Says he will publish a history of all actions by him in highway legislation. Also tracing the history of the man who brought the charge.

The *Evening Post* gladly prints the following letter from Senator Allds, sent to it in reply to its request for a statement and giving it permission to publish the story of the charge against him. He is, however, in error in assuming that any extended conference with him was suggested at the meeting in New York to which he refers, or that there was any such agreement as he alleges. The *Evening Post* made its own investigation of the matter. It notified him verbally, as well as by letter, of Senator Conger's charge just as soon as this was given to the *Evening Post* in Albany last evening. The general nature of the charge was discussed with him last Saturday and he was then asked for any statement he cared to make. Our columns are open to any other statements from him and his side will always be fully represented. The *Evening Post* merely performs its duty to the public in publishing the fact that such an accusation is deliberately made by one high public official against another.

—Ed., *The Evening Post*

[Allds' denial letter was printed after this editorial statement.]

"The Treason of the Senate"

Progressive reformers used popular periodicals to expose political corruption and build support for reform. In New York, they attacked "political bossism" that allegedly dominated both main political powers. They insisted that business and financial interests controlled elected officials, mainly by providing massive funding for their campaigns. This meant that they were responsive to political bosses and businesses' needs, not popular welfare or interests. One of their targets was the US Senate, in those days very protective of business interests and insulated from popular will by being elected by state legislatures rather than directly, at the polls.

David Graham Phillips (1867–1911) was a popular novelist of the day. In 1906, he published a devastating attack on New York Republican Senator Chauncey Depew in the popular magazine Cosmopolitan, *a journal owned by New York's maverick, reform-minded publishing magnate and politician William Randolph Hearst.*

The essay was an unprecedented, accusatory attack on Depew, including his lobbying for the New York Central Railroad (where he served as counsel, lobbyist, and for some years, president) and for the Equitable Life Assurance Company whose corrupt practices had been exposed early in 1906 by a state senate investigation. Phillips' slashing article went after Depew's integrity and character. The article included several photos, one with a caption calling Depew a "Sleek, Self-satisfied American Opportunist in Politics and Plunder." He also took some shots at New York's other senator, Thomas C. Platt, as well (he called the two men "New York's misrepresentatives"). Phillips wrote later pieces on other senators and published the essays as a book, The Treason of the Senate *(1906).*

Phillips' narrative was brisk, his style was engaging, and the picture he painted devastating to his subjects. His work helped pave the way, in 1913, for the Seventeenth Amendment to the Constitution, which provided for direct election of US senators.

∽

From "The Treason of the Senate: New York's Misrepresentatives," *Cosmopolitan Magazine* (March 1906) by David Graham Phillips

The Treason of the Senate!

Politics does not determine prosperity. But in this day of concentrations, politics does determine the distribution of prosperity. Because the people have neglected politics, have not educated themselves out of credulity to flimsily plausible political lies and liars, because they will not realize that it is not enough to work, it is also necessary to think, they remain poor, or deprived of their fair share of the products, though they have produced an incredible prosperity. The people have been careless and unwise enough in electing every kind of public administrator. When it comes to the election of the Senate, how describe their stupidity, how measure its melancholy consequences?

The Senate is the most powerful part of our public administration. It has vast power in the making of laws. It has still vaster power through its ability to forbid the making of laws and in its control over the appointment of the judges who say what the laws mean. It is, in fact, the final arbiter of the sharing of prosperity. The laws it permits or compels, the laws it refuses to permit, the interpreters of laws it permits to be appointed—these factors determine whether the great forces which modern concentration has produced shall operate to distribute prosperity equally or with shameful inequality and cruel and destructive injustice. The United States Senate is a larger factor than your labor or your intelligence, you average American, in determining your income. And the Senate is a traitor to you.

The treason of the Senate! Treason is a strong word, but not too strong, rather too weak, to characterize the situation in which the Senate is the eager, resourceful, indefatigable agent of interests as hostile to the American people as any invading army could be, and vastly more dangerous; interests that manipulate the prosperity produced by all, so that it heaps up riches for the few; interests whose growth and power can only mean the degradation of the people, of the educated into sycophants, of the masses toward serfdom. . . .

No one would pretend for an instant that [New York Senator Chauncey] Depew sits in the Senate for the people. Indeed, why should he, except because he took an oath to do so—and among such eminent respectabilities as he an oath is a mere formality, a mere technicality. Did the people send him to the Senate? No! The Vanderbilt [owners of the New York Central Railroad] interests ordered Platt to send him the first time; and when he came up for a second term the Vanderbilt-Morgan [finance banker J. P. Morgan] interests got, not without difficulty, [railroad magnate Edward H.] Harriman's O.K. on an order to [Republican leader and governor Benjamin] Odell to give it to him. Since he became a large public figure, the only time he has presented himself to the people, he was overwhelmingly beaten. In no part of the state of New York, these thirty-five years, would the people have elected him to any office of trust, great or small. Except, then, for the negligible reason of his oath, he has no reason to represent the people. . . .

Depew became a "lawyer" for the New York Central, with headquarters at Albany, of course. In view of the true nature of old Commodore [Cornelius] Vanderbilt's "business" activities, Depew's fairly accurate description of his own position becomes interesting. "My duties," says he, "covered everything official or personal in which the commodore was interested. For the last eleven years of his life I was in daily consultation with this remarkable man." Further: "Vanderbilt cared little for details and speedily wearied of them. He stated in general terms the results he desired, and then expected the officers of the companies to work them out. It was impossible to explain to him a failure." . . .

The Vanderbilts' Creature

Now followed a quarter of a century of arduous and most adroit lobbying, as counsel and then as figurehead president of the Vanderbilt road, and finally as "honorary" chairman of it. He got for the Vanderbilts, with ever increasing facility and ever decreasing public clamor, free franchises large and small, large free grants of land, immensely valuable shore rights and rights to land under water, authorizations of more consolidations and of more issues of watered stock, exemptions from taxation, etc., etc., etc. Also he was always on hand to cover the operations of the bribe-brigade with speeches full of catching sophistries against any and all legislation seeking to lessen the oppressive burdens imposed by the Vanderbilts upon the people. He managed it all most ably.

He grew more and more respected. By generous, even wholesale, distribution of passes, by cultivating editors and reporters, by ingratiating himself with small politicians and the influential men of little towns and villages, by making popular addresses and after-dinner speeches, by the thousand and one devices which his ingenious mind and his expansive temperament and his passion for public applause suggested, he made himself a popular figure.

Everyone knew he was the Vanderbilts' creature.

Direct Primaries

One central tenet of the progressive movement was that voters should select candidates for political offices. Of course, qualified voters could vote in general elections, but often they had to choose between two candidates who had been selected by the political bosses of the Democratic or Republican parties. Progressive Republican governor Charles Evans Hughes (1907–1910) set out to change that. He was elected in 1906 after serving as counsel to legislative committees that had exposed the connection between boss-dominated politics and corrupt business. In his gubernatorial campaign, he had promised to reform government to make it more responsive to the people's will and needs. In 1907, he proposed a system of "direct primaries" under which enrolled party members would select nominees at the polls. The legislature ignored his recommendation. He renewed his proposal with a strong appeal in 1909, included below.

Neither Hughes' Republican party nor the Democrats, both dominated by political bosses, responded positively. New York did not enact its first direct primary law until two years later, in 1911, after Hughes had left office, under a Democratic legislature and governor, after party leaders recognized a strong increase in popular demand for it. But it was a weak law with partial coverage. The first modern direct primary law came two years after that, in 1913. But governor Hughes had planted the seed in 1909.

〜

From "Message to the Legislature" (January 6, 1909) in *Public Papers of Charles E. Hughes, Governor* by Governor Charles Evans Hughes

Primaries

One of the most striking developments of recent years is the rapid growth of the demand for improved methods of nominating candidates for public office. It is a late phase of the long struggle against the control of the powers of government by selfish interests. Methods which make easy this control are doomed, for the people will not be content with the mere forms of self-government.

There has been a notable progress in perfecting our electoral machinery and in the reduction of opportunities for corruption in connection with elections. But the part played by political parties in nominating candidates makes it necessary to regulate the nominating machinery as well, if the public interest is to be properly protected. As our citizens in general make their choice between the candidates offered by the opposing parties, we, must ultimately depend for truly representative government upon the selection of these candidates in accordance with the wishes of the members of the respective parties.

This is recognized in theory and denied in practice. In theory party candidates are selected by those who have been chosen by the party voters to represent them in conventions. In practice the delegates to nominating conventions are generally mere pieces on the political chess board and most of them might as well be inanimate so far as their effective participation in the choice of candidates is concerned. Party candidates are in effect generally appointed, and by those who have not been invested with any such appointing power.

This practice is attended with serious consequences. It has a disastrous effect upon party leadership. The power of selecting candidates is so important that there is a constant temptation to protect it by such manipulations of the party machinery as will make it serve individual interests. Party principles and the essentials of successful administration of office are too largely subordinated to the necessities of political leaders and their retention of control. The fine service of party loyalty is prostituted to the base uses of those who make the maintenance of their individual power paramount to, true party interests. And the just strength and dignity of party leadership often fails by reason of public contempt for methods frequently used to secure support for its counterfeit. Real leadership of ability and force of character suffers from such methods and would largely gain by increasing the difficulty of their pursuit.

The present system tends to discourage participation by the party voters in the affairs of the party. Entrenched power is so strong and the influence upon the choice of party candidates is so remote that it requires an unusual situation to call forth the activities of the party members to the extent desirable.

The candidates selected by the present method too often and not unnaturally regard themselves as primarily accountable, not to their constituents nor even, broadly speaking, to their party, but to those individuals to whom they feel they owe their offices and upon the continuance of whose good will they deem their political future to depend.

But the most serious consequence is to the people at large. To the extent that party machinery can be dominated by the few the opportunity for special interests which desire to control the administration of government, to shape the laws, to prevent the passage of laws, or to break the laws with impunity, is increased. These interests are ever at work stealthily and persistently endeavoring to pervert the government to the service of their own ends. All that is worst in our public life finds its readiest means of access to power through the control of the nominating machinery of parties. Party organization needs constantly to defend itself from these encroachments, and the people for their proper security must see that the defenses are built as strongly as possible.

There have been and are conspicuous illustrations of party leadership won and held in opposition to those who have represented special interests, and endeavoring faithfully and honorably to perform its proper function. But this does not alter the fact that our present method facilitates the control of government by those whose purposes are antagonistic to the public welfare. Nor should we be unmindful of the extent through which the force of enlightened public sentiment in indirect ways mitigates the evils inherent in our present system. But this sentiment works under conspicuous disadvantages, and it is a defect in our system requiring remedy that the actual power of nomination should reside with those who are under strong temptation to disregard the public interest in favor of private advantage so far as that course may be deemed to be safe.

When we inquire what remedy is available, it may be said that there is none which can be considered as complete, because human nature cannot be changed by legislation and opportunities for political mischief will exist under any system. But we may make improvement' and these opportunities may be diminished. We should perfect our primary laws by providing for an official primary ballot, by extending our enrollment system and by placing our primary elections under substantially the same restrictions as our general elections. But we should go beyond this. As the evil so largely resides in the perversion of representation we should further proceed along the line of progress by restoring effectively to the many the powers which properly belong to them and have been usurped by the few. What history has shown to be essential to the protection of the people is likewise needed for the protection of parties, and thus ultimately for the re-enforcement of public rights. We have decided not to trust despotism, though occasionally it may be benevolent, nor do we favor government by aristocracy. Experience has shown that the people can be better trusted than their self-constituted guardians.

The rule of the people involves vigorous discussion and popular contests, but we are finally committed to it because in the long run our safety depends upon it.

If we apply these principles to our party activities we shall make them the more wholesome, as they will more readily respond to the intelligent and conscientious purposes of the party members. The time has come, I believe, when nominations by all parties for elective offices should be made directly by the enrolled voters of the parties respectively. This will promote true party representation. It will tend to strengthen and dignify party leadership by making it less susceptible to misuse and more in accord with general party sentiment. By increasing the direct influence of the party voters their participation in party affairs will be encouraged. It will make the elective officer more independent of those who would control his action for their selfish advantage, and enable him to appeal more directly to his constituency upon the basis of faithful service. It cannot fail in the main to prove a strong barrier against the efforts of those who seek, by determining the selection of candidates, to pervert administration to the service of privilege or to secure immunity for law-breaking. It is a reform which is instinct with the spirit of our institutions, and it is difficult to see how any party man, however earnest in his partisanship, can oppose the right of the voters of the party really to decide who shall represent them as candidates.

A Day of Reform Triumphs

The Democrats gained control of the governorship and the legislature in 1911 and passed several labor reform bills over the next two years. They had enacted a partial direct primary law in 1911 but balked at enacting a stronger one and stalled on other political reforms.

That changed in 1913. The Democratic legislature impeached and removed from office Democratic governor William Sulzer (elected in 1912) for campaign law violations. In the fall 1913 elections, the voters, impatient with the party's stalling on political reform and its infighting over Sulzer, elected a Republican majority in the Assembly. The change in leadership would take place on January 1, 1914. Majority Republicans in the Assembly would be likely to halt the advance of the progressive agenda. The writing was on the wall for the Democrats: act now while you still have the majority in both houses of the legislature.

Martin H. Glynn, the lieutenant governor who succeeded Sulzer, called the legislature into special session and sent a stern message on December

8, 1913, calling for action, particularly on a statewide direct primary. He emphasized that the public demanded action. The party's leader, Tammany Hall head Charles F. Murphy, and his followers begrudgingly fell into line.

On a single day, December 13, the legislature enacted a strong direct primary, workers' compensation, and ballot reform. Another law passed the same day enabled direct election of US Senators in New York. In addition, another statute authorized a popular vote on holding a state constitutional convention (which voters approved the next year, 1914, and the convention was held the following year).

December 13, 1913, was a day of progressive achievement.

∽

From "Message to the Legislature" (December 8, 1913) in *Public Papers of Martin H. Glynn, Governor* by Governor Martin H. Glynn

For years there has been crystallizing, and there is today a pronounced and insistent demand for legislation which will insure to members of political parties equality of participation in party activities. Legislation, now and then, in the years that have passed, although wholly inadequate to meet the demand, has nevertheless established it as the public policy of the State to throw around party management and party primaries the protection of the law. At your session in the year 1911, the first direct primary election law was passed. It evidenced in a pronounced degree the advance of public sentiment upon this subject. But it falls far short of the requirements of today. I need not say to you, for it is known of all men, that public opinion will not now be satisfied with less than a direct primary law, state-wide in its application, which will require the nomination of every candidate for public elective office in the organized parties by the direct vote of the enrolled members of the parties in their party primaries, without the intervention of delegates or conventions, and with the absolute assurance of exact equality to all candidates for party nominations.

The existing Primary Law has abolished all nominating conventions, except the State convention. Legislation, responsive to unmistakable public opinion, is now demanded which will abolish State conventions and leave to party membership in the party primaries the direct nomination of candidates to be elected by the entire State. . . .

Public opinion demands such a direct primary law with the details worked out to make it fair and efficient for the accomplishment of the general purpose. I am well aware that there is a very respectable difference of opinion as to the wisdom of some of these changes, notably as to the abolition of State conventions. I need not recount the arguments, pro and con, for they are well known. It is my conviction that the people, whose servants we are, have weighed all these arguments and have If I am right in my estimate of public opinion, I am sure that you will readily respond to it by the enactment into law of this public desire. The sufficient reason is that the public demands it. The justification for it, I am confident, will be found in the equality of participation which it will insure to party members, thereby making party management reflect party sentiment, and giving to party activities the vigor, strength, virtue and enthusiasm which will promote the general welfare and make our institutions of government better, safer and more surely enduring.

FROM "ALL GLYNN BILLS TO PASS THIS WEEK," *NEW YORK TIMES* (DECEMBER 10, 1913)

'By order of the Boss' [Tammany Hall leader Charles F. Murphy], the Legislature, as firmly controlled by Tammany as ever, will pass the entire budget of anti-boss legislation recommended by Gov. Glynn in his special message. Furthermore, if present plans are carried out, all the Glynn measures will be passed this week and the legislature will adjourn *sine die* this Saturday.

The political measures include the Direct Primary bill, a bill embodying the Massachusetts ballot act, a bill to render operable in this state the mandate of Congress for the direct election of United States Senators, and a measure providing for a referendum next year to determine whether a Constitutional Convention shall be held in 1915. In addition, the Glynn Workmen's Compensation bill, according to the present outlook, will be passed in both houses on Friday, virtually in the form in which it was submitted to the Legislature last night.

A conference of the Democratic senators today cleared the way for the enactment of the entire legislative program of Gov. Glynn.... All the senators present agreed by unanimous vote on each of the legislative propositions submitted by Gov. Glynn. After the senate conference, Assembly speaker [Alfred E.] Smith and majority leader Aaron J. Levy, declared that the lower house would concur in the senate's action without delay.

Tammany Old-Timers Dazed

This means that with less than week of deliberation, a Tammany-dominated legislature will place on the statute books a series of laws for which Gov. [Charles Evans] Hughes contended for four turbulent years [1907–1910]. The situation is so unusual that the 'old-timers' up here are walking about the Capitol corridors in a daze. The Tammany members, judging from appearances, are consumed by a burning zeal for far-reaching reform and it is only when you get one of the seasoned Tammany members in a corner and ply him with questions that he will confess.

Said one of those old-timers today: 'It is the bitterest doss of medicine that anybody has ever made me swallow. But what's the use? We know that some of these bills are crazy. We know that the abolition of the State Convention is a bad thing, not only for the state but for the people. But what are you going to do about it? The mob upstate seems to want it. I have done my conscientious belief [sic] that these new-fangled ideas are going to wreak havoc in the State. But I am tired of trying to stem the tide; I am tired of being a target for the people to heave bricks at. I am a reformer, indeed.'

An influential upstate leader has seen the light, too. 'I talked the thing over with Mr. Murphy a few days ago. Murphy is willing to go a great deal further than the Governor. He is in favor of the initiative, the referendum and the recall. He is for giving the people everything they want.'

Down in their hearts, many of the Tammany lawmakers who in the Hughes days [Governor Charles Evans Hughes, 1907–1910] and the Dix days [Governor John A. Dix, 1911–1913] and the Sulzer days [Governor William Sulzer, 1913] denounced as heresies the political doctrines they now accept. They believe that the abolition of the state convention and the substitution of a wide-open direct primary system will be a good thing for Tammany in any future effort the organization may make to control the state government. These lawmakers urge that a majority of the vote on the Democratic side always is polled below the Bronx River. They point out that the upstate farmers, who often have to travel a long distance to reach a ballot box, do not come out in force at the primaries.

New York's Progressive Party Presents an Aspirational Agenda

In 1912, a number of progressives bolted from the Republican party to establish their own party and nominate former president Theodore Roosevelt for another term. State-level progressive parties were organized in several states, including New York. The New York Progressive Party was linked closely to the national Progressive Party in part because T. R. was a New Yorker and highly influential in state progressive circles.

The New York Progressives' platform, reproduced in part below, went beyond what either New York Republicans or Democrats, even at their most progressive, had proposed. It represents one of the best statements of the era progressives' goals for streamlining state government, making it more responsive to the people, and enacting state policies to support and protect workers, women, and children.

The New York Progressives fielded a slate of candidates for state office, but the Democrats, whose candidates pledged to a less ambitious agenda of progressive reform, triumphed. Even Republicans, running on a conservative platform, outpolled the Progressives. The Progressives lost at the national level, too, and both the national and the state party soon closed down.

But much of what the New York Progressives advocated was enacted under the Democrats over the next few years, including women's suffrage, workers' compensation, prohibition of night work by women in factories, direct primary, and direct election of senators,. Other reforms, such as streamlining state government, the governor's control over the budget process, and welfare, were enacted in the 1920s and 1930s.

~

From *State Platform, National Progressive Party of the State of New York Adopted by the State Convention, Syracuse, N.Y., Sept. 5, 1912* (1912) by the National Progressive Party of the State of New York

We, the National Progressive Party, in State convention assembled, ratify and reaffirm our national platform, and pledge our support to its candidates, Theodore Roosevelt, for President, and Hiram W. Johnson, for Vice-President. The hopes of a generation are realized in the birth of the new party. Unhampered by any corrupt political past, or by that "invisible government," [the domination of political parties by commercial interests and political bosses] which has so long coerced legislation to serve special and private interests, we present our first State ticket.

In no other State of the Union can citizens place as little trust and hope in the old parties as in New York. Between the "Old Guard," which fought Governor [Charles Evans] Hughes [1907–1910] with Democratic aid, and the Tammany machine dominating Governor [John A.] Dix [1911–1913] with Republican aid, there is no choice. Each promises reforms at conventions and forgets them at Albany.

We pledge ourselves to the elimination of special privilege in every form. We covenant unceasing war against the use of political or governmental power for the private gain of bosses or their friends, who would build up great individual fortunes through monopoly, high prices, and inordinate profits.

We propose to use the powers of the government to protect property rights no less than heretofore, but seek also to serve human welfare more.

We covenant with the people as follows:

The Rule of the People

(1) A Real Direct Primary Law. We denounce the so-called Direct Primary Act of 1911 as a deliberate attempt to discredit the principle of direct nominations and retain boss control. We pledge the enactment of a real Direct Primary Law applicable to every elective office, and a presidential preference primary law.

(2) The Election Law. We denounce the Levy Election Law [a 1911 statute that discouraged fusion movements by making it unlawful for a candidate to appear twice on a ballot] as a bi-partisan conspiracy; we pledge its repeal and the enactment of a fair and understandable statute.

(3) Direct Election of United States Senators. We favor the election of United States Senators by direct vote of the people.

(4) An Office Group Ballot For All Elections. We favor the type of Massachusetts ballot.[2]

(5) Corrupt Practices and Election Expenses. We pledge the enactment of a Corrupt Practices Act by which election abuses shall be clearly defined and bribe-giving punished by imprisonment only; legislation requiring the publication at least once a week during the campaign of all receipts and disbursements by committees, candidates and workers, together with full accounting within ten days after election; the use of public buildings for political meetings, primaries and elections, thus adding dignity to the voting function and reducing the expenses of campaigns.

(6) Woman Suffrage. We pledge our party and its candidates to support loyally and work for the women's suffrage constitutional amendment at all stages.

(7) The Initiative, Referendum and Recall. To give the people an effective ultimate check upon the abuses of governmental power, we favor the Initiative, Referendum and Recall and hereby specifically reaffirm our national platform. We would give the Governor, under proper restrictions, the power directly to invoke the Referendum as to a legislative measure recommended by him, but not enacted by the legislature. We favor a constitutional amendment enabling the people to propose constitutional amendments by petition and to adopt or reject at the polls amendments so proposed.

(8) Responsive and Efficient State Government Through Simplifying its Organization. We favor the Short Ballot principle and appropriate constitutional amendments.

(9) Municipal Home Rule. Municipalities should be given power to adopt and amend their charters in matters pertaining to their powers and the duties, terms of office and compensation of officials; incurring of obligations; methods and subjects of local taxation; and the acquisition and management of municipal properties, including public utilities. We are opposed to special legislation dealing with such subjects. We would make it possible for any city to adopt the Commission form of government.

(10) Civil Service. We pledge ourselves to administer and uphold the civil service laws of the State; to extend the competitive list; and to make examinations an efficient test of real qualifications for appointment.

(11) Reform of Legislative Procedure. The present rules of legislative procedure have been instruments by which the bi-partisan machine has carried out in legislation the sinister purposes of the "invisible government."

We favor just rules of procedure; a public record of the votes of all legislative committees and the abolition of every secret point of access to legislation. We believe that to prevent raids upon the public treasury the Governor should have power to reduce items in the appropriation bills.

(12) Legislative Reference and Drafting Bureau. We favor the creation of a permanent Legislative Reference and Drafting Bureau to aid in the drafting of legislation, with authority to make public its report upon any bill.

(13) The Courts and The People. We endorse the declarations of our national platform respecting the judiciary, and favor their embodiment in the organic law of this State.

The selection of judges by amicable understanding between the bosses of both political parties and lawyers of easy partisanship but ardent devotion to corporate interests, we denounce as a fraud and travesty upon the principle of non-partisanship in the choice of judicial officers. To secure real non-partisanship, the nomination and election of judges should be wholly apart from party columns or party designations on the ballot.

We favor the simplification of civil procedure to eliminate the delays and expensiveness of litigation; the reform of criminal procedure to the end that a speedy trial upon the merits shall be assured to the accused and punishment follow swiftly upon conviction.

(14) Corporation Control. We pledge our support to the Public Service Commissions Law. The highest standards applicable to appointments to a court of justice should apply to the Public Service Commissions. Appointments thereto should not be used as political rewards or partisan prizes. . . .

(16) Social and Industrial Justice. Our National Platform embodies the following program of social and industrial justice, to which we pledge our unceasing efforts:

1. Effective legislation to prevent industrial accidents, occupational diseases, overwork, and involuntary unemployment.
2. The prohibition of child labor.
3. Minimum wage standards providing a "living wage" for working women.
4. The prohibition of night work for women, and the establishment of an eight-hour day for women and young persons.
5. One day's rest in seven for all wage workers.
6. The eight-hour day in continuous twenty four-hour industries.
7. The application of prisoners' earnings to the support of their dependent families.
8. Publicity as to wages, hours and conditions of labor.
9. Full reports of industrial accidents and diseases, and the opening to public inspection of all tallies, weights, measures and check systems on labor products.
10. The protection of the home by a system of insurance against sickness, irregular employment and old age, suited to American conditions.

11. Compensation for death by accident and injury and trade diseases.

12. Continuation of schools for industrial education under public control.

13. Organization of workers, men and women. This far-reaching, but wholly practical program, every portion of which is in successful operation elsewhere, places on the State greater responsibility for action than on the national government.

To do its part in carrying out this program, the Department of Labor should be reorganized: wholly separated from politics; new divisions created; and equipped with an adequate number of inspectors. It should be given full powers for the efficient enforcement of the labor law. It should have authority to make and enforce regulations subject to legislative control, adjusting general laws to particular localities and trades.

We favor immediate investigation of industrial disputes by the Department of Labor and the prompt publication of its findings.

We favor the prompt passage of the pending constitutional amendment relating to workmen's compensation, and the enactment thereupon of a thorough-going workmen's compensation act.

We pledge ourselves to laws securing adequate fire protection to the factory workers of the state.

We favor radical and persistent attack on congestion of population, bad housing, and all other preventable causes of poverty.

We favor the enforcement in letter and spirit of the Empire State's laws forbidding discriminations on account of race, creed or color.

We favor, as a factor in reducing the cost of living, a better supervision of the marketing of food products.

(17) Education. The public school is the most efficient aid to democracy, and we favor its maintenance everywhere at a high standard. We favor practical instruction in matters of immediate concern to each community—agriculture and forestry in rural regions and smaller towns; industry and commerce in the cities; home-keeping and citizenship everywhere.

The movement for the wider use of school houses has our hearty endorsement.

(18) Health. We favor vigorous State and local activity in the protection of public health. Tuberculosis can and must be eliminated. There should be expert medical inspection of all school children.

(19) Conservation. Our water power and other natural resources are the heritage of the people. They should be dedicated to the common benefit, and developed under State control. The policy should be enforced that neither State nor privately owned natural resources can be used to the detriment of the public welfare.

The State holdings in the forest reserve should be greatly extended and so administered as to combine intelligent conservation with a wider public use. The reckless deforestation of privately owned forest lands should be prevented by a careful regulation in the common interest. Franchises for the public use of natural resources should not be granted for nothing and forever.

(20) Immigration. We favor the development of the State Bureau of Immigration and Industries. We favor the education and protection of the immigrant, and the intelligent distribution of alien labor through State employment exchanges or otherwise.

(21) The Unfortunate. We favor liberal provision by the State for its dependents. In mediate institutional provision should be made for all the feeble minded, unsuitable for home life.

Veering Away from Progressivism

The progressive era opened with an aura of excitement and hope. It achieved a good deal during the next two decades. But it closed, around 1920, on a note of disillusionment and apprehension. The public was growing weary of reform after two decades. People seemed to feel that enough had been accomplished for now and it was time for a pause. The traumas of the First World War, followed by political unrest and the rise of labor activism and radicalism, added to the desire for turning away from expansive progressive reforms. Republican President Warren Harding, elected in 1920, called for "normalcy." That bland term summed up the consensus of public opinion.

In New York, control of the legislature shifted from the Democrats to the Republicans in 1915, and progressive Democratic Governor Alfred E. Smith, elected in 1918, was defeated by conservative Republican Nathan Miller in 1920 (governors were elected every two years in those days).

In 1919, the legislature established a committee to investigate and report on organizations suspected of undermining American institutions and plotting the overthrow of American government. The committee capitalized on overblown public fear of radicalism to subpoena witnesses, raid organizations' offices, and seize documents. Its report, issued in 1920, portrayed multiple threats, including socialists and teachers who taught students to disrespect the nation's historical leaders and institutions. The report led to legislation curbing radical organizations and requiring teacher loyalty oaths. It had a chilling effect on radical proposals and progressive reform initiatives as well.

It also marked a dramatic conclusion to the progressive thrust in New York. It would emerge again but in a much different form in the New Deal in the 1930s, led by many of the people who had gotten their experience in reform in New York a couple of decades earlier.

∽

FROM *REVOLUTIONARY RADICALISM* (1920) BY THE JOINT LEGISLATIVE COMMITTEE INVESTIGATING SEDITIOUS ACTIVITIES

General Introduction

In the report here presented the Committee seeks to give a clear, unbiased statement and history of the purposes and objects, tactics and methods of the various forces now at work in the United States, and particularly within the State of New York, which are seeking to undermine and destroy, not only the government under which we live, but also the very structure of American society. It also seeks to analyze the various constructive forces which are at work throughout the country counteracting these evil influences and to present the many industrial and social problems that these constructive forces must meet and are meeting.

The Great War has shaken the foundation of European civilization. The same forces which promote civil strife in many of the countries of Europe are at work on this side of the ocean seeking to create a division in our population, stimulating class hatred and a contempt for government, which, if continued, must necessarily result in serious consequences to the peace and prosperity of this country. In doing this they are taking advantage of the real grievances and natural demands of the working classes for a larger share in the management and use of the common wealth.

The problems which were submitted by the Legislature to this Committee for investigation are vital to the country's life. Upon the steps taken toward their solution, the Committee feels depends the perpetuation of our institutions. We therefore urge members of the Legislature and those into whose hands this report may come, to consider thoughtfully the facts here presented, in order to become acquainted with the subversive forces at work within our boundaries, and to give them careful and devoted study, so as to determine what steps shall and must be taken towards the solution of the problems they create.

In the section of this report dealing with American conditions, the Committee has attempted to describe in detail the various organizations masquerading as political parties, giving the principles and objects for which they stand as well as the tactics they employ or advocate in order to bring about the social revolution. In every instance the Committee has relied upon the so-called party or organization's own statements with respect to these matters. They are permitted to speak for themselves. These organizations fall into two principal classes. The first group composes the Socialist movement; the second consists of the American adherents of the Anarchist philosophy.

Those representing the Socialist point of view are the Socialist Party of America, the Communist Party of America, the Communist Labor Party and the Socialist Labor Party. Each of these groups claims to be the most modern and aggressive body representing the Marxian doctrines. A study of their platforms and official pronouncements shows that they do not differ fundamentally in their objectives. These objectives are: the establishment of the co-operative commonwealth in place of the present form of government in the United States; the overthrow of what they are pleased to call the capitalist system, namely, the present system under which we live; and the substitution in its place of collective ownership, and the management of means of production and distribution by the working class. These organizations differ but slightly in the means advocated to bring about the social revolution. All are agreed that success can be obtained only through the destruction of the present trade union organizations of the working class, and by creating in their stead revolutionary industrial unions having the power (through industrial action involving the general strike and sabotage) to so cripple the government as to render it powerless to prevent the establishment of the cooperative commonwealth and the working class rule.

A study of the chapters dealing with these organizations reveals the fact that they differ slightly in the matter of emphasis. The Socialist Party, the Socialist Labor Party and the American Labor Party believe that parliamentary action, participation in elections offering candidates for public office, and taking part in legislative activities, afford an added weapon for the carrying on of revolutionary propaganda. On the other hand, the Communist Party and the Communist Labor Party feel that the time is ripe for immediate action, and in large measure deny the value of parliamentary action, laying the entire stress upon industrial organization and the mass action of revolutionary organizations. The anarchist movement repudiates parliamentary or political action altogether. It seeks the overthrow of present organized society and the substitution for it of an ill-defined cooperative-commonwealth. It is at one with the Socialist group, however, in advocating revolutionary industrial unionism as the means for accomplishing the destruction of the present form of government and the present system of society.

General strikes and sabotage are the direct means advocated. Anyone who studies the propaganda of the various groups which we have named will learn that the arguments employed are the same; that the methods and tactics advocated cannot be distinguished from one another and that articles or speeches made on the question of tactics or methods by anarchists could, with propriety, be published in Socialist or Communist newspapers without offending the membership of these organizations. The result of the propaganda of the quasi-political organizations which has been spread throughout the country broadcast to the working class organizations, and particularly among the foreign groups, has been to undermine the confidence of these workers in the conservative trade union organizations and lead to the formation of a large number of powerful and independent revolutionary industrial unions. These organizations are treated in this report in the sub-section dealing with revolutionary Industrial Unionism.

The most successful of these organizations is the Industrial Workers of the World. Its propaganda is world-wide. Its members have invaded the membership of conservative organizations of labor, with the view of agitating within trade unions so as to weaken control of conservative labor leaders over a considerable number of their workmen. This method of "boring from within" has been extremely effective and has in large measure permeated the Central Federated Union of New York City as well as many union groups in other parts of the State, engendering radical and revolutionary spirit in their rank and file. It is this phase of the movement which presents the most serious aspect. These tactics are the ones which offer at least a promise of success in their undermining of society and of our present form of government.

The effect of this propaganda is particularly pernicious because it undermines and destroys the moral responsibility of the workers. The motto "a fair day's pay for a fair day's work" is described as "impossible."

Men are taught that they must strike for higher and higher wages, shorter and shorter hours and slow up at the same time the working pace, ignoring the quality of work they turn out and in every way possible lowering production.

The avowed purpose is to drive business into bankruptcy, when it would be taken over by the workers. Strikes are called not with the idea of obtaining what is demanded but for the express purpose of failure—a failure that will leave the workman poorer and more embittered, will increase class hatred and make the workmen feel that only by violent revolution can they gain their demands.

It should not be necessary to point out the logical consequences of such propaganda. The per capita production of the men in industry is necessarily lowered and the cost of the product many times increased. This in the opinion of the Committee is one of the largest factors responsible for the high cost of living which is now a matter of grave concern to all classes of society in this country. While the Committee has been unable in the course of its investigation to make a study of the effects of profiteering and improper and useless handling of manufactured products and raw materials in the course of their distribution, it is certain that these elements also contribute toward the prevailing high prices. It is a matter of regret to the Committee that there has been no thorough investigation into the various elements which go to make up the costs of necessaries of life. It feels that no complete solution of the existing social and economic problems can be offered or suggested until all the facts bearing on this important question have been thoroughly studied and analyzed.

While the nature of this investigation has led the Committee to lay its emphasis upon the activities of subversive organizations, it feels that this report would not be complete if it did not state emphatically that it believes that those persons in business and commercial enterprise and certain owners of property who seek to take advantage of the situation to reap inordinate gain from the public, contribute in no small part to the social unrest which affords the radical a field of operation which otherwise would be closed to him. . . .

Seeing the situation as we do, as something transcending not only the State but the nation, and as reaching down to the fundamentals of man's nature and of the organization of society, the Committee feels that it must appeal in the strongest way to every member of the Legislature, to every man who holds any position of authority or of influence, to take every possible step, not only to understand the cardinal facts of the situation but to devote his thoughts and his acts to a crusade in support of every agency, every policy, that will counteract and defeat this movement. Only complete knowledge will give us the leadership that is absolute, a leadership that will be based on clear conviction and a feeling for the necessity of action; a leadership that will understand that there must be a revival of religious and moral standards as the basis of any political and economic program. The community must be appealed to must be given the facts, must be made to see the causes and the remedies, must be made to hand itself together as a civic force in every center of the State in action that shall not be the action of individuals, the sporadic, ineffectual duplicating action that will lead us nowhere. If American ideals of individual freedom and initiative are to be maintained, every citizen must be militant in their defense.

But the very fact of organizing for social defense and for social offense against those who are attacking our life is in itself dangerous, because unless we are keen of insight, these very organizations are going to be, as they have been in the past, taken possession of by astute, hardworking, clearheaded revolutionists, and turned from the purposes of reconstruction to purposes of contamination.

As much energy and organized thought and action must be put by our leading men into the solution of economic and sociological problems as they have given to the solution of their own business problems. They must show as much altruistic energy in the defense as the radical leaders have been showing in the attack. The disjointed, unprincipled, unpractical or sentimental altruism which is doing so much harm as practiced in university, in church, in philanthropic and in social circles must be shown up or made to understand the realities and dangers of its efforts, and be led, by this new insight, to shift to the camp of constructive action.

The re-education of the educators and of the educated class must go hand in hand with the reorganization and extension of our educational system. We cannot give the right point of view to our foreign population and to our children unless it is clearly and firmly ingrained in all of us. Knowledge and convictions based on knowledge must be gained by the whole nation. This report aims to give this knowledge as far as it was humanly possible to do in the spheres it undertook to investigate. This Committee feels that it has only begun the work that the country as a whole must take up and carry on, heart and soul, beginning with the renovation and elevation of our school system, based on a generous and wise understanding of its financial needs. It therefore backed with all its influence the legislation granting increased salaries to public school teachers. Party differences, local claims, appropriations not fundamentally necessary, should be set aside until more than living wage is secured for those on whose teaching the spiritual and material prosperity of this country so largely depends.

Notes

1. "Black Horse Cavalry" was the name reformers called an informal alliance of corrupt Republican and Democratic legislators at the turn of the century. They extorted money from corporations and lobbyists by introducing "strike" bills with regulatory measures designed to overly restrict or harass business operations. Bribes were demanded for the "strike" bills to be scuttled in legislative committee or on the floor of either house.

2. The Massachusetts Ballot was a ballot advocated by some reformers on which the candidates, with their party designations, are listed alphabetically under the office for which they were nominated instead of by political party.

Sources

"All Glynn Bills to Pass This Week," *New York Times*, December 10, 1913.

"Allds is Accused; Charges of Bribery by Senator Conger; Asserts Personal Knowledge of Corruption," *New York Evening Post*, January 18, 1910.

Joint Legislative Committee Investigating Seditious Activities, *Revolutionary Radicalism: Its History, Purposes and Tactics, With an Exposition and Discussion of the Steps Being Taken and Required to Curb It. Part I: Revolutionary and Subversive Movements Abroad and at Home* (Albany: J. B. Lyon, 1920), 7–11, 14–15. Available at HathiTrust, https://babel.hathitrust.org/cgi/pt?id=mdp.39015008795158&view=page&seq=5.

McClure, Samuel S. (S. S.), "Concerning Three Articles in this Number of McClure's and a Coincidence That May Set Us Thinking," *McClure's Magazine* 20 (January 1903), 136. Available at HathiTrust, https://babel.hathitrust.org/cgi/pt?id=uc1.b000705947&view=page&seq=11.

National Progressive Party of the State of New York, *State Platform, National Progressive Party of the State of New York Adopted by the State Convention, Syracuse, N.Y., Sept. 5, 1912* (New York: National Progressive Party State

Committee, 1912), 3–8. Available at HathiTrust, https://babel.hathitrust.org/cgi/pt?id=uc1.c046726571&view=page&seq=3.

Phillips, David Graham, "The Treason of the Senate: New York's Misrepresentatives," *Cosmopolitan Magazine* 40 (March 1906), 488, 491, 495, 496, 498–99. Available at HathiTrust, https://babel.hathitrust.org/cgi/pt?id=uva.x000455323&view=page&seq=498.

Plunkett, George Washington, and William L. Riordon, *Plunkett of Tammany Hall: A Series of Very Plain Talks on Very Practical Politics. . . . Recorded by William L. Riordon* (New York: McClure, Phillips, 1905), Chapter 1, "Honest Graft and Dishonest Draft." Available at Project Gutenberg, https://www.gutenberg.org/ebooks/2810.

State of New York, *Public Papers of Charles E. Hughes, Governor, 1909* (Albany: J. B. Lyon, 1910), "Message to the Legislature," January 6, 1909, 36–39. Available at HathiTrust, https://babel.hathitrust.org/cgi/pt?id=coo1.ark:/13960/t7hq4j35h&view=page&seq=5.

State of New York, *Public Papers of Martin H. Glynn, Governor, 1913–1914* (Albany: J. B. Lyon, 1925), "Message to the Legislature," December 8, 1913, 43–53.

4

Improving People's Lives

Figure 4. Lillian D. Wald led the establishment of settlement houses, initiated the visiting nursing service, and championed child labor reform and other progressive initiatives to improve people's lives. Source: Harris & Ewing, Library of Congress Prints and Photographs Collection.

The progressive era witnessed a growing public consensus that New Yorkers' lives could and should be improved. People could help themselves through individual initiative, hard work, and moral behavior. But many people needed more than that: help from others. Voluntary organizations, such as charities and settlement houses, had an important role to play. A great deal of the responsibility, though, gradually shifted to government, particularly state government. This was one of the major accomplishments of the New York progressives. New York State took on major new or significantly expanded responsibilities for its youngest citizens, poor people, adequate housing, and public health.

The state also provided guidance, and sometimes requirements, about how people should live. These initiatives, including prohibition and censorship, infringed on personal liberties. Progressives concluded that sometimes state government had to curtail those liberties for the greater good—the health and welfare of people and the overall welfare of everyone in New York State. Sometimes the new regulations proved to be problematic and difficult to enforce.

Educating Young New Yorkers

Getting children out of the factories and strengthening compulsory school attendance were an important prelude to strengthening education. New York State's responsibility for sound, progressive public education grew during the 1900–1920 period. The State Education Department was established in 1904, consolidating the functions of two previous agencies that had exercised uncoordinated supervision over the state's public schools. The first Commissioner of Education, Andrew S. Draper, who served from 1904 to 1913, was a forceful, proactive leader who built the new department into a model progressive agency. The department worked to consolidate school districts, expand access to high school, raise standards for teachers, and expand teacher training opportunities. It issued curriculum guidelines for schools to follow. Draper also secured support for construction of a magnificent new State Education Building across Washington Avenue from the Capitol in Albany. New York soon had the nation's best public school system.

Draper was an articulate champion of public education. He supported the traditional work of local school boards but also insisted on New York State government's overarching responsibility for public education and his department's authority to set high quality standards. His 1909 book, American Education, *set the tone for an assertive state government role and is something of a handbook for progressive education.*

From *American Education* (1909) by Andrew S. Draper

The United States [government] is powerless to *control* and does not assume to *manage* the educational interests of the people; the states have full authority to do so.

Cities and towns and districts have no power in themselves to erect schools. The original theory that education is a matter of private or parental concern was abandoned with the advent of manhood suffrage, or as soon as the power of the voter began to be felt. The later theory that government might appropriately encourage education by gifts, and ought to see that the children of the poor are given the privileges of the schools, has been supplemented by the broader and nobler theory that the state is bound to exercise its sovereign prerogative to take so much of the property of the people as may be necessary to provide the best educational facilities which the world's experience has devised for every child, not as a benefaction, but in satisfaction of the natural and inherent rights of American citizenship. And this is equally for the good of the citizen and for the security of the state. The only instrument with which this theory is or can be carried out is the sovereign power of direct taxation, and that power vests in the state government exclusively.

The power which can levy taxes is bound to see that the taxes are wisely used to advance the common good. There is a wide difference between the people of a local community being a law unto themselves and being the supporters and executors of a general policy of the state. There is abundant play for "home rule" in wisely carrying out the fundamental principles of the whole people. No home rule can be accepted which is not in line with general rule or is not wise rule; certainly this is true in matters educational.

The functions of an American state touching education run into every instrumentality which makes for physical, intellectual, and moral advancement in harmonious company. They have rapidly multiplied in recent years, and they will continue to multiply.

It is fundamental, as we have already seen, that the state is bound to see that a suitable elementary school is maintained within reach of every home, and, to have a suitable school, a house must be provided which is sufficient and which is hygienically above reproach. The school must be in the hands of one who can teach, and its work must be in harmony with such general plans as lead toward ideal results. This means much in the way of general authority, and it points to an infinite variety of details. It involves the making of plans, the nourishing of a system to its fullest completeness and effectiveness; and it involves the exercise of the power of general taxation and the right of local direction. It makes necessary a knowledge of the world's ripest experience touching schoolhouses, the training and treatment of school-teachers, and the trend and quality of school work. All this implies knowledge and powers which are not to be supposed to be common in local communities, for the knowledge is expert and the powers are general.

Unless the state is moving, the purposes of the state are not being fulfilled. The state which is not inspecting and improving its schoolhouses; which is not preparing, regulating, and advancing its teaching service; which is not shaping and stimulating and systematizing the work of its schools, through a department of the state government, and through universal expert supervision, to which it has given a dignity of standing and authority sufficient to justify the theories upon which its every act is taken, is a state whose government is in hands that are nerveless, or whose people are strangely and basely indifferent to the evolution of educational thought and to the stern logic of educational events.

It is the function of the state to define the platform upon which the public schools stand and promulgate the theories upon which they operate. It is to keep their territory free from religious intolerance while it advances the common belief in the reality of a living and omniscient God. It is to banish partisanship from the council chamber. It is to train teachers. It is to let experienced teachers determine the fitness of beginners. It is to lay stress upon spirit and adaptation as well as upon readiness to answer troublesome conundrums. It is to put teachers upon the merit basis; let the incompetent resign; absolve the successful from frequent examinations and from competition with the worthless in the matter of pay; assure them immunity from harassing annoyances, and guarantee them entire security of position, while directing their intellectual activity and stimulating their moral sense so that the whole body may continually advance to a higher and yet higher plane of professional standing and usefulness.

It is to keep the work upon scientific lines, anchored to earth, yet abreast of the world's matured thought. It should do things as well as discuss them. It should make brain culture and spirit culture easier and more far-reaching through the exercise of the eye and the use of the hand,

and it should dignify the manual industries by putting a knowledge of good English and an appetite for learning behind them.

It should make the work of the schools ethical as well as intellectual. They must know the history and the traditions of the race, that they may inspire respect for the institutions of human society. They must know the value of free thought, but they must remember that the quantity of real liberty which people enjoy is likely to be proportioned to the quantity of restraint they will suffer, if the schools would fulfill their mission and develop respect for the law, while they impress upon youth the invaluable prerogatives of American citizenship and the awful responsibility of the exercise of governmental power.

Revealing How Poor New Yorkers Live

One strategic thread in the progressive movement was initiatives to investigate problems and publish reports about them. The immediate goal was to inform people about the nature of the issues, their ramifications for New York, and what needed to be done to address them. The ultimate goal was something more: to get the people to demand and support action.

Journalist and social reformer Jacob A. Riis (1848–1914) added a new element to investigatory reports: documentary photography. He was a police reporter for the New York Tribune *and the* Evening Sun *for several years. He saw firsthand the impact of poverty and squalid living conditions in New York's crowed high-rise apartments, known as tenements, particularly on the Lower East Side of Manhattan. Riis began photographing what he saw and soon hired other photographers to help him. In 1890, he published an unprecedented book,* How the Other Half Lives, *with vivid written descriptions of what he witnessed along with detailed drawings made from his photos and some of the photos themselves. Later editions substituted photos for the drawings, making the book a dramatic photo documentary of sorts.*

Riis described tenements, back alleys, orphans, paupers, ruffians, and the circumstances of newly-arrived immigrants such as Italians and Jews as well as Blacks. The book's introduction, included below, provided an overview and challenged the public: "What are you going to do about it?"

Riis attracted attention and support from the city's growing reform community. Riis's book helped lead to the New York Tenement House Acts of 1901, which imposed state standards for new tenement house buildings.

From *How the Other Half Lives: Studies Among the Tenements of New York* (1901) by Jacob Riis

Long ago it was said that "one half of the world does not know how the other half lives." That was true then. It did not know because it did not care. The half that was on top cared little for the struggles, and less for the fate of those who were underneath, so long as it was able to hold them there and keep its own seat. There came a time when the discomfort and crowding below were so great, and the consequent upheavals so violent, that it was no longer an easy thing to do, and then the upper half fell to inquiring what was the matter. Information on the subject has been accumulating rapidly since, and the whole world has had its hands full answering for its old ignorance.

In New York, the youngest of the world's great cities, that time came later than elsewhere, because the crowding had not been so great. There were those who believed that it would never come; but their hopes were in vain. Greed and reckless selfishness wrought like results here as in the cities of older lands. . . .

Of one thing New York made sure at that early stage of the inquiry: the boundary line through the tenements.

It is ten years and over, now, since that line divided New York's population evenly. Today three-fourths of its people live in the tenements, and the nineteenth century drift of the population to the cities is sending ever-increasing multitudes to crowd them. The fifteen thousand tenant houses that were the despair of the sanitarian in the past generation have swelled into thirty-seven thousand, and more than twelve hundred thousand persons call them home. The one way out he saw—rapid transit to the suburbs—has brought no relief. We know now that there is no way out; that the "system" that was the evil offspring of public neglect and private greed has come to stay, a storm-centre forever of our civilization. Nothing is left but to make the best of a bad bargain.

What the tenements are and how they grew to what they are, we shall see hereafter. The story is dark enough, drawn from the plain public records, to send a chill to any heart. If it shall appear that the sufferings and the sins of the "other half," and the evil they breed, are but as a just-punishment upon the community that gave it no other choice, it will be because that is the truth! The boundary line lies there because, while the forces for good on one side vastly outweigh the bad—it were not well otherwise—in the tenements all the influences make for evil; because they are the hot-beds of the epidemics that carry death to rich and poor alike; the nurseries of pauperism and crime that fill our jails and police courts; that throw off a scum of forty thousand human wrecks to the island asylums and workhouses year by year; that turned out in the last eight years around half million beggars to prey upon our charities; that maintain a standing army of ten thousand tramps with all that that implies; because, above all, they touch the family life with deadly moral contagion.

This is their worst crime, inseparable from the system. That we have to own it, the child of our own wrong, does not excuse it, even though it gives it claim upon our utmost patience and tenderest charity.

"What are you going to do about it?" is the question of today. It was asked once of our city in taunting defiance by a band of political cutthroats [the 1870s "Tweed Ring" of New York City officials and corrupt contractors], the legitimate outgrowth of life on the tenement-house level. Law and order found the answer then and prevailed. With our enormously swelling population held in this galling bondage, will that answer always be given? It will depend on how fully the situation that prompted the challenge is grasped.

Forty per cent of the distress among the poor, said a recent official report, is due to drunkenness. But the first legislative committee ever appointed to probe this sore went deeper down and uncovered its roots. The "conclusion forced itself upon it that certain conditions and associations of human life and habitation are the prolific parents of corresponding habits and morals," and it recommended "the prevention of drunkenness by providing for every man a clean and comfortable home." Years after, a sanitary inquiry brought to light the fact that "more than one-half of the tenements with two-thirds of their population were held by owners who made the keeping of them a business, generally a speculation. The owner was seeking a certain percentage on his outlay, and that percentage very rarely fell below fifteen per cent, and frequently exceeded thirty. . . . The complaint was universal among the tenants that they were entirely uncared for, and that the only answer to their requests to have the place put in order by repairs and necessary improvements was that they must pay their rent or leave. The agent's instructions were simple but emphatic: 'Collect the rent in advance, or, failing, eject the occupants.'

Upon such a stock grew this [toxic] Upas-tree. Small wonder the fruit is bitter. The remedy that shall be an effective answer to the coming appeal for justice must proceed from the public conscience. Neither legislation nor charity can cover the ground. The greed of capital that wrought the evil must itself undo it, as far as it can now be undone. Homes must be built for the working masses by those who employ their labor; but tenements must cease to be "good property" in the old, heartless sense. "Philanthropy and five per cent" is the penance exacted.

If this is true from a purely economic point of view, what then of the outlook from the Christian standpoint? Not long ago a great meeting was held in this city, of all denominations of religious faith, to discuss the question how to lay hold of these teeming masses in the tenements with Christian influences, to which they are now too often strangers. Might not the conference have found in the warning of one Brooklyn builder, who has invested his capital on this plan and made it pay more than a money interest, a hint worth heeding: "How shall the love of God be understood by those who have been nurtured in sight only of the greed of man?"

The Benefits of Tenement House Reform

Following the revelations about crowded city housing conditions by Jacob Riis and other investigative journalists, Governor Theodore Roosevelt appointed a tenement house commission in 1900 to investigate conditions. The commission recommended, and the legislature enacted, a sweeping law in 1901 to ban the construction of dark, poorly ventilated tenement house buildings not only in New York City but throughout the state. The statute required that new apartment buildings must be built with outward-facing windows in every room, an open courtyard, adequate ventilation systems, indoor toilets, and fire safeguards.

The state requirements were strengthened and expanded in 1903. New city and state regulations gradually encouraged the upgrading of existing tenement buildings. New York's building code became a model for the nation.

Robert W. DeForest, an attorney, financier, and philanthropist, chaired the Tenement House Commission and shaped the 1901 law. He then served for several years as New York City's first Tenement House Commissioner. He continued to campaign for housing reform. He summarized the benefits of tenement house regulation in 1908.

∾

FROM *THE TENEMENT HOUSE PROBLEM* (1908) EDITED BY
ROBERT W. DEFOREST AND LAWRENCE VEILLER

The report of the New York State Tenement House Commission of 1900 was adopted in its entirety. Its proposed Tenement House Law for cities of the first class was passed with substantial unanimity by both branches of the legislature, and was approved by the governor on April 12, 1901. The law finally proposed by the Commission and enacted was a general law applicable to all cities of the first class, instead of the special law applicable only to New York City. Its proposed separate Tenement House Department for the city of New York was made part of the new charter of that city which went into effect on January 1, 1902. Seth Low was elected first mayor of the city under that new charter, and he appointed the chairman of the State Commission first Tenement House Commissioner of New York City, who in turn named the Secretary of the State Commission as his first deputy.

By this unusual and unexpected conjunction, tenement house reform became a part of the fundamental law of the State of New York in the shape proposed by the reformers, and the execution of that law in the city of New York was placed in their hands.

More than two years have now elapsed since that law went into effect, and for more than eighteen months its enforcement in the largest city of the State has been in the hands of its framers. During that period there have been two sessions of the Legislature, at each of which the provisions of this law have been an important issue. Numerous amendments have been proposed, all more or less hostile to the new law. The contest has been a bitter one from start to finish. When the new law was introduced in 1901 it aroused strong opposition in the building trades and among owners of unreformed tenement houses, and an effort was made at that time to defeat [repeal] it. Failing in this, the attack was renewed in 1902 and again in 1903. The main sources of opposition in these two years were certain building interests in Brooklyn, and the owners of the old houses in Manhattan. A fierce and bitter campaign was waged during both sessions of the Legislature, and had it not been for strong public opinion, voiced by the press and supported by Governor Odell and the city administration, the cause of tenement house reform might have been lost. No amendments, however, were adopted except those sanctioned by its friends and introduced at their instance.

The results of these legislative contests, the amendments to the law which have been proposed and those which have finally been adopted, the extent to which the new law has improved the type of new tenement houses and bettered the condition of old ones, its effect on the interests of the landlord classes, who build and rent, and of the tenant classes, who occupy and pay the rent, must necessarily form an impressive object-lesson in the development of housing reform. This book would not serve its purpose as a record of progress made, and as a guide toward progress still to come, unless it summarized the results thus far accomplished, outlined the story of tenement reform in New York since the adoption of the new law, and pointed out some of its instructive lessons.

The evils of New York's tenement houses as observed in 1900 were summed up as follows: "Insufficiency of light and air due to narrow courts or air shafts, undue height, and to the occupation by the building or by the adjacent buildings of too great proportion of the lot area; danger from fire; lack of separate water-closet and washing facilities; overcrowding; foul cellars and courts; and other like evils, which may be classed as bad housekeeping." The laws passed as a result of the Commission's investigations and on their recommendation sought primarily to remedy these evils so far as they might be remedied by legislative intervention.

The results accomplished have more than fulfilled the anticipations of the framers of the law. The discredited and horrible "dumb-bell" tenement, the prevailing type of house built in New York from 1879 until 1901, is now a thing of the past. At one stroke it was wiped out of existence as a type of future multiple dwelling. In its place is the new-law tenement, with large courts providing adequate light and ventilation for every room in the building.

What this one change means to the future social and sanitary welfare of the city cannot be overstated. No longer can new buildings be erected with two-thirds of the rooms dark, with narrow air shafts spreading contagion and disease throughout the community, with the windows of one house looking directly into the windows of a house opposite, twenty-eight inches away, destroying privacy and frequently subjecting children to sights and sounds of a debasing influence.

Instead, sanitary, comfortable, and decent houses are being rapidly built all over the city. In these every room is light. The great improvement in ventilation was vividly impressed upon a recent observer, who noticed, with amazement, all the window shades blowing out of the front windows of a row of these houses, so great was the circulation of air in the rooms. To anyone familiar with the heavy, fetid air which prevailed in the old houses, the contrast is striking. Instead of windows opening in close proximity to windows of adjoining houses, no window now opens within twelve feet of a window opposite, and generally they are twenty-five feet apart.

The air shaft is no more. It should have gone years ago. In fact it never should have existed. Thus has been removed from future buildings one of the most potent sources of danger in case of fire, as well as a prolific source of disease. Narrow and confined as it was, it acted in such cases as a flue, conveying the flames and smoke throughout the building.

Overcrowding has been materially checked and the population more widely distributed. Where before twenty-six families lived on a plot of ground 25 feet wide and 100 feet deep, there are now but twenty-two families, and in many cases not more than sixteen. This result has been accomplished by reducing the height of the prevailing type of new tenement house from seven stories to six stories, and by not permitting so great a portion of the lot to be built upon.

In place of common water-closets located in the public halls, without sufficient privacy, and shared by two families, each family has now its own closet facilities within its own apartment and entirely within its own control. This is a gain for decency. It assures the tenant the benefits of his own care and neatness. It enables the landlord to place responsibility for abuse where it belongs.

The dark halls, with all their moral and sanitary evils, can no longer be reproduced. In their place are light halls, having windows at each floor opening upon large courts. Greater fire protection has been afforded to the community in the new houses. The cellars of such houses, where one-fourth of all fires start, are completely shut off by a fireproof floor from the rest of the building, and the public halls and stairs are completely and entirely fireproof. Probably no better contrast between the old and the new could be afforded than by the difference in the kind of fire escapes required. Instead of light vertical ladders connecting the fire escape balconies, which in case of fire would not be used by women, children, or aged persons, there are now substantial stairs.

The extent to which the tenement house problem in New York is thus being solved by "providing proper types of new tenement houses for the future, through adequate restrictive legislation, and by forbidding the erection of any others," is best appreciated when it is borne in mind that during the year 1902, 543 new tenement houses were built, at an estimated cost of over $20,000,000, and during the first half of 1903, plans were filed for a still larger number, 699, at an estimated cost of $20,837,270.

The new-law houses have been an unqualified success. Builders and owners who were at first bitterly opposed to the law are now outspoken in its approval, and many of them state that the new houses are more remunerative than the old ones. The demand for the new accommodations on the part of the tenants has been overwhelming. Not only have the apartments been rented in many cases before the buildings have been completed, but in some instances the apartments have been rented from the plans before the buildings were even started. Such a thing has never before been known to occur in the tenement districts.

On the Lower East Side, where the new houses have been built in greatest number, it is a Sunday diversion of the people to take their families and friends to see them, and to wonder at and admire the light rooms, the bathtubs, and the other improvements. The rents in the new buildings are slightly higher than the rents in houses recently erected under the old law in similar neighborhoods, and rightly so because they give better accommodation. Moreover, there is a general rise in rents throughout the city which has no relation to the new tenement law or to the new-law house; it is due to a variety of causes, among which may be noted the general increase of prices and cost of living, and the displacement of large numbers of the population by the destruction of many houses for extensive public improvements. The approach for the Delancey Street bridge on the Lower East Side alone displaced 10,000 people. It is, of course, obvious that until the supply of new-law houses in certain neighbor hoods equals the demand, rents will tend to rise. It would be a sorrowful comment on the intelligence of the working people if they were not willing to pay a little more for vastly improved living accommodations.

Charitable Assistance for New York's Poor

New York in 1900 had no significant state government welfare or relief programs. "Poor relief," as it was sometimes called, was the responsibility of local governments, and their programs were usually very limited. Reformers and social-minded philanthropists began establishing charitable organizations to aid the poor and unfortunate and to reduce poverty.

This led to the need for cooperation among them. The nation's first comprehensive charity society was established in 1877 in Buffalo. Others were initiated in New York City in subsequent years. The New York City Charity Organization Society, established in New York City in 1882, coordinated the work of charitable organizations there, publicized living conditions in the city's overcrowded tenements, and highlighted the needs of the poor. One of its goals was to encourage charitable work but also to make sure the poor did not receive unwarranted assistance from more than one charitable group. Another was to encourage individual and family self-reliance. Its "friendly visitors" took an active interest in people with whom they worked and became a model for later social caseworkers. It opposed government assistance except in cases where private sources could not meet the needs.

The Society's 1908 report highlighted the impact of the national recession that began in 1907 but emphasized the adequacy of charitable organizations to meet the problems, at least for the time being. Its overall goal, as noted at the end of this excerpt, "an independent life from start to finish" for every New Yorker.

∾

From Twenty-Sixth Annual Report for the Year Ending September 30, 1908 (1908) by the Charity Organization Society of the City of New York

The past year in social work has been a period of extraordinary activity. There have been more people than usual in need of help, and there has been greater sympathy with their troubles, showing in more vigorous and more varied activity and closer cooperation in their behalf, with remarkably little of an objectionable or ill-advised character; and there has also been at the same time an unprecedented interest in poverty, disease, and crime as social problems, and in the social conditions which favor their persistence.

The Charity Organization Society has shared in the general increase of work which has come on account of the contraction in industry; it has tried to find those families, naturally so appealing, and generally believed to be so numerous, who need help but will not ask for it; it has made every effort to ensure for each of the 5,773 families in charge of the districts during the year as careful consideration as each of the 3,336 received the year before, and to adapt the work of all departments to the needs of the situation; it has kept in close touch with the various sources of information about labor conditions; it has urged on the city authorities the prosecution of public works already determined on, and on employers the resumption of activities, as measures of relief for the situation; and it has given increasing attention to the study of general social conditions and the devising and promoting of measures for their improvement.

We are able to record that we have not been obliged, by lack of resources, to refuse assistance to any family in need who has come to our notice. There is, on the contrary, evidence in our case records that relief has been given more liberally than in years of general prosperity; emergent aid has been given more frequently than in other years to families who were found, after thorough inquiry, not to have needed it, and cases were "taken up" who under ordinary circumstances might profitably have been "left to their own resources." The suspension of activities for a week by the United Hebrew Charities and certain limitations which they found necessary to observe for a while after resuming work, have increased the number of exceptional instances of Jewish families in the care of the Charity Organization Society. Repeated offers of assistance for families in need, sent to hospitals, dispensaries, schools, churches day nurseries, and settlements, have brought to the Society some families, though fewer than might have been expected, who would not otherwise have found their way.

Our financial statements show that the expenses of the Society have materially increased, but that the contributions have come within four thousand dollars of keeping up with the new demands. The increase in the number of contributors is especially gratifying, and is especially noticeable in the case of relief obtained, that list being about five times as long as it was the year before. . . .

The year has been a hard one for the poor in New York City, as it has been also for many of the well-to-do [due to the national recession that began in 1907]. A much larger number of families than in any of the ten or twelve years preceding have had to ask for help; many others have been able to maintain independence only by unwonted economies, amounting not infrequently, we must believe, to deprivation. How much actual suffering there has been this year, how much more than last year, no one knows, nor even how much has come to the notice of public and private charities and been relieved. Still less is it possible to estimate how many people have been living in poverty, in the sense of having had less food and fuel and clothing and other necessities than they required to maintain their efficiency; and still less, how many of these have been in poverty on account of the conditions of the labor market.

What we do know, from our own experience, is that since last October our districts have had seventy-three per cent more families in care than they had the year before; that whereas in recent years an able-bodied man has been almost an unknown character among our district families, he has this year been an increasingly conspicuous and increasingly perplexing factor, present in a fourth or a fifth of the families; that in other families the trouble has been that boys and girls have lost their work in factories; that homeless men have come to the Joint Application Bureau in three and four and five times their usual numbers; that the Wood Yard has given employment to three and four and five times as many men during the winter months as it did the year before; that able-bodied men and women have been applying at the Employment Bureau for the Handicapped; that the reception agent has had a long line of callers who did not want relief, but information as to where to find work, or how to collect wages due them, or how to get a small loan; and that the deposits in the Penny Provident Fund have been smaller and the withdrawals heavier in proportion, especially at the settlement stations.

We know, furthermore, from our conferences and correspondence and observation, that other charitable societies have felt a similar increase in the demands on them; that the Municipal Lodging House has on many nights been unable to accommodate all its applicants; that many small deposits have been withdrawn gradually from the savings banks until accounts were exhausted; that immigration fell off in the winter months while eastern bound steamers carried back to Europe unprecedented numbers of recent immigrants; that the Provident Loan Society has made many thousands of small loans, which indicated stress among wage-earners, and that the percentage of loans unpaid was considerably larger than for several years past; that a visitor going from house to house among families who had no connection with relief agencies found women and children sitting in rooms without a fire; that other visitors, in various parts of the city, commonly found the man of the family at home in the daytime. . . .

The most pressing needs in the charitable resources of the city at present are institutions for the care of consumptives in all stages of the disease, homes for the aged, temporary homes for respectable women and girls. The diet kitchens and the day nurseries are finding themselves hard pressed to meet the demands on their resources. . . .

We are not developing a "pauper class." A "hard year," such as we have just finished, makes us realize that unemployment, in the sense of lack of work for men able and willing to work, is not, in our country, a large permanent problem, but confronts us only temporarily, at long intervals; and furthermore, and most encouraging of all, the temporary increase in dependence has not interfered with the progress of movements for the general improvement of social conditions.

The individual families in need have not been neglected, but there has been time and thought and money also for the work which will keep down the numbers of families who will need help in future years. The increased effectiveness of the organized movements for a better distribution of population; for abolishing premature and unsuitable employment for women and children; for preventing preventable disease and accidents; for ensuring decent and sanitary dwellings, and spaces for play and recreation; for protecting all consumers against impurities and adulterations in food and drugs; for keeping families together; for discrimination in relief; for the establishment of new charity organization societies and the renascence of existing ones which have lost their original spirit; for providing a useful and adequate education for all children—this is the most hopeful feature of the year's work.

And this, together with the increased knowledge of social conditions, and the increased enthusiasm for social service, which have also characterized the year, is the best guarantee that we shall not find it necessary to provide a government pension for all our old men and women, and that we may work, with increasing confidence of success, towards the ideal, for every man and woman of normal health and ability, of "an independent life from start to finish."

Helping People Take Care of Themselves

The Charity Organization Society of New York, discussed above, coordinated relief efforts. But it also stressed personal responsibility, self-help and what people could and should do for themselves. One of its interests was showing people how to stay healthy, take care of their apartments, and stretch their scarce, hard-earned dollars. This resulted in publications that gave fairly detailed advice about how people should take care of themselves. But the Society also tried to educate people about their rights, how to deal with landlords and, when necessary, how to contact the police.

∽

From *For You: It is Hard to Get Money, It is Harder to Spend it Right, Health is Wealth* (1910) by Charity Organization Society of New York and New York City Tenement House Department

Do you want to get sick? Do you want to lose a day's pay? Do you want to risk losing your job? Or, do you want to keep well? Do you know that the working people of America lose $772,892,860 a year because of sickness? Light, clean rooms with plenty of fresh air, day and night, will help to keep you well.

Don't Rent Dark Rooms

Fresh air and light in every room are better than medicine. Plants do not grow well in the dark, neither do children. Have you gone to a doctor during the last year? Ask him about dark rooms. A dark room is a Consumption Factory. There germs thrive and flourish.

Gas bills and medicine bills soon equal the difference in rent between good, light rooms and dark, unhealthy ones.

Sick people need sunlight and fresh air. They cannot keep well if they sleep in an inside bedroom. Bad air makes the baby cross. It will pay you to move where the children can have sunshine and fresh air to grow strong. Try it and see the difference.

Poor eyesight and need for glasses often come from bad light. Save your eyes and money by letting in all the light possible. The man with poor eyes can't earn as much as the man with good ones. Do you want your children to have poor eyes? It is better to pay rent for light rooms than to pay bills for glasses and bad eyes.

Give the light a chance to get it. When you hang heavy curtains which shut out the light you hide dust and disease germs. When you nail down the window to save heat, you shut in poisonous air which makes you sick. Windows are intended to admit light and air. Let them do it.

Open your windows often during the day to let in fresh air. Keep some windows open both day and night, summer and winter. At night open a window in every bedroom not less than three inches at the bottom and three inches at the top—more would be better. You will not take cold when you sleep in a room that has plenty of fresh air if you have warm bed clothes. . . .

Don't Take Chances on Getting Sick

[A] dirty sink with old pans, wet rags and mops under it makes a home for roaches and water bugs. Keep it clean above and below. Once a week pour strong washing soda and hot water down the pipes to cut out the grease. Keep food covered. Leave nothing around to attract roaches or flies.

Do you like to see garbage and papers scattered in the street or yard? Do the people living in your house put the garbage in cans or throw it out of the window? Do you? Keep the house clean and make the children do so, too. Clean halls, yards, courts and streets make the home better to live in. Put nothing but garbage in the garbage cans. Don't throw scraps of paper in the street. Don't build bonfires in the street or in the yard. If you see anyone knocking covers off of garbage cans or ash cans or upsetting them, tell the policeman.

Plenty of good clean water is necessary for health. See that you have it. Drinking impure water is sure to cause sickness. The man who bathes every day works better and can earn more money than the man who doesn't. He also stands a better chance of keeping well. If you haven't a bathtub, next time you move try to get in a house where there is a bath in each tenement. Most of the new houses have them. Even without a tub, one can take a bath. . . .

Good Housekeeping

If you keep your rooms tidy, the wall paper clean, the woodwork washed, the windows polished, and the floors scrubbed, your landlord will know you are a good tenant and will be more willing to make repairs for you. He also will not be likely to increase your rent, as he will wish to keep good tenants in his house.

Your husband will like to come to a comfortable place, and the children will be proud of their home. Everyone likes a light, cheerful room. That is why theatres, saloons and stores are brightly lighted.

When the landlord agrees to paint the walls for you, ask for a light color—white, or cream color, or light gray. It will make the room lighter. If you are wise, you will not use wall paper. Disease germs stay there for months. Bugs love the sweet paste, and are often found under wall paper in great quantities. Bedbugs are dangerous as well as annoying.

You must do your part in keeping clean the floors and walls of the halls and stairs if you want to be proud of the house where you live. Do not let the children carry in dirt or mark the walls or break plaster, leaving holes for bugs or dirt.

Don't sweep dirt into the halls from your rooms. Carry garbage or rubbish to the garbage cans and ashes to the ash cans; don't leave it on the stairs. Don't throw it out of the window just because it is easy.

Don't think if you live on the upper floors garbage and filth in the yard will do no harm. It is certain to make the air you breathe bad, and bad air may make you sick. . . .

If Things Are Wrong

If anything is wrong, tell the landlord. If he doesn't do what is right, report it to the Charity Organization Society. You do not have to sign your name; they will pay attention to your complaint just the same. Be sure to give the address of the house by street and number and floor or the Society cannot help you. State clearly what is the matter. If nothing is done at once, don't think they are paying no attention to it. Don't make spite complaints because you are angry at your neighbors or the landlord. They can do them no harm and you no good.

If you have any complaint to make about bad plumbing, dirty stairs or yards or unhealthful conditions, you can write or telephone the Board of Health. Bell 2820; Automatic 1295. If you have any complaint to make about stairways or fire escapes or dangerous fire conditions, you can write or telephone the Fire Department. Bell 2280; Automatic 1334. If you have any complaint to make about immoral or disorderly conditions, you can call a policeman or write or telephone the Police Department. Bell 210; Automatic 1311.

You Can Complain

If the stairways or fire escapes above or below your floor are obstructed by boxes, boards, clothes-lines or anything which would prevent using them in case of fire. If any of the doors leading from your tenement to a hall or stairway are nailed up or locked or obstructed. If rags, feathers, feed, hay, straw, excelsior, cotton or paper stock are kept or stored in the cellar or any other parts of the building. If there are a lot of boxes, boards, furniture, mattresses or inflammable material of any kind in the bins or public parts of the cellar. If bakeries do not have fireproof walls and ceilings. If the door, window, or transom from a drug, liquor or paint store to the public hall is not metal covered. . . .

If there are torn and dangerous carpets, oilcloth or other coverings on the halls or stairs. If there are broken stairs or loose or broken balusters. If there is plaster about to fall. If there are leaky roofs, skylights or scuttles. If there are broken or stopped-up rain leaders or gutters, making the walls damp. . . .

When You Rent a Tenement Make Sure

That you have your own toilet. That you have a sink with running water in your kitchen. That the house is kept clean. That the landlord is a good one. That the landlord keeps his house in proper condition. Ask some of the other tenants. That all the rooms are light and have plenty of air. That there is a back yard for the children to play in. These things are more important than wallpaper or the appearance of the front of the building. If you can't find what you want in one neighborhood, try another. There are always plenty of vacant flats. Be sure to get the right kind of home so you won't have to move often. Moving costs money.

Settlement Houses and Visiting Nurses Ease City Life

In the closing years of the nineteenth century, some reformers began establishing "settlement houses" in poor, crowded neighborhoods. These institutions provided social services, education, and venues for community events. They often focused on immigrants and first-generation New Yorkers. Nurse, settlement house pioneer, and progressive reformer Lillian D. Wald (1867–1940) joined with a colleague from her nursing school to settle on the Lower East Side and began taking care of sick neighbors. Wald witnessed firsthand the hardship and deprivation experienced by poor immigrant families living in the area. In 1895, she established the Henry Street Settlement, which soon became the headquarters of a new medical service, which she called "public health nurses," who visited sick people, particularly indigent people, in their homes.

Wald's visiting nurses were soon serving thousands of patients. Their services met New York's growing medical needs that the city's doctors and hospitals could not meet. Henry Street also provided a playground, dance hall, kindergarten, savings and loan fund, and cooperative food store. Wald's pioneering operation evolved into the Visiting Nurse Service of New York. Wald became a progressive reform leader, advocating for child's rights, women's rights, and public health care.

Her 1915 book The House on Henry Street *described the settlement house's early years and the strategies it used to establish and build up the nursing service.*

∼

From *The House on Henry Street* (1915) by Lillian D. Wald

When I first entered the training-school my outpourings to the superintendent—a woman touched with a genius for sympathy—my youthful heroics, and my vow to "nurse the poor" were met with what I deemed vague reference to the "Mission." Afterwards when I sought guidance I found that in New York the visiting (or district) nurse was accessible only through sectarian organizations or the free dispensary.

As our plan crystallized my friend and I were certain that a system for nursing the sick in their homes could not be firmly established unless certain fundamental social facts were recognized. We tried to imagine how loved ones for whom we might be solicitous would react were they in the place of the patients whom we hoped to serve. With time, experience, and the stimulus of creative minds our technique and administrative methods have naturally improved, but this test gave us vision to establish certain principles, whose soundness has been proved during the growth of the service.

We perceived that it was undesirable to condition the nurse's service upon the actual or potential connection of the patient with a religious institution or free dispensary, or to have the nurse assigned to the exclusive use of one physician, and we planned to create a service on terms most considerate of the dignity and independence of the patients. We felt that the nursing of the sick in their homes should be undertaken seriously and adequately; that instruction should be incidental and not the primary consideration; that the etiquette, so far as doctor and patient were concerned, should be analogous to the established system of private nursing; that the nurse should be as ready to respond to calls from the people themselves as to calls from physicians; that she should accept calls from all physicians, and with no more red-tape or formality than if she were to remain with one patient continuously.

The new basis of the visiting-nurse service which we thus inaugurated reacted almost immediately upon the relationship of the nurse to the patient, reversing the position the nurse had formerly held. Chagrin at having the neighbors see in her an agent whose presence proclaimed the family's poverty or its failure to give adequate care to its sick member was changed to the gratifying consciousness that her presence, in conjunction with that of the doctor, "private" or "Lodge,"[1] proclaimed the family's liberality and anxiety to do everything possible for the sufferer. For the exposure of poverty is a great humiliation to people who are trying to maintain a foothold in society for themselves and their families.

My colleague and I realized that there were large numbers of people who could not, or would not, avail themselves of the hospitals. It was estimated that ninety per cent of the sick people in cities were sick at home, an estimate which has been corroborated (1913–14) by the investigation of the Committee of Inquiry into the Departments of Health, Charities, and Bellevue and Allied Hospitals of New York, and a humanitarian civilization demanded that something of the nursing care given in hospitals should be accorded to sick people in their homes.

We decided that fees should be charged when people could pay. It was interesting to discover that, although nominal in amount compared with the cost of the service, these fees represented a much larger proportion of the wage in the case of the ordinary worker who paid for the hourly service than did the fee paid by a man with a salary of $5,000, who engaged the full time of the nurse. Our plan, we reasoned, was analogous to the custom of "private" hospitals, which give free treatment or charge according to the resources of the ward patients. Both private hospitals and visiting nursing are thereby lifted out of "charity" as comprehended by the people.

We felt that for economic reasons valuable and expensive hospital space should be saved for those for whom the hospital treatment is necessary; and an obvious social consideration was that many people, particularly women, cannot leave their homes without imperiling, or sometimes destroying the home itself.

Almost immediately we found patients who needed care, and doctors ready to accept our services with probably the least amount of friction possible under the circumstances; for those doctors who had not been interns in the hospitals were unfamiliar with the trained nurse, whose work was little known at that time outside the hospitals and the homes of the well-to-do.

Despite the neighborhood's friendliness, however, we struggled not only with poverty and disease, but with the traditional fate of the pioneer: in many cases we encountered the inevitable opposition which the unusual must arouse.

It seems almost ungracious to relate some of our first experiences with doctors. No one can give greater tribute than do the nurses of the settlement to the generosity of physicians and surgeons when we recall how often paying patients were set aside for more urgent non-paying ones; the counsel freely given from the highest for the lowliest; the eager readiness to respond. Occasionally sage advice came from a veteran who knew the people well and lamented the economic pressure which at times involved, to their spiritual disaster, doctors as well as patients.

The first day on which we set out to discover the sick who might need a nurse, my comrade found a woman with high temperature in an airless room, more oppressive because of the fetid odor from the bed. Service with one of New York's skilled specialists had trained the nurse well and she identified the symptoms immediately. "Yes, there was a Lodge doctor. He had left a prescription. He might come again." With fine diplomacy an excuse was made to call upon the doctor and to assume that he would accept the nurse's aid. My colleague presented her credentials and offered to accompany him to the case immediately, as she was "sure conditions must have changed since his last visit or he would doubtless have ordered "so-and-so," suggesting the treatment the distinguished specialists were then using. He promised to go, and the nurse waited patiently for hours at the woman's bedside. When he arrived he pooh-poohed and said "Nothing doing." We had ascertained the financial condition of the family from the evidence of the empty push-cart and the fact that the fish-peddler was not in the market with his merchandise. Five dollars was loaned that night to purchase stock next day.

My comrade and I decided to visit the patient early the next morning, to mingle judgments on what action could be taken in this serious illness with due respect to established etiquette. When we arrived, the Lodge doctor and a "Professor" (a consultant) were in the sickroom, and our five dollars, left for fish, was in their possession. Cigarettes in mouths and hats on heads, they were questioning husband and wife, and only [English novelist Charles] Dickens could have done justice to the scene. We were not too timid to allude to the poverty and the source of the fee, and felt free when we were told to "go ahead and do anything you like." That permission we acted upon instantly and received, over the telephone, authority from the distinguished specialist to get to work. We were prudent enough to report the authority and treatment given, with solemn etiquette, to the physician in attendance, who in turn congratulated us on having helped him to save a life.

Restricting Alcoholic Beverages

By the advent of the progressive era, New Yorkers had long differed about restricting or prohibiting the sale and consumption of alcoholic beverages. Some believed that people (mostly men) had a right to drink. Others thought alcohol was harmful and favored education to reduce its use. Still others, particularly ministers, pushed voluntary abstinence or moderation. For a while, a majority of New Yorkers favored state government prohibition, but an 1855 law imposing that was soon declared unconstitutional.

The Anti-Saloon League, organized in Ohio in 1895 with a New York branch established four years later, thought it had a better approach, with two strategies. One, push for national prohibition. Two, within New York, provide for "local option" where voters could decide for themselves whether their communities would be "wet" or "dry." That had been tried sporadically in the nineteenth century, with mixed results. The first strategy was accomplished by the Eighteenth Amendment to the Constitution, ratified by the states (including New York) in 1919. The second strategy gradually advanced through legislation, including a 1917 law that expanded the range of local options.

The New York League's aggressive superintendent, William H. Anderson, was adept at marshalling support for "dry" candidates for legislature and governor and at getting favorable legislation enacted. He was also skilled at getting attention and claiming credit for his organization.

∽

From "New York" in Proceedings of the Nineteenth National Convention of the Anti-Saloon League of America (1919) by William H. Anderson

New York State is the liquor stronghold of America, the financial capital of the traffic and the national headquarters of the "Imperial German brewers" in America. It was under Prohibition some fifty years ago, but the law was declared unconstitutional.

In 1896 the Raines law was passed.[2] This created an excise department with a commissioner of excise to issue all liquor tax certificates. The law was repeatedly amended in behalf of the liquor interests and eventually developed a great political machine, through which the power of the state was thrown against any effort to curtail the liquor traffic for fear it would reduce the revenue, aggregating some twenty million dollars, and divided between the state and the various localities.

The township option feature contained in the liquor tax law, as it was officially called, was so fixed as to try to get some kind of a license into every community. It provided for a vote on four propositions—the sale of liquor: (1) to be drunk on the premises; (2) in wholesale quantities not to be drunk on the premises; (3) in drug stores on physicians' prescriptions; (4) in hotels only, provided the vote was adverse on Proposition 1. The feature of this law permitting hotels to sell liquor to guests on Sunday resulted in the development of a new abuse known throughout the civilized world as "Raines Law Hotels," through the use for immoral purposes of the additional rooms that saloons had to have to secure hotel privileges.

For twenty years the liquor interests, aided by most of the politicians, successfully resisted all efforts to extend the voting privilege [to restrict or outlaw sale of alcoholic beverages] to other units, but in 1917 a city local option law was passed, and in 1918 twenty of the fifty-seven cities in the state voted dry under it. In 1917 and 1915 approximately three hundred new townships voted dry, making a total of over six hundred and fifty out of nine hundred and thirty-two in the state. In two years, October 1, 1916, to October 1, 1918, due to the effect of Prohibition, to the higher license fee, and to restrictive measures passed by the wets in a desperate effort to head off Prohibition, the number of bar licenses decreased by 8,734, meaning a barroom funeral every two hours, night and day, week days, Sundays and holidays, for two years in preparation for National Prohibition.

New York State with only three votes out of forty-three members of the lower house of Congress in favor of submission of the National Prohibition Amendment in 1914, gained eleven in 1917, or more than the margin of safety by which the amendment was submitted—a case of the liquor "stronghold" breaking the back of the liquor traffic. . . .

The Anti-Saloon League, as the representative of the moral forces, cleaned out the entire wet leadership of the state senate in the primaries of 1918, and nominated and then elected a legislature in favor of ratification.

New York was not one of the first 36 states to ratify the Prohibition amendment, but it did ratify within the first month of the legislative session of 1919, consummating ratification on the 29th day of January as the 29th state to ratify after January 1. Ratification was only made possible through the action of the Republican party representatives in both houses of the Legislature making it a party issue in view of the fact that the Democratic party, controlled by the [New York City] Tammany [Hall] organization, which depends for its campaign funds and its power upon the traffickers in liquor and vice, had made a party issue of it by putting an anti-ratification plank into the Democratic platform and lost the Legislature, whereas the Republican party primaries resulted in overwhelming victory for ratification candidates. The Prohibition candidate for governor [incumbent Charles S. Whitman], who won renomination on the Republican ticket by nearly three to one, was defeated because his managers, instead of following up his splendid record, tried to placate the wets in defiance of the advice of the Anti-Saloon League.

Immediately after ratification by New York there was a tremendous counterattack stirred up by the German brewers and the liquor interests generally, and some of the big hotel men of New York City, backed up by some of the leading New York newspapers, and a most desperate effort was made to pass a bill purporting to legalize beer with 3 per cent by weight of alcohol, which effort was only defeated within the last twenty-four hours of the legislative session. A good enforcement bill has been worked out by the Anti-Saloon League and enforcement will be the main issue until adequate legislation is passed, and we predict that the people of New York City when they become adjusted to the situation will cheerfully obey the law and will welcome the positive benefit as readily as the people of any other city.

Ratification by New York was the hardest blow struck the liquor traffic. It destroyed forever the plea that it was not fair for small states to put National Prohibition over on the big states. The victory is a victory of the united moral forces. It was won by out-guessing and out-generaling the foe, by organization, by hard-hitting and merciless fighting. It has put a premium on Christian citizenship everywhere. To win, it was necessary to build the greatest permanent Anti-Saloon League organization ever built in any state, and do it in the shortest time on record. We are proud to present the Empire State as a self-determining commonwealth on this greatest moral issue.

Censorship Impacts Lives

One of the undercurrents of progressive thinking was that organizations and, sometimes, the government, could improve people's lives. Usually this could be accomplished through education and advice, sometimes by government regulation, but occasionally by firm requirements, limits, and coercion, such as through prohibition, as noted in the document immediately above. The coercive approach was faint and intermittent in New York, where people tended to resent fussy interference in their personal lives, but it did play out in some unfortunate ways.

Anthony Comstock (1844–1915) emerged by the turn of the century as the nation's leading anti-vice activist and censor. He exercised enforcement powers in his roles as secretary of the New York Society for the Suppression of Vice (the law creating the organization bestowed enforcement powers) and as a United States Postal Inspector. Comstock spearheaded efforts to censor publications, performances, and even art works. He gave particular emphasis to suppressing what he judged to be pornographic photos, obscene works, and birth control information. His work was endorsed by clergy, churches, and some of New York's leading and influential citizens. It was widely supported by financial contributions. Comstock usually prevailed when he hauled accused malefactors into court.

Supporters said he was sincere, committed, and determined. Critics called him a snoopy busybody who ran roughshod over freedom of speech and people's rights. His role as enforcer of what he defined as the prevailing morality often met with scorn, ridicule, and opposition, particularly in New York, which tended toward tolerance. The example below demonstrates Comstock's overreach and New Yorkers' occasional pushback.

∽

From *Anthony Comstock: Roundsman of the Lord* (1927)
by Heywood Broun and Margaret Leech

While he may have honestly pictured himself as an obscure weeder in God's garden, he could not escape the deeper conviction that he was an important and aggressive member of God's patrol. But, weeder or constable, his belief in his good judgment was complete and unassailable. As the years brought him experience, this confidence in his own competence was hardened and confirmed. Usually the court decisions were on his side. He grew more and more expert in preparing his cases and to Comstock soon after God came the Law.

Nevertheless, he was to lose one important case, a case occasioning a storm of publicity which shook and nearly shattered the fabric of his life-work. In 1906, Comstock was so imprudent as to arrest a woman. A cry of persecution again went up, and there was foolish talk about dragging off an unoffending girl to prison. But the events were, this time, not tragic; rather they were cast in a vein of comedy.

In the summer of 1906, the eye of the crusader fell upon a pamphlet issued by the Art Students' League [in New York City], and found it very objectionable indeed. The studies of nudes which it contained he considered unfit for general distribution. These pamphlets, according to the official biographer, [James]Trumbull [in his 1913 book, *Anthony Comstock, Fighter*], were being sent "apparently to people of all sorts, whether known to be lovers of art or not." Investigation revealed that "girls and unmarried women" were on the mailing list.

The agents of the Society made an honest effort to find a man connected with this case. The pitfalls connected with arresting women they recognized. But both the mailing department at the League's offices on West Fifty-seventh Street and the desk where catalogues were given away were in charge of women. At length, with some trepidation the risky step was taken. The young bookkeeper of the League was taken into custody. "No one was more regretful or sought more earnestly to relieve this young woman of any embarrassment in the matter than did the Agent of this Society," asserted the Annual Report for the year 1906. To her counsel it was suggested that she might be spared the disgrace of appearing under her own name; and the newspapers carried the announcement that a Miss Robinson had been arrested. It was also suggested that a plea of guilty might be entered in court without the young woman appearing, and that the Society would consent to a suspended sentence. The catalogues would then be legally condemned, and could be destroyed.

The so-called Miss Robinson, however, duly appeared in court, where she was reported as being in a highly nervous condition. Indeed so hysterical did she become that a doctor was subsequently called. She was, it appeared, only nineteen years old. Next morning, when Mr. Comstock arrived at his office he greeted the waiting reporters with angry frowns. Here he was, once more embroiled in persecuting a woman! The role of ogre to a frail and innocent girl did not please him. "I'd like to know who gave that out to the papers," the [New York] World reported that he said. "I thought it was going to be kept quiet."

Quiet, however, was the last thing that Anthony might expect from this unfortunate affair. Dubious as the Society must have been about the popularity of their course, the League felt that it had nothing to lose by publicity. Officers and students alike were ill-disposed to endure this assault in silence. For years they had been circulating pamphlets similar to those which Comstock had seized; and they asserted that they were sent through the mails with the knowledge and consent of the postal authorities. Alarmists were disposed to view the raid as the beginning of a concerted attack on art schools. An emergency meeting of the officers of the League was called. Mr. Comstock's society was threatened with the revoking of its charter; and Mr. Comstock himself with the loss of his commission as Post Office inspector. An interview with Gutzon Borglum appeared in the New York World of August 3, 1906. "My God, what are we coming to?" was one of his comments, and another was the inevitable "Comstock is the one who is lewd." With withering scorn, he inquired why the crusader, instead of interfering with art, did not confiscate Boccaccio, the Heptameron, Rabelais and Balzac. The sculptor's irony, however, failed of its purpose. Mr. Comstock had already attended to literature.

The art students avenged themselves with malicious caricatures of a pious old gentleman with sideburns, wings and a halo. A fat effigy of Comstock was hung outside a third-story window of the League, bearing a placard with the current witticism, "23 for Comstock." The World of August 4, 1906, carried on its front page a full-length photograph of the vice "chaser" flanked by equally large photographs of the Venus de Milo and the Apollo Belvedere, with the suggestion that he would arrest them if they appeared outdoors. Not only in terms of art were the attacks on Comstock expressed. An organization of artists and sculptors suggested that he should be boiled in oil. And one of the art students composed a sonnet, dedicated to the crusader, which contained a scathing reference to "sexless clowns who shun love's hallowed fire."

If Anthony had embarked on this enterprise with trepidation, he was by the time that the [court] hearing was held clearly eager to be done with it. In the courtroom he called for the employer of the young bookkeeper to come forward and take her place at the bar. "I want to get at the sneaking hounds behind this woman's skirts," the New York Sun of October 30 quoted him as saying. There was laughter in court. There was more laughter at the newspaper's ridicule of the case. Yet, in spite of everything, the prosecution did not relent until the offending pamphlets had been destroyed. This end accomplished, Comstock quickly extricated himself from his position as a prosecutor of innocent womanhood. He asked that further proceedings against Miss Robinson be dismissed.

Reverberations of this case were long in dying. Naturally, much of the criticism sprang not from the fact that he had arrested a woman, but from resentment at his having arrested anyone at all. Miss Robinson's connection with the case served to heighten the general indignation, and make Comstock's action appear more tyrannical and absurd. The following spring, at a burlesque exhibition held at the League, a student dressed to represent the vice-hunter stamped about the gallery, affecting to regard the pictures with shame and horror. A statuette caricaturing Comstock had been presented to Miss Robinson. In this presentation, Anthony is shown clasping a sculptor's mallet with which he has apparently shattered the Venus de Milo, on which one foot—a cloven one—is resting. Underneath runs the legend, "Do you love this old man?" But though the statuette caused wide amusement, it is evident that its creator had never seen his subject. The meager ascetic in plaster is no kin to the stout and stalwart vice-hunter, whose legs were like tree-trunks.

Strengthening Public Health

In the closing years of the nineteenth century, much of the state's public health responsibilities were carried out by city and county health commissioners. New York City had a particularly strong program. In the new century, the state's public health role expanded and by 1920 New York had one of the strongest state public health programs in the nation.

Much of that progress was due to Dr. Hermann M. Biggs (1859–1923), who served as New York City health commissioner from 1902 to 1913. Biggs was responsible for the first use of diphtheria antitoxin in the nation, carried on a campaign to eradicate tuberculosis, emphasized preventive medicine, initiated school nurses, and undertook public education initiatives.

In 1913 he headed a New York state task force which made recommendations to strengthen the state health department and, after the legislature enacted them, moved on to serve as New York State Commissioner of Health from 1914 to 1924. In that role, he expanded the role of public health authorities, strengthened public health laws, and continued the work of public education to prevent spread of contagious diseases. His motto was

"Public health is purchasable. Within natural limitations a community can determine its own death-rate."

In his first report as state health commissioner, Biggs reviewed progress in recent years and advanced recommendations to further strengthen public health work.

~

FROM *THIRTY SIXTH ANNUAL REPORT OF THE STATE DEPARTMENT OF HEALTH FOR THE YEAR ENDING DECEMBER 31, 1915* (1915) BY NEW YORK STATE DEPARTMENT OF HEALTH

During the year the work has been actively prosecuted along the lines previously undertaken and has been extended in several directions. A gratifying reduction in the number of deaths and the death rate outside of New York City has taken place and a diminished amount of illness has occurred. It seemed possible a year and a half ago to predict that, with adequate financial support, 25,000 lives in New York State outside of New York City could be saved within five years. The reduction of .9 of a point from the average death rate prevailing for the three years preceding 1913 in a population of nearly 4,700,000 indicates a saving of approximately 4000 lives for the year 1915. This reduction is largely due to the more efficient work performed by the 1100 health officers in 1443 different municipalities, and to the activities of the staff of the State Department of Health.

More specifically with reference to the reduction in deaths and death rates taking place in 1915, I would refer to the following:

> The general death rate was the lowest in the history of the State.
> The infant death rate was the lowest in the history of the State.
> The death rate from tuberculosis was the lowest in the history of the State.
> The death rate from typhoid fever was the lowest in the history of the State.
> The death rate from diphtheria was the lowest in the history of the State.
> The death rate from measles was the lowest in the history of the State.
> The death rate from scarlet fever was the lowest in the history of the State.

> The death rate from whooping cough was the lowest in the history of the State.
>
> Notwithstanding an increase in population (outside of New York City) of nearly 60,000 annually, there was the smallest number of deaths from the six most important communicable diseases for 18 years, a period extending as far back as the comparison can be made [back to the formation of Greater New York, 1898].

In recent years there has been a remarkable expansion in the conception of the responsibility of the State and municipal governments in matters of public health; an expansion in the direction of a broad-minded socialism. Today we find many activities which are generally and properly regarded as belonging to the health authorities, which in former years were either untouched or were considered matters of individual responsibility.

With the great material prosperity and progress and the rapid increase in population of the country, and the higher standards of intelligence and education among the people, together with more accurate knowledge of the possibilities of preventive medicine, furnished by the developments in science, there has come an imperative demand in the larger and more prosperous communities for the practical adaptation and application of scientific discoveries to the prevention of diseases.

More enlightened communities have come more and more to realize the possibilities and their responsibilities in the protection of all classes of citizens, not only to the dangers incident to the prevalence of communicable diseases, but to the even greater possibilities in the prevention of other disease and to the prolongation of life. Years ago, when means of communication were more primitive, the smaller rural communities were often for long periods of time almost free from many of the communicable diseases and only suffered from outbreaks or epidemics when such diseases were introduced from without.

Greater reliance was placed upon quarantine both by sea and by land for the restriction of disease, although the measures adopted were more often unsuccessful than successful, because of the lack of accurate knowledge as to the causation of the various infectious diseases and the methods and means by which they were transmitted. In the presence of epidemics all efforts to cope successfully with these diseases were ineffectual, and the population of an affected area was often decimated before an epidemic subsided, but with increasing knowledge this situation gradually changed until now it is not the lack of sufficient knowledge if these diseases prevail, but lack of means to deal with them or the failure to utilize well-understood methods of prevention.

Gradually in large communities it has become more and more clearly recognized that the material prosperity and happiness of the community are primarily dependent upon the health of the community and that this in turn is dependent upon the standards of sanitary administration. Certain essentials are now demanded as minimum sanitary requirements in a modern city or village, such as a pure and an abundant water supply, a proper drainage and sewerage system, clean and well-paved streets, proper housing for the poor and proper supervision of the food supplies, especially milk.

Less generally recognized are certain other essentials to the welfare of the community, such as ample parks and playgrounds, abundant and ample hospital accommodations for the care of the sick and especially for the care of those sick with communicable disease, and adequate supervision and isolation of cases of contagious disease.

With the improvement in the sanitary conditions in the larger communities, and with increasing knowledge, there has been a gradual disappearance, one after another, of the great epidemic diseases which formerly decimated civilized communities. Bubonic plague, typhus fever, cholera, yellow fever, smallpox and epidemic dysentery are among the communicable diseases which have been gradually restricted through earlier years until now they no longer constitute a serious menace in any of the civilized communities of the world.

When we recall that these diseases alone formerly caused a higher death rate than now exists from all causes, we realize what the eradication of these diseases really means. As we come to more recent years we find that while the changes have been less spectacular than the earlier ones, yet the results have been no less important.

The history of the decreasing death rate in New York City does not differ in any way from the history of other great cities, excepting that it is perhaps more striking than is to be found in most other cities. The significance is perhaps greater because in New York the financial authorities for a number of years have shown great enlightenment and have made more generous appropriations for various phases of sanitary work, and because the difficulties in the accomplishment of results are undoubtedly greater there than in any other city in this country and, perhaps, than in any other city of the world.

The practical demonstration, therefore, may be said to have a broader meaning and greater value to the authorities of other localities.

In 1865 and 1866 in the old City of New York the death rate was about 35 in each 1000 of the population. Today it is scarcely more than one-third this; in fact, it is about 13 in each 1000. This change indicating a reduction in the death rate of more than 20 in each 1000 of the population means an annual saving of 100,000 lives a year as compared with what would have occurred if the rates had continued which prevailed at the end of the Civil War. And when we come to an analysis of the death rates, to see where this saving has been brought about, we find that it is almost solely in the class of diseases known as infectious diseases.

A steady improvement in the quantity and quality of the health officers throughout the State has resulted from the continued and increased demands made upon them by the Department, and the constant supervision and assistance given them by the District Sanitary Supervisors and the administrative officers of the Department. Every effort has been made during the past year to secure the appointment of more efficient local health officers and to eliminate those, comparatively few in number, who are incompetent or negligent in the discharge of their duties. Four health officers were removed for cause during the year 1915.

The competent health officer of today must be much more than a well-trained practicing physician; he must have a knowledge not only of the nature and the methods of control of the more readily communicable diseases, but also of vital statistics, water supplies, sewage disposal, child hygiene and tuberculosis. He must also be familiar with the nature of sanitary surveys and reports, the sanitary control of milk supplies, the recognition and abatement of nuisances, and the methods of public health education. No one of these special topics comes within the scope of the curriculum of even the best medical schools.

The Public Health Council has, therefore, in accordance with the power granted by the Public Health Law, prescribed a series of qualifications to be required of health officers to be appointed on and after November, 1916. The qualifications require that health officers either shall have taken a college degree in public health or have taken an approved correspondence course of six months in public health or a residence course of six weeks, or shall present evidence (by examination or otherwise) satisfactory to the Council that they are qualified to satisfactorily perform the duties of health officer. It is gratifying to note that courses have been established for this purpose at New York University and Bellevue Medical College and at the Medical Department of Syracuse University, which have been approved by the Council, and over 200 health officers are enrolled for these courses. . . .

An extension of the laboratory service has been made possible by larger sums appropriated by the Legislature for this purpose; and in addition to the diphtheria and tetanus antitoxin formerly prepared, it has been possible also to furnish health officers and physicians with typhoid vaccine, whooping cough vaccine and antimeningococcus [sic] serum for the prevention or treatment of typhoid fever, whooping cough, and cerebrospinal meningitis. The diagnostic work of the laboratories has also been extended, and routine examinations of specimens were made during the year for the diagnosis and surveillance of diphtheria, typhoid fever, tuberculosis, syphilis, gonorrhea, malaria and a number of other disease conditions.

Protecting Rural New York

By 1900, New York's cities had police forces but the rest of the state was unevenly protected by town constables and sheriffs in each county. Governor Charles Whitman (1915–1919), citing rising crime in rural areas, proposed creation of a new State Police force in 1915. Some New Yorkers were skeptical—state police in some other states had identified with political parties or been used to break labor strikes. But the legislature approved the governor's proposal and the new force—called State Troopers—took to the field in 1917.

An advocacy group called the "Committee for State Police" pushed for the legislation and then served as an oversight, advocacy, and publicity entity. Its first report highlighted the Troopers' professionalism, integrity, and accomplishments during its first year. The report also included endorsements from state and local officials and the media. That report helped lead to more public support and expansion of the force.

∽

FROM *POWERS AND TERRITORY OF THE NEW YORK STATE TROOPERS* (1918) BY COMMITTEE FOR STATE POLICE

If you need POLICE PROTECTION in the rural districts, call up Central [the telephone company's switchboard] and you will be put in communication with Troop Headquarters in your district. If you know of a violation of the law near you, write stating the facts clearly and you will receive attention.

The Committee for State Police offers with unmixed pleasure its first report for the year 1918. The New York State Troopers, only five months in uniform, have made a record with which the State may well be pleased. They have won the commendation of every departmental head in whose work they have been called upon to cooperate. They have won the liking and good will of law-abiding people wherever they have gone. In four months they have patrolled 99,567 miles of country roads; and they have made 522 arrests, resulting in 423 convictions, with 70 cases pending.

Far more and better than this, their influence as a deterrent of crime and a preventive of evil and disorder is already widely felt. To their service through the counties, the county press bears testimony. And a happy augury conspicuous through it all is the high quality in service that the counties both expect and applaud.

The people of this State did not create their State Police blindly. Our Legislature, enacting the law, obeyed a strong and intelligent popular demand based on wide popular knowledge of what such a force both can and should be. If, in the actual making and running of the organization, any but the highest standard had been sought, or if any slightest taint had appeared of willingness to lend the force to baser use, then, in the voice of the people, jealously watching, would have been heard, sharp and quick, the voice of the men behind the guns.

On November 1, 1917, Major George F. Chandler, Superintendent of New York State Troopers, issued the following "bulletin" for the guidance of his men:

> A physician aims to save life and cure disease; a lawyer helps people out of trouble; a clergyman tries to make people better; a soldier fights for his country in time of war. These are fine professions, all of them. They are professions of service.
>
> The service a State Trooper renders to his community is an auxiliary to all these, and his duty in a measure embraces the work of these four great professions.
>
> You who wear the uniform of the State Troopers must be ready to render first aid pending the arrival of the doctor; you must maintain the law which the lawyer expounds; you

must instruct people to do right, and, if the need arrives, you must fight.

You must have the confidence in yourself which comes from knowing you are a trained horseman, a good shot, and a judge of what is right and wrong in the matter of simple laws.

Go about with the idea of helpfulness and a friendliness that wins the confidence of the people. Never permit a child to be afraid of you.

Never hesitate to render assistance of any kind, and let nothing be too much trouble which you can do for the people you come in contact with.

Always be a gentleman, courteous, kind, gentle, fair, keep yourself clean and neat, you and your horse equally well groomed, stand erect, put snap and vigor into your movements. Avoid the appearance of lounging. Keep your mind calm and free from excitement. Do not be carried away by rumors but investigate every story and hear both sides before you believe it.

Remember that you represent the authority of the Governor, that you are an executive officer and a State official. Be proud of it, live up to it, work in harmony with your officers and the other troopers for the good of the service and for the honor of the great State of New York.

"This Commonwealth is greatly interested in its new State Constabulary," said the *New York Evening World*, dwelling once again on Major Chandler's oft-reiterated pledge to keep the force free from politics and from any veering from the highest and sternest ideals. "That is as solid a platform as any Superintendent of Police need ever build for himself. Major Chandler can be sure New York will back him as long as he stands on it."

After eight months of close and careful observation this Committee is prepared to say that the Force is making good that it has been wisely, effectively and honestly guided, that the men are full of that enthusiasm for the service that can only come from inspiring leadership and from the belief that their leader is himself inflexible in holding to his principle and his word—that he will back, without fear or favor, or shadow of turning the man who makes that principle his guide and that word his dependence.

Major Chandler is now asking for an increase of one troop, or fifty-eight men, to secure the completely effective functioning of his organization and to round out his scheme of service by extending over the entire rural State, simultaneously, the protection now so frankly appreciated by the greater part.

On this point the Committee has to say that experience shows no wisdom in saving fire insurance money till the house burns down, or in waiting till the horse is stolen before buying a lock for the barn door. In prevention of crime and its consequences, in the saving of life and property, and in rapid and practical extension of the effectiveness of other State departments, a good State Police saves its own yearly cost many times over.

Notes

1. The "Lodge" doctor is the physician provided by a mutual benefit society or "Lodge" to attend to its members.
2. The 1896 "Raines Law," named after its sponsor, State Senator John Raines, increased the cost of liquor licenses, raised the drinking age from sixteen to eighteen, and prohibited the sale of alcoholic beverages on Sundays except in hotels. Many saloons skirted the law by adding a few sparsely furnished rooms and serving small portions of food with their drinks, thereby qualifying as a "hotel" eligible to apply for a liquor license under the law which would enable them to serve patrons on Sundays.

Sources

Anderson, William H., "New York," *Proceedings of the Nineteenth National Convention of the Anti-Saloon League of America, June 3–6, 1919* (Westerville, OH.: Anti-Saloon League, 1919), 296–97. Available at HathiTrust, https://babel.hathitrust.org/cgi/pt?id=umn.31951002194797j&view=page&seq=5

Broun, Heywood, and Margaret Leech, *Anthony Comstock: Roundsman of the Lord* (New York: A & C Boni, 1927), 215–19. Available at HathiTrust, https://catalog.hathitrust.org/Record/001120379.

Charity Organization Society of New York and New York City Tenement House Department, *For You. It is Hard to Get Money. It is Harder to Spend it Right. Health is Wealth* (New York: Charity Organization Society, n.d., ca. 1910), 1–8, 17–19, 22–26. Available at Internet Archive, https://archive.org/details/ldpd_9361284_000/page/n1/mode/2up?view=theater.

Charity Organization Society of the City of New York, *Twenty-Sixth Annual Report for the Year Ending September 30, 1908* (New York: The Society, 1908),

"Review of the Year," 9–12, 15, 22. Available at HathiTrust, https://babel.hathitrust.org/cgi/pt?id=ucl.$b600324&view=page&seq=9.

Committee for State Police," *Powers and Territory of the New York State Troopers* (New Bedford, N.Y. Committee for State Police, 1918). Available at HathiTrust, https://babel.hathitrust.org/cgi/pt?id=nyp.33433075964019&view=page&seq=12

DeForest, Robert W., "Tenement House Reform in New York Since 1901," in Robert W. DeForest and Lawrence Veiller, eds., *The Tenement House Problem* (New York: Macmillan, 1908), xii–xvi. Available at Hathi-Trust, https://babel.hathitrust.org/cgi/pt?id=ien.35556036620797&view=page&seq=9.

Draper, Andrew S., *American Education* (New York: Houghton, Mifflin Company, 1909), "The Functions of the State," 39–42. Available at HathiTrust, https://babel.hathitrust.org/cgi/pt?id=loc.ark:/13960/t76t1gd88&view=page&seq=9.

New York State Department of Health, *Thirty-Sixth Annual Report of the State Department of Health for the Year Ending December 31, 1915*, vol. 1 (Albany: J. B. Lyon, 1916), "Report of the Commissioner of Health," 1–6. Available at HathiTrust, https://babel.hathitrust.org/cgi/pt?id=mdp.39015068194466&view=page&seq=9.

Riis, Jacob A., *How the Other Half Lives: Studies Among the Tenements of New York With Illustrations Chiefly From Photographs Taken By the Author* (New York: Charles Scribner' Sons, 1890), Introduction, 1–4. Available at HathiTrust, https://babel.hathitrust.org/cgi/pt?id=mdp.39015005156107&view=1up&seq=7.

Wald, Lillian D., *The House on Henry Street* (New York: Henry Holt and Company, 1915), ch. II, "Establishing the Nursing Service," 26–32. Available at HathiTrust, https://babel.hathitrust.org/cgi/pt?id=ucl.31158002063344&view=page&seq=11.

5

Strengthening Women's Status

Figure 5. Margaret Sanger's crusade a century ago for women's right to choose ignited a campaign that continues today. *Source*: Library of Congress Prints & Photographs Collection.

Women gained the right to vote in New York in 1917, one of the greatest achievements of the progressive era. But suffrage was only one of several ways in which women's status changed and advanced in New York during that time period. Women were moving forces behind the settlement house movement, child labor reform, legal limits on working hours in factories, workers' compensation, and the labor union movement. They led the Charity Organization Society, the Consumers' League, the Citizens Union, and other groups that helped the disadvantaged and lobbied for government programs. They became increasingly influential in advancing broad social and labor reforms, though their power was often exercised behind-the-scenes—for example, through preparing studies and reports showing needs and advancing solutions and through organizing advocacy efforts.

The right to vote would give women more visibility and influence in public life and enable them to advance initiatives to move them closer to the goal of equality with men. But their role in public life was still limited. For instance, women seldom ran for elected office, and during the period covered in this book, there were no women state legislators.

Women faced a range of challenges every day. They had to balance jobs, careers, and their personal lives. If they married and had children, as most did, they assumed responsibilities for home and family. When they advanced into the professions, they found most fields closed to them or restricted. Others such as teaching and nursing were more open. Professions such as journalism attracted many women, but they found achieving equality with men and advancement major challenges.

Women Struggle for Equality in the Workplace

Women gradually made headway in New York workplaces in the progressive era. Some secured professional positions—for example, as teachers. A few women advanced into the field of journalism, but they were usually given lower-visibility assignments and sometimes not allowed to sign their columns. Other times, they were required to use their first initial rather than their full first name or to write under pseudonyms to conceal their gender. They were usually paid less than men and often encountered what would later be called the "glass ceiling," with their advancement beyond entry and second-level positions blocked.

Rheta Childe Dorr (1866–1948) was a good example. Educated in Nebraska, she moved to New York in 1890 and did intermittent newspaper writing jobs until she joined the staff of the New York Evening Post *in 1900. Her journalistic talent was evident, her writing sprightly and engaging. By then she was divorced and supported a young son as a single mother. She merited and needed a job with adequate pay.*

The Evening Post *had the reputation of being an enlightened journal under a progressive-minded publisher, Oswald Garrison Villard. Dorr expected a salary and advancement commensurate with her abilities. As the excerpt below from her autobiography indicates, though, it was not to be. She asked for a raise; the editor refused and instead offered her more work at the same rate she was making. It was clear she could not expect to advance and that there was no real future for her at the* Evening Post. *A few years later, she resigned.*

But Dorr went on to a distinguished career as a journalist and activist. She wrote for several journals. She became a champion for women's suffrage and labor reform. She served as a European correspondent during World War I, with her writing syndicated to several newspapers. Her 1917 book, Inside the Russian Revolution, *provided an inside account of that epochal event.*

∼

From *A Woman of Fifty* (1924) by Rheta Childe Dorr

Chapter VI. Are Women Wage Earners Accidents?

At last, I was a real newspaper-woman, not an unwelcome hanger-on in editorial anterooms, but a reporter with a desk and a salary. It was a very small salary but money went farther in those days than it does now, and on twenty-five dollars a week, paid regularly, I could make a budget, and, living very frugally, provide for myself, buy clothes for the little boy [her son] and even, once a month or so, spend a weekend with him. Mr. [Hammond] Lamont [editor] gave me enough to do and he never let me forget that I had to do it well enough to attract department store advertising. Women's clubs were just coming into prominence and I had to follow club activities, local and national, and write two columns and a half about them for the Saturday Supplement. I wrote also about two columns a week of fashions and a column and a half of housekeeping stuff. These had to be altogether different from the ordinary because I was writing for the class that buys at expensive shops, patronizes the smartest milliners and keeps house with many servants.

Besides these departments I wrote editorial paragraphs and special articles of interest to women. These related to women's philanthropies, college women's activities and particularly to any profession or business in which women were beginning to shine. They really were beginning but in such small numbers that a single success was worth a special article.

Even the newspapers were admitting that women were getting to have a certain news value and one after another they began to take on women reporters. I found that I had quite a group of colleagues.

Even the *Sun*, the classic "Evening" as well as the "Morning," had a woman reporter, but she never was allowed to enter the city-room. She got her assignments and wrote her copy in the office-boy's dark cubbyhole. Most of these women reporters were inclined to envy me because I signed my stuff. Every Wednesday I wrote a signed article which went in under the heading of "Women and Work." I enjoyed this because it brought me in contact with people worth knowing. . . .

To the erudite and conservative members of the *Evening Post* staff my stuff probably seemed of little importance, but the business office let me know that I was getting results. Once in a while my status as a "new woman" was languidly acknowledged by the editors. Mr. Rankin Towse, dramatic critic, sometimes gave me tickets for an Ibsen or a Hauptmann play with a plea to "see it and tell me what the stuff is about." Mr. Paul Elmer More, literary editor, whose long, thin nose seemed perpetually sniffing at modernists in fiction, sometimes gave me a book or a magazine story, as for example [English writer Rudyard] Kipling's [short story] "They" with the lofty confession: "I don't know what this sort of thing means. Do you?"

Still I was always conscious that I was not the equal of any of these men. I was not the equal of an ordinary reporter, and the proof was that my salary was lower than that of any man on the paper. I had gladly accepted twenty-five dollars a week, because I knew that a woman on the staff was an experiment. I assumed that when the experiment justified itself the salary would be raised, but it never was. After about a year and a half I found myself in a position where I had to have more money to meet weekly bills. The little boy was growing and it was taking more and more money to supply his needs. Within a year or two he would be going to school. I had to earn more, so I went to the managing editor and asked for a raise. Mr. Lamont shook his head. "We could easily fill your place," he said. "Scores of college women are trying to get into journalism and, as you know, the positions are very few."

"But," I argued, "even if you did fill my place you would never find a capable woman content to remain on half the salary you are paying men."

Mr. Lamont thought otherwise. "Women are not paid the same salaries as men," he said, "nor can they ever expect to be. This may seem hard but after all there is a rough justice in it. Men are permanent industrial factors, women mere accidents. Men work all their lives, women only until it becomes unnecessary for them to do so. These young men of ours to whom we pay higher salaries will all marry some day and have children. They must save money against that time."

"But Mr. Lamont," I cried, "that's no argument in my case. They may marry and have children. I have been married and I have a child. I support him, and I must save money for his education. I'm no accident, and if I am there are many more like me. I know personally five women who are exactly in my position, widows or abandoned wives with babies to support. There must be thousands like them. What is to become of them and their children if their work is not paid for at its proper value?"

"Frankly I don't know," said Mr. Lamont. "I only know that the situation is all wrong. The present state of things is abnormal, temporary. It must change."

"It isn't going to change," I persisted. "You will have to change. And meanwhile isn't it rather inconsistent for a paper with such high ethical ideals to monopolize all my time, make money out of my ability, and yet pay me less than a living wage?"

Mr. Lamont said there was no use in discussing the matter. Wages were dependent on the law of supply and demand, and he knew he could never persuade the trustees to pay me more than they had to. "But I'll tell you what I'll do," he added. "I'll see that more editorial writing and a certain amount of book-reviewing is thrown your way and that will mean increased income."

I was silenced; for the moment almost convinced. I knew that there were plenty of women to take my place, women of fewer responsibilities perhaps with small incomes of their own. I knew also that the chances were greatly against my getting another job. So I took on the extra work. My evenings, Saturday afternoons, and Sundays thenceforth were devoted to reading and reviewing books, writing more special articles for the Saturday Supplement, and paragraphs to lighten the editorial page. I was able some weeks to earn as much as ten dollars extra, but this meant that I had no holidays, no recreations.

I used to watch the men on Saturday mornings when the pay envelopes were handed around, counting out substantial sums to send to the bank, and afterwards going off to an afternoon of tennis or golf, and I repeated to myself like a lesson: "This is a man's world. You are an accident in it." But always something deep within me said, "No! No!"

Women Already Influence Public Policy; They Should be Able to Vote

Many leaders of the suffrage movement urged that women should be able to vote as a matter of right, the same as men. That view ultimately prevailed in New York, which gave women voting rights in 1917, and nationally in 1920.

New York historian and women's suffrage activist Mary Ritter Beard (1846–1948) took a different approach. In this essay, published in 1914, when she was Secretary of the Legislative Committee of the Women's Trade Union League of New York, she made the case that women's groups were already influential as effective advocates for measures to reform government and improve people's lives. Their behind-the-scenes lobbying was often decisive in getting men legislators to support key bills. Women's concerns, their deep understanding of key issues, and their good judgment added to the case that they should also be able to vote.

Beard became a pioneer in women's history, later writing On Understanding Women *(1931),* America through Women's Eyes *(editor, 1933), and* Woman as Force in History: A Study in Traditions and Realities *(1946). She also published a number of history books with her husband, Charles A. Beard.*

∽

From "The Legislative Influence of Unenfranchised Women" (1914) by Mary Ritter Beard

The forces which actually mold and determine legislative policies in modern society are among the deepest mysteries of political science. Generally speaking, men have had the suffrage for nearly a century in the United States, and yet we still talk, and with reason, of "invisible government," "government by public opinion," "government by common counsel," wondering how much numerical majorities at the polls really count for after all. That the "invisible government" is forceful enough and keen enough to defeat again and again solemn judgments made at the polls is patent to all. Our talk about "bossism" and "big business in politics" is not mere gossip. Investigation after investigation has revealed the reality of the economic influences in modern legislation. Even the late [New York] Senator [Thomas C.] Platt, always reticent in the presence of inquisitors, admitted that the large sums which he received from the life insurance companies "might" have had some influence on legislation at Albany.

Anti-lobby legislation is another piece of testimony to the effect that the "popular will 'registered at the polls' " is not always the "will" registered at the state capitol. The growth of direct government is an evidence of the voters' suspicion that other influences than those of the ballot box operate on their "representatives."

If it is true that powerful economic interests organized and always alert, have often written their will into law, through popular representatives and in spite of popular will, what can we say of the weight of beneficent influences, and particularly the influence of voteless women?

If we cannot estimate accurately the weight of popular will expressed at the polls on legislation, or the weight of determined economic interests, how can we hope, with any degree of success, to gauge the intermittent efforts of women to advance or retard the progress of legislation in many fields? In the absence of data of a scientific character, we can only fall back upon certain more or less popular conclusions about women's influence, some of which have arisen from vague opinion or uncertain feelings, only slightly tinged with information.

These conclusions rest in fact upon such readily available data as the following: the testimony of politicians and legislators as to the extent of women's influence which they have been compelled to recognize; individual examples of moral persuasion or statesmanlike wire-pulling on the part of women; organized efforts of women for the accomplishment of definite programs; lobbies in legislative chambers maintained by women; and cooperation with men in organized legislative effort.

Only the most striking instances can be given of the testimony of legislators as to the influence exercised upon them by women. The first example, and probably the most forceful one, that comes to mind is in connection with the extension of the privilege of voting to women. "When women want it they will get it" is admitted even by the most hardened anti-woman suffrage men on platform committees, men at the primaries, men at the polls, men in their legislative halls and in judiciary committees would gladly escape the importunities of the persistent hordes of women who descend upon them to question them as they go into meeting places or polling booths about their intentions and question them again as they come forth about their acts with regard to the enfranchisement of women. Where women in large organized groups protest vigorously against the extension of the suffrage, their influence is undoubtedly felt in the legislatures and at the polls, and the cry of defense by the legislator and the voter becomes: "Women do not want to vote."

In either case, the proposition in the popular mind is left to the decision of women. Suffrage, when submitted at the polls, is generally won by women through their activity in persuading voters to ballot in its favor. Without their constant hammering at every man whom they can reach, women know, and men know and admit, that the franchise would never be extended to women. . . .

Of course women are not the only senders of appeals to congressmen. They are wise enough to know that, in most cases, congressmen are more affected by men whose votes elect or defeat them. Women therefore prod busy men into letter writing—and the transmission of telegrams. They seek out influential men and see that their messages are sent. The congressman, therefore, who is anxious to represent the people, lays before his colleagues this combined evidence of what his "people" want. The existence of a certain degree of "government by petition" is disclosed by statements made to women lobbyists by legislators that they see "little popular interest" in a proposed kind of legislation because more appeals have come to them for "bird protection" or for the appointment of a commission to study the subject further than for immediate legislation upon it. This is submitted in evidence that what the people including women, want, they get unless the interests arrayed against it are too powerful. . . .

[An] example of personal influence on legislation exerted by women is that of Frances Perkins of New York in her fight for the Fifty-Four Hour bill [limiting women's factory work to 54 hours per week] for the women workers of her state. Miss Perkins represented a society—the Consumers League—which asked for this measure, and she was supported in her demand by the Women's Trade Union League and other organizations. The measure would have been defeated, however, as is widely known and acknowledged in New York, had it not been for the personal sagacity and watchfulness of Miss Perkins who captured a senator of dominating power [Democratic Senator Timothy Sullivan] and prevented his escape in a taxi to the station in time to restore him to his seat in the chamber his vote on the floor bringing with him the votes he controlled.

More than one refugee has been escorted back to his duties by women sentinels when legislation on which they were determined has been up for a vote. In such cases the woman's influence lies not in physical force, for she has never been seen to lay hands upon the recalcitrant legislator, but in the occasional subservience of the mind of man to the actual presence of amoral force. . . .

In addition to these general clubs and societies, there are special women's organizations, such as the Women's Christian Temperance Union, the Council of Jewish Women, and the Women's Trade Union League. The first of these associations has stood for better protective laws for women and children as well as for measures directed against the liquor traffic. In their warfare upon liquor, women have discovered the relation of wages, overcrowding, long hours and other economic factors to the consumption of alcoholic stimulants; and are considering preventive as well as prohibitory legislation. The second of these associations, while concerned primarily with the safeguarding of Jewish immigrant women and girls, has been drawn more and more into the development of social and correctional legislation. The Women's Trade Union League, in addition to organizing wage working women, devotes special efforts to obtaining protective labor legislation, including an eight-hour day for women and woman suffrage.

It is safe to say, therefore, that in the progress of modern social legislation of all kinds—the extension of educational functions, pure food laws, mothers' pensions, development of recreational facilities, labor laws, particularly for women and children, and measures directed against prostitution—not a single important statute has been enacted without the active support of women, organized and unorganized.

This much we may say without attempting to apportion to women the exact weight of their influence. Important as has been that influence, there can be no doubt that in cases of serious labor legislation affecting large employing interests women's weight has been almost negligible in many instances. Indeed, one of the New York legislators, in a very friendly and confidential talk with the representatives of the Women's Trade Union League, told them that the 35,000 voteless women whom they represented naturally could not carry the same weight as thirty five voting men. It was just such frank statements as this that turned Florence Kelley and many leading social workers, who sought legislation in their various fields, into ardent suffragists.

Making the Case for Women's Suffrage

Women's rights organization, particularly the New York Woman Suffrage Party, the lead advocacy organization in New York, pushed for the right to vote in the new century. They held public rallies and parades, appealed to the press, and lobbied individual legislators. The legislature put the suffrage question on the ballot in 1915. New York's (all male) voters rejected it that time but approved it when the legislature endorsed it and put it on the ballot again in 1917. This time, it passed.

Much of the strength of the 1915 and 1917 suffrage campaigns came from the advocacy information women's organizations disseminated. They emphasized that voting should be a woman's right, echoing sentiments dating back to the Seneca Falls women's rights convention of 1848. But the emphasis shifted and expanded somewhat in the 1915 and 1917 campaigns, citing men's inability to represent women at the polls, the improvements in civic life likely to flow from women's influence in the elections, and women's service during World War I.

Four 1917 campaign booklets by the New York Woman Suffrage Party illustrate the broad appeal.

~

From "What Woman Suffrage Stands For" (1917) booklet by New York State Woman Suffrage Party

The protection of the home—Women want to vote because it will double the home vote.

The protection of all children—Women want every child to have a chance to grow up sound in body and mind.

Economy in government—Women want lower taxes and economical use of public finds.

A square deal for every man and woman—Women want equal rights for all and special privileges for none.

The only plank in the suffrage platform is Votes for Women, which means the right of every woman to have her opinion and to have it counted on election day.

Work for Woman Suffrage. Vote "Yes" on Woman Suffrage November 6th.

~

From "Twelve Reasons Why Women Should Vote" (1917) booklet by New York State Woman Suffrage Party

BECAUSE

1. It is the foundation of all political liberty that those who obey the law should have a voice in choosing those who make the law.

2. Most laws affect women as much as men, and some laws affect women more than they do men.

3. The laws which affect women are now passed without consulting them.

4. Laws affecting children should be regarded from a woman's point of view as well as the man's.

5. Questions affecting the home come up for consideration in every session of the Legislature and Congress.

6. Women which should be helpfully brought to bear on legislation.

7. To deprive women of the vote is to lower their position in common estimation.

8. The possession of the vote would increase the sense of responsibility among women toward questions of public service.

9. Public-spirited mothers mean public-spirited sons.

10. Large numbers of intelligent, thoughtful, hard-working women desire the franchise.

11. The objections raised against their having the franchise are based on sentiment, not on reason.

12. To sum up all reasons in one—IT IS FOR THE COMMON GOOD OF ALL.

∽

FROM "MODERN REPRESENTATIVE GOVERNMENT" (1917) BOOKLET BY NEW YORK STATE WOMAN SUFFRAGE PARTY

[Initial letters were boldface in original to spell out "IDIOTIC" vertically]

Question: If a man represents the women of a household, how can he represent himself?

It is a common notion that men represent women at the polls.

Did you ever know a man who asked his wife how she wished him to vote?

If a man votes as his wife wishes him to, he doesn't represent himself.

Or, if a man votes to please himself, he doesn't represent his wife.

The predicament of a man who attempts to represent a family consisting of a wife, mother and daughters who hold different opinions, is conclusive that it cannot be done.

If there are any sons, the idea of a family vote isn't applied; they vote for themselves.

Can you see any sense to the argument that men represent women at the polls? Of course not; there isn't any sense to it.

∼

From "Suffrage as a War Measure" (1917) booklet by New York State Woman Suffrage Party

Since the war began woman suffrage has been sweeping over the civilized world. Women are now voters in Canada, Russia, Norway and Denmark; all constitutional liabilities have been removed from them in Holland; and government bills to allow woman suffrage are under way in France and Italy.

The women of New York State have no less patriotism, courage or ability than the women of England, Russia or Canada.

They ask the men of New York to recognize this and vote for woman suffrage on election day.

Where do New York women come in? During the past four years the women of New York State have made a continuous campaign for Woman Suffrage. By sheer hard work a huge organization has been built up which includes every one of the one hundred fifty Assembly Districts and extends into most of the polling precincts in the State. . . .

In every other country at war the vote has either been given to women or is under consideration. Are New York women going to be classed as the only women among civilized nations unworthy of the vote?

Give votes to women as part of the nation's defense.

Men have denied votes to women because they said that women are not called to serve the State and therefore not entitled to vote.

This war has proved that women must serve the state equally with men.

The Census taken by New York State of its Military Resources included both men and women.

The government is calling on women to help in factories, in the production and conservation of food, to make munitions, and, hardest of all, to give their sons to war.

Women are responding to the call. They are eager to serve. Either in war or peace they wish to serve their country.

Men of New York, don't wait until the war is over to admit the justice and necessity of woman suffrage here. For the sake of the strength it will add to the nation, vote for woman suffrage November 6th.

Securing the Right to Vote

The campaign for women's suffrage dated back to the famous 1848 Seneca Falls, New York, convention that demanded the right to vote for women. A half century later, a new generation of women leaders, many of them living in New York, reenergized the suffrage movement in the new century. Many were active in other areas of progressive reform beyond suffrage. They were well organized and effective. Their strategies included political lobbying, petitions to the legislature with thousands of signatures, and large public rallies and parades that got lots of media attention.

Carrie Chapman Catt (1859-1947) was born in Iowa but moved to New York in 1892. She led the women's suffrage movement and was a skilled organizer and strategist. Catt served as president of the National American Woman Suffrage from 1900 to 1904 and again from 1915 to 1920. Women's suffrage slowly gained adherents, and by 1910 a number of states had adopted it. Under Catt's leadership, one of the key strategies was achieving victory in New York as a prelude to achieving it nationally. She called this a "winning strategy." Catt organized the New York City Woman Suffrage

Party in 1909 and worked to win over Tammany Hall, the powerful New York City Democratic organization. In 1915, Tammany opposed suffrage, but in 1917 Tammany leader Charles Murphy announced they would no longer oppose it. Catt's work was a major factor in Tammany's change of direction.

New York voters turned down a suffrage amendment to the state constitution in 1915. Advocates redoubled their efforts and it passed in 1917. The New York City vote, heavily influenced by Tammany Hall's changed position, overwhelmingly in favor of suffrage, was decisive. Catt was right—New York's move helped pave the way to securing the right in Washington three years later.

Catt and another leader of the movement, Nettie Rogers Schuler (1862–1939), described the New York campaign in a 1923 book.

~

From *Woman Suffrage and Politics: The Inner Story of the Suffrage Movement* (1923) by Carrie Chapman Catt and Nettie Rogers Schuler

Chapter XIX. The Decisive Battle

The [1915] City campaign was more intensive than in any other part of the State, as its political unit organization had been established longer and therefore worked more smoothly. There were barbers' days, days for firemen, street cleaners, bankers, brokers, business men, clergymen, street car men, factory workers, students, restaurant and railroad workers, ticket sellers and choppers, lawyers, ditch diggers and longshoremen. No voter escaped. Each one of these days had its own literature and attractions and called forth columns of comment in the newspapers. Evening demonstrations took place daily and brought interested and thoughtful crowds. There was a bonfire on the highest hill in each Borough, with balloons flying, music, speeches, and tableaux illustrating women's progress from the primitive campfire to the council of State. Torchlight processions were formed upon twenty-eight evenings with Chinese lanterns, balloons, banners and decorations in yellow and ending in a street rally at some important point in the City. There were street dances on the lower East Side, in honor of political leaders; there were Irish, Syrian, Italian, Polish rallies; there were outdoor concerts, a series of small ones culminating in a big one given in Madison Square Park where a full orchestra played, opera singers sang and many distinguished orators spoke on a platform erected for the purpose.

There were open air religious services on Sunday evenings, with the moral and religious aspect of suffrage discussed; there was a fête in beautiful Dyckman Glen; there were flying squadrons of speakers from the Battery to the Bronx; there was an Interstate Rally where the suffragists of Massachusetts, New Jersey and New York met publicly in picturesque formation; there was the New York to San Francisco trip of the dancer Joan Sawyer to whom a letter was given at Times Square from eastern suffragists for western suffragists. Bottles containing suffrage messages were consigned to the waves from boats and wharves with appropriate speeches. Sandwich girls advertised meetings and sold papers. Sixty playhouses had theatre nights, many with speeches between the acts. There were innumerable movie nights with speeches and suffrage slides; "flying canvass wedges," "hikes" and automobile tours. The entire State was stirred by the activities. Many things easy to do won widest publicity, as when college women in cap and gown visited naturalization courts where hordes of ignorant men, anxious to escape conscription in Europe where the great war was now raging, were being speedily manufactured into American citizens and voters. There were other things that helped the agitation which had no publicity value, such as traveling libraries and the correspondence classes of the Equal Franchise Society. There were German and French Committees, and Committees to work with the Protestant and Catholic Churches. "What rot!" said some. "What ingenuity!" said others. "Surely the women have gone stark mad," said others. . . .

The campaign of 1915 thus kept itself before the public on the plane of the public every hour of every day. Suffragists themselves were passing through an unforgettable experience. To this day they close their eyes and hear again the thrill of martial bugles, the tread of marching thousands, and see the air once more ablaze with the banners of those spectacular years. Just before election day a great procession possessed Fifth Avenue, the entire suffrage forces of the State uniting in it. Every Assembly District in the State sent its women. Twenty-five bands made music for 30,000 marching men and women. The streets and windows of the buildings on both sides were filled with lookers-on and there were more tears than jeers in that contemplation. In the Union League Club a group of the great men in City affairs somewhat cynically watched the procession. A break caused a lull in the interest, then another band marched forward and behind it came 5,000 of the public school teachers of the city. They were soberly garbed in dark gowns with white hats and gloves. Their banners were blackboards and on them their mottoes and messages were penciled in chalk. They knew American history and they were telling it to the public. . . .

No political party had endorsed the amendment, but in New York women could serve as watchers at the polls, because a special law to that effect had been passed. It was estimated that 2,500 women had held official positions in the organization of the Empire State Campaign Committee, that 200,000 women had aided the campaign, and on election day 6,330 women served as watchers or workers at the polls, some serving from 5 A.M. until midnight. The total cost of the campaign was about $95,000. Headquarters filled with anxious men and women on election night. A few of the younger workers wept as adverse returns kept coming in, but the older heads counseled, "Don't give up. Forward march," and when at midnight it was certain that the amendment was lost a group of young State and City women went forth to a public square, where suffrage rallies had been a familiar sight, called together the late street crowd, homeward bound from theatres, announced the result and declared that gathering the first meeting of the new campaign. On Friday night, three days later, an overflowing meeting was held in Cooper Union where $100,000 was pledged for the new campaign. Every campaign district in the State offered its quota and no note of surrender was heard. The New York amendment of 1915 was lost by a majority of 194,984. The yes vote was 553,348. The no vote was 748,332. . . .

In April [1917], the nation entered the great World War. The New York State Woman Suffrage Party, following the National Suffrage Association, offered its organization for war service, the State organization to the Governor of the State and the City to the Mayor. War Service Committees were promptly organized. These committees served as registrars in the Governor's Military Census, enrolled volunteered women for all sorts of war work, sold bonds in each Liberty Loan and Thrift Stamp Campaign, and raised money in all the numerous drives for funds for foreign or home relief or helps to the soldiers. "Knitting teams" supplied thousands of woolen garments for the Red Cross. There were war gardens to produce food, canning demonstrations to preserve food, and the distribution of food pledge cards designed to economize food. A recreation hut at Plattsburg for white soldiers and one at Yaphank for colored troops was maintained and money was raised for the overseas hospitals that had been organized and were being maintained by the National Suffrage Association.

But the suffragists of 1917 had read history; they knew how prone men were to accept the help of suffragists in the hour of need and forget women's case for suffrage in the hour of calm. So while working loyally and energetically as special war organizations in support of the needs of the nation in its time of crisis, the New Yorkers did not lay aside their campaign. In the 1915 campaign one of the stock insistences of the indifferent and opposed had been "New York women do not want to vote." To meet it the Empire State Campaign Committee had dared claim "A million New York women want to vote." The claim had been laughed at and poohpoohed but it had had enough vitality to pass into campaign history in the form of a slogan. But, unsupported, the claim was not conclusive. Even in 1915 the need of supplying incontrovertible evidence had been encountered on every hand, and the close of the campaign had found a plan of proof well-matured. This plan, covering no less an undertaking than the assembling of the personal signatures of the million women of the State who wanted to vote, was the heavy heritage of the workers of the 1917 campaign. With dogged endurance, they canvassed door to door in an effort to secure the signatures of women to a petition to voters to vote for suffrage on election day. They climbed stairs, descended into cellars, found their way into the homes of the rich and the incredibly poor, walked country lanes, left no section untouched. In the result they piled up the largest individually signed petition ever collected, 1,030,000 names, all of New York State women appealing to men for the vote.

Next in order was the problem of how to make the public realize the enormous force of that petition. In the City a ceremony was arranged and the Mayor and other prominent officials came to the City Headquarters to verify the numbers. Then all the petitions went to Albany to allow the Governor and State officials to verify them. "Press parties" in New York and Albany gave opportunity to newspaper correspondents and the Associated Press to verify them. At the State Headquarters the petitions were pasted upon huge pasteboards and the general public allowed to inspect them. In the great procession that closed the suffrage campaign the chief feature was the display of these petitions. Each of the placards was borne by two women, marching four abreast in a special section, with banners giving the totals in all the "up state" districts. The City section displayed its petitions in 63 ballot boxes, one for each Assembly District, resting upon a decorated platform, and each borne by four women. The "Procession of the Petitions" alone covered more than half a mile and was the most conspicuous feature of those thousands who went marching by to the music of 40 bands.

Meanwhile 10,000,000 leaflets were distributed, schools for training women watchers were conducted and 10,000 watchers and poll workers were enrolled. Hundreds of newspapers were served with daily news, including 24 foreign language papers. The voters were circularized. Friendly windows were filled with posters, silent speeches and printed appeals; and, as a climax, advertisements announcing the number of women petitioners for the vote and carrying various appeals to the voters were placed in the leading newspapers of the State. Huge billboards advertising suffrage lined the railroads, and street cars and electric signs in the cities emphasized the women's appeal.

Women Can Vote, What Comes Next?

Some reformers saw women's suffrage as the goal and once it was achieved, stopped formulating long-term objectives. But Crystal Eastman (1881–1928), attorney, labor reformer, feminist, socialist, and antimilitarist, reminded everyone that the right to vote was just one milestone on the long road to gender equality. Eastman publicized the issue of workplace accidents and helped lead the development of New York State's first workers' compensation law in 1910. She was one of the founders of the Civil Liberties Bureau, later the American Civil Liberties Union, in New York City in 1917.

In the 1920 article "Now We Can Begin," in The Liberator, *a socialist magazine she had established with her brother Max Eastman in 1918, she outlined the long road ahead. Suffrage was just the beginning, she contended. Now the struggle should move on to reproductive rights, equality of education, and wider career opportunities.*

∽

From "Now We Can Begin," The Liberator (1920)
by Crystal Eastman

Most women will agree that August 23 [1920], the day when the Tennessee legislature finally enacted the Federal suffrage amendment [the final vote needed to add it to the Constitution], is a day to begin with, not a day to end with. Men are saying perhaps "Thank God, this everlasting woman's fight is over!"

But women, if I know them, are saying, "Now at last we can begin." In fighting for the right to vote most women have tried to be either non-committal or thoroughly respectable on every other subject. Now they can say what they are really after; and what they are after, in common with all the rest of the struggling world, is freedom. Freedom is a large word. Many feminists are socialists, many are communists, not a few are active leaders in these movements. But the true feminist, no matter how far to the left she may be in the revolutionary movement, sees the woman's battle as distinct in its objects and different in its methods from the workers' battle for industrial freedom.

She knows, of course, that the vast majority of women as well as men are without property, and are of necessity bread and butter slaves under a system of society which allows the very sources of life to be privately owned by a few, and she counts herself a loyal soldier in the working-class army that is marching to overthrow that system. But as a feminist she also knows that the whole of woman's slavery is not summed up in the profit system, nor her complete emancipation assured by the downfall of capitalism. Woman's freedom, in the feminist sense, can be fought for and conceivably won before the gates open into industrial democracy.

On the other hand, woman's freedom, in the feminist sense, is not inherent in the communist ideal. All feminists are familiar with the revolutionary leader who "can't see" the woman's movement. "What's the matter with the women? My wife's all right," he says. And his wife, one usually finds, is raising his children in a Bronx flat or a dreary suburb, to which he returns occasionally for food and sleep when all possible excitement and stimulus have been wrung from the fight. If we should graduate into communism tomorrow this man's attitude to his wife would not be changed. The proletarian dictatorship may or may not free women. We must begin now to enlighten the future dictators.

What, then, is "the matter with women"? What is the problem of women's freedom? It seems to me to be this: how to arrange the world so that women can be human beings, with a chance to exercise their infinitely varied gifts in infinitely varied ways, instead of being destined by the accident of their sex to one field of activity: housework and child-raising. And second, if and when they choose housework and child-raising, to have that occupation recognized by the world as work, requiring a definite economic reward and not merely entitling the performer to be dependent on some man. This is not the whole of feminism, of course, but it is enough to begin with.

"Oh, don't begin with economics," my friends often protest, "Woman does not live by bread alone. What she needs first of all is a free soul." And I can agree that women will never be great until they achieve a certain emotional freedom, a strong healthy egotism, and some un-personal sources of joy; that in this inner sense we cannot make woman free by changing her economic status. What we can do, however, is to create conditions of outward freedom in which a free woman's soul can be born and grow. It is these outward conditions with which an organized feminist movement must concern itself.

Freedom of choice in occupation and individual economic independence for women: How shall we approach this next feminist objective? First, by breaking down all remaining barriers, actual as well as legal, which make it difficult for women to enter or succeed in the various professions, to go into and get on in business, to learn trades and practice them, to join trades unions. Chief among these remaining barriers is inequality in pay. Here the ground is already broken. This is the easiest part of our program. Second, we must institute a revolution in the early training and education of both boys and girls. It must be womanly as well as manly to earn your own living, to stand on your own feet. And it must be manly as well as womanly to know how to cook and sew and clean and take care of yourself in the ordinary exigencies of life.

I need not add that the second part of this revolution will be more passionately resisted than the first. Men will not give up their privilege of helplessness without a struggle. The average man has a carefully cultivated ignorance about household matters—from what to do with the crumbs to the grocer's telephone number—a sort of cheerful inefficiency which protects him better than the reputation for having a violent temper. It was his mother's fault in the beginning, but even as a boy he was quick to see how a general reputation for being "no good around the house" would serve him throughout life, and half-consciously he began to cultivate that helplessness until today it is the despair of feminist wives. A growing number of men admire the woman who has a job, and, especially since the cost of living doubled, rather like the idea of their own wives contributing to the family income by outside work. And of course for generations there have been whole towns full of wives who are forced by the bitterest necessity to spend the same hours at the factory that their husbands spend.

But these bread-winning wives have not yet developed homemaking husbands. When the two come home from the factory the man sits down while his wife gets supper, and he does so with exactly the same sense of fore-ordained right as if he were "supporting her." Higher up in the economic scale the same thing is true. The business or professional woman who is married, perhaps engages a cook, but the responsibility is not shifted, it is still hers. She "hires and fires," she orders meals, she does the buying, she meets and resolves all domestic crises, she takes charge of moving, furnishing, settling. She may be, like her husband, a busy executive at her office all day, but unlike him, she is also an executive in a small way every night and morning at home. Her noon hour is spent in planning, and too often her Sundays and holidays are spent in "catching up." Two business women can "make a home" together without either one being over-burdened or over-bored. It is because they both know how and both feel responsible. But it is a rare man who can marry one of them and continue the homemaking partnership. Yet if there are no children, there is nothing essentially different in the combination. Two self-supporting adults decide to make a home together: if both are women it is a pleasant partnership, more fun than work; if one is a man, it is almost never a partnership, the woman simply adds running the home to her regular outside job. Unless she is very strong, it is too much for her, she gets tired and bitter over it, and finally perhaps gives up her outside work and condemns herself to the tiresome half-job of housekeeping for two. Cooperative schemes and electrical devices will simplify the business of homemaking, but they will not get rid of it entirely. As far as we can see ahead people will always want homes, and a happy home cannot be had without a certain amount of rather monotonous work and responsibility.

How can we change the nature of man so that he will honorably share that work and responsibility and thus make the homemaking enterprise a song instead of a burden? Most assuredly not by laws or revolutionary decrees. Perhaps we must cultivate or simulate a little of that highly prized helplessness ourselves.

But fundamentally it is a problem of education, of early training—we must bring up feminist sons. Sons? Daughters? They are born of women. How can women be free to choose their occupation, at all times cherishing their economic independence, unless they stop having children? This is a further question for feminism. If the feminist program goes to pieces on the arrival of the first baby, it is false and useless. For ninety-nine out of every hundred women want children, and seventy-five out of every hundred want to take care of their own children, or at any rate so closely superintend their care as to make any other full-time occupation impossible for at least ten or fifteen years. Is there any such thing then as freedom of choice in occupation for women? And is not the family the inevitable economic unit and woman's individual economic independence, at least during that period, out of the question?

The feminist must have an answer to these questions, and she has. The immediate feminist program must include voluntary motherhood. Freedom of any kind for women is hardly worth considering unless it is assumed that they will know how to control the size of their families. "Birth control" is just as elementary an essential in our propaganda as "equal pay." Women are to have children when they want them, that's the first thing. That ensures some freedom of occupational choice; those who do not wish to be mothers will not have an undesired occupation thrust upon them by accident, and those who do wish to be mothers may choose in a general way how many years of their lives they will devote to the occupation of child raising.

But is there any way of insuring a woman's economic independence while child-raising is her chosen occupation? Or must she sink into that dependent state from which, as we all know, it is so hard to rise again? That brings us to the fourth feature of our program, motherhood endowment. It seems that the only way we can keep mothers free, at least in a capitalist society, is by the establishment of a principle that the occupation of raising children is peculiarly and directly a service to society, and that the mother upon whom the necessity and privilege of performing this service naturally falls is entitled to an adequate economic reward from the political government. It is idle to talk of real economic independence for women unless this principle is accepted. But with a generous endowment of motherhood provided by legislation, with all laws against voluntary motherhood and education in its methods repealed, with the feminist ideal of education accepted in home and school, and with all special barriers removed in every field of human activity, there is no reason why woman should not become almost a human thing. It will be time enough then to consider whether she has a soul.

Public Support Encourages Women's Labor Activism

Women staged strikes several times during the progressive era. Often, the workers were mostly young women, many of them Jewish or Italian immi-

grants, working for low wages in garment manufacturing factories. The women workers were determined to improve things.

Most of the factories were in New York City but Rochester was also a notable textile making center.

Rochester labor activists and social reformers Edwin and Catherine Rumball, editors of a local reform journal, The Common Good, *published reports on women's low wages and poor working conditions. They also showed that the women were dependent on the meager income from their jobs and merited something better. The* Common Good *encouraged public pressure on the employers to improve things and advocated collective bargaining.*

The women's confidence and determination were enhanced by local public support. In January 1913, thousands of garment workers, mostly women, struck for lowered hours, salary increases, and other benefits. Factories closed, garment production dwindled, and public sentiment solidified behind a settlement. The United Garment Workers of America, a labor union of mostly men up to that time, assisted the women strikers. The strikers and owners agreed to mediation by the New York State Board of Mediation and Arbitration. In the spring, an agreement was reached granting many of the strikers' demands.

∽

From "The Working Girls and Women of Rochester" by Edwin and Catherine Rumball, The Common Good: An Independent Magazine of Civic and Social Rochester (1913) by Edwin and Catherine Rumball

One of the best things being done today is that so many are willing to admit the social responsibility. The more publicity that we have on the life of the working women of our land, the harder it will be for exploitation to take place. But in order to have this we must have our working women standing before their employers on a different status to what they do in Rochester today. We not only refer to the equality which will come to them with the granting of the suffrage but to the equality which will be theirs when they are organized. No amount of welfare work, which many of our Rochester factories have taken up, can atone for the refusal to recognize collective bargaining and organized workers. Welfare work usually is paternalism in its origin yet the moment that the principle of paternalism is applied to the owners and the State is urged to have a paternalistic power over the wages they shall give and the working conditions they shall provide, their enthusiasm for paternalism often disappears. Paternalism seems to be wanted only if the employers can be the fathers. We know that after they are started, many of these welfare experiments have the cooperation of the workers and we have much sympathy and encouragement for it, but there is one feature of it that arouses indignation. Wherever employers are dealing in these "philanthropies" for the sole purpose of staving off organization and destroying labor unions, they are worthy of the indignation of the community. . . .

Our girls must soon refuse to be the helpers-out with their wages and insist on the same wage as men for the same work, and then unite with the men for the maximum wage for all. The women who trim hats and work in the factories of Massachusetts, New York, Connecticut and Pennsylvania have already come to their responsibility as workers. . . .

What we want in Rochester is an increase of the public opinion which shall say "Progress is measured by the constantly increasing organization both of capital and labor and the increased effectiveness of each. The organization of capital may be interpreted as the increased ability through corporations to direct capital in the most intelligent and efficient manner, and the organization of labor as the increased ability of labor to arrive at an intelligent basis for collective bargaining." Our employers need an organization among their employees, because they know their own needs best. We want a public opinion which shall make a man an outcast from respectable society who lives well himself and yet who does not know the needs of our womanhood enough to pay a living wage. . . .

We want to close on a different strain. For after all, the greatest need is not more information, investigations everywhere show the same facts, what happens if poor wages are paid. We know what happens if the working girls are made to speed beyond their strength. The facts regarding the struggle of womanhood in the past and in the present we know. What we want now and want badly, is the will to do and hearts unafraid to do it. The woman's cause is not only man's it is the cause of all of us together and in this city at least it awaits the energy of those who have the knowledge and leisure and money and life to respond.

Advocating for "Voluntary Motherhood"

In early twentieth century America, advocating for birth control and publicizing contraceptives were illegal. New York nurse, social activist, and women's rights advocate Margaret Sanger (1879–1966) set out to change that. Through her writings, lectures, and other work, she pushed for sex education and a woman's right to choose when to have children, and she helped coin the phrase birth control. On the pages of a journal she founded, Woman Rebel, *she defended contraception and challenged the government's censorship of information on contraceptions and sexuality. With other activists, she opened the nation's first birth control clinic, in Brooklyn, in 1916. She founded the American Birth Control League, which later evolved into the Planned Parenthood Federation of America. She supported child planning and opposed abortion, which some critics said limited her credibility and influence.*

Sanger argued that "voluntary motherhood" was a woman's right. But she also argued that children should be conceived in love and born under conditions that assured their health and welfare. Liberating women from the risk of unwanted pregnancy would improve their lives, strengthen marriage, and lead to children who would grow up to be healthy, happy, responsible adults who, in turn, would foster the betterment of society.

She expounded on her views of the broad and long-term benefits of voluntary motherhood in her 1921 book Woman and the New Race. *The final chapter, titled "The Goal," excerpted below, summarized her case.*

Sanger was a pioneer and much of her agenda was fulfilled in later years, but a good deal of it still has not been accomplished.

∽

FROM *WOMAN AND THE NEW RACE* (1921) BY MARGARET SANGER

The Goal

What is the goal of woman's upward struggle? Is it voluntary motherhood? Is it general freedom? Or is it the birth of a new race? For freedom is not fruitless, but prolific of higher things. Being the most sacred aspect of woman's freedom, voluntary motherhood is motherhood in its highest and holiest form. It is motherhood unchained—motherhood ready to obey its own urge to remake the world.

Voluntary motherhood implies a new morality—a vigorous, constructive, liberated morality. That morality will, first of all, prevent the submergence of womanhood into motherhood. It will set its face against the conversion of women into mechanical maternity and toward the creation of a new race.

Woman's role has been that of an incubator and little more. She has given birth to an incubated race. She has given to her children what little she was permitted to give, but of herself, of her personality, almost nothing. In the mass, she has brought forth quantity, not quality. The requirement of a male dominated civilization has been numbers. She has met that requirement.

It is the essential function of voluntary motherhood to choose its own mate, to determine the time of childbearing and to regulate strictly the number of offspring. Natural affection upon her part, instead of selection dictated by social or economic advantage, will give her a better fatherhood for her children. The exercise of her right to decide how many children she will have and when she shall have them will procure for her the time necessary to the development of other faculties than that of reproduction. She will give play to her tastes, her talents and her ambitions. She will become a full-rounded human being.

Thus and only thus will woman be able to transmit to her offspring those qualities which make for a greater human race.

The importance of developing these qualities in the mothers for transmission to the children is apparent when we recall certain well established principles of biology. In all of the animal species below the human, motherhood has a clearly discernible superiority over fatherhood. It is the first pulse of organic life. Fatherhood is the fertilizing element. Its development, compared to that of the mother cell, is comparatively new. Likewise, its influence upon the progeny is comparatively small. There are weighty authorities who assert that through the female alone comes those modifications of form, capacity and ability which constitute evolutionary progress. It was the mothers who first developed cunning in chase, ingenuity in escaping enemies, skill in obtaining food and adaptability. It was they also who attained unfailing discretion in leadership, adaptation to environment and boldness in attack. When the animal kingdom as a whole is surveyed, these stand out as distinctly feminine traits. They stand out also as the characteristics by which the progress of species is measured.

Why is all this true of the lower species yet not true of human beings? The secret is revealed by one significant fact—the female's functions in these animal species are not limited to motherhood alone. Every organ and faculty is fully employed and perfected. Through the development of the individual mother, better and higher types of animals are produced and carried forward. In a word, natural law makes the female the expression and the conveyor of racial efficiency.

Birth control itself, often denounced as a violation of natural law, is nothing more or less than the facilitation of the process of weeding out the unfit, of preventing the birth of defectives or of those who will become defectives. So, in compliance with nature's working plan, we must permit womanhood its full development before we can expect of it efficient motherhood. If we are to make racial progress, this development of womanhood must precede motherhood in every individual woman. Then and then only can the mother cease to be an incubator and be a mother indeed. Then only can she transmit to her sons and daughters the qualities which make strong individuals and, collectively, a strong race.

Voluntary motherhood also implies the right of marriage without maternity. Two utterly more different functions are developed in the two relationships. In order to give the mate relationship its full and free play, it is necessary, that no woman should be a mother against her will. There are other reasons, of course reasons more frequently emphasized—but the reason just mentioned should never be overlooked. It is as important to the race as to the woman, for through it is developed that high love impulse which, conveyed to the child, attunes and perfects its being.

Marriage, quite aside from parentage, also gives two people invaluable experience. When parentage follows in its proper time, it is a better parentage because of the mutual adjustment and development—because of the knowledge thus gained. Few couples are fitted to understand the sacred mystery of child life until they have solved some of the problem arising out of their own love lives.

Maternal love, which usually follows upon a happy, satisfying mate love, becomes a strong and urgent craving. It then exists for two powerful, creative functions. First, for its own sake, and then for the sake of further enriching the conjugal relationship. It is from such soil that the new life should spring. It is the inherent right of the new life to have its inception in such physical ground, in such spiritual atmosphere. The child thus born is indeed a flower of love and tremendous joy. It has within it the seeds of courage and of power. This child will have the greatest strength to surmount hardships, to withstand tyrannies, to set still higher the mark of human achievement.

Shall we pause here to speak again of the rights of womanhood, in itself and of itself, to be absolutely free? We have talked of this right so much in these pages, only to learn that in the end, a free womanhood turns of its own desire to a free and happy motherhood, a motherhood which does not submerge the woman, but which is enriched because she is unsubmerged. When we voice, then, the necessity of setting the feminine spirit utterly and absolutely free, thought turns naturally not to rights of the woman, nor indeed of the mother, but to the rights of the child—of all children in the world. For this is the miracle of free womanhood, that in its freedom it becomes the race mother and opens its heart in fruitful affection for humanity.

How narrow, how pitifully puny has become motherhood in its chains! The modern motherhood enfolds one or two adoring children of its own blood, and cherishes, protects and loves them. It does not reach out to all children.

When motherhood is a high privilege, not a sordid, slavish requirement, it will encircle all. Its deep, passionate intensity will overflow the limits of blood relationship. Its beauty will shine upon all, for its beauty is of the soul, whose power of enfoldment is unbounded.

When motherhood becomes the fruit of a deep yearning, not the result of ignorance or accident, its children will become the foundation of a new race. There will be no killing of babies in the womb by abortion, nor through neglect in foundling homes, nor will there be infanticide. Neither will children die by inches in mills and factories. No man will dare to break a child's life upon the wheel of toil.

Voluntary motherhood will not be passive, resigned, or weak. Out of its craving will come forth a fierceness of love for its fruits that will make such men as remain unawakened stand aghast at its fury when offended. The tigress is less terrible in defense of her offspring than will be the human mother. The daughters of such women will not be given over to injustice and to prostitution; the sons will not perish in industry nor upon the battlefield. Nor could they meet these all too common fates if an undaunted motherhood were there to defend. Childhood and youth will be too valuable in the eyes of society to waste them in the murderous mills of blind greed and hate.

This is the dawn. Womanhood shakes off its bondage. It asserts its right to be free. In its freedom, its thoughts turn to the race. Like begets like. We gather perfect fruit from perfect trees. The race is but the amplification of its mother body, the multiplication of flesh habitations—beautified and perfected for souls akin to the mother soul.

The relentless efforts of reactionary authority to suppress the message of birth control and of voluntary motherhood are futile. The powers of reaction cannot now prevent the feminine spirit from breaking its bonds. When the last fetter falls, the evils that have resulted from the suppression of woman's will to freedom will pass. Child slavery, prostitution, feeblemindedness, physical deterioration, hunger, oppression and war will disappear from the earth.

In their subjection women have not been brave enough, strong enough, pure enough to bring forth great sons and daughters. Abused soil brings forth stunted growths. An abused motherhood has brought forth a low order of humanity. Great beings come forth at the call of high desire. Fearless motherhood goes out in love and passion for justice to all mankind. It brings forth fruits after its own kind. When the womb becomes fruitful through the desire of an aspiring love, another Newton will come forth to unlock further the secrets of the earth and the stars. There will come a Plato who will be understood, a Socrates who will drink no hemlock, and a Jesus who will not die upon the cross. These and the race that is to be in America await upon a motherhood that is to be sacred because it is free.

Sources

Beard, Mary R., "The Legislative Influence of Unenfranchised Women," in *Women in Public Life: The Annals,* 61 (Philadelphia: American Academy of Political and Social Science, 1914), 54–60. Available at HathiTrust, https://babel.hathitrust.org/cgi/pt?id=hvd.li4mkr&view=page&seq=9&skin=2021.

Dorr, Rheta Childe, *A Woman of Fifty* (New York: Funk & Wagnalls Company, 1924), 95–100. Available at HathiTrust, https://catalog.hathitrust.org/Record/000243477.

Eastman, Crystal, "Now We Can Begin," *The Liberator: A Journal of Revolutionary Progress* 33 (December 1920), 23–24, Carrie Chapman Catt Center, Iowa State University, https://awpc.cattcenter.iastate.edu/2017/03/09/now-we-can-begin-1920_.

New York State Woman Suffrage Party, "Modern Representative Government," broadside, 1915, Cornell University, Woman Suffrage at Cornell University collection, https://rmc.library.cornell.edu/suffrage/exhibition/earlyyears/index.html#modalClosed.

New York State Woman Suffrage Party, "Suffrage as a War Measure," booklet, 1917. Available at HathiTrust, https://babel.hathitrust.org/cgi/pt?id=uc1.31175035167512&view=page&seq=1.

New York State Woman Suffrage Party, "What Woman Suffrage Stands For," broadside, 1917, Cornell University, Woman Suffrage at Cornell University collection, https://rmc.library.cornell.edu/suffrage/exhibition/earlyyears/index.html#modalClosed.

New York Woman Suffrage Party, "Twelve Reasons Why Women Should Vote," broadside, undated, probably 1915, Museum of the City of New York, https://www.mcny.org/story/100-years-19th-amendment F2011.16.2.

Rumball, Edwin and Catherine, "The Working Girls and Women of Rochester," *The Common Good: An Independent Magazine of Civic and Social Rochester* VI (February 1913), "What to Do," 155–57. Available at HathiTrust, https://babel.hathitrust.org/cgi/pt?id=nyp.33433086642612&view=page&seq=29.

Sanger, Margaret, *Woman and the New Race* (New York: New York Truth Publishing Company, 1921), 226–34. Available at HathiTrust, https://hdl.handle.net/2027/uva.x002526013.

6

Welcoming Newcomers

Figure 6. Immigrants at Ellis Island, the entry point for millions of newcomers in the early twentieth century. *Source*: Library of Congress Prints and Photograph Division.

Between 1900 and 1915, more than fifteen million immigrants arrived in the United States, most of them through New York City. Many hailed from southern and eastern Europe, unlike most of the previous waves of immigrants who had come from northern and western Europe. Many of the newcomers stayed in New York City and had children who stayed in the city as adults. New York City was probably the most diverse, cosmopolitan city in the nation in the progressive period. The rest of the state, particularly the cities, was also marked by diversity. New York mostly welcomed newcomers.

Some immigrants tended to band together and settle in particular neighborhoods—for example, on the Lower East Side of Manhattan, which became one of the most densely populated areas in the world. But others dispersed throughout the city or moved beyond it. Immigrants sought opportunities to work and struggled to reconcile retaining some of the language, customs, and cultures they brought with them with the adopting the norms and expectations of their new homes.

New York tended to be an accommodating place, mostly spurning racial and ethnic animosity. New Yorkers were mostly tolerant, more interested in what they had in common than in their differences. But immigrants endured hostility and discrimination as already-established groups opposed large-scale immigration or determined to "assimilate" the newcomers into the state and nation. Several organizations were created to help particular ethnic groups with immigrant origins. Progressives understood that immigration and diversity contributed to the vibrance of their state and nation. But they also favored "Americanization," integrating the newcomers into American society and culture. Progressives also advocated for limited state government intervention to address immigrant-related issues.

Immigrants Encounter New York

Between 1880 and 1915, more than two million Jews left their homes in Europe, mostly Russia, fleeing persecution and seeking economic opportunity in the United States. Most of them entered through New York City, and large numbers stayed there, many settling on the Lower East Side. Jewish immigrants brought a shared heritage and commitment to hard work. Many started out in the garment industry. Many went on to advance in the garment trades, business, journalism, and other careers. A number emerged as leaders of the progressive movement.

Some later recalled their first experiences in New York. Abraham Cahan (1860–1951) arrived from Lithuania (then part of the Russian empire) in 1882. He eventually became an outstanding editor and novelist and was a founding editor of the Jewish Daily Forward, *geared toward a*

Jewish-American audience. His 1917 novel, The Rise of David Levinsky, *was a semiautobiographical account that mirrored his own experience of immigration and Americanization and reflected the experiences of immigrants in general. In the book, the main character, David Levinsky, a Russian Jew who immigrates from Russia to New York, rises from rags to riches. Cahan has Levinsky recall a sense of apprehension coupled with wonder as he set foot in New York. Levinsky's experiences mirrored those of thousands of other immigrants well into the twentieth century.*

∼

From *The Rise of David Levinsky* (1917) by Abraham Cahan

When the ship reached Sandy Hook, I was literally overcome with the beauty of the landscape. The immigrant's arrival in his new home is like a second birth to him. Imagine a new-born babe in possession of a fully developed intellect. Would it ever forget its entry into the world? Neither does the immigrant ever forget his entry into a country which is, to him, a new world in the profoundest sense of the term and in which he expects to pass the rest of his life. I conjure up the gorgeousness of the spectacle as it appeared to me on that clear June morning: the magnificent verdure of Staten Island, the tender blue of sea and sky, the dignified bustle of passing craft above all, those floating, squatting, multitudinously windowed palaces which I subsequently learned to call ferries. It was all so utterly unlike anything I had ever seen or dreamed of before. It unfolded itself like a divine revelation. I was in a trance or in something closely resembling one.

"This, then, is America!" I exclaimed, mutely. The notion of something enchanted which the name had always evoked in me now seemed fully borne out. . . .

When I say that my first view of New York Bay struck me as something not of this earth it is not a mere figure of speech. I vividly recall the feeling, for example, with which I greeted the first cat I saw on American soil. It was on the Hoboken pier, while the steerage passengers were being marched to the ferry. A large, black, well-fed feline stood in a corner, eying the crowd of newcomers. The sight of it gave me a thrill of joy. "Look! There is a cat!" I said to Gitelson [a fellow immigrant from the ship]. And in my heart I added, "Just like those at home!" For the moment the little animal made America real to me. At the same time it seemed unreal itself.

We were ferried over to Castle Garden [in New York harbor, at that time, the reception center for arriving immigrants]. One of the things that caught my eye as I entered the vast rotunda was an iron staircase rising diagonally against one of the inner walls. A uniformed man, with some papers in his hands, ascended it with brisk, resounding step till he disappeared through a door not many inches from the ceiling. It may seem odd, but I can never think of my arrival in this country without hearing the ringing footfalls of this official and beholding the yellow eyes of the black cat which stared at us at the Hoboken pier.

The harsh manner of the immigration officers was a grievous surprise to me. As contrasted with the officials of my despotic country, those of a republic had been portrayed in my mind as paragons of refinement and cordiality. My anticipations were rudely belied. "They are not a bit better than Cossacks," [a group in Russia known for their rough manners] I remarked to Gitelson. But they neither looked nor spoke like Cossacks, so their gruff voices were part of the uncanny scheme of things that surrounded me. These unfriendly voices flavored all America with a spirit of icy inhospitality that sent a chill through my very soul.

The stringent immigration laws that were passed some years later had not yet come into existence. We had no difficulty in being admitted to the United States, and when I was finished I was loath to leave the Garden.

Many of the other immigrants were met by relatives, friends. There were cries of joy, tears, embraces, kisses. All of which intensified my sense of loneliness and dread of the New World. . . .

I led the way out of the big Immigrant Station. As we reached the park outside we were pounced down upon by two evil-looking men, representatives of boarding houses for immigrants. They pulled us so roughly and their general appearance and manner were so uninviting that we struggled and protested until they let us go, not without some parting curses. Then I led the way across Battery Park and under the Elevated railway to State Street. A train hurtling and panting along overhead produced a bewildering, daunting effect on me. The active life of the great strange city made me feel like one abandoned in the midst of a jungle. Where were we to go? What were we to do? But the presence of Gitelson continued to act as a spur on me. I mustered courage to approach a policeman, something I should never have been bold enough to do at home. As a matter of fact, I scarcely had an idea what his function was. To me he looked like some uniformed nobleman, an impression that in itself was enough to intimidate me. With his coat of blue cloth, starched linen collar, and white gloves, he reminded me of anything but the policemen of my town. I addressed him in Yiddish, making it as near an approach to German as I knew how, but my efforts were lost on him. He shook his head. With a witheringly dignified grimace he then pointed his club in the direction of Broadway and strutted off majestically. . . .

Ten minutes' walk brought me to the heart of the Jewish East Side. The streets swarmed with Yiddish speaking immigrants. The sign-boards were in English and, some of them in Russian. The scurry and hustle of the people were not merely overwhelmingly greater, both in volume and intensity, than in my native town. It was of another sort. The swing and step of the pedestrians, the voices and manner of the street peddlers, and a hundred and one other things seemed to testify to far more self-confidence and energy, to larger ambitions and wider scopes, than did the appearance of the crowds in my birthplace. The great thing was that these people were better dressed than the inhabitants of my town. The poorest looking man wore a hat (instead of a cap), a stiff collar and a necktie, and the poorest woman wore a hat or a bonnet. . . .

My intention was to take a long stroll, as much in the hope of coming upon some windfall as for the purpose of taking a look at the great American city. Many of the letters that came from the United States to my birthplace before I sailed had contained a warning not to imagine that America was a "land of gold" and that treasure might be had in the streets of New York for the picking. But these warnings only had the effect of lending vividness to my image of an American street as a thoroughfare strewn with nuggets of the precious metal. Symbolically speaking, this was the idea one had of the "land of Columbus." It was a continuation of the widespread effect produced by stories of Cortes and Pizarro in the sixteenth century, confirmed by the successes of some Russian emigrants of my time.

Adjusting to American Ways

David Blaustein (1866–1912) emigrated to Boston from Prussia, became a rabbi, and in 1898 moved to New York City to become head of the Educational Alliance. The Alliance's initial main purpose was to serve as a settlement house for eastern European Jewish immigrants. But under Blaustein, who directed the Alliance until 1907, it expanded well beyond that initial mission to provide classes and other educational and cultural opportunities and to help newcomers assimilate to their new state and nation.

Blaustein was concerned with the process through which immigrants became Americans. That was essential, he maintained, because the future of the country depended on immigrants retaining some of the best aspects of their cultures but also assimilating with their fellow Americans and adopting their ways. The tension between retaining the old and adopting the new was serious. It was particularly notable in New York, probably the nation's most diverse city, where thousands of new immigrants were arriving each year. Blaustein described the challenges and offered some strategies for addressing it in a 1903 address to the New York Conference of Charities.

∽

From "The Making of an American," Outlook (1903)
by David Blaustein

To him who would consider the problem of the making of Americans, there is no saner point of departure than that of asking the immigrant, "What does America mean to you?" The traveler who visits Eastern or Southern Europe, whether it be Italy or Roumania [Romania], Galicia or Western Russia, will realize and perhaps can then only realize the meaning which that eastern world has given to the word "America."

In the land of persecution he hears of America as the land that is free. In the land of despotism and militarism and police surveillance, he hears of America as the land where the spirit as well as the body is free. If he visits a land where the heavy scourge of famine has fallen, he hears of America as the land of plenty and prosperity. . . . Whatever evils, economic, moral, political, or even religious, he finds in Eastern Europe, there also he finds the deep-seated faith akin to that of the ancient Greeks, that in the "land beyond the ocean" none of these prevail. What the old, who with the eyes of faith see beyond the grave in the hereafter, the young, with eyes still fixed on life, see in America. . . .

Having thus sketched in rough that succession of circumstances which result in the failure of the immigrant to become an American, it remains to propose that remedy that shall bridge the gulf of centuries, races, and nationalities, the simple bridge of education in its oldest sense, the "leading out" of the immigrant into America. The plan of which I speak is the plan we have devised and which I have personally applied in dealing with the Jews, who come from Eastern Europe. Those who work among other nationalities can, I believe, devise a similar scheme, adapted to their own problem. The first barrier which meets the Jewish immigrant is the barrier of language. In his own country, his people, living in many lands, spoke one language of their own, Yiddish. We must teach them:

1. The language of America; and this teaching the children receive in the public schools, the older people should obtain in evening classes.

2. Many come from lands where they were either deprived from citizenship or were residents of an absolute monarchy where representative government, which, when they understand, they will realize that they are a constituent part of, and so we teach them civics. Teach them the spirit as well as the law and the history of the American Republic.

3. The Jew of Russia is forced to live in the city, he may not till the field, his life is set within the pale of the city. To meet this, we have the Jewish Agricultural and the Jewish Industrial Removal Societies, organized to turn the Jew back once more to his ancient pursuit of agriculture, to send him to the smaller towns over the country and to break up the tradition-enforced Ghetto.

4. National holidays express national tradition, as well as recall national history. It is part of our work in the making of Americans, to make the immigrant understand and feel what a victory was won for his country at Concord and Lexington, what a deliverance was secured for his children in the Declaration of Independence, that he may feel his share in the glory of America, of which he is a part.

5. In Europe, as we have said, the necessity of military service created a philosophy of unfitness as a means of escape. In America, where it is the "survival of the fittest," physical culture plays an important part and when we are striving to make an American, we strive to make a physically strong American, and our physical culture is by no means one of the minor branches of our work.

6. Social life in a tenement in a crowded city falls far short even of the social life of the immigrant at home. To give

him that social life, we have our roof concerts on summer nights, our entertainments, our receptions, our dances. Community and village life are thus made possible for the tenement dweller.

7. In Europe, religion is the fundamental fact of the Jew's existence. Vaguely he hears that in America the State is separated from the Church. The younger generation, his children, separated by a gulf from their parents, grasp the phrase and not the fact of religion in American life. We meet in our system by those classes in which we teach progress to the older, and the value, the sincerity and the power of religious tradition to the younger.

8. In Eastern Europe, especially in Russia, the "ukase" is the wing which shelters the petty official. The immigrant at home believes the lowest official issues the order. Government to him means the official with whom he comes in contact, by necessity a minor one. He learns the value of bribery, the absolute necessity of corruption in all Europe. In America, he puts his old-world philosophy to work. The official who enforces the law is to him the man who invents it. The court that applies the statute, the judge who interprets it, is to him the despot who willed it. We teach him whence comes the authority of the court. We advise him in his legal difficulties. We do not litigate for him, but we help him to the proper steps.

There is no greater change from Eastern Europe to America than the change in the life of the women. It might be fairly termed an improper fraction, if one tried to contrast the fractional part woman played in the foreign life and in the American. But American schools and American traditions certainly bring the woman from the nonentity to a powerful factor. If we take her from the home, in the reaction against the old semi-bondage, we tend to create a neglect of those domestic sciences, on which the American we are going to make, must finally depend. To meet this, our system embraces classes in Domestic Art and Science in practical problems of home life.

In all that our tentative system has so far dealt, we have considered private activity, not public. There remains one phase wherein the State and not the individual, in my opinion, should take a hand in the making of Americans; for education, according to every American tradition is a public, not a private, affair. Public schools meet the necessities of the younger generation, but these are "born," not "made" Americans. Evening schools as they are now conducted seem to me to fall far short of the necessity. They should, in part at least, be especially adapted to the needs of the race that attends them, should teach not merely the "three R's," but should develop the latent talents of the nationalities with which they deal, and should have something of the complete science that is now used in kindergartens and which should be for larger [older] children who are yet young in the meaning and lesson they are learning of "America."

I am presenting no system of perfection, no system of accurately determined methods, but only a few practical ways that in my own experience seem to help in the one problem for the solution of which we are working. We are not making Americans for the best good of America, that they, when they are perfectly amalgamated with that America, may themselves be come not merely a receptive, but a contributory force. In its last analysis, the "Making of Americans" must inevitably mean "The Making of America."

Aiding Immigrants

Like newcomers before and after them, the immigrants who entered during the progressive era often encountered scorn and difficulties in finding work and adjusting to the new nation. A group of concerned citizens founded the Society for the Protection of Italian Immigrants in 1901. The organization offered advice and assistance to newly-arrived immigrants, helped them find housing and jobs, and kept them out of the clutches of padrones (unscrupulous labor agents) and other exploiters.

Gino Speranza, an Italian-born but American-educated lawyer and journalist, served as the society's director and spokesman. He emphasized that America benefitted from immigrants but that the newcomers needed more understanding and assistance, as this 1904 article shows.

Later, in the 1920s, Speranza, like some other immigration advocates, shifted his views and came to favor immigration restriction and emphasized the need for immigrants to assimilate into American culture.

∼

From "Solving the Immigration Problem," *Outlook* (1904)
by Gino Carlo Speranza

We hear a great deal nowadays of the "problem of immigration." Orators and statesmen, newspapers and magazines, never lose the opportunity of talking of the "foreign peril," of the danger from an influx of immigrants who do not readily assimilate with the elements and institutions of the Republic.

Indeed, many of our sins we conveniently saddle on the stranger, finding in him the responsibility for some of the evils of our own making. And so a thoughtless majority fails to see that such procedure can result only in race prejudice, and prevent rather than foster that very assimilation which we all desire.

On the other hand, how seldom do we hear of the work of those men and women who, while their companions discuss, are toiling to solve, this problem of the incoming stranger. It is true that, now and again, we get picturesque descriptions of what the agents of the various immigrant societies do at our ports of entry, or of the scenes, pitiful or humorous, witnessed before the Courts of Special Inquiry at our immigration stations.

Our knowledge of the field of labor of immigration societies, however, stops there. We know, in a vague way, that the Irish and the Scandinavians and the Jews maintain missionaries or agents who welcome the immigrant of their respective nationality, and perhaps find him work. But there is much more than this that such societies do, as a brief history of one of them and of its work will show. . . .

I choose the Society for the Protection of Italian Immigrants for other reasons than that my knowledge of its work is more extensive than that of no less beneficent ones.

This is . . . an encouraging sign of a practical solution to the immigration problem. My choice was determined, moreover, by the fact that Italian immigration is decidedly on the increase, and any body of men actively engaged in solving the peculiar questions which the Italian immigrant presents deserve special attention.

The Society for the Protection of Italian Immigrants was founded about two years ago by some fifteen people, most of whom were that type of men and women whom many would have classified as "dreamers"—settlement workers, reformers, philanthropists! They, however, had the wisdom to formulate a constitution setting forth such practical objects as these:

The objects of this Society shall be:

I. To afford advice, information, aid, and protection of all kinds to Italian immigrants.

II. By assisting, wherever possible, such immigrants as are unfamiliar with the language and customs of the country to a practical knowledge thereof.

III. By learning the character of the labor for which each individual immigrant is best fitted, and endeavoring to procure for said immigrant employment, at his particular trade or calling, or at some remunerative occupation, that he may not, through want of work, become a charge to the State or an enemy of society.

IV. By investigating and remedying, if possible, all abuses to which Italian immigrants are exposed, and all wrongs inflicted upon them.

V. By familiarizing immigrants with their rights and duties under the State and Federal Constitutions, and securing for them the entire enjoyment of all their constitutional rights.

All these seem simple enough on reading; indeed, it might be said that, being for the immigrant's benefit, the immigrant will be only too glad to meet the Society's efforts. But this reasoning overlooks the forces which operate against the exercise of such good intentions and purposes.

First of all, you must overcome the immigrant's suspicions, and this is not a simple matter. The examination he undergoes by the Federal officials is a valuable and necessary thing, but put yourself in his place and you will see that if you had to answer the questions put to him, either you would refuse to answer them as impertinent, or else assault the official for making them; at all events, you would not think you were being welcomed to the new land.

Then, having passed this necessary examination, his first experience in the land of the free is likely to be his acquaintance with the boarding-house "runner," who will force him to go with him, or the crook who will exchange his foreign money into Confederate notes or take it without even such souvenirs of the transaction, or the "friend" who will take him to the banker and padrone who want to "sell" his labor, or the district boss who will "Americanize" him for the sake of his vote.

Perhaps if he is fortunate in escaping these, he will experience the pleasure of what it means not to understand the policeman's "gaw on!" ["Go on!"].

It is obvious, though too often forgotten, that the first impression the foreigner gets of a new country will tend to color all his future opinions of and experiences in that country. It is natural, therefore, that immigrants' societies should concentrate their efforts in minimizing the bad impression that the alien is apt to get on his arrival. This is especially important as regards the Italian, who is proverbially sensitive and inexperienced. Yet the work the representatives of the various immigrants' societies have to do at the landing station is, in a sense, very simple. It may be summed up in the words "lending a helping hand." In the rush and excitement of handling some four thousand immigrants in a day by the Federal authorities, a little kindness, a word of advice, a reassuring promise in the tongue of the immigrant, will go far not only in helping the alien but also in aiding the authorities in expediting the trying work of examination.

In the case of Italians, the absence of a correct address to which they may be sent is a common source of trouble. This is due either to the use of phonetic spelling of American names or the absence of the house number. Thus "Chrippocricks" may be the immigrant's address for Cripple Creek or it may be simply Elizabeth Street. In that case the Agent of the Society goes to that section of Elizabeth Street where the fellow-townsmen of the new arrival reside, and there generally finds the immigrant's friends or relatives.

The Agent's work is not, however, always so simple. There are immigrants who, through failure properly to present their case, are ordered deported, or others against whom a strict application of the Federal laws would work an injustice. The Agents take up such cases before the Immigration Boards and endeavor to overcome the obstacles, which often are due to misunderstanding.

The moment the immigrant is "passed" by the authorities, he ceases to be in charge of Uncle Sam, and it is then that the immigration societies have to exercise special vigilance to save their charges from those various persons who are ready to pounce upon them at the landing.

The Italian Society has established at Ellis Island a corps of uniformed watchers who take in charge all those immigrants who desire to place themselves in the care of the Society. These watchers put tags of identification on the immigrants, and bring them over from Ellis Island to the Battery Landing in New York, where other uniformed guards take them in charge and conduct them to the Society's office at 17 Pearl Street. It is at the Battery Landing that, before the corps of watchers had been organized and the efficiency of the police increased there, open fights used to take place between the Agents who had charge of the immigrants and the "runners" and crooks who tried to get them away.

To give an idea of the aggressiveness of the powers that prey there, I might cite an instance where, of thirty-six immigrants in charge of the Society's Agents, only seventeen were left after an encounter with the runners. On another occasion the police reserves had to be called out. Nor is the drawing of weapons and the slashing with knives entirely done away with even now.

From the office of the Society the various immigrants are sent to their destination in the care of guides whose possible dishonesty is checked by a system of cards and receipts and whose charges for services are fixed by the Society. By this method the usual rate charged immigrants for transportation to their destination has been cut down from an average of $4.50 a head charged by the runners to about 34 cents each.

An immigrant society could hardly render efficient service without what is known as an information bureau. Only men of the utmost patience and of pretty wide knowledge can be employed in such a bureau. To it the foreign-born goes for almost anything he does not know. Ostensibly it exists to supply information to friends and relatives of expected or detained immigrants. Actually it is a dispenser of all sorts of information. Foreigners come to it for legal advice, for financial aid, for instruction regarding how to act or what to do in the new land, even for matrimonial advice. In the Society for the Protection of Italian Immigrants the man in charge of the information bureau also performs the important function of transmitting or distributing money from friends of detained immigrants. Last year it handled over ten thousand dollars in sums not exceeding fifty dollars.

An employment bureau is a necessary adjunct of every immigrant society. In the Jewish society young immigrants are sent out to try their luck as peddlers, being entrusted with a small stock. This is a most practical method for people of that race.

The Austro-Hungarian and Irish societies try to supply the servant demand. The employment bureau of the society for Italians has a peculiarly difficult problem. It has made it a fundamental rule to place applicants only in out-of-town work; it will do nothing for men who want to labor in the city. In this it again contributes to the solution of the problem of immigration. For it cannot be denied that the problem of immigration with us is essentially one of distribution.

The demand for laborers is great outside of the cities, but the gregarious Italian prefers to increase our urban congestion instead of going to the country. The Society, in its endeavors to relieve such congestion, is forced to find work for large gangs of men as an inducement for them to leave the city.

An even greater difficulty lies in the fact that a successful labor bureau for Italians in competent American hands means the breaking up of the much talked-of padrone system. The padrones recognize this, and are actively using their great influence against the Italian labor bureau.

It will be apparent, after this summary, that the underlying aim of the work of immigrant societies, and more especially of the society for Italians, is to make their wards feel that their advent into a strange land does not mean their coming among those who wish them ill. By practical work the societies engender a feeling in the newcomer that the Republic holds friends ready to help him.

But with the sensitive Italian the work of friendly aid cannot stop here. He is probably the most complex character that comes to our shores, and the least understood by us. In a way he is the most helpless, not because he lacks strength or intelligence, but because he is often ignorant, childlike in his confidence once won, and highly impressionable to small matters. Moreover, he is helpless in the sense that, unlike the Germans and the Irish, he possesses no political influence whatsoever, and his race in America has not yet won the prestige which would come from having among us many Italians or Italian-Americans either of affluence or distinction.

It is in supplying this very prestige that the Society for the Protection of Italian Immigrants, as a body of Americans of distinction, is really performing its greatest good. And it is this peculiar function which differentiates it from other similar societies; it is in this regard that we must look upon it as the most practical example of a way out of the immigration difficulty. . . .

The way out seems to me to lie in approaching the immigration problem from the point of friendliness rather than of defense. That is, in doing things that will tend to make the foreigner feel that he is among friends. Assimilation is a mutual process; it depends for success not only on what the foreign body will do to be absorbed into the greater body, but upon what the greater body will do to attract it. . . .

Explaining the Immigrant Experience

Some immigrants who entered New York in this era later recorded their experiences. Marcus Eli Ravage (1884–1965), a Jewish immigrant who came from Romania to New York in 1900 at age sixteen, went further. He contended in his account that it was immigrants rather than native-born people who really understood the promise of America because they experienced it. The American population as a whole needed a better understanding of immigrants' experience and culture and the fact that immigrants changed and transformed America.

Ravage recounted his early, hard years in New York, working as a peddler, bartender, and textile sweatshop worker. But then he moved on to another sweatshop where the pay and conditions were better. He described the work as a hard but rewarding because, in his free time, he had the opportunity to take in the city's cultural attractions and benefit from available educational opportunities.

Ravage's message was that immigrants had dreams and aspirations, worked hard, and improved their status. His life, described in the book, was a model of immigrants' advancement. After the schooling described in the book (below), he went to college and became a prolific writer and defender of Jewish rights.

∼

From *An American in the Making: The Life Story of an Immigrant* (1917) by Marcus Eli Ravage

Introduction

When I hear around me the foolish prattle about the new immigration—"the scum of Europe," as it is called—that is invading and making itself master of this country, I cannot help saying to myself that Americans have forgotten America. The native, I must conclude, has, by long familiarity with the rich blessings of his own land, grown forgetful of his high privileges and ceased to grasp the lofty message which America wafts across the seas to all the oppressed of mankind. What, I wonder, do they know of America, who know only America?

The more I think upon the subject the more I become persuaded that the relation of the teacher and the taught as between those who were born and those who came here must be reversed. It is the free American who needs to be instructed by the benighted races in the uplifting word that America speaks to all the world. Only from the humble immigrant, it appears to me, can he learn just what America stands for in the family of nations. . . .

Yes, we immigrants have a real claim on America. Every one of us who did not grow faint-hearted at the start of the battle and has stuck it out has earned a share in America by the ancient right of conquest. We have had to subdue this new home of ours to make it habitable, and in conquering it we have conquered ourselves. We are not what we were when you saw us landing from the Ellis Island ferry. Our own kinsfolk do not know us when they come over. We sometimes hardly know ourselves.

XII. Shirts and Philosophy

. . . I soon found myself very happy in my new surroundings. Those novelists and sentimentalists who slander the sweat-shop and the tenement should take notice. We certainly had a very much more human time of it in the old days than we did later on in the high-ceilinged, many-windowed, electric fanned, palatial prisons that conformed to the factory laws. The reasons were these: In the sweat-shop the hand and the boss belonged to the same class. That made a big difference. There were no spying "foreladies" and no rules, no peremptory calls to the office and no threats of discharge. You did not have to stand in line with hat in hand for the wages of your toil.

If we were hard up after a long, slack season, we could get all our meals on credit from the old shop peddler, who sold baked liver by the slice, brandy, bananas, and rolls, and sometimes lent us even a bit of cash. The number of workers was small, so that everybody knew everybody else. During the lunch hour we visited, and fell into violent arguments about the labor movement and socialism and literature, and mocked good-naturedly at the "capitalist" when he ventured to put in a word (as he always did); and each of us, except the girls, took his turn in going for the can of beer. All this tended to preserve the human dignity and the self-respect of the worker. . . .

My earnings kept gradually rising, until (with the standards of barroom wages in my mind) they attained dizzying heights. With softer materials, to be sure, I might have turned out more dozens per day, but I comforted myself with the thought that the work would be more "particular," so that the net results would probably be about the same. The "slack," indeed, was longer and more thoroughgoing than at the better lines. For the two whole months of January and February that temperamental gentleman in the South seemed to be dispensing with shirts. But while that meant going into debt and cutting down on luxuries, there were compensating circumstances even then, as we shall see. . . .

There was no denying that, for all its good things to eat and drink, and its lazy afternoon hours, and educational opportunities, the saloon could not hold a candle to the two-needle machine. Indeed, the sweat-shop was for me the cradle of liberty. It was more, it was my first university. I was not long there before I discovered that there were better things I could do with my free evenings than to frequent the cozy hang-outs of my fellow-countrymen. When I overheard a dispute between the young buttonhole-maker and the cadaverous, curly-haired closer, on the respective merits of the stories of Tchekhov and Maupassant; and when, another day, the little black-eyed Russian girl who was receiving two cents per dozen shirts as a finisher boldly asserted that evolution pointed the way to anarchism and not to socialism, and cited the fact that Spencer himself was an anarchist, my eyes were opened and I felt ashamed of my ignorance.

I had been rather inclined hitherto to feel superior to my surroundings, and to regard the shop and the whole East Side as but a temporary halt in my progress. With my career looming on the horizon, and my inherited tendency to look down upon mechanical trades, I had at first barely given a tolerant eye to the sordid men and girls who worked beside me. I had not realized that this grimy, toil-worn, airless Ghetto had a soul and a mind under its shabby exterior. It knew everything and talked about everything. Nothing in the way of thought-interest was too big or too heavy for this *intelligentsia* of the slums.

I made an effort to listen attentively in the hope that I might get some hint as to where my fellow-operatives got all their knowledge. I observed that nearly all of them brought books with them to work—Yiddish, Russian, German, and even English books. During the lunch-hour, if the disputatious mood was not on them, the entire lot of them had their heads buried in their volumes or their papers, so that the littered, un-swept loft had the air of having been miraculously turned into a library. While waiting for my next bundle of shirts, or just before leaving the shop, I would stealthily glance at a title, or open a pamphlet and snatch a word or two. I was too timid to inquire openly. Once a girl caught me by the wardrobe examining her book, and asked me whether I liked books and whether I went to the lectures. I became confused and murmured a negative. "You know," she said, "Gorky is going to speak to-night," and held out a newspaper to show me the announcement.

So they were going to lectures! I began to buy newspapers and watch for the notices. I took to reading books and attending meetings and theaters. There were scores of lectures every week, I found, and I went to as many as I could. One night it was Darwin, and the next it might be the principles of air pressure. On a Saturday night there were sometimes two meetings so arranged that both could be attended by the same audience. I remember going once to a meeting at Cooper Union to protest against the use of the militia in breaking a strike somewhere in the West, and then retiring with a crowd of others to the anarchist reading-room on Eldridge Street to hear an informal discussion on "Hamlet versus Don Quixote." It did not matter to us what the subject was. There was a peculiar, intoxicating joy in just sitting there and drinking in the words of the speakers, which to us were echoes from a higher world than ours. Quite likely most of us could not have passed an examination in any of the subjects we heard discussed. It was something more valuable than information that we were after. Our poor, cramped souls were yearning to be inspired and uplifted. Never in all my experience since, though I have been in colleges and learned societies, have I seen such earnest, responsive audiences as were those collarless men and hatless girls of the sweat-shops.

The East Side theater was another educational institution. It was seldom that an attempt was made to entertain us there, and whenever it was made we expressed our resentment by hooting. We did not go to the theater for amusement any more than we read books or listened to lectures for amusement. It was art and the truthful representation of actual life and the element of culture that we demanded, and the playwrights who satisfied us we rewarded by our homage and our devotion. No American dramatist was ever worshiped by his public as Jacob Gordin was. I remember that when a reactionary newspaper tried to stab him in the back by raising a cry of immorality against one of his plays, the whole progressive element in the Ghetto came as a unit to his support by packing his theater and clamoring for his appearance. The sheet that dared attack him was nearly boycotted out of existence. And when, some years later, Gordin died, every shop was closed on the East Side and a hundred thousand followed his hearse in genuine mourning. There is no parallel, I think, in the whole history of the American drama to this testimonial of popular devotion to an intellectual leader.

Nor was Gordin the only divinity on our dramatic Olympus. There were younger men like Libin and Kobrin, who, while they might be said to have been members of Gordin's realistic school, had made some interesting departures in subject-matter by laying emphasis on the humor and pathos of life in the New World as affecting the immigrant. These two had for a long time been principally occupied with fiction, but had turned to the stage because of the greater educational possibilities of the drama. The Russians, too, kept in touch with their exiled brethren and saw to it that our souls did not starve for lack of spiritual sustenance.

Not only did the Canal Street publishers bring out the beautiful humorous tales of Sholom Aleichem and Mendele Mocher Sforim and the poetry of Frug and Peretz, several amateur organizations—precursors of the numerous "advanced" playhouses now fashionable everywhere—were formed for the purpose of producing the poetic dramas of Hirshbein and Peretz and the symbolic plays of Asch and Pinsky which, owing to their extreme literary character, were not adapted to the regular theaters. Notably the Progressive Dramatic Club conducted readings and performances of choice tragedies "from home," which, although they were intended for the elect, were attended by as large audiences as ever went to the Thalia and People's theaters.

I saw more good literature on the stage in those days while I was sewing sleeves into shirts than I saw in all my subsequent career. When the original playwrights could not fill the demand, the lack was supplied by the translators. While Broadway was giving Ibsen the cold shoulder, the East Side was acclaiming him with wild enthusiasm. I saw "Monna Vanna" on the Bowery before the Broadway type of theater-goer had ever heard the name of Maeterlinck. Many foreign writers—Hauptmann, Sudermann, Gorky, Andreiyev, Tolstoy—had their premieres in the Ghetto. The same was true of actors; I saw Nazimova in "Ghosts" before she could speak English. And I made my first acquaintance with Greek tragedy when I had not yet learned how to speak English.

Documenting Immigrants' Challenges in New York

One of the tenets of the progressive movement was attention to the welfare of individuals. Progressives recognized that massive change, including the influx of millions of newcomers, mostly from Europe, could be unsettling to both the people arriving and the people already residing here.

Immigration policy was largely a federal matter and, after the establishment of Ellis Island as the main point of entry into the United States in 1906, the flood of newcomers increased. But progressive New York reformers maintained that state government could take steps to ease immigrants' entry and adjustment to their new home.

Investigating conditions and issuing reports was a common progressive strategy. In 1908, progressive Republican governor Charles Evans Hughes appointed a commission to study the issue. Chaired by prominent New York attorney Louis Marshall, it produced a substantive report the next year, much of it drafted by the commission's secretary, labor reformer Frances A. Kellor.

The commission emphasized immigration's benefit for New York, detailed challenges facing immigrants, and recommended state action to meet them. It set the tone: immigrants were welcome in New York but they faced major challenges. The excerpt below summarizes some of the issues.

The 1910 legislature established a new Bureau of Industries and Immigration to assist immigrants, identify employment opportunities, and address exploitation. It also passed laws to regulate steamship ticket agents and private bankers who sometimes exploited immigrants.

∼

From *Report of the Commission of Immigration of the State of New York* (1909)

The Alien in New York State

New York is pre-eminently the State most affected by immigration and where the alien has been a most important factor. There are today approximately five hundred thousand aliens in New York State, or about six per cent. of the total population. Four-fifths of all aliens arrive at the port of New York. Nearly one-third on landing express the intention of settling within the state. Ellis Island, as formerly Castle Garden, is the main gateway through which they come. In New York, too, are located hundreds of agents who distribute laborers throughout the country, and who facilitate their return to their native land.

The industrial, political and social history of the alien in this state constitutes an important chapter in the history of the State. The alien has become a constituent force in every field of American endeavor. On the farm, in the factory, in the mine, in the construction of railroads and other public works, he has been indispensable. He has not only proven a valiant soldier in the army of industry, but he has also borne arms in defense of the land of his adoption. He has become rapidly assimilated with the great body of our citizenship, and has intelligently furthered the progress of the nation. His children, indistinguishable from those of the earlier settlers, now constitute an integral part of the American people.

Indeed, the word "American" does not apply to racial stock, or to creed or belief, or to length of residence, but to citizenship in this, our Republic. For the majority of aliens no special protection has ever been, or perhaps ever will be, necessary. Upon the whole, the attitude of the native-born has been and is friendly to them. As a rule, aliens arrive in the prime of life, and have been courageous and self-reliant. They have availed themselves of the opportunities here with remarkable avidity, contributing in return to the prosperity and intellectual development of this country.

Granting in the fullest measure the achievements of aliens in the face of difficulties which have hitherto confronted them, they nevertheless encounter obstacles which will be best overcome, with resultant benefits to the State and alien alike, through a sympathetic attitude toward and intelligent co-operation with the alien on the part of the State and its citizens. Aliens born and reared in rural communities have been suddenly transplanted into great cities, and peasants have become factory operatives. The movement from Europe to America has been but a part of the world-wide movement from country to city. The alien who reaches the city is often permanently held there by poverty, ignorance of conditions, timidity or social attraction, even when his best interests might have led him elsewhere. Not knowing the language of the country and unacquainted with its legal and social institutions, he has often been despoiled, and the records are replete with instances of gross fraud perpetrated upon him. Today, despite the better legislation and better administration, the difficulties persist and call for more adequate remedy.

The American spirit is adverse to the granting of special privileges to, or withholding of general rights from, any class of the population, for it is not consonant with our American institutions to favor special legislation save under exceptional circumstances. Our alien population, however, occupies in many respects a distinct if not an anomalous position. Alienage is a status preparatory to citizenship, involving certain political and industrial disabilities. To these may be added disadvantages due to the alien's ignorance of our language and institutions.

It may be said that laws which adequately protect the citizen are equally effective for the alien. The Commission believes that its investigation does not support this contention. The experiences of the alien, until he becomes habituated to his new surroundings, are not paralleled by those of any other group of our population. Upon arriving at the Battery, the jurisdiction of the Federal government ceases, and he is thrown upon his own resources, practically bereft of speech. At this point congregate runners and sharpers, native Americans as well as countrymen of the alien, eager to exchange his money for counterfeit or Confederate notes; to substitute a subway ticket for his full railway ticket, and to indulge in all manner of misrepresentation.

He is defrauded by unscrupulous employment agents, charged exorbitant rates, sent to labor camps where conditions are unsanitary and the hours of labor excessive, where his wage is unreasonably low and irregularly paid, and where he is subjected to gross extortion. The padrone and the commissary, who practically own him, do not exist for the American workman. The alien woman incurs even greater danger through the employment agency, for she may be sent to immoral places to work.

If the alien accumulates savings he is liable to exploitation by bankers, who accept his money on deposit or for transmission abroad, and fail to repay or transmit it. When he is finally able to send for his family he is often defrauded by dishonest steamship ticket agents who sell him invalid tickets, and the family is stranded far from home and unable to join him. Owing to the congestion prevailing in cities, and the trend of aliens toward the unskilled and sweated trades which are there established, he is unable to avail himself of the demand for his labor which exists throughout the State and nation. He, therefore, lives and works under conditions which by reason of the complete change in his environment affect him and his family injuriously, and practically cut him off from the opportunity of selecting more favorable surroundings.

Finally, if the alien desires to return to his native land he is exploited at the docks and ferries, and if he works his way on board ship he is charged exorbitant rates by employment agents and is frequently subjected to brutal treatment and spoliation. The facilities afforded by the courts to aliens ignorant of the language are also inadequate. Justice is a costly privilege to the mute and illiterate alien, and the lack of proper interpretation often deprives him of the equal protection of the law; while his lack of knowledge or opportunity to become acquainted with the general nature of our system of laws, frequently leads him, though desirous of yielding obedience, unintentionally to become a violator of its prohibitions.

The Commission has dealt with the subject referred to it from a broader point of view than the mere need of the alien, though that is vital. A large proportion of the aliens now in the State will soon be citizens and will be called upon to perform the duties of citizenship. Hence the welfare of the State demands that they shall do so intelligently and possessed of the true spirit of our institutions. The future of the State depends in no small degree upon the manner in which this commonwealth deals with the situation and imbues the citizen in embryo with trust and confidence. The present let-alone attitude of the State toward the alien, which enables a small group of men to exploit him, is also to its material detriment, because it tends to send out of the country millions of dollars which with better protection and some encouragement might be safely invested here.

It seems, therefore, desirable from the standpoint of the State, as well as that of the alien, that it makes special provision to secure to him such measure of protection, education and industrial opportunity as will tend toward the equalization of the standard of living, and insure to the State his full value, and to him recognition of his manhood.

Economic Conditions

The alien, though a rural worker at home, here to a large extent remains in the city. This permanency of urban residence is due to various causes, including ignorance of opportunities and resources in other parts of the country; lack of incentive, or the means to go elsewhere; reluctance to leave the small colony to which he first attaches himself, and where he can have association with his own nationality and race, and especially those of his native province; the lack of protection from the pitfalls which beset him when seeking to make his way alone among strangers; and the self-interest of those who profit by his remaining in the city.

As a consequence, although the alien works to a large extent in industries grouped about small towns and villages, he forms a large proportion of the city workers. The existence in New York and other cities of the State of large numbers of persons unable to seek their best economic advantage, leads to their employment in the so-called sweated trades. This term is used to denote industrial conditions involving hard-driven workers, who labor long hours for low wages, usually in their living quarters in tenements under unsanitary conditions. These trades have developed with the increase of immigration, and in this State during the last generation these workers have been most largely recruited from the most recent immigration. Wages are low and factory conditions, though much improved, are far from good. Men, women and children labor long hours under unsanitary conditions, and earn wages in many cases materially below the current wages of the community. Whole families work in sleeping rooms temporarily converted into workshops, sometimes in the midst of filth and dirt. The work during certain seasons lasts until late at night, and sometimes long after the workers' reserve of physical strength and nervous energy is exhausted. Children are, in some sections of the city, kept at work to the injury of their health.

Chapter 415 of the Laws of 1897 regulates certain phases of home work in tenements, and prohibits work in any tenement house unless it be licensed by the Department of Labor upon the application of the owner of the tenement, while the manufacture of certain specified articles is entirely prohibited. The law does not apply to dwelling-houses, and, therefore, its application is largely limited to New York City. In his report for 1907 the Commissioner of Labor of New York states that of a large number of home workers in Buffalo investigated, 677 were found to be in dwelling houses and only 77 in tenements.

The staff of the Commissioner of Labor is not sufficient to enforce certain provisions of the law, and the Commissioner further states that, while the evil conditions have been grossly exaggerated, a number of the licensed houses are found in an unsanitary condition, much prohibited work still continues in unlicensed houses, home work is in many cases, and especially in the worst sections of New York City sweated, and constitutes an economic evil, and child labor, while absent in many sections of the city, is very prevalent in others; that in one section of the city, a special investigation of 241 houses revealed 119 boys and girls under fourteen at work, their average age being from ten years to eleven years, and some of them as young as five and six, and that, in a second district, 157 houses were investigated, and revealed 325 children at work. The average age was from nine to ten, and some children were as young as four. Practically all the children in the family worked, though most of them irregularly and without set tasks. Night work was common and the proportion of children at work was exceedingly high.

Another occupation which is largely carried on by aliens is that of peddling with push-carts. Under the ordinances of New York City, no person can secure a push-cart license unless he is a citizen or has declared his intention of becoming one. A traffic in licenses has grown up, and a number of aliens operate push-carts, either directly or as agents of others, under licenses not legally belonging to them. According to the report of the Push-Cart Commission appointed in 1905, 97 per cent of the peddlers were "foreigners," principally Jews, Italians and Greeks, but the majority were not newly-arrived aliens, but had lived in the United States from five to ten years.

Since the report made by the Push-Cart Commission, many districts of the city formerly free from push-cart congestion are now crowded. A system of graft in the granting of push-cart licenses and their renewals and in the charge of rental for desirable positions on the street has grown up to the detriment of the licensee.

Asserting That Some Newcomers Are a Threat

Madison Grant (1865–1937), a lifelong New York City resident, lawyer, and scholar, was a pioneering conservationist and environmentalist. But he is best known for his 1916 book The Passing of the Great Race, *which he asserted was a historical account of the origins and geographical movements of races of people in Europe.*

The book was not an easy read; it was laden with dense pseudoscientific and contrived historical analyses. But it was widely popular and influential in part because racist and anti-immigration forces picked up on its central thesis about racial differences and one race being superior to others. The book promoted the idea that the "Nordic race," a loosely defined biological-cultural group that began in Scandinavia, was the key group in the development of Western civilization. The first European settlers in America, and most immigrants since then, brought with them "Nordic" traits and values, said Grant. But more recently, immigrants from southern and eastern Europe, from different and lesser racial stocks, Grant said, were threatening to undermine American civilization.

Grant's book popularized the emerging pseudoscience of eugenics. Eugenicists asserted that the tone of people's skin and other racial characteristics revealed the level of their intelligence. The "white" race was being threatened, they said. Eugenics became an insidious part of the popular culture at the end of the progressive era. It led to racial misunderstanding and animosity and contributed to immigration restriction in the 1920s and a decade later to the Holocaust.

Grant's malignant ideas and proposals have long been discredited, but some of the reverberations of The Passing of the Great Race *are still with us.*

∽

FROM *THE PASSING OF THE GREAT RACE* (1916)
BY MADISON GRANT

We have shown that the Mediterranean race entered Europe from the south and forms part of a great group of peoples extending into southern Asia, that the Alpine race came from the east through Asia Minor and the valley of the Danube, and that its present European distribution is merely the westernmost point of an ethnic pyramid, the base of which rests solidly on the round skulled peoples of the great plateaux of central Asia. Both of these races are, therefore, western extensions of Asiatic subspecies, and neither of them can be considered as exclusively European.

With the remaining race, the Nordic, however, the case is different. This is a purely European type, and has developed its physical characters and its civilization within the confines of that continent. It is, therefore, the *Homo europoeus*, the white man par excellence. It is everywhere characterized by certain unique specializations, namely, blondness, wavy hair, blue eyes, fair skin, high and narrow and straight nose, which are associated with great stature, and a long skull, as well as with abundant head and body hair. . . .

THE EXPANSION OF THE NORDICS. The men of Nordic blood today form all the population of Scandinavian countries, and also a majority of the population of the British Isles, and are almost pure in type in Scotland and eastern and northern England. The Nordic realm includes all the northern third of France, with extensions into the fertile southwest; all the rich lowlands of Flanders; all Holland; the northern half of Germany, with extensions up the Rhine and down the Danube; and the north of Poland, and of Russia. Recent calculations show that there are about 90,000,000 of purely Nordic physical type in Europe out of a total population of 420,000,000.

Throughout southern Europe a Nordic nobility of Teutonic type everywhere forms the old aristocratic and military classes, or what now remains of them. These aristocrats, by as much as their blood is pure, are taller and blonder than the native populations, whether these be Alpine in central Europe or Mediterranean in Spain or in the south of France and Italy. . . .

Mental, spiritual, and moral traits are closely associated with the physical distinctions among the different European races, although like somatological [a branch of anthropology focused on the comparative study of human evolution, variation, and classification] characters, these spiritual attributes have in many cases gone astray. Enough remain, however, to show that certain races have special aptitudes for certain pursuits. The Alpine race is always and everywhere a race of peasants, an agricultural and never a maritime race. In fact, they only extend to salt water at the head of the Adriatic. The coastal and seafaring populations of north Europe are everywhere Nordic as far as the coast of Spain, and among Europeans this race is preeminently fitted to maritime pursuits. The Nordics are, all over the world, a race of soldiers, sailors, adventurers, and explorers, but above all, of rulers, organizers, and aristocrats in sharp contrast to the essentially peasant character of the Alpines. Chivalry and knighthood, and their still surviving but greatly impaired counter parts, are peculiarly Nordic traits, and feudalism, class distinctions, and race pride among Europeans are traceable for the most part to the north. The mental characteristics of the Mediterranean race are well known, and this race, while inferior in bodily stamina to both the Nordic and the Alpine, is probably the superior of both, certainly of the Alpines, in intellectual attainments. In the field of art its superiority to both the other European races is unquestioned. . . .

The continuity of physical traits and the limitation of the effects of environment to the individual only are now so thoroughly recognized by scientists that it is at most a question of time when the social consequences which result from such crossings will be generally understood by the public at large. As soon as the true bearing and import of the facts are appreciated by lawmakers, a complete change in our political structure will inevitably occur, and our present reliance on the influences of education will be superseded by a readjustment based on racial values.

Bearing in mind the extreme antiquity of physical and spiritual characters and the persistency with which they outlive those elements of environment termed language, nationality, and forms of government, we must consider the relation of these facts to the development of the race in America. We may be certain that the progress of evolution is in full operation today under those laws of nature which control it, and that the only sure guide to the future lies in the study of the operation of these laws in the past. We Americans must realize that the altruistic ideals which have controlled our social development during the past century, and the maudlin sentimentalism that has made America "an asylum for the oppressed," are sweeping the nation toward a racial abyss. If the Melting Pot is allowed to boil without control, and we continue to follow our national motto and deliberately blind ourselves to all "distinctions of race, creed, or color," the type of native American of Colonial descent will be come as extinct as the Athenian of the age of Pericles, and the Viking of the days of Rollo.

Defining New York's "Cultural Pluralism"

Some New Yorkers and other Americans were uneasy as the number of newcomers from foreign lands increased. Many of the new immigrants hailed from southern and eastern Europe rather than northern and western Europe—for example, English and Germans—like most of the previous waves of immigrations. Would the newcomers "assimilate," maintaining what some called the American "melting pot"? Or would they cluster together in ethnic groups and cling to their own languages and culture? Edward A. Ross's 1914 book The Old World in the New *raised the specter of new immigrants threatening America's sense of identity. It was moderate in tone but previewed the sort of analysis of Madison Grant's* The Passing of the Great Race *(summarized above) would advance two years later.*

Political philosopher Horace M. Kallen (1882–1974) refuted Ross and others like him in an eloquent 1915 essay, "Democracy Versus the Melting Pot." Kallen suggested that history demonstrated that people from different cultures and backgrounds could blend smoothly into a pluralistic society. Minority groups can maintain some of their distinctive cultural identities and at the same time fit into the majority culture—for example, through use of the English language, public education, and ubiquitous ready-made clothes. America should not aim to be a "melting pot" where all cultures were amalgamated into one "American" culture. Instead, said Kallen, America would be like an orchestra, a "culture of cultures" in a sense, richer and stronger because of the newcomers.

Kallen later used the term "cultural pluralism" to describe his concept and expanded his ideas into a book. It was a good fit for progressive-era

New York. Kallen was persuasive and the New York progressive community quickly endorsed and disseminated his ideas. Kallen moved from Wisconsin to New York and was a founding member of the New School for Social Research in 1919.

∽

FROM "DEMOCRACY VERSUS THE MELTING POT," *THE NATION* (1915) BY HORACE KALLEN

Immigrants appear to pass through four phases in the course of being Americanized. In the first phase they exhibit economic eagerness, the greed of the unfed. Since external differences are a handicap in the economic struggle, they "assimilate," seeking thus to facilitate the attainment of economic independence. Once the proletarian level of such independence is reached, the process of assimilation slows down and tends to come to a stop. The immigrant group is still a national group, modified, sometimes improved, by environmental influences, but otherwise a solitary spiritual unit, which is seeking to find its way out on its own social level. This search brings to light permanent group distinctions, and the immigrant, like the Anglo-Saxon American, is thrown back upon himself and his ancestry.

Then a process of dissimilation begins. The arts, life, and ideals of the nationality become central and paramount; ethnic and national differences change in status from disadvantages to distinctions. All the while the immigrant has been using the English language and behaving like an American in matters economic and political, and continues to do so. The institutions of the Republic have become the liberating cause and the background for the rise of the cultural consciousness and social autonomy of the immigrant Irishman, German, Scandinavian, Jew, Pole, or Bohemian. On the whole, Americanization has not repressed nationality. Americanization has liberated nationality. . . .

We are, in fact, at the parting of the ways. A genuine social alternative is before us, either of which parts we may realize if we will. In social construction the will is father to the fact, for the fact is nothing more than the concord or conflict of wills. What do we will to make of the United States—a unison, singing the old Anglo-Saxon theme "America," the America of the New England school, or a harmony, in which that theme shall be dominant, perhaps, among others, but one among many, not the only one? The mind reverts helplessly to the historic attempts at unison in Europe—the heroic failure of the pan-Hellenists, of the Romans, the disintegration and the diversification of the Christian Church, for a time the most successful unison in history; the present-day failures of Germany and of Russia.

Here, however, the whole social situation is favorable, as it has never been at any time elsewhere—everything is favorable but the basic law of America itself, and the spirit of American institutions. To achieve unison—it can be achieved—would be to violate these. For the end determines the means, and this end would involve no other means than those used by Germany in Poland, in Schleswig-Holstein, and Alsace-Lorraine; by Russia in the Pale, in Poland, in Finland. Fundamentally it would require the complete nationalization of education, the abolition of every form of parochial and private school, the abolition of instruction in other tongues than English, and the concentration of the teaching of history and literature upon the English tradition. The other institutions of society would require treatment analogous to that administered by Germany to her European acquisitions. And all of this, even if meeting with no resistance, would not completely guarantee the survival as a unison of the older Americanism. For the program would be applied to diverse ethnic types, and the reconstruction that, with the best will, they might spontaneously make of the tradition would more likely than not be a far cry from the original. It is, already.

The notion that the program might be realized by radical and even enforced miscegenation, by the creation of the melting-pot by law, and thus the development of the new "American race," is, as Mr. Ross points out, as mystically optimistic as it is ignorant. In historic times, so far as we know, no new ethic types have originated, and what we know of breeding gives us no assurance of the disappearance of the old types in favor of the new, only the addition of a new type, if it succeeds in surviving, to the already existing older ones. Biologically, life does not unify; biologically, life diversifies; and it is sheer ignorance to apply social analogies to biological processes.

In any event, we know what the qualities and capacities of existing types are; we know how by education to do something towards the repression of what is evil in them and the conservation of what is good. The "American race" is a totally unknown thing; to presume that it will be better because (if we like to persist in the illusion that it is coming) it will be later, is no different from imagining that, because contemporary, Russia is better than ancient Greece.

There is nothing more to be said to the pious stupidity that identifies recency with goodness. The unison to be achieved cannot be a unison of ethnic types. It must be, if it is to be at all, a unison of social and historic interests, established by the complete cutting-off of the ancestral memories of our populations, the enforced, exclusive use of the English language and English and American history in the schools and in the daily life. The attainment of the other alternative, a harmony, also requires concerted public action. But the action would do no violence to our fundamental law and the spirit of our institutions, nor to the qualities of men. It would seek simply to eliminate the waste and the stupidity of our social organization, by way of freeing and strengthening the strong forces already in operation. Starting with our existing ethnic and cultural groups, it would seek to provide conditions under which each may attain the perfection that is proper to its kind. The provision of such conditions is the primary intent of our fundamental law and the function of our institutions. And the various nationalities which compose our commonwealth must first of all learn this fact, which is perhaps, to most minds, the outstanding ideal content of "Americanism"—that democracy means self-realization through self-control, self-government, and that one is impossible without the other. For the application of this principle, which is realized in a harmony of societies, there are European analogies also. I omit Austria and Turkey, for the union of nationalities is there based more on inadequate force than on consent, and the form of their organization is alien to ours. I think of England and of Switzerland. England is a state of four nationalities—the English, Welsh, Scotch, and Irish (if one considers the Empire, of many more), and while English history is not unmarred by attempts at unison, both the home policy and the imperial policy have, since the Boer War, been realized more and more upon the voluntary and autonomous cooperation of the component nationalities.

Switzerland is a state of three nationalities, a republic as the United States is, far more democratically governed, concentrated in an area not much different in size. I suspect, from New York city, with a population not far from it in total. Yet Switzerland has the most loyal citizens in Europe. Their language, literary and spiritual traditions are on the one side German, on another Italian, on a third side French. And in terms of social organization, of economic prosperity, of public education, of the general level of culture, Switzerland is the most successful democracy in the world. It conserves and encourages individuality. The reason lies, I think, in the fact that in Switzerland the conception of "natural rights" operates, consciously or unconsciously, as a generalization from the unalterable data of human nature.

What is inalienable in the life of mankind is its intrinsic positive quality—its psychophysical inheritance. Men may change their clothes, their politics, their wives, their religions, their philosophies, to a greater or lesser extent: they cannot change their grandfathers. Jews or Poles or Anglo-Saxons, would have to cease to be. The selfhood which is inalienable in them, and for the realization of which they require "inalienable" liberty, is ancestrally determined, and the happiness which they pursue has its form implied in ancestral endowment. This is what, actually, democracy in operation assumes. There are human capacities which it is the function of the state to liberate and to protect; and the failure of the state as a government means its abolition. Government, the state, under the democratic conception, is merely an instrument, not an end. That it is often an abused instrument, that it is often seized by the powers that prey, that it makes frequent mistakes and considers only secondary ends, surface needs, which vary from moment to moment, is, of course, obvious; hence our social and political chaos. But that it is an instrument, flexibly adjustable to changing life, changing opinion, and needs, our whole electoral organization and party system declare.

And as intelligence and wisdom prevail over "politics" and special interests, as the steady and continuous pressure of the inalienable qualities and purposes of human groups more and more dominate the confusion of our common life, the outlines of a possible great and truly democratic commonwealth become discernible. Its form is that of the Federal republic; its substance a democracy of nationalities, cooperating voluntarily and autonomously in the enterprise of self-realization through the perfection of men according to their kind. The common language of the commonwealth, the language of its great political tradition, is English, but each nationality expresses its emotional and voluntary life in its own language, in its own inevitable aesthetic and intellectual forms. The common life of the commonwealth is politico-economic, and serves as the foundation and background for the realization of the distinctive individuality of each nation that composes it.

Thus "American civilization" may come to mean the perfection of the cooperative harmonies of "European civilization," the waste, the squalor, and the distress of Europe being eliminated—a multiplicity in a unity, an orchestration of mankind. As in an orchestra, every type of instrument has its specific timbre and tonality, founded in its substance and form; as every type has its appropriate theme and melody in the whole symphony, so in society each ethnic group is the natural instrument, its spirit and culture are its theme and melody, and the harmony and dissonances and discords of them all make the symphony of civilization, with this difference: a musical symphony is written before it is played; in the symphony of civilization the playing is the writing, so that there is nothing so fixed and inevitable about its progressions as in music, so that within the limits set by nature they may vary at will, and the range and variety of the harmonies may become wider and richer and more beautiful.

But the question is, do the dominant classes in America want such a society?

Sources

Blaustein, David, "The Making of Americans," November 19, 1903, in Miriam Blaustein, ed., *Memoirs of David Blaustein: Educator and Communal Worker* (New York: McBride, Nast & Co., 1913), 127, 133–37. Available at HathiTrust, https://catalog.hathitrust.org/Record/100484506.

Cahan, Abraham, *The Rise of David Levinsky* (New York: Harper & Brothers, 1917), 86–90, 93, 95. Available at Project Gutenberg, https://www.gutenberg.org/files/2803/2803.txt.

Grant, Madison, *The Passing of the Great Race* (New York: Charles Scribner's Sons, 1916), 150, 170, 197–98, 227–28. Available at HathiTrust, Https://babel.hathitrust.org/cgi/pt?id=mdp.39015005011880&view=page&seq=9.

Kallen, Horace M., "Democracy Versus the Melting Pot: A Study of American Nationality," *The Nation* 100 (February 25, 1915), 218–20, New School for Social Research, http://newschoolhistories.org/wp-content/uploads/2018/04/kallen_democracyvmeltingpot.pdf.

Ravage, Marcus Eli, *An American in the Making: The Life Story of an Immigrant* (New York: Harper and Brothers, 1917) Introduction, 173–78. Available at HathiTrust, https://babel.hathitrust.org/cgi/pt?id=yale.39002003576460&view=page&seq=9.

Report of the Commission of Immigration of the State of New York (Albany: J. B. Lyon, 1909), 4–7, 12–15, Available at HathiTrust, https://babel.hathitrust.org/cgi/pt?id=ucl.b3126386&view=page&seq=7. (Note: Several long footnotes in the original have been omitted here.)

Speranza, Gino Carlo, "Solving the Immigration Problem," *Outlook* 76 (April 19, 1904), 928–33. Available at HathiTrust, https://babel.hathitrust.org/cgi/pt?id=nyp.33433081671459&view=page&seq=7.

7

Reckoning with Race

Figures 7a and 7b. Civil rights activist and writer W. E. B. Du Bois (left) and educator Elise Johnson McDougald (right) were leaders in the campaign for equality for Blacks in New York and across the nation. *Source:* National Portrait Gallery.

Blacks constituted a sizeable minority in the state's cities, particularly New York City. New York was more tolerant than most places in the nation, but Blacks experienced considerable prejudice and racism, some of it overt, some less obvious. There was de facto housing and school segregation. Many Blacks were trapped in menial jobs; advancing was a challenge because skin color held them back. Blacks were discouraged from entering many hotels and restaurants, sometimes by being refused service, other times by being told facilities were full. That was illegal under New York's civil rights laws, but Blacks seldom forced the issue in courts. There were also other forms of racism and discrimination. New York fell far short of racial equality.

But three countervailing trends made New York different. One, in part because of massive immigration from Europe, New York City was much more diverse than most other cities and New York State was more diverse than other states. This predisposed people toward acceptance and toleration. Two, the Harlem area of northern Manhattan was becoming an enclave of outstanding Black musical, artistic, and literary talent in what was soon called the "Harlem Renaissance." Three, a new campaign for racial equality and justice was spearheaded by a group of determined reformers, mostly New Yorkers, who founded the National Association for the Advancement of Colored People (NAACP) in 1909 and the Committee on Urban Conditions Among Negroes (which soon evolved into the National Urban League) in 1910.

Note: In the texts that follow, writers sometimes used the terms *Negro, Negro Race*, and *colored*, which were in common use at that time.

Probing Black New Yorkers' Burdens

Suffragist and social reformer Mary White Ovington (1865–1951) was a strong proponent of the rights of Black Americans. She was one of the founders of the NAACP in New York City in 1909 and later served as a board member, executive secretary, and chairman. An investigator and writer, she published a study in 1911 of the condition of Blacks living in New York City, excerpted below.

Ovington showed the realities in New York of community segregation, substandard education, and obstacles to obtaining employment and advancing in professional career fields. The title she chose for her book, Half a Man: The Status of the Negro in New York, *denoted her thesis that New York needed to do much better.*

In her concluding chapter, she noted the prevalence of white prejudice against young Blacks from the time they started grade school. This type of prejudice got minority children off to a weak start in life. But at the end

Ovington expressed hope that New York's "cosmopolitan spirit" would one day mean full equality for its Black residents.

∽

FROM *HALF A MAN: THE STATUS OF THE NEGRO IN NEW YORK* (1911) BY MARY WHITE OVINGTON

A new little boy came two years ago into our story-book world. When Miss North, taking Ezekiel by the hand, led him into her school-room, we met a child full of what we call temperament; dreaming quaint stories, innocently friendly, anxious to please for affection's sake, in his unconscious way something of a genius. We saw his big musing eyes looking out upon a world in which his teacher stood serene and reasoning, but a little cold like her name; his friend, Miss Jane, kind and very practical; his employer, Mr. Rankin, amused and contemptuous; all watching him with the impersonal interest with which one might view a new species in the animal world. For Ezekiel, unlike our other story-book boys, had a double being, he was first Ezekiel Jordan, a little black boy, and second, a Representative of the Negro Race.

Ezekiel was too young to understand his position, but the white world about him never forgot it. When he arrived late to school, he was a dilatory representative; when, obliging little soul, he promised three people to weed their gardens all the same afternoon, he was a prevaricating representative. He never happened to steal ice cream from the hoky-poky man or to play hookey, but if he had, he would have been a thieving and lazy representative. Always he was something remote and overwhelming, not a natural growing boy.

Ezekiel's position is that of each Negro child and man and woman in the United States today. I think we have seen this as we have reviewed the position of the race in New York; indeed, the very fact of our attempting such a review is patent that we see and feel it. We white Americans do not generalize concerning ourselves, we individualize, leaving generalizations to the chance visitor, but we generalize continually concerning colored Americans; we classify and measure and pass judgment, a little more with each succeeding year.

Now if we are going to do this, let us be fair; let us try as much as possible to dismiss prejudice, and to look at the Ezekiels entering our school of life, with the same impartiality and the same understanding sympathy with which we look upon our own race. And if we are to place them side by side with the whites, let us be impartial, not cheating them out of their hard-earned credits, or condemning them with undue severity. Let us try, if we can, to be just.

When we begin to make this effort to judge fairly our colored world, we need to remember especially two things: First, that we cannot yet measure with any accuracy the capability of the colored man in the United States, because he has not yet been given the opportunity to show his capability. If we deny full expression to a race, if we restrict its education, stifle its intellectual and aesthetic impulses, we make it impossible fairly to gauge its ability. Under these circumstances to measure its achievements with the more favored white race is unreasonable and unjust, as unreasonable as to measure against a man's a disfranchised woman's capabilities in directing the affairs of a state.

The second thing is difficult for us to remember, difficult for us at first to believe; that we, dominant, ruling Americans, may not be the persons best fitted to judge the Negro. We feel confident that we are, since we have known him so long and are so familiar with his peculiarities; but in moments of earnest reflection may it not occur to us that we have not the desire or the imagination to enter into the life emotions of others? "We are the intellect and virtue of the airth [earth], the cream of human natur', and the flower of moral force," Hannibal Chollup [a fictional character invented by English novelist Charles Dickins] still says, and glowers at the stranger who dares to suggest a different standard from his own. Hannibal Chollup and his ilk are ill-fitted to measure the refinements of feeling, the differences in ideals among people.

This question of our fitness to sit in the judgment seat must come with grave insistence when we read carefully the literature published in this city of New York within the past two years. Our writers have assumed such pomposity, have so reveled in what Mr. [English writer G. K.] Chesterton calls "the magnificent buttering of one's self all over with the same stale butter; the big defiance of small enemies," as to make their conclusions ridiculous. Ezekiel entering their school is at once pushed to the bottom of the class, while the white boy at the head, Hannibal Chollup's descendant, sings a jubilate of his own and butters himself so copiously as to be as shiny as his English cousin, Wackford Squeers [another Dickins character]. . . .

In short there is nothing evil that Ezekiel is not at the bottom of. Sometimes, poor little chap, he tries to sniffle out a word, to say that his family is doing well, that he has an uncle who is buying a home, and a rich cousin in the undertaking business, but such extenuating circumstances receive scant attention, and we are not surprised to find, the class dismissed, that Ezekiel and the millions whom he represents, are swiftly shuffled off the earth, victims of "disease, vice, and profound discouragement."

Now this is not an exaggerated picture of much that has recently been printed in newspaper and magazine, and does it not make us feel the paradox that if we are to judge the Negro fairly, we must not judge him at all, so little are we temperamentally capable of meeting the first requirement? "My brother Saxons," says [English poet] Matthew Arnold, "have a terrible way with them of wanting to improve everything but themselves off the face of the earth." And he adds, "I have no such passion for finding nothing but myself everywhere." Among our American writers a few, like Arnold, do not care to find only themselves everywhere, and these have told us a different story of the American Negro. They are poets and writers of fiction, men and women who are happy in meeting and appreciating different types of human beings.

If these writers were to instruct us, they would say that we must individualize more when we think of the black people about us, must differentiate. That, too, we must remember that when we pass judgment, we need to know whether our own standard is the best, whether we may not have something to learn from the standards of others. Supposing Ezekiel is deliberate and slow to make changes or to take risks; are we who are "acceleration mad," who acquire heart disease hustling to catch trains, who mortgage our farms to buy automobiles, who seek continually new sensations, really better than he? Is it not a matter of difference, just as we may each place in different order our desires, the one choosing struggle for power and the accumulation of wealth, the other preferring serenity and pleasure in the immediate present?

And lastly, after having praised our own virtues and our own ideals, must we not beware that we do not blame the Negro when he adopts them, that we do not turn upon him and fiercely demand only servile virtues, the virtues that make him useful not to himself but to us?

No one can talk for long of the Negro in America without propounding the all-embracing question, What will become of him, what will be the outcome of all this racial controversy? It is a daring person who attempts to answer. We, who have studied the Negro in New York, may perhaps venture to predict a little regarding his future in this city, his possible status in the later years of the century; whether he will lose in opportunity and social position, or whether he will advance in his struggle to be a man.

Looking upon the great population of the city, its varied races and nationalities, I confess that his outlook to me begins to be bright. New York is still to a quite remarkable extent dominated socially by its old American stock, its Dutch and Anglo-Saxon element. Few things strike the foreign visitor so forcibly as that despite its enormous European population, American society is homogeneous. But this is not likely to continue for very long. When the present demand for exhausting self-supporting work becomes less insistent, we shall feel in a deeper, more vital way the influence of our vast foreign life. With a million Jews and nearly a million Latin peoples, we cannot for long be held in the provincialism of today. I suspect that to many Europeans New York seems still a great overgrown village in "a nation of villagers," pronouncing with narrow, dogmatic assurance upon the deep unsolved problems of life.

But in the future it may take on a larger, more cosmopolitan spirit. Its Italians may bring a finer feeling for beauty and wholesome gayety, its Jews may continue to add great intellectual achievements, and its people of African descent, perhaps always few in number, may show with happy spontaneity their best and highest gifts. If New York really becomes a cosmopolitan city, let us believe the Negro will bring to it his highest genius and will walk through it simply, quietly, unnoticed, a man among men.

An Outburst of Cultural Achievement

The Harlem neighborhood in upper Manhattan became a mecca for Black families, musicians, artists, writers, and businessmen during the progressive era. An outburst of artistic, music, and literary creativity activity known as the "Harlem Renaissance" began there around 1920.

Alain Locke (1885–1954) was a New York writer and philosopher. He was the first Black American Rhodes Scholar, a professor at Howard University, a writer, and a champion of Black equality. Locke emphasized the need for more Black self-consciousness and political awareness and the value of self-expression and creativity. One of his contributions was to describe and call public attention to the "Harlem Renaissance," where he saw all those themes unfolding in the World War I era and the 1920s. He covered them in a landmark 1925 book, The New Negro. *The purpose of the book was to document the outstanding achievements of Black poets, artists, and writers, and it consisted mainly of samples of their works. Locke's "Foreword," reproduced in part below, set the stage.*

∼

FROM *THE NEW NEGRO: AN INTERPRETATION* (1925)
BY ALAIN LOCKE

This volume aims to document the New Negro culturally and socially, to register the transformations of the inner and outer life of the Negro in America that have so significantly taken place in the last few years. There is ample evidence of a New Negro in the latest phases of social change and progress, but still more in the internal world of the Negro mind and spirit. Here in the very heart of the folk-spirit are the essential forces, and folk interpretation is truly vital and representative only in terms of these. Of all the voluminous literature on the Negro, so much is mere external view and commentary that we may warrantably say that nine-tenths of it is about the Negro rather than of him, so that it is the Negro problem rather than the Negro that is known and mooted in the general mind. We turn therefore in the other direction to the elements of truest social portraiture, and discover in the artistic self-expression of the Negro today, a new figure on the national canvas and a new force in the foreground of affairs. Whoever wishes to see the Negro in his essential traits, in the full perspective of his achievement and possibilities, must seek the enlightenment of that self-portraiture which the present developments of Negro culture are offering. In these pages, without ignoring either the fact that there are important interactions between the national and the race life, or that the attitude of America toward the Negro is as important a factor as the attitude of the Negro toward America, we have nevertheless concentrated upon self-expression and the forces and motives of self-determination. So far as he is culturally articulate, we shall let the Negro speak for himself.

Yet the New Negro must be seen in the perspective of a New World, and especially of a New America. Europe seething in a dozen centers with emergent nationalities, Palestine full of nascent Judaism. These are no more alive with the progressive forces of our era than the quickened centers of the lives of black folk. America, seeking a new spiritual expansion and artistic maturity, trying to found an American literature, a national art, and national music implies a Negro-American culture seeking the same satisfactions and objectives. Separate as it may be in color and substance, the culture of the Negro is of a pattern integral with the times and with its cultural setting.

The achievements of the present generation have eventually made this apparent. Liberal minds today cannot be asked to peer with sympathetic curiosity into the darkened Ghetto of a segregated race life. That was yesterday. Nor must they expect to find a mind and soul bizarre and alien as the mind of a savage, or even as naive and refreshing as the mind of the peasant or the child. That too was yesterday, and the day before. Now that there is cultural adolescence and the approach to maturity. There has come a development that makes these phases of Negro life only an interesting and significant segment of the general American scene.

Until recently, except for occasional discoveries of isolated talent here and there, the main stream of this development has run in the special channels of "race literature" and "race journalism." Particularly as a literary movement, it has gradually gathered momentum in the effort and output of such progressive race periodicals as *Crisis* under the editorship of Dr. Du Bois and more lately, through the quickening encouragement of Charles Johnson, in the brilliant pages of *Opportunity, a Journal of Negro Life*. But more and more the creative talents of the race have been taken up into the general journalistic, literary and artistic agencies, as the wide range of the acknowledgments of the material here collected will in itself be sufficient to demonstrate. Recently in a project of *The Survey Graphic*, whose Harlem Number of March, 1925, has been taken by kind permission as the nucleus of this book, the whole movement was presented as it is epitomized in the progressive Negro community of the American metropolis. Enlarging this stage we are now presenting the New Negro in a national and even international scope. Although there are few centers that can be pointed out approximating Harlem's significance, the full significance of that even is a racial awakening on a national and perhaps even a world scale.

That is why our comparison is taken with those nascent movements of folk-expression and self-determination which are playing a creative part in the world today. The galvanizing shocks and reactions of the last few years are making by subtle processes of internal reorganization a race out of its own disunited and apathetic elements. A race experience penetrated in this way invariably flowers. As in India, in China, in Egypt, Ireland, Russia, Bohemia, Palestine and Mexico, we are witnessing the resurgence of a people. It has aptly been said, "For all who read the signs aright, such a dramatic flowering of a new race-spirit is taking place close at home, among American Negroes." Negro life is not only establishing new contacts and founding new centers, it is finding a new soul. There is a fresh spiritual and cultural focusing. We have, as the heralding sign, an unusual outburst of creative expression. There is a renewed race-spirit that consciously and proudly sets itself apart. Justifiably then, we speak of the offerings of this book embodying these ripening forces as culled from the first fruits of the Negro Renaissance.

The New Negro

. . . Take Harlem as an instance of this. Here in Manhattan is not merely the largest Negro community in the world, but the first concentration in history of so many diverse elements of Negro life. It has attracted the African, the West Indian, the Negro American; has brought together the Negro of the North and the Negro of the South; the man from the city and the man from the town and village; the peasant, the student, the business man, the professional man, artist, poet, musician, adventurer and worker, preacher and criminal, exploiter and social outcast. Each group has come with its own separate motives and for its own special ends, but their greatest experience has been the finding of one another. Proscription and prejudice have thrown these dissimilar elements into a common area of contact and interaction. Within this area, race sympathy and unity have determined a further fusing of sentiment and experience. So what began in terms of segregation becomes more and more, as its elements mix and react, the laboratory of a great race-welding. Hitherto, it must be admitted that American Negroes have been a race more in name than in fact, or to be exact, more in sentiment than in experience. The chief bond between them has been that of a common condition rather than a common consciousness; a problem in common rather than a life in common.

In Harlem, Negro life is seizing upon its first chances for group expression and self-determination. It is, or promises at least to be, a race capital. That is why our comparison is taken with those nascent centers of folk-expression and self-determination which are playing a creative part in the world today. Without pretense to their political significance, Harlem has the same role to play for the New Negro as Dublin has had for the New Ireland or Prague for the New Czechoslovakia. . . .

Harlem Becomes a Center of Black Culture

James Weldon Johnson (1871–1938) was a civil rights activist and writer. He began working for the NAACP in 1916 and served as its executive from 1920 to 1930. Johnson excelled in many areas. He was a lawyer, teacher, writer, and editor. He was known during the Harlem Renaissance for his poems, novel, and anthologies of the poems and spirituals of black writers. Later he taught at New York University and Fisk University.

One of his goals was to publicize Blacks' achievements, which he felt seldom received enough recognition in the public at large. This would achieve two things: encourage more Black self-confidence and creativity, and demonstrate to the white majority Blacks' accomplishments, contributions, and potential. His essay "Harlem: The Cultural Center," published in the 1925 book The New Negro, *edited by Black activist Alain Locke, reflected the progress and potential of Harlem in encouraging and showcasing Black talent. Harlem was becoming the "cultural center," something of a self-identified, self-contained center of achievement, said Johnson. That demonstrated the accomplishments and potential of Blacks, given opportunities and venues to excel.*

∼

From "Harlem: The Cultural Center," in Alain Locke, ed., The New Negro (1925) by James Weldon Johnson

In the history of New York, the significance of the name Harlem has changed from Dutch to Irish to Jewish to Negro. Of these changes, the last has come most swiftly. Throughout colored America, from Massachusetts to Mississippi, and across the continent to Los Angeles and Seattle, its name, which as late as fifteen years ago had scarcely been heard, now stands for the Negro metropolis. Harlem is indeed the great Mecca for the sight-seer, the pleasure-seeker, the curious, the adventurous, the enterprising, the ambitious and the talented of the whole Negro world; for the lure of it has reached down to every island of the Carib [Caribbean] Sea and has penetrated even into Africa.

In the make-up of New York, Harlem is not merely a Negro colony or community, it is a city within a city, the greatest Negro city in the world. It is not a slum or a fringe, it is located in the heart of Manhattan and occupies one of the most beautiful and healthful sections of the city.

It is not a "quarter" of dilapidated tenements, but is made up of new law apartments [built after the 1901 Tenement House Law, which required new buildings meet minimum space, ventilation, and other standards] and handsome dwellings, with well-paved and well-lighted streets. It has its own churches, social and civic centers, shops, theaters and other places of amusement. And it contains more Negroes to the square mile than any other spot on earth. A stranger who rides up magnificent Seventh Avenue on a bus or in an automobile must be struck with surprise at the transformation which takes place after he crosses One Hundred Twenty Fifth Street. Beginning there, the population suddenly darkens and he rides through twenty-five solid blocks where the passers-by, the shoppers, those sitting in restaurants, coming out of theaters, standing in doorways and looking out of windows are practically all Negroes; and then he emerges where the population as suddenly becomes white again. There is nothing just like it in any other city in the country, for there is no preparation for it; no change in the character of the houses and streets; no change, indeed, in the appearance of the people, except their color.

Negro Harlem is practically a development of the past decade, but the story behind it goes back a long way. There have always been colored people in New York. In the middle of the last century they lived in the vicinity of Lispenard, Broome and Spring Streets. When Washington Square and lower Fifth Avenue was the center of aristocratic life, the colored people, whose chief occupation was domestic service in the homes of the rich, lived in a fringe and were scattered in nests to the south, east and west of the square. As late as the 1888's, the major part of the colored population lived in Sullivan, Thompson, Bleecker, Grove, Minetta Lane and adjacent streets. It is curious to note that some of these nests still persist. In a number of the blocks of Greenwich Village and Little Italy may be found small groups of Negroes who have never lived in any other section of the city. By about 1890 the center of colored population had shifted to the upper Twenties and lower Thirties west of Sixth Avenue. Ten years later another considerable shift northward had been made to West Fifty-third Street.

The West Fifty-third Street settlement deserves some special mention because it ushered in a new phase of life among colored New Yorkers. Three rather well-appointed hotels were opened in the street and they quickly became the centers of a sort of fashionable life that hitherto had not existed. On Sunday evenings these hotels served dinner to music and attracted crowds of well-dressed diners. One of these hotels, The Marshall, became famous as the headquarters of Negro talent. There gathered the actors, the musicians, the composers, the writers, the singers, dancers and vaudevillians. There one went to get a close-up of Williams and Walker, Cole and Johnson, Ernest Hogan, Will Marion Cook, Jim Europe, Aida Overton, and of others equally and less known. Paul Laurence Dunbar was frequently there whenever he was in New York. Numbers of those who love to shine by the light reflected from celebrities were always to be found. The first modern jazz band ever heard in New York, or, perhaps anywhere, was organized at The Marshall. It was a playing-singing-dancing orchestra, making the first dominant use of banjos, saxophones, clarinets and trap drums in combination, and was called The Memphis Students. Jim Europe was a member of that band, and out of it grew the famous Clef Club, of which he was the noted leader, and which for a long time monopolized the business of "entertaining" private parties and furnishing music for the new dance craze. Also in the Clef Club was "Buddy" Gilmore who originated trap drumming as it is now practiced, and set hundreds of white men to juggling their sticks and doing acrobatic stunts while they manipulated a dozen other noise-making devices aside from their drums. A good many well-known white performers frequented The Marshall and for seven or eight years the place was one of the sights of New York.

The move to Fifty-third Street was the result of the opportunity to get into newer and better houses. About 1900 the move to Harlem began, and for the same reason. Harlem had been overbuilt with large, new-law apartment houses, but rapid transportation to that section was very inadequate. The Lenox Avenue Subway had not yet been built and landlords were finding difficulty in keeping houses on the east side of the section filled. Residents along and near Seventh Avenue were fairly well served by the Eighth Avenue Elevated [railroad] A colored man, in the real estate business at this time, Philip A. Payton, approached several of these landlords with the proposition that he would fill their empty or partially empty houses with steady colored tenants. The suggestion was accepted, and one or two houses on One Hundred and Thirty-fourth Street east of Lenox Avenue were taken over. Gradually other houses were filled. The whites paid little attention to the movement until it began to spread west of Lenox Avenue; they then took steps to check it. They proposed through a financial organization, the Hudson Realty Company, to buy up all properties occupied by colored people and evict the tenants. The Negroes countered by similar methods. Payton formed the Afro-American Realty Company, a Negro corporation organized for the purpose of buying and leasing houses for occupancy by colored people. Under this counter stroke the opposition subsided for several years. . . .

The question naturally arises, "Are the Negroes going to be able to hold Harlem?" If they have been steadily driven northward for the past hundred years and out of less desirable sections, can they hold this choice bit of Manhattan Island? It is hardly probable that Negroes will hold Harlem indefinitely, but when they are forced out it will not be for the same reasons that forced them out of former quarters in New York City. The situation is entirely different and without precedent. When colored people do leave Harlem, their homes, their churches, their investments and their businesses, it will be because the land has become so valuable they can no longer afford to live on it. But the date of another move northward is very far in the future. What will Harlem be and become in the meantime? Is there danger that the Negro may lose his economic status in New York and be unable to hold his property? Will Harlem become merely a famous ghetto, or will it be a center of intellectual, cultural and economic forces exerting an influence throughout the world, especially upon Negro peoples? Will it become a point of friction between the races in New York?

I think there is less danger to the Negroes of New York of losing out economically and industrially than to the Negroes of any large city in the North. In most of the big industrial centers Negroes are engaged in gang labor. They are employed by thousands in the stockyards in Chicago, by thousands in the automobile plants in Detroit; and in those cities they are likely to be the first to be let go, and in thousands, with every business depression. In New York there is hardly such a thing as gang labor among Negroes, except among the longshoremen and it is in the longshoremen's unions, above all others, that Negroes stand on an equal footing. Employment among Negroes in New York is highly diversified; in the main they are employed more as individuals than as non-integral parts of a gang. Furthermore, Harlem is gradually becoming more and more a self-supporting community. Negroes there are steadily branching out into new businesses and enterprises in which Negroes are employed. So the danger of great numbers of Negroes being thrown out of work at once, with a resulting economic crisis among them, is less in New York than in most of the large cities of the North to which Southern migrants have come.

These facts have an effect which goes beyond the economic and industrial situation. They have a direct bearing on the future character of Harlem and on the question as to whether Harlem will be a point of friction between the races in New York. It is true that Harlem is a Negro community, well defined and stable; anchored to its fixed homes, churches, institutions, business and amusement places; having its own working, business and professional classes. It is experiencing a constant growth of group consciousness and community feeling. Harlem is, therefore, in many respects, typically Negro. It has many unique characteristics. It has movement, color, gayety, singing, dancing, boisterous laughter and loud talk. One of its outstanding features is brass band parades. Hardly a Sunday passes but that there are several of these parades of which many are gorgeous with regalia and insignia. Almost any excuse will do—the death of a humble member of the Elks, the laying of a cornerstone, the "turning out" of the order of this or that. In many of these characteristics it is similar to the Italian colony. But withal, Harlem grows more metropolitan and more apart of New York all the while. Why is it then that its tendency is not to become a mere "quarter?"

I shall give three reasons that seem to me to be important in their order. First, the language of Harlem is not alien; it is not Italian or Yiddish; it is English. Harlem talks American, reads American, thinks American. Second, Harlem is not physically a "quarter." It is not a section cut off. It is merely a zone through which four main arteries of the city run. Third, the fact that there is little or no gang labor gives Harlem Negroes the opportunity for individual expansion and individual contacts with the life and spirit of New York. A thousand Negroes from Mississippi put to work as a gang in a Pittsburgh steel mill will for a long time remain a thousand Negroes from Mississippi. Under the conditions that prevail in New York they would all within six months become New Yorkers. The rapidity with which Negroes become good New Yorkers is one of the marvels to observers.

New York's Racial Ambivalence

Walter White (1893–1955) was widely recognized as one the twentieth century's leading civil rights leaders. He was born in Atlanta but moved north, joined the staff of the NAACP in New York in 1918, and served as head of the organization from 1929 to 1955. He spoke out against discrimination and segregation and was a prominent critic of lynching. He favored the full participation of Black people in American culture and society.

White identified and was regarded as a Black man. Because his skin tone was light, though, he could sometimes "pass" as a white person. His writings reflected the complexity of his racial perspective and the diversity of New York City. He was ambivalent about his city, where easy-going toleration mixed with blatant racism. Many Blacks were gravitating to Harlem, which was becoming a center of Black culture and art, part of the city and yet marked by distinctiveness.

The article excerpted below, which he wrote for Alain Locke's edited 1925 book The New Negro, *reflected New York's racial complexity. White attended a theater performance by rising Black actor and singer Paul Robeson in 1924, but afterward he and his party went to Harlem for an after-performance meal rather than be shunned by restaurants in Manhattan. White uses the incident to reflect on the nature and impact of prejudice. White concluded, though, that complex New York was "as nearly ideal a place for colored people as exists in America."*

∽

From "The Paradox of Color," in Alain Locke, ed., The New Negro (1925) by Walter White

The hushed tenseness within the theater was broken only by the excited chattering between the scenes which served as oases of relief. One reassured himself by touching his neighbor or gripping the edge of the bench as a magnificently proportioned Negro on the tiny Provincetown Theatre stage, with a voice of marvelous power and with a finished artistry enacted Eugene O'Neill's epic of human terror, *The Emperor Jones*. For years I had nourished the conceit that nothing in or of the theater could thrill me. I was sure my years of theater-going had made me immune to the tricks and the trappings which managers and actors use to get their tears and smiles and laughs. A few seasons ago my shell of conceit was cracked a little in that third act of Karel Capek's *R. U. R.* [a 1920 science fiction play] when Rossum's automatons swarmed over the parapet to wipe out the last human being. But the chills that chased each other up and down my spine then were only pleasurable tingles compared to the sympathetic terror evoked by Paul Robeson [in a scene in *The Emperor Jones*] as he fled blindly through the impenetrable forest of the "West Indian island not yet self-determined by white marines" [the setting for the play].

Nor was I alone. When, after remaining in darkness from the second through the eighth and final scene, the house was flooded with light, a concerted sigh of relief welled up from all over the theater. With real joy we heard the reassuring roar of taxicabs and muffled street noises of Greenwich Village and knew we were safe in New York. Wave after wave of applause, almost hysterical with relief, brought Paul Robeson time and time again before the curtain to receive the acclaim his art had merited. Almost shyly he bowed again and again. as the storm of handclapping and bravos surged and broke upon the tiny stage. His color—his race—all were forgotten by those he had stirred so deeply with his art.

Outside in narrow, noisy Macdougal Street the four of us stood. Mrs. Robeson, alert, intelligent, merry, an expert chemist for years in one of New York's leading hospitals; Paul Robeson, clad now in conventional tweeds in place of the ornate, gold-laced trappings of the Emperor Jones; my wife and I. We wanted supper and a place to talk. All about us blinked invitingly the lights of restaurants and inns of New York's Bohemia.

Place after place was suggested and discarded. Here a colored man and his companion had been made to wait interminably until, disgusted, they had left. There a party of four colored people, all university graduates, had been told flatly by the proprietress, late of North Carolina, she did not serve [offensive term for Black people]. At another, other colored people had been stared at so rudely they had bolted their food and left in confusion. The Civil Rights Act of New York would have protected us, but we were too much under the spell of the theater we had just quitted to want to insist on the rights the law gave us. So we mounted a bus and rode seven miles or more to colored Harlem where we could be served with food without fear of insult or contumely. The man whose art had brought homage to his feet from sophisticated New York could not enter even the cheapest of the eating places of lower New York with the assurance that some unpleasantness might not come to him before he left.

What does race prejudice do to the inner man of him who is the victim of that prejudice? What is the feeling within the breasts of the Paul Robesons, the Roland Hayes's, the Harry Burleighs [two Black composers and singers], as they listen to the applause of those whose kind receive them as artists but refuse to accept them as men? It is of this inner conflict of the black man in America, or, more specifically in New York City, I shall try to speak. I approach my task with reluctance. It is no easy matter to picture that effect which race or color prejudice has on the Negro of fineness of soul who is its victim. Of wounds to the flesh it is easy to speak. It is not difficult to tell of lynchings and injustices and race proscription. Of wounds to the spirit which are a thousand times more deadly and cruel it is impossible to tell in entirety. On the one hand lies the Scylla of bathos and on the other the Charybdis of insensitivity to subtler shadings of the spirit. If I can evoke in your mind a picture of what results proscription has brought, I am content.

With its population made up of peoples from every corner of the earth, New York City is, without doubt, more free from ordinary manifestations of prejudice than any other city in the United States. Its Jewish, Italian, German, French, Greek, Czechoslovakian, Irish, Hungarian quarters with their teeming thousands and hundreds of thousands form so great a percentage of the city's population that "white, Gentile, Protestant" Nordics have but little opportunity to develop their prejudices as they do, for example, in Mississippi or the District of Columbia. . . . New York's polyglot population . . . by a curious anomaly, has created more nearly than any other section that democracy which is the proud boast but rarely practiced accomplishment of these United States. The Ku Klux Klan has made but little headway in New York City for the very simple reason that the proscribed outnumber the proscribers. Thus race prejudice cannot work its will upon Jew or Catholic or Negro, as in other more genuinely American centers. This combined with the fact that most people in New York are so busy they haven't time to spend in hating other people, makes New York as nearly ideal a place for colored people as exists in America.

Despite these alleviating causes, however, New York is in the United States where prejudice appears to be indigenous. Its population includes many Southern whites who have brought North with them their hatreds. There are here many whites who are not Southern but whose minds have indelibly fixed upon them the stereotype of a Negro. . . . From these the Negro knows he is ever in danger of insult or injury. This situation creates various attitudes of mind among those who are its victims. Upon most the acquisition of education and culture, of wealth and sensitiveness causes a figurative and literal withdrawal, as far as is humanly possible or as necessity permits, from all contacts with the outside world where unpleasant situations may arise. This naturally means the development of an intensive Negro culture and a definitely bounded city within a city. Doubtless there are some advantages, but it is certain that such voluntary segregation works a greater loss upon those within and those without the circle.

Upon those within, it cuts off to a large extent the world of music, of the theater, of most of those contacts which mean growth and development and which denied, mean stagnation and spiritual atrophy. It develops as well a tendency towards self-pity, towards a fatal conviction that they of all peoples are most oppressed.

The harmful effects of such reactions are too obvious to need elaboration. Upon those without, the results are equally mischievous. First there is the loss of that deep spirituality, that gift of song and art, that indefinable thing which perhaps can best be termed the over-soul of the Negro, which has given America the only genuinely artistic things which the world recognizes as distinctive American contributions to the arts. . . .

Black Women Cope with Racism

Elise Johnson McDougald (1885–1971), a New York City writer and educator, was a pioneering teacher and the first Black principal in the city. In a 1925 essay, she discussed the obstacles Black women faced, particularly in the workplace, and their perseverance in dealing with them. She called their dilemma "the double task"—fighting racism and sexual discrimination. Her insights are particularly valuable because she encountered and coped with both forms of discrimination. Her life story is something of a model of perseverance and achievement.

Black women had two burdens to bear, their gender and their skin color, McDougald explained, but they persevered. They were making headway in New York City and particularly in Harlem, which was becoming a mecca for Black men and women. McDougald concluded there was cause for optimism and faith in progress.

∽

From "The Double Task: The Struggle of Negro Women for Sex and Race Emancipation," *Survey Graphic: Harlem Number 1* (1925) by Elise Johnson McDougald

Throughout the long years of history, woman has been the weather-vane, the indicator, showing in which direction the wind of destiny blows. Her status and development have augured now calm and stability, now swift currents of progress. What then is to be said of the Negro woman today?

In Harlem, more than anywhere else, the Negro woman is free from the cruder handicaps of primitive household hardships and the grosser forms of sex and race subjugation. Here she has considerable opportunity to measure her powers in the intellectual and industrial fields of the great city. Here the questions naturally arise: "What are her problems?" and "How is she solving them?"

To answer these questions, one must have in mind not any one Negro woman, but rather a colorful pageant of individuals, each differently endowed. Like the red and yellow of the tiger-lily, the skin of one is brilliant against the star-lit darkness of a racial sister. From grace to strength, they vary in infinite degree, with traces of the race's history left in physical and mental outline on each. With a discerning mind, one catches the multiform charm, beauty and character of Negro phenomenon; and grasps the fact that their problem cannot be thought of in mass.

Because only a few have caught this vision, the attitude of mind of most New Yorkers causes the Negro woman serious difficulty. She is conscious that what is left of chivalry is not directed toward her. She realizes that the ideals of beauty, built up in the fine arts, exclude her almost entirely. Instead, the grotesque Aunt Jemimas [a racist advertising stereotype] of the streetcar advertisements proclaim only an ability to serve, without grace or loveliness. Nor does the drama catch her finest spirit. She is most often used to provoke the mirthless laugh of ridicule; or to portray feminine viciousness or vulgarity not peculiar to Negroes.

This is the shadow over her. To a race naturally sunny comes the twilight of self-doubt and a sense of personal inferiority. It cannot be denied that these are potent and detrimental influences, though not generally recognized because they are in the realm of the mental and spiritual. More apparent are the economic handicaps which follow her recent entrance into industry. It is conceded that she has special difficulties because of the poor working conditions and low wages of her men. It is not surprising that only the determined women forge ahead to results other than mere survival. The few who do prove their mettle stimulate one to a closer study of how this achievement is won in Harlem.

Better to visualize the Negro woman at her job, our vision of a host of individuals must once more resolve itself into groups on the basis of activity. First, comes a very small leisure group the wives and daughters of men who are in business, in the professions and in a few well-paid personal service occupations. Second, a most active and progressive group, the women in business and the professions. Third, the many women in the trades and industry. Fourth, a group weighty in numbers struggling on in domestic service, with an even less fortunate fringe of casual workers, fluctuating with the economic temper of the times.

The first is a pleasing group to see. It is picked for outward beauty by Negro men with much the same feeling as other Americans of the same economic class. [Because men keep] their women free to preside over the family, these women are affected by the problems of every wife and mother, but touched only faintly by their race's hardships. They do share acutely in the prevailing difficulty of finding competent household help. Negro wives find Negro maids unwilling generally to work in their own neighborhoods, for various reasons. They do not wish to work where there is a possibility of acquaintances coming into contact with them while they serve and they still harbor the misconception that Negroes of any station are unable to pay as much as persons of the other race. It is in these homes of comparative ease that we find the polite activities of social exclusiveness. The luxuries of well-appointed homes, modest motors, tennis, golf and country clubs, trips to Europe and California, make for social standing. The problem confronting the refined Negro family is to know others of the same achievement. The search for kindred spirits gradually grows less difficult; in the past it led to the custom of visiting all the large cities in order to know similar groups of cultured Negro people.

A spirit of stress and struggle characterizes the second two groups. These women of business, profession and trade are the hub of the wheel of progress. Their burden is twofold. Many are wives and mothers whose husbands are insufficiently paid, or who have succumbed to social maladjustment and have abandoned their families. An appalling number are widows. They face the great problem of leaving home each day and at the same time trying to rear children in their spare time this too in neighborhoods where rents are large, standards of dress and recreation high and costly, and social danger on the increase.

The great commercial life of New York City is only slightly touched by the Negro woman of our second group. Negro business men offer her most of their work, but their number is limited. Outside of this field, custom is once more against her and competition is keen for all. However Negro girls are training and some are holding exceptional jobs. One of the professors in a New York college has had a young colored woman as secretary for the past three years. Another holds the head clerical position in an organization where reliable handling of detail and a sense of business ethics are essential. For four years she has steadily advanced. Quietly these women prove their worth, so that when a vacancy exists and there is a call, it is difficult to find even one competent colored secretary who is not employed. As a result of opportunity in clerical work in the educational system of New York City a number have qualified for such positions, one being appointed within the year to the office work of a high school. In other departments the civil service in New York City is no longer free from discrimination. The casual personal interview, that tenacious and retrogressive practice introduced in the Federal administration during the World War has spread and often nullifies the Negro woman's success in written tests. The successful young woman just cited above was three times "turned down" as undesirable on the basis of the personal interview. In the great mercantile houses, the many young Negro girls who might be well suited to salesmanship are barred from all but the menial positions. Even so, one Negro woman, beginning as a uniformed maid, has pulled herself up to the position of "head of stock."

Again, the telephone and insurance companies which receive considerable patronage from Negroes deny them proportionate employment. Fortunately, this is an era of changing customs. There is hope that a less selfish racial attitude will prevail. It is a heartening fact that there is an increasing number of Americans who will lend a hand in the game fight of the worthy.

In the less crowded professional vocations, the outlook is more cheerful. In these fields, the Negro woman is dependent largely upon herself and her own race for work. In the legal, dental, medical and nursing professions, successful women practitioners have usually worked their way through college and are "managing" on the small fees that can be received from an underpaid public. Social conditions in America are hardest upon the Negro because he is lowest in the economic scale. This gives rise to a demand for trained college women in the profession of social work. It has met with a response from young college women, anxious to devote their education and lives to the needs of the submerged classes. In New York City, some fifty-odd women are engaged in social work, other than nursing. In the latter profession there are over two hundred and fifty. Much of the social work has been pioneer in nature: the pay has been small with little possibility of advancement. For even in work among Negroes, the better paying positions are reserved for whites. The Negro college woman is doing her bit in this field at a sacrifice, along such lines as these: in the correctional departments of the city, as probation officers, investigators, and police women; as Big Sisters attached to the Childrens' Court; as field workers and visitors for relief organizations and missions; as secretaries for travelers-aid and mission societies; as visiting teachers and vocational guides for the schools of the city; and, in the many branches of public health nursing, in schools, organizations devoted to preventive and educational medicine, in hospitals and in private nursing.

In New York City, nearly three hundred Negro women share the good conditions in the teaching profession. They measure up to the high pedagogical requirements of the city and state law and are increasingly, leaders in the community. Here too the Negro woman finds evidence of the white workers' fear of competition. The need for teachers is still so strong that little friction exists. When it does seem to be imminent, it is smoothed away, as it recently was at a meeting of school principals. From the floor, a discussion began with: "What are we going to do about this problem of the increasing number of Negro teachers coming into our schools?" It ended promptly through the suggestion of another principal: "Send all you get and don't want over to my school. I have two now and I'll match their work to any two of your best whom you name." One might go on to such interesting and more unusual professions as journalism, chiropody, bacteriology, pharmacy, etc., and find that, though the number in any one may be small, the Negro woman is creditably represented in practically everyone. According to individual ability she is meeting with success.

Closing the door on the home anxieties, the woman engaged in trades and in industry faces equally serious difficulty in competition in the open working field. Custom is against her in all but a few trade and industrial occupations. She has, however been established long in the dressmaking trade among the helpers and finishers, and more recently among the drapers and fitters in some of the best establishments. Several Negro women are themselves proprietors of shops in the country's greatest fashion district. Each of them has, against great odds, convinced skeptical employers of her business value; and, at the same time, has educated fellow workers of other races, doing much to show the oneness of interest of all workers. In millinery, power sewing-machine operating on cloth, straw and leather, there are few Negro women. The laissez-faire attitude of practically all trade unions makes the Negro woman an unwilling menace to the cause of labor.

In trade cookery, the Negro woman's talent and past experience is recognized. Her problem here is to find employers who will let her work her way to managerial positions, in tea-rooms, candy shops and institutions. One such employer became convinced that the managing cook, a young colored graduate of Pratt Institute, would continue to build up a business that had been failing. She offered her a partnership. As in the cases of a number of such women, her barrier was lack of capital. No matter how highly trained, nor how much speed and business acumen has been acquired, the Negro's credit is held in doubt. An exception in this matter of capital will serve to prove the rule. Thirty years ago, a young Negro girl began learning all branches of the fur trade. She is now in business for herself, employing three women of her race and one Jewish man. She has made fur experts of still another half-dozen colored girls. Such instances as these justify the prediction that the foothold gained in the trade world will, year by year, become more secure.

Because of the limited fields for workers in this group, many of the unsuccessful drift into the fourth social grade, the domestic and casual workers. These drifters increase the difficulties of the Negro woman suited to housework. New standards of household management are forming and the problem of the Negro woman is to meet these new business-like ideals. The constant influx of workers unfamiliar with household conditions in New York keeps the situation one of turmoil. The Negro woman, moreover, is revolting against residential domestic service. It is a last stand in her fight to maintain a semblance of family life. For this reason, principally, the number of day or casual workers is on the increase. Happiness is almost impossible under the strain of these conditions. Health and morale suffer, but how else can her children, loose all afternoon, be gathered together at night-fall? Through it all she manages to give satisfactory service and the Negro woman is sought after for this unpopular work largely because her honesty, loyalty and cleanliness have stood the test of time. Through her drudgery, the women of other groups find leisure time for progress. This is one of her contributions to America.

It is apparent from what has been said, that even in New York City, Negro women are of a race which is free neither economically, socially nor spiritually. Like women in general, but more particularly like those of other oppressed minorities, the Negro woman has been forced to submit to over-powering conditions. Pressure has been exerted upon her, both from without and within her group. Her emotional and sex life is a reflex of her economic station. The women of the working class will react, emotionally and sexually, similarly to the working-class women of other races. The Negro woman does not maintain any moral standard which may be assigned chiefly to qualities of race, any more than a white woman does. Yet she has been singled out and advertised as having lower sex standards. Superficial critics who have had contact only with the lower grades of Negro women, claim that they are more immoral than other groups of women. This I deny. This is the sort of criticism which predicates of one race, to its detriment, that which is common to all races. Sex irregularities are not a matter of race, but of socio-economic conditions. . . .

We find the Negro woman, figuratively, struck in the face daily by contempt from the world about her. Within her soul, she knows little of peace and happiness. Through it all, she is courageously standing erect, developing within herself the moral strength to rise above and conquer false attitudes. She is maintaining her natural beauty and charm and improving her mind and opportunity. She is measuring up to the needs and demands of her family, community and race, and radiating from Harlem a hope that is cherished by her sisters in less propitious circumstances throughout the land. The wind of the race's destiny stirs more briskly because of her striving.

The Push for Racial Justice

The National Association for the Advancement of Colored People (NAACP) was established in New York City in 1909, following a deadly race riot in Springfield, Illinois, the previous year. Several progressive New Yorkers were among the founders. The organization continues to be headquartered in New York City.

The NAACP fought for racial justice on many fronts, including attacking lynching, prejudice, segregation, and job discrimination. The spearhead of their reforms was a journal, The Crisis. *It was edited by William Edward Burghardt (W. E. B.) Du Bois (1968–1963). DuBois was an outstanding writer, editor, and civil rights leader. He was the first Black person to earn a doctorate at Harvard University. He was a leader of the Niagara Movement, which transformed into the NAACP in 1909. DuBois wanted equal rights for Blacks, and he disagreed with Booker T. Washington and others who wanted to settle for basic educational and economic opportunities. DuBois wanted more: full civil and political rights. He believed this would be brought about by Blacks who were intellectual and political leaders. His 1903 book* The Souls of Black Folk, *a pioneering work in the emerging field of sociology, explored the experiences of Black people in the south. His writings targeted racism, lynching, segregation, and discrimination in education and employment.*

Under DuBois's leadership, The Crisis *became a major source of news about the Black community in the United States as well as articles and advertising aimed at that community. He wrote editorials for each issue, attacking racism, lynching, and inequality and demanding full social equality and educational and career advancement opportunities for Blacks. His message was educational, intended for white people as well as Blacks. The editorials below, from the first two years of the journal, reflect his breadth and persuasiveness.*

∼

FROM *THE CRISIS: A RECORD OF THE DARKER RACES* (1910 AND 1911) BY W. E. B. DUBOIS

"THE CRISIS," The Crisis *1 (November 10, 1910), 10*

The object of this publication is to set forth those facts and arguments which show the danger of race prejudice, particularly as manifested to-day toward colored people. It takes its name from the fact that the editors believe that this is a critical time in the history of the advancement of men. Catholicity and tolerance, reason and forbearance can today make the world-old dream of human brotherhood approach realization; while bigotry and prejudice, emphasized race consciousness and force can repeat the awful history of the contact of nations and groups in the past. We strive for this higher and broader vision of Peace and Good Will.

The policy of *The Crisis* will be simple and well defined: It will first and foremost be a newspaper; it will record important happenings and movements in the world which bear on the great problem of inter-racial relations, and especially those which affect the Negro-American. Secondly, it will be a review of opinion and literature, recording briefly books, articles, and important expressions of opinion in the white and colored press on the race problem. Thirdly, it will publish a few short articles. Finally, its editorial page will stand for the rights of men, irrespective of color or race, for the highest ideals of American democracy, and for reasonable but earnest and persistent attempt to gain these rights and realize these ideals. The magazine will be the organ of no clique or party and will avoid personal rancor of all sorts. In the absence of proof to the contrary it will assume honesty of purpose on the part of all men. North and South, white and black.

"N.A.A.C.P.," The Crisis, *1 (December 1910), 16–17*

What is the National Association for the Advancement of Colored People? It is a union of those who believe that earnest, active opposition is the only effective way of meeting the forces of evil. They believe that the growth of race prejudice in the United States is evil. It is not always consciously evil. Much of it is born of ignorance and misapprehension, honest mistake and misguided zeal. However caused, it is none the less evil, wrong, dangerous, fertile of harm. For this reason it must be combatted. It is neither safe nor sane to sit down dumbly before such human error or to seek to combat it with smiles and hushed whispers. Fight the wrong with every human weapon in every civilized way.

The National Association for the Advancement of Colored People is organized to fight the wrong of race prejudice:

(a) By doing away with the excuses for prejudice.

(b) By showing the unreasonableness of prejudice.

(c) By exposing the evils of race prejudice.

This is a large program of reform? It is, and this is because the evil is large. There is not today in human affairs amore subtle and awful enemy of human progress, of peace and sympathy than the reaction war and hatred that lurks in the indefinite thing which we call race prejudice. Does it not call for opposition—determined, persistent opposition? Are rational beings justified in sitting silently, willingly dumb and blind to the growth of this crime? We believe not. We are organized, then to say to the world and our country:

Negroes are men with the foibles and virtues of men.

To treat evil as though it were good and good as though it were evil is not only wrong but dangerous, since in the end it encourages evil and discourages good.

To treat all Negroes alike is treating evil as good and good as evil. To draw a crass and dogged undeviating color line in human affairs is dangerous—as dangerous to those who draw it as to those against whom it is drawn.

We are organized to fight this great modern danger. How may we fight it?

1. By the argument of the printed word in a periodical like this, and in pamphlets and tracts.

2. By the spoken word in talk and lecture.

3. By correspondence.

4. By encouraging all efforts at social uplift.

5. By careful investigation of the truth in matters of social condition and race contact—not the truth as we want it or you want it, but as it really is.

6. By individual relief of the wretched.

If you think such work is worthwhile, aid us by joining our organization.

"OPPORTUNITY," The Crisis 1 (January 1911), 17

A friend of our Association writes: "While I heartily approve of the colored people being given an opportunity to improve their condition, I feel that after doing what I can to help them to earn a living honorably, they must depend on their own resources to advance themselves." This is the attitude of many excellent friends of humanity, but it assumes that if a man is fairly equipped for earning a living today he will have the opportunity to do so, and that the paths before him will be open so as to make the rise of the deserving possible.

It is precisely because the opportunity to earn a living, even for those equipped to do so, is not given today to thousands of colored people in the United States, that the National Association for the Advancement of Colored People exists. It is wrong and wasteful to do for people what they can and ought to do for themselves, but when the doors of opportunity are so shut in their faces so as to discourage and keep back the hard-working and deserving, then action is called for.

Today, Negroes may work freely as menials at low wages; they may work freely as farm laborers under conditions of semi-slavery; higher than that they meet unusual difficulties, the difficulty of saving capital from low wages to farm or go into business; the difficulty of securing admission to the trades even when competent; the difficulty of securing protection under the law and of rearing a family in decency; the difficulty of educating their children; the difficulty of protecting their rights by the ballot. To be sure, if they are unusually gifted and pushing they may push higher at the risk of insult and bitter opposition. Thus the fact remains that the mass of the willing, eager workers of the race are held back and forced down by a deep and growing race prejudice, and these, pressing down on the lower strata, encourage in them laziness and vagrancy and crime. The National Association for the Advancement of Colored People is an organization for giving the colored race a reasonable opportunity to help itself.

"SEPARATION," The Crisis I (February 1911), 20–21

It is a cruel mental strain to which honest colored men are being put to-day, particularly in the South. They want to come to terms with their neighbors. They are being urged to do this—urged by black leaders and white and by strong public opinion. The South sometimes is represented as aggressively friendly. They are seeking piteously, therefore, to agree with the dominant race and yet preserve something of their self-respect. It is very difficult.

Take, for instance, the letter of an honest colored man in the New Orleans *Times-Democrat*. He says: "Whatever may be the opinion of others concerning the drawing of the color line in the South, the thoughtful Negro has accepted it as a fixed principle, realizing that the race has absolutely nothing to fear or lose by social separation. Social intermingling has always meant social degradation to the less advanced element. It may set the minds of many people at rest to know that the Negro is willing and ready to meet the most advanced thought of the South on its own ground."

He then swallows segregation whole; he would accept separate stores, separate physicians and lawyers, separate schools, separate school superintendents, separate street cars—all and complete, because, as he concludes: "The Negro does not desire racial intermingling. All he wants is a square deal before the law."

Precisely. But the thing that this black man would better ask himself good and hard is this: Is such separation physically and politically possible, and under it is there the slightest likelihood of the segregated getting "a square deal"? No. Such counsellors of surrender stand willing to sacrifice the foundations of democracy for peace. Why does the world ask equality? Out of personal bravado and impudence? No, but for self-protection. If you can separate people by color, you can separate them by birth, by wealth, by ability and any accident. This once done and democracy is dead before Privilege.

Or turn to the other side: the white South does not want Separation, but Subordination. They do not want separate Negro schools, but Negro schools under the control of white superintendents who hold the purse strings. They do not want separate cars, but cars which Negroes may not enter save as servants. They do not want to stop social intermingling, but they do want to prescribe the conditions.

In other words, the separation of the races which would involve political, economic and social independence in the South would be as hateful to them as social intermingling. Every man, then, that bows to the dogma of race separation must accept subordination and humiliation along with the destruction of the best ideals of democracy.

Those who persist in opposition to it need not be scared by bugbears of possible intermarriage. In a true democracy and there alone are sexual relations regulated by giving to all the right to choose their consorts. Only in an oligarchy like Louisiana is race intermingling so endless that they cannot enforce their own race segregation laws.

"EARNING A LIVING," The Crisis 2 (June 1911), 65

"How do Northern colored people earn a living? There is no economic opening in the North. They are being displaced; starvation faces them." These and other phrases we hear continually. Yet colored people continue to come North. They live in better and better homes, they are better dressed, they are growing in intelligence. How do they earn a living? In ways that many do not dream. Turn, for instance, to your last magazine. See the advertisement of the Aeolian organs and piano players. Marvelous, is it not? Great triumph of white brains and ingenuity. Now if Negroes only—stop! The master mechanic in the Aeolian Organ Company's shops at Garwood, N.J., is Joseph H. Dickinson, a colored man. Turn to your telephone—did you know that a black man's patent is included in the transmitter? Scarcely a locomotive rolls in the United States but by aid of a black man's lubricating device, and only recently Edison paid a colored man $62,000 for an improvement on the phonograph.

"SOCIAL EQUALITY," The Crisis 2 (September 1911), 197

A colored physician of Kansas City has made a speech at a large meeting in Denver in which he protests that he does not want "social equality." It happens, however, that social equality is precisely what this gentleman does want and we can prove it; if our readers will turn to the March number of The Crisis they will learn that this same physician got on a

Pullman car to ride into Texas and was ejected. He protested vigorously, as he ought to have done, and brought suit.

Now, riding on a Pullman car is social equality and there is no use in pretending that it is not. Equal civil rights are impossible without social equality. Equal political rights are impossible without social equality. When American Negroes recently sent a protest to England complaining of civil and political degradation what did the South retort? Practically all the Southern white papers said this is "demanding social equality"; and it was. Social equality is simply the right to be treated as a gentleman when one is among gentlemen and acts like a gentleman. No person who does not demand such treatment is fit for the society of gentlemen.

Of course, what the speaker meant to say was that he had no desire to force his company on people unnecessarily if they objected to him, but such a right does not imply "equality" but "superiority," and this speaker knows or ought to know that every time a black man says publicly that he is willing to be treated as a social pariah, he is forging the chains of his social slavery. Let intelligent black men stop this sort of talk. If they are afraid to demand their rights as men, they can, at least, preserve dignified silence.

Sources

DuBois, W. E. Burghardt, editorials in *The Crisis: A Record of the Darker Races*, vols. 1–2, November 1910–October 1911. Available at HathiTrust, https://babel.hathitrust.org/cgi/pt?id=hvd.32044012439774&view=page&seq=11"https://babel.hathitrust.org/cgi/pt?id=hvd.32044012439774&view=page&seq=11.

Johnson, James Weldon, "Harlem: The Cultural Capital," in Locke, *The New Negro*, 301–04, 308–10. Available at HathiTrust, https://babel.hathitrust.org/cgi/pt?id=inu.30000005027994&view=page&seq=9.

Locke, Alain, "Foreword" and "The New Negro," in Alain Locke, ed., *The New Negro: An Interpretation* (New York: Albert and Charles Boni, 1925), ix–xi, 6, 7. Available at HathiTrust, https://babel.hathitrust.org/cgi/pt?id=inu.30000005027994&view=page&seq=9"https://babel.hathitrust.org/cgi/pt?id=inu.30000005027994&view=page&seq=9.

McDougald, Elise Johnson, "The Double Task: The Struggle of Negro Women for Sex and Race Emancipation," in Alain Locke, ed., "Harlem: The Mecca of the New Negro," *Survey Graphic, Harlem Number* (1925), n.p. Available at Internet Archive, https://web.archive.org/web/20080513092856/http://etext.lib.virginia.edu/harlem/McDDoubF.html.

Ovington, Mary White, *Half a Man: The Status of the Negro in New York* (New York: Longmans Green, 1911), ch. IX, "Conclusion," 218–27. Available at HathiTrust, https://babel.hathitrust.org/cgi/pt?id=loc.ark:/13960/t54f1vp-8f&view=page&seq=7. (Note: The chapter's three long footnotes have not been included.)

White, Walter, "The Paradox of Color," in Locke, *The New Negro*, 361–64, 367. Available at HathiTrust, https://babel.hathitrust.org/cgi/pt?id=inu.30000005027994&view=page&seq=9.

8

Regulating Business

Figure 8. Charles Evans Hughes, New York's progressive Republican governor, 1907–1910, initiated new regulations of banks, insurance companies, railroads, and other corporations. Source: Library of Congress Prints & Photographs Collection.

New York businesses were largely unregulated in 1900. There was a strong tradition in New York of laissez-faire and a public consensus that government should not unduly interfere with the management of business. In the new century, however, that consensus shifted and many New Yorkers came to believe that many businesses had grown too large, too committed to making exorbitant profits, too influential in politics, and insufficiently regulated through the natural forces of competition. Some were irresponsibly led by men who served their own interests and made fortunes through their companies. Newspapers and popular magazines, particularly those adept at "muckraking," as the style of investigatory writing came to be called, began exposing abuses and pushing the need for government intervention and regulation.

New York progressives recognized and acknowledged the need for government oversight and began to enact regulatory legislation. It was an idea with limited public support in 1900; by 1920, it was commonplace. Charles Evans Hughes, the Republican New York governor from 1907 to 1910, achieved national recognition for his state's leadership. Often, development of regulation followed a sequence. First, exposure of an issue or problem through the press or investigative studies and reports by progressives. Second, development and passage of legislation, often with support of the progressive-minded press and over the opposition of conservative forces. Third, implementation, which typically involved an expanded or new state agency and tended to be tolerant, giving businesses lots of time and leeway to improve their practices. Fourth, lots of publicity as the regulation went along to show the public that the regulation was working, progress industries were making, and the need for continuing improvement and, sometimes, additional regulation. Fifth, challenge by the industries in court, which almost always sustained the regulation.

It was the advent of extensive government oversight of business, which would expand in the twentieth century in New York and at the federal level.

Regulation of Insurance Companies

Newspapers and magazines began publicizing mismanagement and malfeasance of a number of large New York insurance companies early in the new century. It was a high-visibility issue because so many people in New York and elsewhere held life insurance policies with these companies. The legislature, at the prodding of the media, launched an investigation in September 1905. The investigating committee hired Charles Evans Hughes (1862–1948), a former law professor and corporate lawyer who had proven his ability as counsel for a legislative investigation into gas and electricity companies earlier in the year. Hughes proved even more effective in the insurance investigation. Hughes's probing examination of witnesses revealed mismanagement, misuse of company funds, excessive salaries, and tax evasion. The company managers came across as lax or arrogant. Serving customers was a low priority. The companies spent huge sums on lobbying for favorable legislation and against restrictive regulations.

Hughes produced a persuasive report that led to new regulatory legislation designed to rectify the many insurance company abuses revealed at the hearings, including restricting political contributions and lobbying, covered in the section excerpted below. The new laws significantly increased the authority of the state banking department.

~

From Report of the Joint Committee of the Senate and Assembly of the State of New York Appointed to Investigate the Affairs of Life Insurance Companies (1906)

Political Cont0ributions

Contributions by insurance corporations for political purposes should be strictly forbidden. Neither executive officers nor directors should be allowed to use the moneys paid for purposes of insurance in support of political candidates or platforms. The devious methods taken to conceal the payments of this sort are confessions of their illicit character. They illustrate the manner in which executive officers have treated the funds of the company virtually as their own, abusing their power to disburse them without proper accounting. Whether made for the purpose of supporting political views or with the desire to obtain protection for the corporation, these contributions have been wholly unjustifiable. In the one case executive officers have sought to impose their political views upon a constituency of divergent convictions, and in the other they have been guilty of a serious offense against public morals. The frank admission that moneys have been obtained for use in State campaigns upon the expectation that candidates thus aided in their election would support the interests of the companies, has exposed both those who solicited the contributions and those who made them to severe and just condemnation.

The committee recommends the passage of an unequivocal and drastic measure to remedy this evil. Not only should it be expressly prohibited and treated as a waste of corporate moneys, but any officer, director or agent making, authorizing or consenting to any such contribution should be guilty of a misdemeanor, and the prohibition should be extended to all corporate contributions of this character.

Lobbying

Nothing disclosed by the investigation deserves more serious attention than the systematic efforts of the large insurance companies to control a large part of the legislation of the State. They have been organized into an offensive and defensive alliance to procure or to prevent the passage of laws affecting not only insurance, but a great variety of important interests to which, through subsidiary companies or through the connections of their officers, they have become related. Their operations have extended beyond the State and the country has been divided into districts so that each company might perform conveniently its share of the work. Enormous sums have been expended in a surreptitious manner. Irregular accounts have been kept to conceal the payments for which proper vouchers have not been required. This course of conduct has created a widespread conviction that large portions of this money have been dishonestly used.

Andrew C. Fields, who represented both the *Mutual* and the *Equitable* [two large insurance companies] in legislative matters, and was in control of the supply department of the former company, remained beyond the jurisdiction during the sessions of the committee. The general solicitor of the *Mutual*, to whom the chairman of the committee on expenditures entrusted large sums, died before the beginning of the investigation and apparently left no account as to how the money had been spent.

Andrew Hamilton, who, within ten years, received upwards of $1,000,000 from the *New York Life* [another company] on the warrant of its President in connection with its bureau of legislation and taxation, has remained abroad and has failed to render any proper account showing the disposition of the money. The officers the company say that they have no knowledge of the uses to which it was put. The officers of the *Equitable*, from whom light might have been expected on the disbursements of their company, either have remained out of the jurisdiction or have been disabled by illness. On account of the absence of the necessary witnesses and the lack of proper vouchers, the committee has been unable to trace the moneys said to have been disbursed in connection with legislation. But while it is sufficiently evident that large sums have been disbursed for improper purposes, it is also clear that payments for confidential outlays exempt from audit have furnished abundant opportunities for misappropriations. They suggest the necessity of requiring a strict accounting from those who are responsible for the payments as well as from the agents who have received the moneys.

It has been insisted that the insurance companies have been so continuously menaced by the introduction of improper and ill-advised legislative measures in many states that they have been compelled to maintain a constant watchfulness and to resort to secret means to defeat them. An insurance corporation, however, holds a position of peculiar advantage in opposing any legislative measure which really antagonizes the interests of policy holders. A very large proportion of the voters of the state hold policies of life insurance. It is easy for the company to apprise them of hostile legislative measures, and in addition a department of the state government exists for their protection, whose recommendations have rarely failed to receive proper consideration in the Legislature. It is not a difficult matter to direct public attention to an objectionable bill affecting life insurance corporations or to have opposing argument and criticism effectively presented. Again, if, in spite of argument fairly and publicly presented, the Legislature insists upon passing a law inimical to the true interests of the companies, it is not the officers, but the policy holders, who must bear the loss, and the consequences which can readily be pointed out are almost certain to bring about an early repeal of the obnoxious legislation. The employment of agents to disburse large sums, and of clandestine methods to defeat legislation is wholly inexcusable.

The pernicious activities of corporate agents in matters of legislation demand that the present freedom of lobbying should be restricted. They have brought suspicion upon important proceedings of the Legislature, and have exposed its members to consequent assault. The Legislature owes it to itself, so far as possible, to stop the practice of the lavish expenditure of moneys ostensibly for services in connection with the support of or opposition to bills, and generally believed to be used for corrupt purposes. The Legislature should free itself from the stigma which now attaches to the progress of measures affecting important interests. The laws against bribery and corruption, offenses which are difficult of proof, are sufficiently stringent, but an effort should be made to strike at the root of the evil by requiring under proper penalties full publicity with regard to moneys expended in connection with matters before the Legislature. Corporations should be required to keep accounts and vouchers in which all such payments should be fully detailed and receipted for, and an adequate statement regarding them should form a part of such reports as may be required.

In the case of insurance corporations the remedy lies first, generally, in the requirement of a proper authorization of all expenditures and vouchers, stating in detail the purposes for which moneys paid for legal expenses or in connection with legislative matters have been expended. And, further, the company should be compelled to set forth in its annual statement to the Superintendent of Insurance all sums so disbursed, giving the names of the payees, the amounts paid and the specific purpose of the payment. . . .

The Committee therefore recommends that the Legislative Law be so amended that every person retained or employed for compensation as counsel or agent to promote or oppose the passage of bills or resolutions by either House or executive approval of such measures shall before entering upon the service file in the office of the Secretary of State a writing stating the name or names of his employer, together with a brief description of the legislative matter with reference to which the service is to be rendered. The Secretary of State should be required to provide a docket to be known as the "Docket of Legislative Appearances," with appropriate blanks and indices in which the names of counsel and agent may be properly entered. Fees contingent upon legislative action should be prohibited.

A New Governor Sets a Progressive Tone

Republican Charles Evans Hughes (1862–1948) was New York's first progressive governor, serving in the office from 1907 to 1910. Hughes was something of a scholar (a former professor at Cornell Law School) and a sometime corporate lawyer when he was tapped to serve as counsel to two legislative investigations in 1905. The first explored high prices and uneven services by companies delivering gas for lighting and heating in New York City. The second probed mismanagement of insurance companies (summarized in the document above). Hughes proved to be a brilliant investigator, fair but probing, cutting through complexity, eliciting revealing information about shady practices. He wrote stellar reports at the end of both investigations which documented the abuses and advanced solutions that the public could easily understand. His reports led to legislation fostering better utility services and curbing insurance company abuses. Both laws broke new ground and extended state government well beyond its previous limits.

Republicans dominated at Albany, but they needed someone fresh, unconnected with the conservative politics that had enabled the insurance and gas abuses to grow unchecked. Hughes fit the bill—he was a Republican but had a sterling reputation for independence and sound judgment. He reluctantly accepted the nomination. He campaigned against the Democratic nominee, publisher and former congressman William R. Hearst, who ran on an antibusiness platform. Hughes proved to be an effective, if not charismatic, campaigner and won the election.

His short inaugural speech set the tone for his administration and indeed for much of progressive reform: government must serve the people, not special interests; government must push further into the economic and social arena, but carefully; and the public interest must be redefined and championed. The brief speech distilled Hughes's political philosophy and signaled the reforms he would champion.

∾

From "Inaugural Address" (1907) by Charles Evans Hughes

Fellow-citizens: I assume the office of Governor without other ambition than to serve the people of the State. I have not coveted its powers nor do I permit myself to shrink from its responsibilities. Sensible of its magnitude and of my own limitations, I undertake the task of administration without illusion. But you do not require the impossible. You have bound me to earnest and honest endeavor in the interest of all the people according to the best of my ability and that obligation, with the help of God, I shall discharge.

We have reason to congratulate ourselves that coincident with our prosperity, there is an emphatic assertion of popular rights and a keen resentment of public wrongs. There is no panacea in executive or legislative action for all the ills of society which spring from the frailties and defects of the human nature of its members. But this furnishes no excuse for complacent inactivity and no reason for the toleration of wrongs made possible by defective or inadequate legislation or by administrative partiality or inefficiency.

It is sometimes said that we have laws enough and that the need is not of more law, but of better enforcement of the law. There is abundant occasion for caution against hasty legislation. Whether or not we have laws enough, we certainly have enough of ill-considered legislation, and the question is not as to the quantity, but as to the quality of our present and of our proposed enactments.

The proper confines of legislative action are not to be determined by generalities. Slowly but surely the people have narrowed the opportunities for selfish aggression, and the demand of this hour, and of all hours, is not allegiance to phrases, but sympathy with every aspiration for the betterment of conditions and a sincere and patient effort to understand every need and to ascertain in the light of experience the means best adapted to meet it. Each measure proposed must ultimately be tested by critical analysis of the particular problem, the precise mischief alleged and the adequacy of the proffered remedy. It is the capacity for such close examination without heat or disqualifying prejudice which distinguishes the constructive effort from vain endeavors to change human nature by changing the forms of government.

It must freely be recognized that many of the evils of which we complain have their source in the law itself, in privileges carelessly granted, in opportunities for private aggrandizement at the expense of the people recklessly created, in failure to safeguard our public interests by providing means for just regulation of those enterprises which depend upon the use of public franchises. Wherever the law gives unjust advantage, wherever it fails by suitable prohibition or regulation to protect the interests of the people, wherever the power derived from the State is turned against the State, there is not only room, but urgent necessity for the assertion of the authority of the State to enforce the common right.

The growth of our population and the necessary increase in our charitable and correctional work, the great enterprises under State control—our canals, our highways, our forest preserves—the protection of the public health, the problems created by the congestion of population in our great cities lead to a constant extension of governmental activity from which we cannot have, and we would not seek, escape.

This extension compels the strictest insistence upon the highest administrative standards. We are a government of laws and not of men. We subordinate individual caprice to defined duty. The essentials of our liberties are expressed in constitutional enactments removed from the risk of temporary agitation. But the security of our government despite its constitutional guaranties is found in the intelligence and public spirit of its citizens and in its ability to call to the work of administration men of single-minded devotion to the public interests, who make unselfish service to the State a point of knightly honor.

If in administration we make the standard efficiency and not partisan advantage, if in executing the laws we deal impartially, if in making the laws there is fair and intelligent action with reference to each exigency, we shall disarm reckless and selfish agitators and take from the enemies of our peace their vantage ground of attack.

It is my intention to employ my constitutional powers to this end. I believe in the sincerity and good sense of the people. I believe that they are intent in having government which recognizes no favored interests and which is not conducted in any part for selfish ends. They will not be, and they should not be, content with less.

Relying upon your support and hoping to deserve your continued confidence, with the single desire to safeguard your interests and to secure the honorable administration of the office to which you have called me, I now enter upon the discharge of its duties.

Asserting State Authority over Public Utilities

Public utilities—railroads, rapid transit lines, and the companies that supplied gas and electricity to power homes and factories—were vitally important to New York in the emerging century. They were largely unregulated at the turn of the century, resulting in public dissatisfaction about inadequate service, excessive rates, and inflated stock offerings.

Charles Evans Hughes had served as counsel to a legislative investigation of New York City gas and electricity companies in 1905 and shaped legislation to create a Commission of Gas and Electricity to regulate the companies. The commission worked well, regulating the companies and at the same time holding their critics at bay while they improved services and worked out equitable pricing. But other utilities, particularly railroads, were largely unregulated. There was a state board of railroad commissioners, dating from the nineteenth century, but it had little real power.

Elected governor on the Republican ticket in 1906, Hughes advanced an unprecedented proposal in 1907 to deal with the issue of public utilities broadly defined, including railroads and rapid transit lines in New York City, by taking the "regulation by commission" concept to a higher level: two new "public service commissions," one for New York City, the other for the rest of the state. The commissions would cover gas and electricity (superseding the Commission of Gas and Electricity), rapid transit, and railroad companies (which were among the largest in the state and impacted communities throughout the state). The commissions would have broad power to order changes in rates, mandate better service, and pass on proposed new stock issues. Hughes appealed to public opinion to secure passage of his bill over opposition by Democrats and the conservative wing of his own Republican party. The public was won over and the legislature passed Hughes's bill. The public service commissions constituted leading-edge progressive reform and a significant new approach to regulating.

The new law, and Hughes's skill in getting it passed, brought a good deal of praise from progressive-minded journals. The article excerpted below by Burton J. Hendrick, a "muckraker" of sorts who had helped expose wrongdoing in the insurance and other industries, is a good example.

∾

FROM "GOVERNOR HUGHES," OUTLOOK (1908),
BY BURTON J. HENDRICK

An Attempt to Make Public Service Corporations Subject to Law

The great public service corporations of New York State had led what was virtually a lawless existence for years. The practical explanation for this . . . is that these corporations had always taken an active hand in politics, and had reversed the relative positions of legislative authority and corporate subordination. The history of the Metropolitan Street Railway [operator of surface rapid-transit lines in New York City], recently described in this magazine, is an interesting illustration of what a great public utility corporation had become, merely because the law-making power of the State, so far as that corporation was concerned, had not been used. The Metropolitan had received certain valuable rights in the streets of Manhattan Island, practically without consideration, because the public interest required safe, adequate, and reasonably cheap local transportation.

The Metropolitan had entirely ignored its part of the contract. The last ambition of the speculators who had obtained control of it was to perform these public services. They simply used the company as a convenient medium for creating enormous issues of what was practically fraudulent stock and unloading this upon the unsuspecting investor. In the electric and gas companies, Mr. Hughes had shown [as counsel to a 1905 legislative committee that investigated gas and electricity services and charges] how the rights of the people had likewise been largely disregarded. In the management of the steam railroads, the telephone and telegraph companies, though conditions in these companies has never been so flagrant as in the New York street-railways, the rights of the franchise-granting public had never been adequately protected.

In his first message, Governor Hughes outlined a plan for restoring to the State government its long abandoned rights, and the Public Service Bill, which was soon introduced embodied his ideas. This plan was simplicity itself. It merely proposed that the Legislature should exercise its inherent powers for supervision and regulation. It had the right to insist that the public service corporations should give the people safe, adequate, reasonably cheap non-discriminatory service. It only remained to create the machinery by which this authority should be exercised. Manifestly, the legislature could not supervise the details directly. A body which met only three months in the year, and which changed its membership constantly, could hardly deal intelligently with the hundreds of practical questions that arise every day.

The proposed law, therefore, provided for the delegation of these powers by the Legislature to two commissions. A Public Service Commission of the first district was to have supervision and regulation over all the utility corporations in the city of New York. A second commission was to have similar powers over corporations operating in the rest of the State. In order that these commissions might be kept constantly in touch with their duties, the law stipulated that they should keep their office open every day in the year, Sundays and holidays not excepted, from eight in the morning until eleven at night. They were thus to serve as a perpetual means of communication between the public and the corporations. Anyone who had any grievance against his gas company or trolley road was to have the right of constant appeal to his Public Service Commission. At any time, according to the proposed law, the commission or its representative was to have immediate access to all the books and accounts of the corporations; its powers of investigation were to be unlimited. It could subpoena any officer at any time and demand explanations on any question of service or finance.

Its most important power was to be that of fixing rates and regulating service. It was to determine—if it proved necessary to go to extremes to obtain just treatment—the proper rates for trolley fares, passenger and freight charges on steam-roads [railroads], and the price of gas. The commission would also have the regulation of appliances and equipment. If it found any railroad operating without machinery adequate for insuring the safety of passengers, it could force the railroad to install such machinery. If it found that a trolley line was not running a sufficient number of cars to accommodate its traffic, it could file an order requiring it to do so, specifying the precise number of cars and where they were to go. If it obtained reliable information that a steam-railroad was neglecting its suburban traffic, it could compel it to put on more trains. A gas company which made a habit of supplying bad gas at a high price could be compelled to supply good gas at a reasonable price.

Radical as this measure may seem, Governor Hughes safeguarded it by certain provisions which protected the corporation from unjust treatment. Above all, he stands for the spirit that does not act without investigation and detailed information. The Public Service Law required that the new commissions could take no action for the enforcement of public rights without thorough investigation. Before filing any order the commission must give the corporation notice, in order that the whole subject might be thoroughly canvassed. There were other checks which protected the corporation from hasty action without at the same time preventing the public from obtaining the service to which it was entitled. The new law carefully withheld from the corporations the right of a "court review." In other words, the corporations could not run to the courts for protection against all orders of the commission. On the other hand, the law specifically limited all such orders to those which are "just and reasonable"; that is, the only ground of appeal retained by the corporations was the constitutional provision against the confiscation of property without due process of law. . . .

This proposed legislation did not originate in the brain of a Kansas Populist but in that of a conservative ex-professor of law at Cornell University. In its fundamental principles it involved nothing new; the powers which it assumed had always existed; the Governor's only claim to originality was his determination to make them effective. . . .

Hughes Appeals to the People

[After conservative Republicans who held a majority in the New York State senate initially blocked the governor's bill,] Mr. Hughes now resorted to the only legitimate weapon left to him—a direct appeal to the people over the Senate's head [in a series of public speeches]. He did not belch fire; he made a logical, closely argued explanation of his Public Service Act and the reasons it should pass. He never mentioned his opponents in the Legislature, or in the slightest degree criticized them for fighting the bill. When the Governor finished, however, there was not a more discredited group of men in New York State. He had clearly demonstrated that the public interest required the passage of this law, and he had made the point so plain that, without once hinting at the fact, the whole State saw that any man who was opposing it was not actuated by public-spirited motives. The politicians could easily have survived a tongue-lashing; they could not survive the terrible logic and inevitable conclusion of the Governor's words. . . .

Public Opinion Asserts Itself

And now was heard that voice which, after all is the governing power in the United States and to which Mr. Hughes had so eloquently appealed—public opinion. From all sections of the State "the people" made themselves heard. Thousands of newspapers, Republican, Democratic and independent, leveled their barriers against the Albany politicians. Public meetings denounced them and civic bodies took their stand upon the Governor's side. The fight which Hughes was making against the worst influences at Albany became the one subject of popular discussion and the Albany crowd began to hear from their "constituents." Telegrams and letters poured in upon the anti-Hughes senators threatening them with political extinction if they continued in their course. Two years before, certain senators had outraged public opinion by voting against a bill reducing the price of gas to eighty cents, and had as a result been retired to life at the succeeding election. Forcible reminders of the fate of the "gas senators" were made to those who were opposing Governor Hughes.

Popular indignation was so high that the State Republican leaders, in a panic, rushed to Albany, in the hope of straightening out the situation. [State Senate leader John] Raines and his associates at last perceived that if they continued their opposition, not only would they fail of election to the Senate, but that the whole Republican party would lose public confidence. They did precisely what all shifty politicians do in similar circumstances. They immediately reversed their position, meekly put themselves upon the Governor's side, and announced their willingness to vote for his reforms. When the public service measure—the Governor's bill, not the emasculated affairs which the corporations had favored—came up for consideration, the old guard voted for it with ostentatious eagerness. Thus had Governor Hughes not only secured perhaps the most far-reaching reform ever adapted by an American legislature, but he had given an inspiring object-lesson in the workings of popular government.

Lenient State Regulation

The Public Service Commissions Law and other progressive-era New York state laws initiating or strengthening state oversight provided new state agencies with unprecedented, sweeping powers. The newly regulated companies were at first apprehensive about the possibility of state employees interfering in their business. In practice, though, the agencies usually exercised their powers quietly and with restraint. The preferred approach was to work with companies to get them up to acceptable levels of good service and fair rates rather than coercing them through formal orders. At the same time, the existence of the regulatory bodies discouraged the legislature from enacting direct requirements through new laws.

The Public Service Commissions Law gave the new agencies sweeping authority. But Governor Charles Evans Hughes appointed moderates to both new commissions. He selected Frank W. Stevens, who had served as counsel for a branch of the New York Central Railroad, as chair of the Second District (upstate) commission, whose main work would be regulating railroads. In his first public address, in October 1907, Stevens said the commission's key strategy would be to get the railroads to expand their capacity and correct their own service inadequacies and rate inequities rather than the commission coercing them through regulations and orders. That was a reassuring message to public utility managers, because it signaled the new, powerful commissions were likely to be pragmatic and moderate in exercising their powers.

∼

From "The Work of the Public Service Commission, Second District . . ." (1908) by Frank W. Stevens

The complaint against the corporations has been that they have disregarded the rights of the people; that they have overridden them. If we assume, for the moment, that this is entirely true and that the belief of the public in that respect is justified by the history of the past, still it does not justify the commission in disregarding the rights of the corporation. The great State of New York has not enacted any law to oppress any man or any association of men. The object of the law is to promote justice and to prevent injustice, and no man can conscientiously observe the oath of office which he took, if, in order to correct one injustice he perpetrates another. Corporations have their legal rights and they should be protected in them.

I wish to state with the utmost emphasis, that I do not believe that any commission or commissioners who will ever be appointed in the State of New York, under the law which is now upon the statute books, will upon any occasion attempt to right one wrong by doing another. I have no hesitation in making a statement of that character, and I have no fear that any person will for a moment say that I am in sympathy with corporations and am not in sympathy with the people, because I believe that a true sympathy with the people requires that the ideal which the commission should have before it be to promote the efficiency of the corporations to the utmost, and when corporations are efficient, when they perform the duties with which they are charged and which they ought to perform, I do not believe that they need fear for a moment but that the American people will always be willing to grant them a just and reasonable and a generous reward for the service which they render.

There is another thought with regard to general principles which I wish to impress upon you. I believe that the commission is entitled to the hearty support of the corporations; first, because the Public Service Commission law is the law of the land, and it is the duty of all corporations, as well as the duty of all individuals, so long as a law stands upon the statute books, put there with good intent and with righteous purpose, to give it all the support and upholding which they can; give it a fair show, fair trial, because it is the law of the land and American institutions demand that the law should be respected, obeyed and observed. I wish to say here tonight, as I have said before publicly, and mean to say publicly hereafter so long as it is true, that up to this time there is no indication on the part of the corporations in the second district but that they intend to observe, obey and support the law, and the commission in endeavoring to enforce it. . . .

There is another branch in the work of the commission which attracts the utmost attention, and which is perhaps one of the most important things to the people of the State and to the corporations subject to the law, and that is what is the commission going to do about those things which have excited public discontent, public indignation. Now, it is a fact that there exists through all the State and among all ranks of people who have anything to do with public service corporations a great discontent with their operation. What is the cause of it? With what are the people discontented? Is it a mere wave of passion sweeping over the country without cause, or has it a cause deep-seated in the experience of men? I say emphatically that it has a cause, and that cause is this: I will now refer to the steam railroads—that they have not been and are not performing their work efficiently. They are not and have not been doing their duty by the public. Now, the sole advantage which any commission has regarding this is that it can take a little wider view than the ordinary man.

The situation is something like this: We go into the city of Buffalo and we find great discontent existing, the gravest complaint made that they are not furnished with proper facilities; that they cannot get cars furnished [to] them to transport their freight, and then when cars are finally loaded, they are not transported with sufficient rapidity. They think in Buffalo that they are discriminated against. . . .

The railroads have not been performing their work efficiently and to the satisfaction of the public, and I regret to say that they have not improved in that respect, for the service is worse now than it was two or three years ago. . . .

The cause, primarily is that the business of the country has outgrown the capacity of the railroads. The railroads have not kept up with the business of the country. In other words, perhaps it has been inevitable; perhaps it has been impossible for them to do it. If that is so, let us have that understood and have the public informed of that fact. Perhaps the difficulty arises from a shortage of cars. I don't know; it is impossible for any man at the present stage of the inquiry to say; but if it arises from a shortage of cars, let us know it and let us see that more cars are built. Perhaps it arises from the fact that the traffic has outgrown the economic power of the roads; that there is not trackage enough, not terminals enough to take care of the business. If that is so, let us know it.

It is perhaps true that a large part of these evils and delays arises from an inability on the part of the administration to handle large matters in a large way. If so, let us find that out and let us expose the inefficient weaklings to the public gaze in order that other men may be put in their places. Whatever the cause may be, let us find it out; because there can be no efficient remedy, there can be nothing done which will remove the evils, until the exact cause or causes are found out, and the proper remedy applied. It is impossible for the commission to build the cars; it is impossible for the commission to furnish the cars; it is impossible for the commission to operate them after they are put upon the line. All these things must be done by the railroad companies, and I wish to assure the railroad companies that when they do that work efficiently, in my judgment they are entitled to a fair compensation for that work. But the people are not to be required, and should not be required, to pay a liberal price for poor service. They are willing, in my judgment, to pay a liberal price for good, efficient service. . . .

All of these questions have to be treated in a plain, simple, business-like fashion and no other; without any dramatic strikes or hysterics or without any attempt to coerce the corporations. It must be accomplished with an honest effort to bring [us] up to a realization of the actual conditions which exist in this State and which are hampering trade.

Reigning in the New York-led "Money Trust"

In the opening years of the new century, there was growing public concern over what the media called the "money trust," a community of bankers and financiers, mostly concentrated in New York, that exerted powerful control over the nation's finances. Through a series of strategic consolidations, interlocking directorates, cooperative agreements, and shrewd investment strategies, a few men in charge of the largest banks controlled much of the nation's financial wealth.

Some of the big banks were in Boston, Philadelphia, Chicago, and a few other cities, but most were in New York City. New York financier and investment banker John Pierpont (J. P.) Morgan (1837–1913) dominated corporate finance on Wall Street, where many of the banks and the New York Stock Exchange were headquartered.

New York stepped up its banking regulations under Governor Charles Evans Hughes, in office from 1907 to 1910. But New York banking department reports showed how powerful the financial conglomerate was. The "money trust" was way beyond the power of New York regulators. Solutions would require federal action.

A congressional committee investigated the "money trust" in 1912 and issued its report the next year. It is often called the "Pujo Committee" after its chair, Congressman Arsène Pujo. The committee's counsel, New

York City attorney Samuel Untermeyer, questioned dozens of witnesses and elicited evidence of the dominance of the financial system by an elite group of bankers. He grilled J. P. Morgan himself on the witness stand, eliciting testimony that showed Morgan defending his work and decrying potential government oversight and interference with it.

New York enacted a few Wall Street reforms in 1913 as a result of the Pujo revelations. But the Pujo Committee had exposed the extent of the concentration, as summarized in the section of the report excerpted below, and showed that federal regulation was needed. Over the next two years, federal action included a constitutional amendment that authorized a federal income tax, the Federal Reserve Act, and the Clayton Anti-Trust Act.

～

From REPORT OF THE COMMITTEE APPOINTED PURSUANT TO HOUSE RESOLUTIONS 429 AND 504 TO INVESTIGATE THE CONCENTRATION OF CONTROL OF MONEY AND CREDIT (1913)

Chapter Third:
Concentration of Control of Money and Credit

Section 1. Two Kinds of Concentration

It is important at the outset to distinguish between concentration of the volume of money in the three central reserve cities of the national banking system—New York, Chicago, and St. Louis—and concentration of control of this volume of money and consequently of credit into fewer and fewer hands. They are very different things. An increasing proportion of the banking resources of the country might be concentrating at a given point at the same time that control of such resources at that point was spreading out in a wider circle. Concentration of control of money, and consequently of credit, more particularly in the city of New York, is the subject of this inquiry. With concentration of the volume of money at certain points, sometimes attributed, so far as it is unnatural, to the provision of the national-banking act permitting banks in the 47 other reserve cities to deposit with those in the three central reserve cities half of their reserves, we are not here directly concerned.

Whether under a different currency system the resources in our banks would be greater or less is comparatively immaterial if they continued to be controlled by a small group. We therefore regard the argument presented to us to show that the growth of concentration of the volume of resources in the banks of New York City has been at a rate slightly less than in the rest of the country, if that be the fact, as not involved in our inquiry. It should be observed in this connection, however, that the concentration of control of credit is by no means confined to New York City, so that the argument is inapplicable also in this respect. The resources of the banks and trust companies of the city of New York in 1911 were $5,121,245,175, which is 21.73 per cent of the total banking resources of the country as reported to the Comptroller of the Currency. This takes no account of the unknown resources of the great private banking houses whose affiliations to the New York financial institutions we are about to discuss.

That in recent years concentration of control of the banking resources and consequently of credit by the group to which we will refer has grown apace in the city of New York is defended by some witnesses and regretted by others, but acknowledged by all to be a fact.

As appears from statistics compiled by accountants for the committee, in 1911, of the total resources of the banks and trust companies in New York City, the 20 largest held 42.97 per cent; in 1906, the 20 largest held 38.24 per cent of the total; in 1901, 34.97 per cent.

This increased concentration of control of money and credit has been effected principally as follows:

First, through consolidations of competitive or potentially competitive banks and trust companies, which consolidations in turn have recently been brought under sympathetic management.

Second, through the same powerful interests becoming large stock holders in potentially competitive banks and trust companies. This is the simplest way of acquiring control, but since it requires the largest investment of capital, it is the least used, although the recent investments in that direction for that apparent purpose amount to tens of millions of dollars in present market values.

Third, through the confederation of potentially competitive banks and trust companies by means of the system of interlocking directorates.

Fourth, through the influence which the more powerful banking houses, banks, and trust companies have secured in the management of insurance companies, railroads, producing and trading corporations, and public utility corporations, by means of stockholdings, voting trusts, fiscal agency contracts, or representation upon their boards of directors, or through supplying the money requirements of railway, industrial, and public utilities corporations and thereby being enabled to participate in the determination of their financial and business policies.

Fifth, through partnership or joint account arrangements between a few of the leading banking houses, banks, and trust companies in the purchase of security issues of the great interstate corporations, accompanied by understandings of recent growth—sometimes called "banking ethics"—which have had the effect of effectually destroying competition between such banking houses, banks, and trust companies in the struggle for business or in the purchase and sale of large issues of such securities.

It is a fair deduction from the testimony that the most active agents in forwarding and bringing about the concentration of control of money and credit through one or another of the processes above described have been and are:

J. P. Morgan & Co
First National Bank of New York
National City Bank of New York
Lee, Higginson & Co. of Boston and New York.
Kidder, Peabody & Co. of Boston and New York
Kuhn, Loeb & Co. . . .
Evolution of the Controlling Groups

Your committee is satisfied from the proofs submitted, even in the absence of data from the banks, that there is an established and well defined identity and community of interest between a few leaders of finance, created and held together through stock ownership, interlocking directorates, partnership and joint account transactions, and other forms of domination over bank, trust companies, railroads, and public service and industrial corporations, which has resulted in great and rapidly growing concentration of the control of money and credit in the hands of these few men.

The bulk of the oral and documentary evidence taken before your committee was directed toward ascertaining whether, in current phrase, there is a "money trust." If by such a trust is meant a combination or arrangement created and existing pursuant to a definite agreement between designated per sons with the avowed and accomplished object of concentrating unto themselves the control of money and credit, we are unable to say that the existence of a money trust has been established in that broad bald sense of the term, although the committee regrets to find that even adopting that extreme definition surprisingly many of the elements of such a combination exist. . . .

Under our system of issuing and distributing corporate securities the investing public does not buy directly from the corporation. The securities travel from the issuing house through middlemen to the investor. It is only the great banks or bankers with access to the mainsprings of the concentrated resources made up of other people's money in the banks, trust companies, and life insurance companies, and with control of the machinery for creating markets and distributing securities, who have had the power to underwrite or guarantee the sale of large-scale security issues. The men who through their control over the funds of our railroad and industrial companies are able to direct where such funds shall be kept, and thus to create these great reservoirs of the people's money are the ones who are in position to tap those reservoirs for the ventures in which they are interested and to prevent their being tapped for purposes of which they do not approve. The latter is quite as important a factor as the former. It is a controlling consideration in its effect on competition in the railroad and industrial world.

When we consider, also, in this connection that into these reservoirs of money and credit there flow a large part of the reserves of the banks of the country, that they are also the agents and correspondents of the out-of-town banks in the loaning of their surplus funds in the only public money market of the country, and that a small group of men and their partners and associates have now further strengthened their hold upon the resources of these institutions by acquiring large stock holdings therein, by representation on their boards and through valuable patronage we begin to realize some thing of the extent to which this practical and effective domination and control over many of our greatest financial, railroad, and industrial corporations has developed, largely within the past five years, and that it is fraught with peril to the welfare of the country.

If, therefore, by a "money trust" is meant:

> An established and well-defined identity and community of interest between a few leaders of finance which has been created and is held together through stock holdings, interlocking directorates, and other forms of domination over banks, trust companies, railroads, public-service and industrial corporations, and which has resulted in a vast and growing concentration of

control of money and credit in the hands of a comparatively few men,

your committee, as before stated, has no hesitation in asserting as the result of its investigation up to this time that the condition thus described exists in this country today.

Some of the endless ramifications of this power have been traced and presented and it is upon these that we have based our findings.

Many others can be fully discovered and analyzed only after a close scrutiny of the internal affairs of the great national banks that will disclose the ways in which their resources are used, to whom their funds are loaned, what securities they have been buying and selling and how their vast profits have been earned. Whilst your committee has been denied access to this data, sufficient has been learned to reveal the relations of these banks and of the State banks and trust companies and the use that has been made of them in upbuilding a power over our financial system and in consequence over our railroads and greater industries that permits real competition on a large scale in the various fields of enterprise only by sufferance, if at all.

The parties to this combination or understanding or community of interest, by whatever name it may be called, may be conveniently classified, for the purpose of differentiation, into four separate groups.

First. The first, which for convenience of statement we will call the inner group, consists of J. P. Morgan & Co., the recognized leaders, and George F. Baker and James Stillman in their individual capacities and in their joint administration and control of the First National Bank, the National City Bank, the National Bank of Commerce, the Chase National Bank, the Guaranty Trust Co., and the Bankers Trust Co., with total known resources, in these corporations alone, in excess of $1,300,000,000, and of a number of smaller but important financial institutions. This takes no account of the personal fortunes of these gentlemen. . . .

In the case of the pending New York subway financing of $170,000,000 of bonds by Messrs. Morgan & Co. and their associates, Mr. Davison estimated that there were from 100 to 125 such underwriters who were apparently glad to agree that Messrs. Morgan & Co., the First National Bank, and the National City Bank should receive 3 per cent—equal to $5,100,000—for forming this syndicate, thus relieving themselves from all liability, whilst the underwriters assumed the risk of what the bonds would realize and of being required to take their share of the unsold portion.

This transaction furnishes a fair illustration of the basis on which this inner group is able to capitalize its financial power. Included among the underwriters are the banks and trust companies that are controlled by Messrs. Morgan, Baker, and Stillman under voting trusts, through stock ownerships, and in the other ways described.

Thus, they utilize this control for their own profit and that of the stockholders of the institutions. But the advantage to the depositors whose money and credit may be used in financing such enterprises is not apparent. It may be that this recently concentrated money power so far has not been abused otherwise than in the possible exaction of excessive profits through absence of competition.

Sources

Hendrick, Burton J.. "Governor Hughes," *Outlook* 30 (April 1908), 674–76, 679–81. Available at HathiTrust, https://babel.hathitrust.org/cgi/pt?id=uc1.$b199987&view=page&seq=11.

Hughes, Charles Evans, "Inaugural Address," in State of New York, *Public Papers of Charles E. Hughes, Governor*, January 1, 1907 (Albany: J. B. Lyon, 1908), 5—9. Available at HathiTrust, https://babel.hathitrust.org/cgi/pt?id=coo1.ark:/13960/t7tm7t44p&view=page&seq=5.

Report of the Joint Committee of the Senate and Assembly of the State of New York Appointed to Investigate the Affairs of Life Insurance Companies (New York: M. B. Brown Company, 1906), 284–88. Available at HathiTrust, https://babel.hathitrust.org/cgi/pt?id=mdp.35112105253225&view=page&seq=1.

Report of the [US House of Representatives] Committee Appointed Pursuant to House Resolutions 429 and 504 to Investigate the Concentration of Control of Money and Credit (Washington: Government Printing Office, 1913), 55–56, 129–32. Available at HathiTrust, https://babel.hathitrust.org/cgi/pt?id=mdp.39015056056255&view=page&seq=5.

Stevens, Frank W., "The Work of the Public Service Commission, Second District, and its Policies With Relation To the Corporations Under Its Supervision," in *Discussion of Present Day Problems* (New York: Empire State Gas and Electric Corporation and Street Railway Association of the State of New York, 1908), 6-11. Available at HathiTrust, https://babel.hathitrust.org/cgi/pt?id=nnc1.cu56783248&view=page&seq=1.

9

Helping Workers

Figures 9a and 9b. The State Factory Investigating Commission (1911–1915) documented fire hazards and unsafe working conditions, including these in a rope-making factory in Auburn (left) and a men's clothing factory in Hudson (right). The commission's reports prompted enactment of laws to improve factory safety. *Source*: New York State Archives Digital Collections.

Before 1900, working conditions in New York factories were mostly unregulated. New York had rudimentary sanitary and safety regulations passed in the final two decades of the nineteenth century. But state government was mostly unconcerned with factory conditions. Regulations were laxly enforced due in part to inadequate staffing in the state factory inspector's office. Labor unions were mostly still small or in the process of organization. Working conditions and safety measures varied greatly, depending on the employer.

That began to change with the new century. Labor unions grew in strength and secured higher wages and other benefits for men and women workers through collective bargaining. After 1900, the public grew more concerned about long working hours, unsafe factory conditions, and accidents on the job. Enlightened employers voluntarily improved conditions. An activist press and popular journals published in New York City, in concert with progressive reformers, transformed public concern into demand, jolted more employers into voluntary action, and led to substantial new government regulation in the form of new laws and regulations. This included an expanded Department of Labor that featured a State Board of Mediation and Arbitration to help settle labor disputes, restrictions on working hours, enhanced factory safety and fire protection, a workers' compensation law, and employment offices. New York courts generally supported unions' collective bargaining efforts and the right to strike. By 1920, New York had a very strong industrial code.

Industrial Morality and Social Progress

Progressive reformers advocated reigning in big business, mandating improved factory working conditions, and regulating hours and wages. Often, they made the case for taking a holistic view of needs and opportunities. Shorter working hours, particularly for women, improved working conditions, worker safety requirements, and labor unions would all contribute to stronger families and society.

New York social and political reformer Florence Kelley (1859–1932) was one of the most energetic and effective of the progressive-era leaders. She led in several campaigns of the time, including curtailing child labor, improving factory working conditions and safety, increasing factory inspections, limiting work hours, enacting workers' compensation, and achieving racial equality (she was one of the organizers of the NAACP). Kelley was the founder of the New York-based National Consumers' League, which fought for improved labor working conditions, in 1899 and served as its general secretary from then until 1932.

Kelley had a knack for connecting parts of her agenda so that the relationship among them was clear and mutually reinforcing. She was very adept at explaining things. In a series of 1913 speeches at Columbia University Teachers' College, published as a book the following year, she deftly linked the impact of factory work on workers and their families, the importance of government labor regulations, the value of labor organizations, and the need for change in public opinion about the social responsibilities of industry. She encapsulated several of these themes in the term industrial morality—*more humane, responsible, worker-oriented industrial policies. That was a good fit for progressivism, which emphasized the underlying morality as well as the social benefit of progressive-oriented policies.*

∼

FROM *MODERN INDUSTRY IN RELATION TO THE FAMILY, HEALTH, EDUCATION, MORALITY* (1914) BY FLORENCE KELLEY

Modern Industry and the Family

Modern industry affords, in more generous measure than the human race has before known them, all those goods which form the material basis of family life food, clothing, shelter, and the materials and opportunities for subsistence for husband, wife and children.

But modern industry tends to disintegrate the family, so threatens it that the civilized nations are, and for at least one generation have been, actively building a code intended to save the family from this destructive pressure. This is the paradox of Modern Industry.

It is my object to illustrate this paradox by indicating some forms of the pressure of industry upon the family, and upon each of its elements. The American ideal of the home inherited from the time when we were an agricultural country includes father, mother and children living together in a house; the father the breadwinner, the mother the homemaker, the children at play and at school until they reach a reasonable age for work, boys helping their fathers with the chores and the girls learning under their mothers' eyes the arts of the housewife, the house which shelters this group being the property of the family or in process of becoming their property. Originally, the typical home was a farm which furnished subsistence, and the children received within the family group industrial, religious and moral training. Our departure from this early ideal under the pressure of modern industry is conspicuous.

The paradoxical tendency of the family to disintegrate under pressure of the same industry which affords it infinite material enrichment offers the key to a complex, varied legislative movement going forward in all the civilized nations. Seemingly incoherent, this movement is a ramified effort to safeguard the family. The mind is wearied even by a partial enumeration of the elements of the industrial and political code upon which the modern world is at work to this end. Among those elements, the following are important:

    a. Compulsory arbitration of labor disputes

    b. Workmen's compensation and social insurance, factory inspection and compulsory provision of fire precautions and safety devices

    c. Regulation of working time, including one day's rest in seven, a short working day, prohibition of night work for women and children, and the utmost attainable restriction of night work for men

    d. Prohibition of child labor and of homework under the sweating system

    e. Minimum wage boards and widows' pensions with generous provision for institutional care of certain classes of diseased and defective children

    f. Compulsory education prolonged for part time instruction throughout minority [up to adulthood]

    g. Housing codes

    h. Pure food laws

    i. The enfranchisement of women

Such effort to bulwark the family by comprehensive legislation arises because, all over the modern world, a large and increasing proportion of husbands and fathers are by the nature of their work taken out of their homes, or killed outright, or maimed, or they are disabled by industrial diseases, and thus disqualified for their normal duty of breadwinner.

On throughout long periods of seasonal unemployment they are recurrently without earnings. Even when in health and at work, unskilled laborers and many employees of higher grade are so far underpaid that they cannot maintain their wives and children, who are, therefore, drawn out of the home into industry to supplement the earnings of the father;

or the home is invaded under the sweating system [companies supplying materials, such as cloth to make garments, to workers and paying by the piece for work done at home] for the materials of industry. . . .

Our Preparation for the Change

Our lack is intellectual and spiritual. We distrust ourselves and each other. The mental energy of our ablest men has been too largely expended in industrial organization in the service of greed for dividends. We have been taught too long, and we have believed too credulously, that the profit motive is the best of which we are capable. The failure and crime that we see we attribute to the frailty of human nature, not, as the facts demand, to the corroding power of industry on a basis fundamentally immoral.

We all suffer a lack of moral sensitiveness because we are, throughout our lives, members of a society in which the average length of life of wage earners is conspicuously less than the life of prosperous people. We accept this with equanimity as we accept child labor, and avoidable night work even when performed by young girls, and the monstrous spectacle of wholesale poverty in the midst of riches beyond the power of the mind to compute or to conceive. Our industrial epoch has corroded our morals and hardened our hearts as surely as slavery injured its contemporaries, and far more subtly.

There is grave reason to fear that it may have unfitted us for the oncoming stage of civilization, as slave owning unfitted the white race for freedom and democracy, and left its blight of race hatred from which the Republic still suffers.

Acid tests of the industrial morality of every public movement are the questions: "Does it tend to restore to the people who work a share in the ownership and control of the tools of industry? Does it contribute to the ability of any group of wage earners to fit themselves in mind, character and economic position to participate helpfully in the transition? Does it promote the enactment of the industrial code?" Whatever is calculated to enable us as a people, or any group among us, to make a step forward on the road to peaceful service away from the battlefield of greed, is a contribution to the sum total of industrial morality. And whatsoever hinders a forward step is in itself actively evil, because it prolongs the existing evil. We can retrieve our integrity only as we come to accept as our ideal service instead of profit.

And this can be achieved only as industry becomes a city, state, and national service. We are, indeed, confronted by the task of extending public ownership of industry, and cooperative distribution of products, in the interest of the moral life of the American people.

No one can predict how we, as a nation, shall bear the strain of industry made collective, and permanently a cooperative undertaking of citizens, without the relation of master and men. No prophet can foretell with certainty whether we can make that change peacefully, without a great revulsion and reaction, by reason of the uncooperative spirit in which we have all been bred. In the transition from the old industrial society we need to bring to bear all the wisdom, all the varied experience and discipline, that life has bestowed upon us all. We cannot safely omit from the common task any human soul however humble.

In each generation some cause arises which serves as a touchstone for the genuine democracy of mankind. Such today is the industrial transition. On the Pacific Coast and in the Northwest where the citizens have developed democratic institutions the initiative, the referendum, the recall (including judges), equal suffrage, minimum wage boards, and the short working day they go forward confidently with transition measures. There the conservation battle rages.

Indeed, the most hopeful feature of our outlook is our democracy, the fact that manhood suffrage has long been a matter of course in most of the states, the rapidly developing movement for giving votes to women, and the spread of the new devices of democracy eastward from the Pacific Coast.

It is the teachers' duty to prepare the minds of the next generation for carrying on the further stages of this industrial and political change. But how can the teachers themselves be fitted for their task?

The time of transition needs more than all things else socially minded people, multitudes of average men and women trained to habits of integrity and cooperation. But what preparation has been made for this?. . . .

Ending Child Labor

Progressive reformers undertook several initiatives to improve the condition and prospects of New York's children. One of their targets was child labor. Thousands of children were employed in New York's textile, canning, paint, and other factories and in stores at the beginning of the century. They were paid much less than adults, were required to work long hours, and often skipped school, or dropped out, in order to work. Their parents frequently facilitated this by lying about their kids' ages and claiming they needed the income to support the family. State factory laws prohibited the worst abuses, but they were incomplete, lightly enforced and easily evaded.

The New York Child Labor Committee, an alliance of social workers, settlement house workers, consumer advocates, and children's rights champions, was organized in New York City in 1902 to remedy the situation. Florence Kelley, the progressive leader referenced in the document immediately above; Lillian Wald, founder of a settlement house and a visiting nurse service; and a number of wealthy, influential New Yorkers joined the cause. Like so many progressive reformers, they began by winning over the public through investigations, widely reported in the newspapers, which dramatically highlighted the problem by citing actual examples, as in the examples below. The results were dramatic. The next year, 1903, the legislature passed New York's first child labor laws, prohibiting the employment of children under fourteen in factories, department stores, and other commercial establishments and strengthening New York's compulsory school attendance law. The state Department of Labor was strengthened and enforced the new laws. Employers began to comply voluntarily, seeing the justification for the regulations and not wanting to be exposed in the press or cited by the labor department.

~

"The City's Child Labor," *New York Tribune*, January 2, 1903

Giuseppe is ten years old. He is sent for [to sell] papers [on the street] daily but has no regular stand. Though he may not return home without profits proportionate to the 'stakes' his mother furnishes him, he keeps all his 'odds," that is, the money made over and above the profits. His average earnings are about 20 cents. He is furnished with supper and breakfast at home but buys his dinner for five cents or less. In school he lacks almost wholly concentration and attention and is consequently very unruly and uninterested in school work. He makes an incorrigible truant. The money he makes beyond his normal profit he uses for gambling and cigarettes. He is nervous and irritable. On hard luck nights, he sleeps where he can. Twice he has been caught stealing lead pipe when he had not been able to make enough to take home. His father is able bodied and makes $8 to $10 a week [enough to support the family without the boy's wages, according to child labor reformers].

A local express company employs children of eleven and upward. They begin work at 7 a.m. and make their last trip between 9 and 10 o'clock at night. On Friday and Saturday they work until midnight. If the packages are not all delivered by midnight on Saturday they must return on Sunday morning to finish the task. There are children who deliver milk from 4 a.m. until school time. Other children, both boys and girls, work both before and after school cleaning halls and basements of the poorer flats and hotels or washing dishes there. Some are working so as not to be under their parental control. Others were required to work by parents without regard to their welfare. In cases of actual poverty, where the child's small wage is urgently required, it is a case for charity. The burden is too heavy to be borne by any street boy. The earnings for which all this sacrifice of child health, education and morals is going on are absurdly small.

"LITTLE WAGE EARNERS," *NEW YORK TRIBUNE*, FEBRUARY 13, 1903

Jennie Boose is called a 'turner-in.' She takes the cardboard from a paster [in a box factory] and folds the paper that covers the outside of the box over the edge of the cardboard. The occupation is simple and her employer finds her stature and extreme youth no drawbacks to the accomplishment of the tasks. She is four feet high and twelve years old. According to her employment papers, she is fifteen years old. Her certificate was secured and she began work in the factory when she was still eleven. During the busy season she worked from 7:30 in the morning until 7:00 at night with one half hour off for lunch. She was released from work on Saturday at 5 o'clock. For her week's work, she was paid $2.75. Her regular weekly wage is $2.50 but for the extra work she received 25 cents.

From Tragedy to Action

A tragic fire at the Triangle Shirtwaist textile factory in New York City on March 25, 1911, resulted in the deaths of 146 workers, most of them young women. The fire was the result of overcrowding in the factory, lack of fire prevention and protection, including adequate fire escapes, and, overall, employer and New York state government indifference to the safety and welfare of workers.

At a mass meeting at Metropolitan Opera House in New York City on April 2, several civic and labor leaders put the responsibility for the tragedy, and for making sure it never happened again, on the people of the state. There must be action, said a number of speakers, but they did not emphasize the urgency for doing something dramatic and right away.

But the speech by labor leader and women's rights advocate Rose Schneiderman (1882–1972), vice president of the Women's Trade Union League, was an exception. It was brief but the most notable and moving at the meeting.

Schneiderman, who had been a factory worker as well as a union organizer, decried lax fire and safety standards that led to injuries and deaths on the job. She recalled the role of police in helping employers crush strikes. She practically shouted that the time for talk was past, the time for union organization and government action was now. Her speech led to the group passing resolutions demanding state action and quickly sending a delegation to Albany. Under pressure from the group, the legislature quickly established the Factory Investigation Commission (see the document immediately below). Over the next few years, the commission's work led to New York's adopting the most extensive factory safety code and requirements in the nation.

∽

FROM SPEECH BY ROSE SCHNEIDERMAN IN *THE SURVEY* (1911)

I would be a traitor to these poor burned bodies if I came here to talk good fellowship. We have tried you good people of the public and we have found you wanting. The old Inquisition had its rack and its thumbscrews and its instruments of torture with iron teeth. We know what these things are today; the iron teeth are our necessities, the thumbscrews are the high-powered and swift machinery close to which we must work, and the rack is here in the firetrap structures that will destroy us the minute they catch on fire.

This is not the first time girls have been burned alive in the city. Every week I must learn of the untimely death of one of my sister workers. Every year thousands of us are maimed. The life of men and women is so cheap and property is so sacred. There are so many of us for one job it matters little if 143 [sic] of us are burned to death.

We have tried you citizens; we are trying you now, and you have a couple of dollars for the sorrowing mothers and brothers and sisters by way of a charity gift. But every time the workers come out in the only way they know to protest against conditions which are unbearable the strong hand of the law is allowed to press down heavily upon us.

Public officials have only words of warning to us—warning that we must be intensely orderly and must be intensely peaceable, and they have the workhouse just back of all their warnings. The strong hand of the law beats us back, when we rise, into the conditions that make life unbearable.

I can't talk fellowship to you who are gathered here. Too much blood has been spilled. I know from my experience it is up to the working people to save themselves. The only way they can save themselves is by a strong working-class movement.

A Progressive Industrial Code

After the Triangle Shirtwaist Factory fire on March 25, 1911, claimed the lives of many workers, an outraged public demanded that the state government take action to prevent a recurrence of another tragic factory fire and to improve workers' safety and sanitary conditions.

The Democrats had taken over both the governorship and the legislature in the 1910 elections. The legislature's newly elevated progressive Democratic leaders, Senator Robert Wagner and Assemblyman Alfred E. Smith, created a Factory Investigating Commission to address the issue. Wagner signed on as chair, Smith as vice-chair, to guide the commission. Wagner and Smith hired a cadre of attorneys and factory investigators. Initial legislation required a report (excerpted below) within a year, but the legislature enthusiastically extended the commission's tenure through the end of 1914.

The commission's energetic investigators included emerging industrial reformer Francis Perkins (who would become FDR's Secretary of Labor in the New Deal in the 1930s) and others determined to improve factory conditions. Its recommendations led to tighter enforcement of existing regulations and to new ones on building codes, fire safety, sanitation, lighting, and ventilation, and a new Industrial Commission for enforcement. It also recommended workers' compensation and limits on working hours, which were also enacted into law.

The Factory Investigating Commission produced several reports during its tenure, providing detailed analysis of needs, essays and testimony by experts, photos documenting working conditions, and outlines of proposed new legislation. The reports highlighted the state government's obligations to protect its workers, an underlying theme in the progressive movement.

FROM *PRELIMINARY REPORT OF THE FACTORY INVESTIGATING COMMISSION* (1912)

Creation of Commission

On Saturday afternoon, March 25, 1911, a fire took place in the business establishment of the Triangle Waist Company, at No. 23–29 Washington Place, in the Borough of Manhattan, City of New York, in which 145 employees, mainly women and girls, lost their lives. This shocking loss of life aroused the community to a full sense of its responsibility. The public began to realize that in factories and manufacturing establishments that constituted a daily menace to the lives of the thousands of working men, women and children. Lack of precautions to prevent fire, inadequate fire-escape facilities, insanitary conditions that were insidiously undermining the health of the workers were found existing everywhere. The need of a thorough and extensive investigation into the general conditions of factory life was clearly recognized.

Public-spirited citizens and representatives from the Fifth Avenue Association of the City of New York, the Committee on Safety of the City of New York and other organizations laid these facts before the Governor and Legislature of the State and asked for the appointment of a legislative commission to inquire into the conditions under which manufacturing was carried on in the cities of the first and second class of the State. As a result, the Act creating this Commission (Chapter 561 of the Laws of 1911) was passed and became a law on June 30, 1911. . . .

The Commission was authorized by the Legislature to inquire into the existing conditions under which manufacturing was carried on in so-called loft buildings and otherwise, including matters affecting the health and safety of the operatives as well as the security and best interests of the public, the character of the buildings and structures in which such manufacturing and business takes place, and the laws and ordinances regulating their erection, maintenance and supervision so that, among other things, remedial legislation might be enacted to eliminate existing peril to life and health of operatives and occupants in existing or new structures and to promote the best interests of the community. The Commission was required to report to the Legislature on or before the 15th day of February, 1912. . . .

Scope of the Investigation

The Commission was charged with the duty of inquiring into the following matters:

1. Hazard to life because of fire: covering fire prevention, arrangement of machinery, fire drills, inadequate fire escapes and exits, number of persons employed in factories and lofts, etc.

2. Danger to life and health because of insanitary conditions: ventilation, lighting and heating arrangement, hours of labor, etc.

3. Occupational diseases: industrial consumption, lead poisoning, bone disease, etc.

4. Proper and adequate inspection of factories and manufacturing establishments.

5. Manufacturing in tenement houses.

6. The present statutes and ordinances that deal with or relate to the foregoing matters, and the extent to which the present laws are enforced.

The Commission was to recommend such new legislation as might be found necessary to remedy defects in existing legislation, and to provide for conditions at present unregulated.

The Act creating this Commission limited the scope of its inquiry to cities of the first and second class, although the Commission was authorized to inquire into the conditions surrounding manufacturing in other cities of the State and country if it should so determine.

Importance of the Investigation

New York is the first State in the Union to authorize a general investigation of the conditions in manufacturing establishments within its borders. Several other States have appointed commissions which were limited in the scope of their investigations, such as the Illinois Commission on the subject of occupational diseases, the Massachusetts Commission on Factory Inspection and the various Commissions on accident prevention and employers' liability. It remained for the State of New York to lead the way with an investigation of factory conditions general in its scope and character. According to the preliminary report of the Census of 1910 there were 1,003,981 men, women and children employed in the factories and manufacturing establishments of New York State. This is the average of the number employed during the year. The Commissioner of Labor gives the number of such employees as 1,250,000.

In addition to the actual wage earners concerned, the Commission's inquiry bears indirectly upon the millions of women and children who compose the families of these workers and are dependent upon them for support. Health is the principal asset of the working man and the working woman. The State is bound to do everything in its power to preserve the health of the workers who contribute so materially to its economic wealth and its industrial prosperity. Aside from the humanitarian aspect of the situation, economic considerations demand from the State the careful supervision and protection of its workers. Failure to perform this obligation will produce serious results in the workers of the future. It will affect the working capacity of the future generations.

The State not only possesses the power and the right, but it is charged with the sacred duty of seeing that the worker is properly safeguarded in case of fire; that he is protected from accidents caused by neglect or indifference; that proper precautions are taken to prevent poisoning by the materials and processes of his industry, and that he works under conditions conducive to good health, and not such as breed disease. Indifference to these matters reflects grossly upon the present day civilization, and it is regrettable that our State and national legislation on the subject of industrial hygiene compares so unfavorably with that of other countries. Factory workers particularly need protection and supervision. Among them disease more easily finds its victims than among other classes of workers. Every epidemic has drawn most of its victims from the working classes. Statistics show the greater mortality of those engaged in factory work, as compared with those in other occupations. . . .

New York has already expended great sums of money to conserve its natural resources. The conservation of human life, the most valuable of all things, has received but little attention. The appointment of this Commission was the first comprehensive attempt to investigate the waste of human life in our modern industrial system and to endeavor to devise means to prevent such a sacrifice, surely a matter of equal importance to the preservation of forests and streams.

Fires and industrial accidents are fortunately only occasional and extraordinary events. Their effects are visible and immediate so they are impressed forcibly upon our minds. But the common, everyday incidents of industrial life, the lack of ventilation, the long hours of labor amid insanitary surroundings, the failure to give notice to employees of the dangers of their occupations and how to avoid them, these work unnoticed, but the toll of human life they exact is very great.

The illness and diseases caused by these conditions can in large measure be prevented, and prevention is always better than cure and less costly. In his report on National Vitality, Professor Irving Fisher shows that the economic gain to the nation that would result from proper precaution to prevent sickness and diseases would amount to at least $500,000,000 per annum.

A New York State manufacturer testified before the Commission that he had installed a great many sanitary improvements and labor-saving devices tending to the comfort of his employees. He expressly disclaimed any philanthropical motives in so doing, but said it was a decided benefit to him in his business from a purely dollars-and-cents standpoint.

During the past few decades methods of protecting machinery in use have been vastly improved. Labor-saving devices have been introduced everywhere, but much remains to be done by the manufacturer to conserve the most valuable of all assets the working man and the working woman. It cannot be said that this waste is the result of intentional wrongdoing. It has simply been nobody's business, and therefore has been neglected and unheeded.

The investigation has already produced results. In many cases the manufacturers themselves were unaware of the conditions under which they required their employees to work, or if indeed they were aware of these conditions, did not realize their evil effects. Many did not know what could be done to improve them. They took these conditions as a matter of course.

The authorities in many cities, because of the publicity of the Commission's inquiry, began special investigations, which resulted in many cases in improved conditions. The educational value of the Commission, therefore, has been very great. The manufacturers who had not only complied with the provisions of the law, but had gone beyond its requirements, should feel rewarded by the contrast which was shown.

A general awakening has taken place throughout the State. A far larger number of inspections by authorities have been made than ever before. No great reliance, however, can be placed upon such a momentary or spasmodic awakening. When its cause is no longer present, conditions relapse into their former state, and there is little real improvement. To improve the industrial situation permanently, clear, concise and comprehensive legislation is needed.

Special Protection for Women Workers

Progressive reformers pushed for shorter working hours, better conditions, and higher pay, particularly for women employed in factories. Thousands of women worked in bookbinding factories in New York, particularly New York City, the publishing capital of the nation. To outsiders, the work seemed relatively light and easy, but in reality it could entail long hours, low wages, and operating dangerous machinery.

New York labor reform advocate Mary Van Kleeck (1883–1972) studied women in the New York bookbinding trade in a project sponsored by the Russell Sage Foundation, which was dedicated to improving social and living conditions in the country. Her influential 1913 book, Women in the Bookbinding Trade, *described working conditions in detail, revealed the prevalence of low wages, and advocated for more enlightened owner policies and state action. Soon new state laws, some inspired by the book, restricted women's working hours and mandated improved working conditions. Van Kleeck went on to a long career of advocating for better working conditions and higher wages.*

∼

From *Women in the Bookbinding Trade* (1913)
by Mary Van Kleeck

The conditions of women's work in the bookbinding trade fail in many particulars to measure up to the standard which public opinion has begun to demand. About 10 per cent of the women workers are under sixteen. Careful supervision of learners in the workroom is rare. Processes are so subdivided as to deaden mental faculties rather than to encourage growth in intelligence. As yet the subject of industrial education is discussed only with reference to the men in the trade, and little attention is given to the problem in the women's department.

Operating complicated machines, repeating one process hour after hour, standing at work all day, carrying loads of heavy paper from one part of the shop to another, stooping frequently to lift the folded sections of books, pressing a foot pedal rapidly and incessantly, or handling the completed volumes to wrap them for shipping, these are tasks which would inevitably fatigue girls even though the day never lasted longer than eight hours. Yet only a fourth of the women in the shops investigated had as short a working day as eight hours, and 44 per cent worked longer than forty-eight hours in a week. In fully three-fourths of the binderies the girls worked overtime at some season of the year. More than half of the statements collected regarding this overtime showed an excess above the limit allowed by law. Moreover, flagrant instances are recorded of the employment of women throughout the night.

The average wage reported by the group of girls interviewed by us was $7.22 a week, while the average reported by census enumerators in 1905 was even lower, $6.13. Yet it has been seen that women bookbinders are members of households in which it is difficult to make ends meet, and in which heavy responsibilities fall upon the women wage-earners. Their earnings are reduced still lower by reason of irregular work. Only about a third work in establishments reporting steady employment. Nearly three-fourths of the workers interviewed had frequently lost time in slack seasons. Only one in eight reported no time lost for any cause, while nearly a third reported a loss of one to three months during the year, and more than a fourth lost three months or more. An estimate of the approximate yearly income of bindery women shows that nearly three-fourths receive less than $400 in a year, in spite of their finding employment in other occupations when they have no work in bookbinding. An income of less than $400 a year is distinctly below the generally accepted estimate of $9.00 a week as the minimum wage on which a woman can support herself in New York City. . . .

Scientific men in many countries have proved beyond question that getting tired is a physiological process equivalent to taking poison into the system. The poison is eliminated and the tissues restored only by a period of rest. Furthermore, rest must be taken before fatigue has become so great as to result in an exhaustion from which recovery is difficult. The application of these facts to the regulation of the hours of work of women in industry is obvious. The public welfare demands that work shall cease and rest be permitted before the worker becomes exhausted. No enlightened employer of women can fail to welcome the scientific conclusions already reached on this subject, and to take them into consideration in determining the hours of work in his establishment. . . .

[A new Massachusetts law regulating working hours and conditions] is indicative of a growing demand for the betterment of conditions, a demand in which all classes of the population are now joining, however great may be their differences of opinion as to methods of reform. Reports of the meetings of the National Association of Manufacturers show their interest in the prevention and relief of work-accidents, in a comprehensive plan for industrial education, and in an effort to bring "manufacturers in every department of industry to a higher realization of their social responsibility to their employees and the public." The American Federation of Labor works through its affiliated unions in many trades to prohibit the employment of children under sixteen, to establish an eight-hour day in all trades, and to secure a living wage for every worker. State legislatures are rapidly falling into line in the enactment of laws regarding child labor, the introduction of industrial education in public schools, the regulation of the hours of work of women, compensation for accidents, and the maintenance of sanitary conditions in factories. . . .

All these expressions of opinion of manufacturers, workers, and citizens are signs of the times, a promise of better things to come in industry. Following the general statement of principles, however, is the more difficult task of applying these principles in all the various fields of employment into which the world's work is divided. For this application, detailed studies must be made of conditions in each occupation. Reform must necessarily come not in industry as a whole, but trade by trade, since that is the way economic life is organized. Moreover, each trade has its peculiar problems.

To establish proper standards in the bookbinding trade would require certain definite changes, which may be thus summarized:

- Prohibition of the employment of children under sixteen.

- Careful supervision of learners to insure thorough training.

- Cooperation with the public schools in efforts to supply additional opportunities to those who have left school at the age of sixteen.

- Limitation of the hours of work of all women to eight in a day, without permitting overtime.

- Provision for a definite rest period of at least eight hours during the night for all women, irrespective of age.
- Planning the work so as to obviate the ill effects due to specialized tasks and to guard against the dangers peculiar to the trade.
- Provisions for adequate light, ventilation, and space in the workroom and dressing rooms, and for proper toilet facilities.
- Protection against fire assured.
- Resolute efforts to prevent unemployment, and to steady the seasons.
- Payment of adequate wages, with full recognition of the fact that the public welfare requires a living wage for every worker.

To raise all binderies to the level here indicated will require the cooperation of employers, workers, and the public. That the suggestions are practicable is proved by the fact that almost every one of them has been tried to some degree in at least one bindery in New York. No establishment combines them all. The whole trade cannot be suddenly transformed, but a few important changes which would mark a decided advance should now be made general throughout the trade by means of legislation.

No revolutionary reforms are necessary to make state intervention practicable. To strengthen the present laws regarding women's work in factories in New York, and to enforce them strictly, would markedly improve conditions in the bookbinding trade. Many persons now believe that the employment of children under sixteen ought to be prohibited in any occupation, and especially in connection with machines, or in lifting or carrying heavy weights. It seems obvious that a child of fourteen or fifteen should not be employed for such heavy work as that required in binding books. In any case, the present legal provision requiring that no employment certificate shall be issued unless the child "is in sound health and is physically able to perform the work which it intends to do" should be more actively enforced.

The law regarding the hours of work of women ought to be amended for the benefit not only of bindery women but of all women at work in factories. Night work should be prohibited in order to assure an adequate rest period in every twenty-four hours, and to make possible the strict enforcement of the fifty-four-hour law [maximum of fifty-four hours of work per week]. The exception to the nine-hour law permitting a maximum working day of ten hours should be repealed. Prosecutions should be in a reasonable ratio to the number of violations, in order to prove to employers that the law is alive. Public opinion should express itself strongly enough to reach the magistrates' courts, in order that the results of convictions may not be nullified by an unwise use of the suspended sentence.

Workers' Compensation for On-the-Job Injuries

Railroads and factories, which powered New York industry in the new century, were dangerous places for workers. Modern industry relied on high-speed machinery that could injure or kill in an instant. Safety practices varied greatly from one company to the next; in most, safety was not a high employer concern. A few companies adequately compensated workers for their injuries or their families in case of death, but most did not. Workers found buying accident insurance too expensive. Suing an employer for damages in court was costly and usually unsuccessful.

Progressive reformers realized there had to be a better way. They used one of their most common strategies to address the problem: a blue-ribbon study commission. Governor Charles Evans Hughes appointed one to advance recommendations for workers' compensation in 1909. It included a number of progressive stalwarts, most notably women's suffrage and labor reform leader Crystal Eastman, who drafted much of its report. Eastman, an attorney, was an effective investigator, a very skilled writer, and a persuasive behind-the-scenes advocate as well as a public champion for women's suffrage, workers' rights, and international peace. The report on workers' compensation was a model of progressive approaches: reasonable and persuasive in tone, well-researched, describing the problem, advancing a solution, and explaining its merits.

The legislature passed New York's first workers' compensation law that year based on the report, the first state law of its kind in the nation. It was invalidated as unconstitutional by the Court of Appeals (Ives v. South Buffalo Railway Company, 1911). But the public by then wanted a state liability law. The voters approved a state constitutional amendment in 1913 to clearly authorize it, the legislature soon passed a new law that was stronger than the original one, and the Court of Appeals upheld its constitutionality (Matter of Jensen v. Southern Pacific Company, 1915). Workers' compensation, proposed in 1909, became a permanent feature of New York state policy.

From *Report to the Legislature . . . by the Commission Appointed Under Chapter 518 of the Laws of 1909 to Inquire Into the Question of Employers' Liability* (1910)

The Commission is strongly of opinion that the present legal system of employers' liability in force in this State (and practically everywhere else in the United States) in industrial employments is fundamentally wrong and unwise and needs radical change.

The workman injured in his employment must of necessity bear the burden of his injury. The pain and suffering are his, and no system of law can change or shift that burden. But if that injury be not one which he has willfully brought on himself, but has arisen from the hazard of his work, we are unanimously of opinion that the workman should be so placed by the law that he shall have the right to call for and receive such prompt and certain compensation as will keep him and those dependent on him from destitution.

We are further convinced that in industries in this State as they now exist, the workmen are not able to solve this accident difficulty for themselves. Were the laissez faire system of political economy working without friction, a workman engaged in hazardous employments would command and receive wages high enough to enable him to carry the risks of trade accident and insure them and there would be no problem. The accident relief burden reflected in wages would be an element in the cost of the industrial product which the consumers of that product must pay.

But that theory does not work out. Wages are not relatively higher in the most dangerous trades. The accident risk is a minor element in fixing wages, and the workers in dangerous trades are in the majority of cases not able to carry adequate insurance, and in a large proportion of cases seem to carry no insurance.

In view of that fact, we are convinced that the wise policy for the State should be to throw the burden of accident relief in dangerous trades on the industry in another way. Though the workman cannot shift this accident burden upon the cost of the product or upon the trade, the employers can through their power to fix the selling price of the product; just as employers now fix their selling price with reference to the cost of replacing and repairing machinery, so we would have them make an element of the price of the product the cost of relieving the injured workers of hazardous industry.

Our present system of dealing with this question in New York (and the same system prevails in all the United States) is to make no such provision, to require that the workman assume the risks of the trade, and to give him a right to sue his employer at law only when the accident is due to fault of the employer and to recover from his employer such a sum as shall compensate him for the damage suffered. That system discarded in almost every other industrial country, we regard as inherently unfitted to modern industrial conditions in dangerous employments, and grossly unfair to workmen injured by trade risks. In practice our system with its lawsuits is so uncertain, so full of vexatious delays and so wasteful and extravagant, that as a whole it is satisfactory to no class in the community. Moreover, no change in it can cure its greatest defects unless the change amounts to abandoning the theory that the employer shall pay only when the accident is due entirely to his negligence or fault. . . .

Conclusion

The summary of our investigation on employers liability then is:

First, that the present system in New York rests on a basis that is economically unwise and unfair and that in operation it is wasteful, uncertain, and productive of antagonism between workmen and employers.

Second, that it is satisfactory to none and tolerable only to those employers and workmen who practically disregard their legal rights and obligations and fairly share the burden of accidents in industries.

Third, that the evils of the system are most marked in hazardous employments, where the trade risk is high and serious accidents frequent.

Fourth, that, as matter of fact, workmen in the dangerous trades do not, and practically cannot, provide for themselves adequate accident insurance, and therefore, the burden of serious accidents falls on the work men least able to bear it, and brings many of them and their families to want.

These results can, we think, be best avoided by compelling the employer to share the accident burden in intrinsically dangerous trades, since by the fixing of the price of his product the shock of the accident may be borne by the community. In those employments which have not so great an element of danger, in which, speaking generally, there is no such imperative demand for the exercise of the police power of the state for the safeguarding of its workers from destitution and its consequences, we recommend, as the first step in this change of system, such amendment of the present law as will do away with some of its unfairness in theory and practice, and increase the workman's chance of recovery under the law.

With such changes in the law, we couple an elective plan of compensation which if generally adopted, will do away with many of the evils of the present system. Its adoption will we believe be profitable to both employer and employee, and prove to be the simplest way for the State gradually to change its system of liability without disturbance of industrial conditions.

Not the least of the motives moving us is the hope that by these means a source of antagonism between employer and employed, pregnant with danger for the State, may be eliminated.

Documenting the Harmful Effects of Long Working Hours

Many progressive reformers concentrated on reducing long working hours in factories and other industries, particularly for women. At first they were defeated by business leaders who claimed the reformers lacked solid evidence that long hours were really harmful. The reformers set out to remedy that by referencing studies, conducting their own investigations, and presenting the evidence.

New York labor law reform advocate Josephine Goldmark (1877–1950) worked against child labor and for legislation limiting working hours, particularly for women. She assisted her brother-in-law, activist labor attorney (later Supreme Court Justice) Louis Brandeis in preparing a number of court briefs that assembled and presented systematic evidence and convinced judges to uphold the regulatory laws, including a New York law forbidding night work by women in factories (People v. Charles Schweinler Press, 1915).

Her 1912 book, Fatigue and Efficiency, *documented the weariness and health impacts of overly long hours. It also made the case, persuasive to an increasing number of employers, that long hours actually brought diminished productivity. The book cited dozens of studies and reports, including several from Europe, to make its case and also to show that the United States generally—and New York in particular—lagged behind enlightened industrial nations. Goldmark's analysis led to both more enlightened employer policies and expanded government regulation.*

FROM *FATIGUE AND EFFICIENCY: A STUDY IN INDUSTRY* (1912)
BY JOSEPHINE GOLDMARK

The aim of this book is to present, as a new basis for labor legislation, the results of the modern study of fatigue. It seeks to show what fatigue is, its nature and effects, and to explain the phenomena of overwork in working people. It draws upon the scientific study of fatigue—one of the most modern inquiries of physiological, chemical, and psychological science—for aid in the practical problem of reducing the long working day in industry.

Such a scientific basis of legislation has been almost wholly absent during the century which has elapsed since the first factory laws were enacted. First for lack of the necessary scientific equipment, and in recent times, for lack of that coordination of knowledge which should apply the teaching of science to the problems of a new industrial order, labor legislation has been deprived of the authoritative sanction which it might have. In this country, at least, the laws of fatigue, verified by years of experiment in the seclusion of the laboratory, have been practically unknown to those who have been most active in preserving for working people a minimum of human leisure.

Yet such scientific authority is precisely what is most needed today for a more rational progress in the future than in the past; something more exact and demonstrable than the appeal to pity, less subject to temporary variations than what the Italian physiologist Treves calls the "illusory profits of long hours." Just because the more cruel, dramatic exploitation of workers is in the main a thing of the past, exact scientific proof is needed of the more subtle injuries of modern industry, its practically illimitable speed and strain. After a hundred years of human experience throughout the world, it remains true in our own country that the most helpless workers are still, in respect to the length of their working hours, the least protected.

The most recent government investigation of the iron and steel industry in the United States shows that of the 172,671 employees whose hours of labor were reported in May, 1910, nearly one-half (42.58 per cent) were kept at work seventy-two hours a week or over; that is, at least twelve hours daily on six days of the week. Nearly a quarter of all the workers (20.59 per cent) were kept employed eighty-four or more hours in the week; that is, at least twelve hours each day, including Sundays. In the largest single department in the industry, the blast furnaces, 88 per cent of the 31,321 employees, engaged in both productive and general occupations, were regularly kept at work seven days in the week.

These prodigious and terrible figures concern the work of men. It might reasonably be supposed that the century long effort to gain legal protection for women and children in industry would have safeguarded them from the bare possibility of such inhuman usage.

But, to mention only random examples, young boys of fourteen years may still be employed all night long in Pennsylvania, West Virginia, and other great glass producing states; girls upon reaching their sixteenth birthday in New York state may be employed twelve hours a day during five days of the week in factories, and unlimited hours in stores during the season of "rush" before Christmas. The decision of the Illinois Supreme Court in 1910, upholding the constitutionality of the ten-hour law for women employed in factories and laundries, is estimated to have freed from over strain in Illinois alone more than 30,000 working women who were employed over ten hours a day. Some great manufacturing states such as Alabama and Mississippi in the south, and New Jersey in the north, set no legal limitation whatsoever upon the hours of women's employment. This is true also of other states, such as Delaware, Kansas, and Iowa, where manufacture is not yet foremost but where thousands of women are working overlong hours in laundries, restaurants, and department stores. Indeed, only 15 states have enacted laws to check the overwork of women in the exhausting service of the modern department store; and conspicuous by their absence from among these, are states with large commercial centers, such as Maryland, New York, Ohio, and Rhode Island.

Like most human institutions, factory legislation has been founded on no *a priori* logic. It has been, rather, essentially illogical, the result of half-way measures and opposing forces. During the nineteenth century, while agricultural Europe and America were gradually becoming industrial and the whole face of nature reflected the new order, the history of factory legislation—the state's defense of its workers—has been devious advance and compromise. Self-interest on the one side, self-defense and philanthropy on the other, hampered by prejudices of every sort—these for the most part have brought about such protection as exists today. Not man's foresight, but the inexorable results of labor long carried on counter to nature's laws, have been on the whole responsible for the meager protection which industrial communities have granted their workers.

In the main, opposition to laws protecting working women and children has come from the unenlightened employer, who has been blind to his own larger interests and who has always seen in every attempt to protect the workers an interference with business and dividends. To this day, it is the shortsighted and narrow-minded spirit of money-making that is the most persistent enemy of measures designed to save the workers from exhaustion and to conserve their working capacities. Work itself is of the essence of life; without it, man's physical as well as his moral nature decays. Regular continuous labor and exertion is as necessary for the worker's health as it is for subsistence, and if legislation regulating the workday had sought to invade legitimate work, it would long ago have defeated its own end. What it does seek is to check and control overwork, to conserve the workers from labor which leaves them spent and worn at thirty-five and forty years, when they should be in their prime. . . .

First the new industry, then exploitation, then the demand for some measure of protection—such is the universal story. Nor is this a chance sequence. It is the relentless record of history, the more impressive for its unconscious testimony to a waste of human effort and experience, in retrospect scarcely credible among a thinking people, yet in our very midst persisting steadily to this day.

Workers Take Direct Action

The organized labor union movement gained momentum in New York in the progressive era. Some unions targeted men workers; others, women workers; and still others both men and women. Routine collective bargaining was still mostly in the future and strikes were rare. But in November 1909, thousands of workers in shirtwaist factories launched a strike. Shirtwaists were a popular style of women's blouses, and their production was centered in dozens of factories in New York. Most of the workers were young women who had arrived in New York from Russia and Italy. Wages were low, working conditions harsh, and owners frequently exploited their workers. The strike began with a spontaneous protest in a few factories but quickly spread, eventually being called "The Uprising of the 20,000."

Employers struck back by hiring men to attack the strikers, police arrested them, and judges imprisoned them. Two fledgling unions, the Women's Trade Union League and the International Ladies' Garment Workers Union, supported them. The strikers' pleas garnered attention from the press and civic leaders. The strike lasted until February 1910 with mixed results:

higher wages, shorter hours, and better conditions in some shops, no progress in others, but thousands joining the ILGWU, significantly strengthening the organized labor movement.

∼

From "The Spirit of the Girl Strikers," Outlook (1910) by Miriam Finn Scott

The "Grand American Palace" was packed with a strangely unaccustomed crowd. . . . Strikers were there—a group of shirtwaist makers whose strike in New York has been the biggest and most bitter strike of women in the history of American labor troubles.

And the faces of this group were fixed on the stage and on that stage stood a single, pale girl of perhaps nineteen, her dark eyes flashing. "Girls, from the bottom of my heart," she cried, "I beg you not to go back to work. We are all poor, many of us are suffering hunger, none of us can afford to lose a day's wages. But only by fighting for our rights, and fighting all together, can we better our miseries; and so let us fight for them to the end!"

The strikers applauded long, and in scores of other East Side dancehalls at the time the strike was at its height and forty thousand girls were out, just so at this same time were other speakers applauded by other groups; and by meetings such as this was the spirit kept in the girls for their remarkable fight. When the girl left the platform, I edged my way to her and asked for her story. She had come from Russia, she told me, come with her parents who had found life in the land of the Czar no longer endurable.

"Close your eyes and point to any girl in this hall," said the little shirtwaist maker, "and my story will be her story. We are all the same. Why do we strike? I will tell you where we work, how we work; and from that perhaps you will understand. My shop is on a long and narrow loft on the fifth floor of the building, with the ceiling almost on our heads. In it one hundred electric-power machines are so closely packed together that, unless I am always on the lookout, my clothes or hair or hand is likely to catch in one of the whizzing machines. In the shop it is always night. The windows are only on the narrow ends of the room, so even the few girls who sit near them sew by gaslight most of the time, for the panes are always so dirty the weak daylight hardly goes through them.

The shop is swept only once a week; the air is so close that sometimes you can hardly breathe. In this place I work from eight to six o'clock six days a week in the ordinary season; and in the busy season, when we are compelled to work nights and Sundays, I put in what equals 38 workdays in the week. Thirty minutes is allowed for lunch which I must eat in the dressing-room four flights above the shop, on the ninth floor. These stairs I must always climb; the elevator, the boss says, is not for the shopgirls.

I began as a shirtwaist maker in this shop five years ago. For the first three weeks I got nothing, though I had already worked on a machine in Russia. Next the boss paid me three dollars a week. Now, after five years' experience, and I am considered a good worker, I am paid nine dollars. But I never get the nine dollars. There are always 'charges' against me. If I laugh or cry or speak to a girl during working hours, I am fined ten cents for each 'crime.' Five cents is taken from my pay every week to pay for the benzine which is used to clean waists that have been soiled in the making; and even if I have not soiled a waist for a year, I must pay the five cents just the same. If I lose a little piece of lining, that possibly is worth two cents, I am charged ten cents for the goods and five cents for losing it. If I am one minute late, I am fined one cent, though I only get 15 cents an hour; and if I am five minutes late, I lose half a day's pay. Each of these things seems small, I know, but when you only earn ninety dimes a week, and are fined for this and fined for that, why, a lot of them are missing pay when it comes, and you know what it means when your money is the only regular money that comes in a family of eight."

She told me other grievances, many of them. And as I went from meeting to meeting talking with the girls, as I walked with them on picket duty, I found that she had spoken truly when she said "My story is their story!". . . .

There is one very simple explanation for the wretched conditions under which these girls have worked—they have been very easy to exploit. Ninety percent of the workers are Russian and Italian girls between eighteen and twenty-five. These girls enter the shop almost immediately after landing in America. They come from great poverty and oppression where they were compelled to accept conditions without complaint. And so, accustomed to fear and [to] obey, these girls have for years suffered their grievances here, and kept silent.

Now and then in the past there have been attempts made by the workers to fight the conditions, but the individual uprisings had no effect. The spirit of discontent among the workers grew and continued to grow deeper and wider; it set the girls thinking, and finally they realized the only possible remedy for these conditions was for all of them to stand together and make common demands—to organize a strong union and gain recognition for it.

Everywhere was ferment. The girls were ripe for the strike, as was shown by the quickness and unanimity with which the girls responded to the call for the strike. . . .

Of all the wearing duties that have devolved upon the girls, none has been so trying and dangerous as the duty of picketing. It means long and weary hours of walking and waiting, often in bitter cold and rain, and often with little food to keep you warm and too little clothing to protect you from without. It means exposure to the street loafer; it often means abuse and insult from the boss; it has meant, as has been shown, suffering from the lawlessness of the police and magistrates, for merely performing an act which is a legal act according to the statutes of the State of New York; it has meant being thrown into cells with the most degraded women of the street, and finally, for many, a sentence to five days in the workhouse [prison-like city facilities for poverty-stricken people]. . . .

Some of the actions of the magistrates seem almost unbelievable, but they are only too sadly, too frequently true. There is one little girl who is always doing something at the union's headquarters—you can distinguish her from the rest because she wears her coat like a cape. There is a reason for that, for her right arm is in a sling. When she arose in her shop to announce to the workers that a strike had been called and asked them to join her, the boss in his fury threw a pair of scissors at her, which inflicted a deep wound in her forearm. When she applied at court for a warrant for the arrest of her assailant, the magistrate expressed himself as follows:

"You cannot have a warrant. You are a criminal, and you have got no more than your own just deserts. God says in the Bible that by the sweat of his brow, every man must earn his bread. You are keeping the girls from earning their bread. Your strike is a strike against God!"

But despite it all—despite cold, hunger, police brutality, magisterial insult and injustice, the shame and degraded companionship of the workhouse—these girls have kept up their spirit, a spirit that has brought them much sympathetic outside aid, a spirit that is, as I write, bringing toward a successful close the longest, biggest, bitterest struggle for better living conditions ever waged by women in America.

Unions Advance Labor

Trade unions played a major role in New York in the progressive era. They included carpenters, cigar-makers, iron molders, garment-makers, printers, and other skilled and semiskilled trades. Through collective bargaining and, occasionally, strikes, they gradually secured higher wages and shorter hours for their members.

Samuel Gompers (1850–1924) was the nation's most prominent labor leader in this period. He had immigrated with his family from England in 1863. They settled on the Lower East Side, and Gompers soon apprenticed in cigar-making. He became a labor organizer, starting with the United Cigar Makers in 1873. In 1881 he founded the Organized Trades and Labor Union and was a leading architect of the American Federation of Labor in 1886. He served as AFL president almost continually from then until his death, running the union for many years from his New York City home.

Under Gompers's leadership, the AFL and its New York-based affiliates, including the New York State Federation of Labor and the International Ladies' Garment Workers, focused on collective bargaining (strikes were sometimes used but regarded as a last resort) and legislative issues impacting workers such as higher wages, shorter hours, and safe working conditions. Workers just wanted an adequate standard of living, Gompers contended, so that they could maintain a good home, purchase enough food and clothing, and support their families. That message resonated with the progressive movement generally, which emphasized the need for a higher standard of living. Gompers mostly steered clear of broader social and political issues. The AFL and other trade unions concentrated on getting higher wages, better conditions, and safer conditions.

Gompers set the tone with an emphasis on the need to keep striving. "The cry of the toilers is for More!" as he noted in the 1904 essay excerpted below.

∽

FROM ORGANIZED LABOR: ITS STRUGGLES, ITS ENEMIES AND ITS FOOL FRIENDS (1904) BY SAMUEL GOMPERS

There is no necessity to worry about how labor and capital can be reconciled, for they are one and the same. How the laborers and the capitalists can be reconciled is entirely within the scope of proper inquiry, and to which the attention of both and of all students of economics and devotees to the social welfare may well give their best thought and attention. And it may lead to the conclusion that despite the clamor which we hear, and the conflicts which occasionally occur, that there is a constant trend toward agreement between the laborers and capitalists, employed and employer, for the uninterrupted production and distribution of wealth, and, too, with ethical consideration for the common interests of all the people.

No body of men deplores strikes more than do the organized workers, and one of their chief aims is to endeavor to reduce the number, if not to entirely obliterate strikes; but thinking men have no sympathy with the unqualified condemnation with which the dilettante in society, the professoriate, the open and covert enemies of the workers, denounce them.

A strike or lockout is a disagreement between the buyer and seller of labor power in order to arrive at what each or both may determine to be a more rational and equitable condition upon which production and distribution shall proceed. There has never yet been full harmony between the buyers and sellers of anything in this world. When a strike or lockout occurs, wages and production are not destroyed; they are deferred. . . .

The best organized workers, those who are better prepared to enter into strikes or to resist lockouts, are those who have least occasion to engage in them, and yet are the greater beneficiaries from modern civilization in the form of higher wages, shorter hours of daily labor, and Sunday rest. They attain a higher plane of morality, economic, political and social independence.

Thousands of agreements reached, the many more thousands of strikes averted through organization, are lost sight of by the sophists and superficial observers and strikes regarded as the sum total, the Alpha and Omega of the labor movement, when, as a matter of fact, as already indicated, strikes are a few of the failures to agree on terms upon which industry shall be continued.

While some may assert that the strike is a relic of barbarism, I answer that the strike is the most highly civilized method which the workers, the wealth producers, have yet devised to protest against the wrong and injustice, and to demand the enforcement of the right.

The strike compels more attention and study into economic and social wrongs than all the essays that have been written. It establishes better relations between the contending parties than have theretofore existed; reconciles laborers and capitalists more effectually, and speeds the machinery for production to a greater extent; gives an impetus to progress and increases power. . . .

In this world of ours those who do not make themselves heard have no grievance to redress. Those who are not willing to bear burdens and even temporary sacrifices in striking for their rights may be given a passing word of sympathy; books and essays may be written upon social inequalities, and the awful condition of the slums; but they are usually "passed by on the other side," and left in their squalor and misery. The workers, or the people of a nation who, knowing their rights, have the courage and the fortitude and the willingness to assert and defend them, are always the most respected among the peoples on the face of the earth. . . .

The workers are sometimes accused of unwillingness to make concessions. To this we answer that so far as it is possible, the workers ought not to concede; in fact, their conditions are such that they have exceedingly little to concede.

The cry of the toilers is for More! The organized movement of the workers is to obtain more of the advantages which result not only from their labor, but from the combined genius of the past and present.

The movement of labor organization began with those who, through the rudest form of association, pledged to each other the effort to lighten their burdens, mitigate their woes, and resist the common oppressor. It has moved along with the increased aspirations, wants and demands of the most intelligent among us.

None will dispute that the trade unions comprise the most moral and intelligent of the working class; that they represent the highest practical hopes, and aim to achieve them in the most reasonable and civilized manner. All really educated and honest men admit that the thorough organization of the wage-workers tends to render employment and the means of subsistence less precarious, and secures a larger share of the fruits of their toil.

Organized labor helps to reduce class, race, creed, and political prejudices. It aids and supports its fellow-workers morally and financially. It raises wages and lowers usury. It fosters education and uproots ignorance; increases independence and decreases dependence. It develops manhood, and balks tyranny. It shortens hours of toil and lengthens life. It lightens and brightens man. It establishes fraternity, and discourages blind selfishness. It makes manhood more independent, womanhood more beautiful and healthful, and childhood more hopeful and bright. It cheers the home and tends to make the world better.

Unions of labor endow the workers with individual dignity, and individual freedom. The unions prescribe a minimum, living wage; not a maximum wage. They insist upon a living rate, and never interfere with an employer desiring to reward superior skill or merit, the charge of labor's enemies to the contrary notwithstanding.

Where are the evidences or manifestations then of harm done by organized labor? Production has more than kept pace with population, and the growing demands at home or abroad.

The toilers will contest for full and unqualified recognition of all their rights. They will win in the future as they have won in the past. Nor will they transgress beyond the limits of legal and strictly industrial warfare. Not one school of political economy in any era of our industrial and commercial life has advanced the wage-earners one jot in their material interests. It has been the persistent plodding and sacrifices of the organized labor movement which has secured for the workers a general discussion of their rights and their wrongs, and has given the keynote and proven the open sesame to the student in all the walks of life. . . .

Strong Unions Get Results through Collective Bargaining

New York–based unions sometimes resorted to strikes but more often worked out new contracts through collective bargaining with employers. The State Labor Department encouraged and sometimes facilitated that process. Part of the union's strategy was to appeal to the public with the message that the unions and the workers they represented were just seeking a living wage, that the companies were very profitable and could afford it (without raising prices to customers), and that, overall, the economy and society benefited from unions' work. The editorial reproduced below is an example.

∽

From "Editorial: Manufacturers Plunged Cloak Industry Into War," *The Ladies' Garment Worker* (1916)

The chaos of industrial strife, into which the cloak and suit industry of New York has been plunged, was not of the union's making. All the responsibility for this war, and any dislocation of business it shall entail, rests entirely on the shoulders of the Cloak, Suit and Skirt Manufacturers'

Association. It was they who chose the barbarous method of the lockout as a means of becoming "masters in their factories," however un-American the term "masters" as applied to the industry, may be. On April 29th, they locked out 30,000 workers from their 409 shops. Thus the union had no alternative than to declare a general strike. The war was forced upon us.

The policy of our union has been all the time a policy of discussing grievances in conference with employers and negotiating settlements peacefully. We hold the strike as a weapon of last resort, and use it effectively only when every expedient for arriving at an amicable settlement has failed. Primarily, we stand for peace; not out of weakness, not because of inability to conduct a spirited fight, and not for lack of courage, faith and discipline in the organized ranks. Our union is well known for some very hard blows it has delivered at various times in our history. Only this year a number of our locals have acquitted themselves with credit in industrial warfare. We are for peace because we have been trained to regard trade matters and union affairs from a business viewpoint, and we are susceptible to every fair and reasonable attempt to preserve and even perpetuate peace in the industry on the basis of fairness and justice.

For six years we have responded to every impulse making for peace. Within the last two years our General Officers have concluded some fifteen collective agreements in various trades and centers of industry, and signed a large number of agreements with individual employers. In most of these cases, no strikes have occurred. Conciliation and arbitration have taken the place of force and all disputes between employers and employees are now adjusted peacefully by these methods with profit to the employers and benefits to the workers. . . .

Within recent years, the public has been educated to the enlightened modern view that troubles between capital and labor can best be adjusted by conciliation and the collective bargaining process. The feeling has grown immensely that industrial disputes and unrest can never be solved by the arbitrary methods such as the cloak manufacturers want to force on the industry; that such methods must only intensify the bitterness between employer and employees and keep aflame the passions of strife and turmoil. The Protective Association spurned that enlightened view and must be saddled with the entire responsibility for the presented distracted state of the cloak industry. . . .

The union is fighting for its rights to bargain for the workers with the employers collectively or individually, for the right to protect the workers against harsh treatment and vengeful discrimination in the shops, and for every humane principle, implied in conciliation and arbitration, that has generally governed the industry in the last six years.

The employers are fighting for the rule of the Bourbons in industry, the freedom to crush the spirit out of the workers, their unchecked power to overawe them into submitting to any wages, hours and conditions that it would please them to grant.

Sources

"Editorial: Manufacturers Plunged Cloak Industry Into War," *The Ladies' Garment Worker* VII (June 1916), 1–2, 6. Available at HathiTrust, https://babel.hathitrust.org/cgi/pt?id=hvd.li239p&view=page&seq=1.

Goldmark, Josephine, *Fatigue and Efficiency: A Study in Industry* (New York: Russell Sage Foundation, 1912), "Introductory," 3–6, 8, Footnotes have not been included. Available at HathiTrust, https://babel.hathitrust.org/cgi/pt?id=uga1.32108001725293&view=page&seq=5. (Footnotes not included.)

Gompers, Samuel, *Organized Labor: Its Struggles, Its Enemies and Fool Friends* (Washington: American Federation of Labor, 1904), 1–7. Available at HathiTrust, https://catalog.hathitrust.org/Record/001345226.

Kelley, Florence, *Modern Industry in Relation to the Family, Health, Education, Morality* (New York: Longmans, Green and Company, 1914), 3–5, 133–38. Available at Internet Archive, Archive.org, https://ia803108.us.archive.org/24/items/modernindustryin00kellrich/modernindustryin00kellrich.pdf.

"Little Wage Earners," *New York Tribune*, February 13, 1903.

New York State Legislature, *Report to the Legislature . . . by the Commission Appointed Under Chapter 518 of the Laws of 1909 to Inquire Into the Question of Employers' Liability and Other Matters. First Report* (Albany: J. B. Lyons, 1910), 7–8, 68–69. Available at HathiTrust, https://babel.hathitrust.org/cgi/pt?id=uc1.c2629875&view=page&seq=7&skin=2021.

Rose Schneiderman speech, "Citizens' Mass Meeting Stands for Prevention," *The Survey* 26 (April 8, 1911), 84–85. Available at Internet Archive, https://archive.org/details/thesurvey26survuoft/page/82/mode/2up.

Scott, Miriam Finn, "The Spirit of the Girl Strikers," *Outlook* 94 (February 18, 1910), 392–93, 394, 396–97. Available at HathiTrust, https://babel.hathitrust.org/cgi/pt?id=uc1.31822025100330&view=page&seq=1.

State of New York, *Preliminary Report of the Factory Investigating Commission*, vol. 1 (Albany: Argus Company, 1912), 13–15, 18–20. Available at HathiTrust, https://babel.hathitrust.org/cgi/pt?id=uc2.ark:/13960/t3hx17p6q&view=page&seq=13.

"The City's Child Labor," *New York Tribune*, January 2, 1903.

Van Kleeck, Mary, *Women in the Bookbinding Trade* (New York: Survey Associates, 1913), Chapter IX, "Summary and Outlook," 219–21, 226, 229–32, 235–36, Available at Internet Archive, https://ia802609.us.archive.org/31/items/womeninbookbindi00vankrich/womeninbookbindi00vankrich.pdf. (Two lengthy footnotes are not included.)

10

Appealing to History

Figure 10. A replica of Dutch explorer Henry Hudson's *Half Moon*, the ship he sailed in 1609 into what would later be called New York Harbor was one of the many historical attractions during the 1909 Hudson-Fulton Celebration. Source: Stereo-Travel Company, Library of Congress Prints & Photographs Division.

One of the quiet trends of the progressive era was a transition to a new way of looking at history. Historians shifted away from traditional themes of studying great documents and great men and toward detailed, engaging history of political and social movements and the historical experiences of common people. They explored more archival sources to get at details. Some historians began emphasizing the complexity of history and the multiple motives behind major historical developments. They highlighted reform and change in history, explaining that New York, and the nation, were constantly evolving. That reinforced and dovetailed with the progressive movement's rationale of evolution and change. It was an example of using history to reinforce the notion of continued change being the norm.

A number of university history departments in New York, particularly Columbia University, emerged as academic leaders in this "new history" movement. The New York State Historical Association was founded by a group of men in 1899 to promote greater public knowledge of New York's colonial and early state history. The state legislature established the position of official state historian in 1895 to edit and publish documents from the state's early history. The office was shifted to the State Education Department, which already included the State Library and the State Museum, in 1911. The Education Department expanded the coverage of American history in the schools. A 1919 state law authorized towns, cities, and counties to appoint their own official local historians.

The "New History" Makes History More Relevant

Before 1900, the study of history had mostly consisted of a focus on the actions of great men and key events. James Harvey Robinson (1863–1936), a history professor at Columbia University, and a number of his colleagues there, including Charles A. Beard, began advocating for a different, more progressive, timely approach. They espoused a strategy that would draw on a wider array of historical evidence, place more emphasis on social and economic trends, provide more coverage of the lives of ordinary people in history, draw on allied social sciences such as economics and sociology, dovetail with the emerging field of social studies, and demonstrate the relevance of history for providing insights into contemporary affairs and problems.

The fresh, new approach, introduced in New York mainly by Robinson and his Columbia colleagues, gradually became known as the "new history." The name was derived from a highly influential article Robinson wrote in

1911, excerpted below. Here, Robinson ranged widely over European and US histories to discern trends pointing toward, or demonstrating the need for, the new approach. Identifying "the value of historical study" for insight into the present in the first sentence as the key theme set the stage for the rest of the article and the new approach to history it introduced. Robinson later expanded his concept into a book and wrote a number of other history books, including some widely used texts, that spread and popularized the idea.

∽

FROM "THE NEW HISTORY" IN *PROCEEDINGS OF THE AMERICAN PHILOSOPHICAL SOCIETY* (1911)
BY JAMES HARVEY ROBINSON

I propose to discuss in this paper the value of historical study. The question has long haunted me and certainly merits a more careful consideration than it has, so far as I can discover, hitherto received. It will be impossible to do more here than to analyze the problem and briefly state the general conclusions which that analysis suggests.

The older traditional type of historical writing was narrative in character. Its chief aim was to tell a tale or story by setting forth a succession of events and introducing the prominent actors who participated in them. It was a branch of polite literature, competition with the drama and fiction, from which, indeed, it differed of only in the limitations which the writer was supposed to place upon his fancy. As Professor McMaster has recently said: "It was no mere accident that Motley began his literary career with a so called 'Merry-Mount,' and Parkman his with 'Vassall Morton.' These bespoke their type of mind. The things that would interest them in history would be, not the great masses of toiling men, not the silent revolutions by which nations pass from barbarism to civilization, from ignorance to knowledge, from poverty to wealth, from feebleness to power, but the striking figures of history, great kings queens, the leaders of armies, men renowned for statescraft, and dramatic incidents in the life of nations. Each must have his he and his villain, his plots, conspiracies and bloody wars. . . . History as viewed by writers of this school is 'a series of dramas in each of which a few great men perform the leading parts and use the rest of mankind as their instruments.'"[1]

[The article proceeds to discuss several of these examples of "epic history."]

These genial speculations of the philosophers have rested usually upon no very careful study of historical sources and their conclusions now seem very hazardous even if we grant the correctedness [sic] of the data upon which they relied. It was inevitable that these historical students who, about the middle of the nineteenth century, commenced to feel the influence of the general scientific spirit of the period, should begin to look very sourly upon the earlier attempts to bring order and beauty out of a mass of historic assertions which were commonly either erroneous or unproved and to establish laws for events which one could not be sure had ever happened. The reaction against the dreams of the philosophers of history was, and still is, very clear. . . .

Along with more exacting criticism and the repudiation of supernatural considerations and explanations came a revulsion against the older epic or dramatic interest in the past. The essential interest and importance of the normal and homely elements in human life became apparent. The scientific historian no longer dwells by preference on the heroic, spectacular, and romantic episodes, but strives to reconstruct past conditions. This last point is of such importance that we must stop over it a moment.

History is not infrequently still defined as a record of past events and the public still expects from the historian a story of the past. But the conscientious historian has come to realize that he cannot aspire to be a good story teller for the simple reason that if he tells no more than he has good reasons for believing to be true his story is usually very fragmentary and uncertain. Fiction and drama are perfectly free to conceive and adjust detail so as to meet the demands of art, but the historian should always be conscious of the rigid limitations placed upon him. If he confines himself to an honest and critical statement of a series of events as described in his sources it is usually too deficient in vivid authentic detail to make a presentable story.

The historian is coming to see that his task is essentially different from that of the man of letters. His place is among the scientists. He is at liberty to use only his scientific imagination, which is surely different from a literary imagination. It is his business to make those contributions to our general understanding of mankind in the past which his training in the investigation of the records of past human events especially fit him to make. He esteems the events he finds recorded not for their dramatic interest but for the light that they cast on the normal and prevalent conditions which gave rise to them. It makes no difference how dry a chronicle may be if the occurrences that it reports can be brought into some assignable relation with the more or less permanent habits of a particular people or person. . . .

The kind of history, accordingly, the practical value of which we shall attempt roughly to estimate, and which for convenience sake, we may call the 'new' history is scientific in its methods, exacting in regard to the inferences it makes from its material; it rejects supernatural explanations and an anthropocentric conception of the universe; it studies by preference the normal and long-enduring rather than the transit and exceptional. . . . So much for the attitude of mind of the modern historian who realizes the changes which have overtaken his subject during the past fifty or sixty years. . . .

History in its broadest sense, is, in short, nothing less than the experiences of our race, so far as we can determine or surmise them. And what uses are we to make of the experiences of the race? The same kind that we make of our own personal history. We may question it as we question our memory of our personal acts, situations, and past ideals. But those things we recall from the superabundant fund of our own experiences vary continually with our moods and preoccupations. We instinctively adjust our recollections to our immediate needs and aspirations and ask from the past light on the particular problems that face us. Just as our individual history is thus not immutable but owes its value to its adaptability, so with the history of mankind. . . .

History is then not fixed but reducible to outlines and formulas but it is ever-changing, and it will, if we will permit it, illuminate and explain our lives as nothing else can do. For our lives are made up almost altogether of the past and each age should feel free to select from the annals of the past those matters which have a bearing on the matters it has specially at heart.

If we test our personal knowledge of history by its usefulness to us, in giving us a better grasp on the present and a clearer notion of our place in the development of mankind, we shall perceive forthwith that a great part of what we have learned from historical works has entirely escaped our memory, for the simple reason that we never had the least excuse for recollecting it. The career of Ethered the Unready, the battle of Poitiers, and the negotiations leading to the treaty of Nimwegen are for most of us forgotten formulae, no more helpful, except in a remote contingency, than the logarithm of the number 57.

The ideal history for each of us would be the facts of past human experience to which we should have recourse oftenest to our endeavors to understand ourselves and our fellows. No one account would meet the needs of all, but all would agree that much of what now passes for the elements of history meet the needs of none. . . . History has a disintegrating effect on current prejudices which is yet scarcely appreciated. It makes both for understanding and for intellectual emancipation as nothing else can.

Obviously history must be rewritten, or rather, innumerable current issues must be given their neglected historic background. Our present so-called histories do not ordinarily answer the questions we would naturally and insistently put to them. When we contemplate the strong demand that women are making for the right to vote, do we ask ourselves how did men win the vote? The historians we consult have scarcely asked themselves that question and so do not answer it. We ask how did our courts come to control legislation in the exceptional and extraordinary manner they do? We look in vain to most histories for a reply. No one questions the inalienable right of the historian to interest himself in any phase of the past that he chooses. It is only to be wished that a greater number of historians had greater skill in hitting upon those phases of the past which serve us best in understanding the most vital problems of the present.

Putting History to Work for Progressivism

A number of leading progressive historians wrote books that advanced new interpretations of history and that also furnished a historical context for progressive reform. The most prominent was An Economic Interpretation of the Constitution *(1913) by Columbia University professor Charles A. Beard (1874–1948). Beard carried out extensive research in the papers and records of the founding fathers. He contended they were motivated primarily by personal financial interests and that the Constitution was intended to protect vested interests rather than a framework for popular democracy. His book, still controversial today, dovetailed well with progressivism. One of the movement's aims was to loosen the grip that the rich and powerful had on government. Beard's book enabled them to assert that the control reached back to the origins of the country.*

Beard clashed with the conservative president of Columbia University, Nicholas Murray Butler, and charged that the university was a defender of the status quo. Beard and his colleague, James Harvey Robinson, noted above, also became disillusioned with Columbia. They left Columbia in 1919 to join other progressive-minded scholars to found the New School for Social Research, which became a bastion of progressive scholarship.

The first chapter of An Economic Interpretation of the Constitution of the United States, *excerpted below, set forth Beard's contention about the economic motives of the founding fathers.*

∽

FROM *AN ECONOMIC INTERPRETATION OF THE CONSTITUTION OF THE UNITED STATES* (1913) BY CHARLES A. BEARD

Different degrees and kinds of property inevitably exist in modern society; party doctrines and "principles" originate in the sentiments and views which the possession of various kinds of property creates in the minds of the possessors; class and group divisions based on property lie at the basis of modern government; and politics and constitutional law are inevitably a reflex of these contending interests. Those who are inclined to repudiate the hypothesis of economic determinism as a European importation must, therefore, revise their views, on learning that one of the earliest, and certainly one of the clearest, statements of it came from a profound student of politics [James Madison] who sat in the Convention that framed our fundamental law.

The requirements for an economic interpretation of the formation and adoption of the Constitution may be stated in a hypothetical proposition which, although it cannot be verified absolutely from ascertainable data, will at once illustrate the problem and furnish a guide to research and generalization.

It will be admitted without controversy that the Constitution was the creation of a certain number of men, and it was opposed by a certain number of men. Now, if it were possible to have an economic biography of all those connected with its framing and adoption—perhaps about 160,000 men altogether—the materials for scientific analysis and classification would be available. Such an economic biography would include a list of the real and personal property owned by all of these men and their families: lands and houses, with incumbrances, money at interest, slaves, capital invested in shipping and manufacturing, and in-state and continental securities.

Suppose it could be shown from the classification of the men who supported and opposed the Constitution that there was no line of property division at all; that is, that men owning substantially the same amounts of the same kinds of property were equally divided on the matter of adoption or rejection. It would then become apparent that the Constitution had no ascertainable relation to economic groups or classes, but was the product of some abstract causes remote from the chief business of life gaining a livelihood.

Suppose, on the other hand, that substantially all of the merchants, money lenders, security holders, manufacturers, shippers, capitalists, and financiers and their professional associates are to be found on one side in support of the Constitution and that substantially all or the major portion of the opposition came from the non-slaveholding farmers and the debtors. Would it not be pretty conclusively demonstrated that our fundamental law was not the product of an abstraction known as "the whole people," but of a group of economic interests which must have expected beneficial results from its adoption? Obviously all the facts here desired cannot be discovered, but the data presented in the following chapters bear out the latter hypothesis, and thus a reasonable presumption in favor of the theory is created.

Of course, it may be shown (and perhaps can be shown) that the farmers and debtors who opposed the Constitution were in fact, benefited by the general improvement which resulted from its adoption. It may likewise be shown, to take an extreme case, that the English nation derived immense advantages from the Norman Conquest and the orderly administrative processes which were introduced, as it undoubtedly did; nevertheless, it does not follow that the vague thing known as "the advancement of general welfare" or some abstraction known as "justice" was the immediate, guiding purpose of the leaders in either of these great historic changes. The point is, that the direct, impelling motive in both cases was the economic advantages which the beneficiaries expected would accrue to themselves first, from their action. Further than this, economic interpretation cannot go. It may be that some larger world process is working through each series of historical events; but ultimate causes lie beyond our horizon.

Public Pageants Boost New York History

In the early years of the new century, public officials often employed patriotic history festivals to bring people together and encourage them to appreciate their American heritage. Organizers often gave priority to young people (in part to make them informed, responsible citizens as adults) and to immigrants (to "Americanize" them through exposure to American history, culture, and values). A good example is the Hudson-Fulton Celebration in New York in September and October 1909. It commemorated the of the three hundredth anniversary explorer Henry Hudson's discovery of the river that was later named after him and one hundredth anniversary of Robert Fulton's development of the first paddle steamer.

Organizers used the celebration to highlight the achievements of the two men but also display the status of New York City as a city of global importance and the importance of the Hudson River in state and national history. The organizers were in part trying to compensate for the fact that there was at that time no comprehensive New York State history book.

Dazzling electric lights (electric lighting was still something of a novelty) illuminated the city's streets at night. There were speeches, pageants, and fireworks in New York, Albany, and other cities. Highlighting history in public forums was a key component. There was a special "History Parade" in New York and reenactments of historical events. Students wrote historical essays in schools.

∽

From *The Hudson-Fulton Celebration, 1909* (1910)
by Herman Hagaman Hall

From Saturday, September 25, to Monday, October 11, 1909, the State of New York commemorated, under the auspices of the Hudson-Fulton Celebration Commission, the 300th anniversary of the discovery of the Hudson River by Henry Hudson in 1609 and the 100th anniversary of the first successful application of steam to navigation upon that River by Robert Fulton in 1807. As a stimulus to its four years of devoted labor in preparing for the Celebration, the Commission had the inspiration of two eminent events in human history. The first of these, which brought the Hudson River to the knowledge of Europe and opened the adjacent region to European settlement, was well calculated to appeal to the imagination and arouse popular interest. In contemplating it the mind instinctively compared conditions at the time of Hudson's advent with conditions at present and marveled at the change.

Three hundred years ago, when civilization was hoary upon the banks of the Thames, the Rhine, the Seine, the Tiber, the Nile, and the Ganges, the primeval forests of the Hudson River gave shelter to no higher culture than the middle status of barbarism. Here was a virgin soil, seemingly reserved by Destiny in order that Civilization might here plant herself anew, and here cultivate in a freer air the institutions for which she had qualified herself by hard and painful schooling in the Old World. Then came Hudson's little ship and then the magic of three centuries of change. And in the harbor where Hudson saw only the hollow-log canoes of the native Indians, to-day float the treasure-laden argosies of the world; where he saw the rude bark habitations of the aborigines [a term then in use to refer to native peoples], now rises the second—soon to be the first—city of the world; and upon the banks of the river and in the tributary region where 300 years ago the barest necessities of precarious human existence were the measure of industry and the simplest requirements of personal adornment, the chase, and primitive warfare were the measure of art and science, now dwells a civilization which rivals that of any other part of the world.

The contrasts thus presented by conditions at the two extremities of the period and the consciousness of the phenomenal development of our people in the multifarious departments of human activity during the three centuries intervening, could not but arouse civic pride and inspire civic enthusiasm. . . .

The Commission arranged its plans with definite ends in view. The first was to make the Celebration educational, not commercial. . . . In the educational conception of the Celebration, much to Create emphasis was laid on its historical side for the very natural reason that historical events were being commemorated. But there were additional reasons for this emphasis. The State of New York, as compared with her neighbors on the east and south, has heretofore shown questionable modesty in refraining from exploiting her own history. A glance at the book shelves of any great public library will show how industrious the historians of Massachusetts and Pennsylvania and Virginia have been in recording the annals of which they are justly proud and how comparatively indifferent our own writers have been in this field. And this disparity has resulted in a very general ignorance of the full part played by our Colony and State in our national history.

Furthermore, it has led to a positive and unfortunate misconception by many persons of the dignity of our State history. . . . For many years, the best known—if not the best loved—book of New York history was a satire on New York history. The misfortune of [Washington] Irving's *Knickerbocker's History of New York* [1809, a satirical fictional account of the Dutch colonial period] was not so much its satire, which any person with a reasonable sense of humor can appreciate, as the period at which it appeared—a period barren of any worthy and serious history of New York. The result was that many persons derived their impressions of the character of the founders of New York from Irving's whimsical conceptions. . . .

A third object sought to be attained by the educational features was to promote the assimilation of our adopted population. Knowledge of the history of a city, or a state, or a nation conduces the love of country, civic pride and loyalty to established institutions. It serves to bind a people together, make it more homogeneous and give it stability. And it makes the inhabitants better citizens by holding up to their eyes lofty traditions to enlist their affections and inspire their imitation. With over 26 per cent of the population of the State foreign born, and 33 per cent more born here of foreign parents, it was felt that such a Celebration as was planned would result in great and far-reaching good.

Still further to emphasize this phase of the Celebration, the people of every nationality were invited to take part in the parades and festivals, and an effort was made to make them feel that the Celebration belonged to them as much as to the older inhabitants; that by adopting our citizenship they adopted our traditions and institutions; and that their pride and loyalty should be as great as those of the descendants of the pioneer settlers.

It requires but little reflection to perceive the great value of acquainting our adopted citizens with the fact that we have a body of worthy traditions and attaching them to those traditions. The power of tradition has been one of the most fundamental and conservative forces of all peoples of all times. As a body propelled through space tends to travel in a direct line unless diverted by some force other than that which drives it, so a people naturally tends to follow the impulses of the past and to adhere to tradition unless turned therefrom by other influences. Therefore the ingrained history of a nation, which in a broad sense we call tradition, serves as a balance wheel, tending to restrain sudden and spasmodic departures from the normal mode of progress. Historical culture thus materially promotes the welfare of the Commonwealth.

Students Need to Study History

New York's first Commissioner of Education, Andrew S. Draper, who served from 1904 to 1913, transformed New York's educational system, including increasing funding, raising standards for teachers, and issuing statewide educational goals and standards. One goal was to increase students' understanding of the state's rich history. Draper, like many progressive reformers, was particularly interested in informing young foreign-born and first-generation New Yorkers.

The place to begin, Draper explained, was in the public schools. Students should be taught lively history that would inspire respect and pride in their state and nation. Engaging narrative writing rather than dense historical chronologies and analysis were needed to engage students during their school years. This approach to history education would ensure that future citizens were well versed in their nation's and their state's past and also inspire an interest in continuing to study history.

∼

From *No Mummified History in New York Schools* (1912)
by Andrew S. Draper

[A New York State Education Department priority is] quickening and improving the teaching of history in the schools. There is no state with a more resplendent history than New York. The story of the first settlements, of the progress of pioneer farming, of the dealings and conflicts with the Indians, of the upbuilding of our commerce and manufactures, of the development of our religious and political institutions, of the old roads which foreshadowed the newer and greater ones, of the habits and customs of early generations which have influenced the doings of the present generation, of the deadly battles fought and the political policies established by our fathers which settled the character of the State and nation, is an inheritance which is not exceeded by that of any people in the world.

All of this splendid story cannot be understood by the children in the schools, for that requires long lives and mature minds, but we may have the satisfaction of knowing that if we teach little parts of it so children become readily interested in them, they will go on and learn about other parts without other helps than such as they will find on their own account. The story truly told is so fascinating that it is irresistible. The point of this little paper is not so much to extend the courses in history as it is to make the teaching vital and the history irresistible. . . .

The thing we are speaking of is not an exclusive trade at all: it is to be saved from being professionalized; it is far more a matter of knowledge, of intelligent interest and literary accomplishment, than of balancing evidence or of expert training. History consists of facts infused with life rather than of mere opinions. Of course there is such a thing as a philosophy of history, a treatment of causes and effects, a connecting of results and an explaining of consequences, but that is wholly beyond the children in the elementary or secondary schools; and, aside from that, it is in the province of historical or philosophical speculation, and not in the field of historical fact at all.

The same considerations govern the teaching as the writing of history. To be effectively taught it will have to be done by partisans, whose hearts quicken with the teaching and are quickened by it as it progresses. The thing taught will have to be within a compass which pupils can grasp, and it will have to be made so clear, so full of human action and interest, will have to move in such an orderly and convincing way, that normal children must be enlightened, entertained, and convinced by it.

We have 2,000,000 children in our New York schools. Large numbers of them are the children of parents who are new in the State and know little of the facts and the spirit of our history. We had 1,800,000 souls added to the population of New York State, and 1,300,000 added to the population of New York City, between 1900 and 1910. In other words, the decade's increase alone would make great cities and states as the world goes. And there are vast numbers of children descended from early settlers in the State who know little of the facts and feel little of the inspiration of our history. It is very vital to the State that they shall know these facts and feel this inspiration.

No civilization lives unto itself alone. It is a matter on intelligence, of feeling, and of relations and outlook. A civilization treasures what its fathers did for it, and it is urgent about what it aspires to do for its children and their children. Indeed, loyalty to and intelligence about this line of teaching in the homes and in the schools goes farther than anything else to determine the power and the right of a civilization to endure.

The schools of all peoples are expected to attend to the matter. Frankly, I do not think we attend to it as well as we ought. We are as prodigal of our history as of our lands, woods, waters and children. We need to conserve and care more for all of them. The people need to help the schools to do it better. . . .

The history of Holland and Britain, indeed the history of all intellectual and constitutional progress in all lands, is our inheritance. But we have to go no farther back than the first settlements upon the Hudson River to find both great and picturesque events to illustrate the evolution of the material state, and fascinating stories to quicken the commercial, scholarly, political, and military doings of the people. We are plutocrats in the materials that must touch the pride, quicken the heartbeats, and enlarge the sense of responsibility of every one who is worth his salt and lives upon New York soil.

There is hardly a town in the State that is without its historic episodes and traditions. There is hardly a county that has not a shrine made sacred, not a stream that has not been crimsoned by blood spilt for the rights of man. To say nothing of the names of men, think of what Morningside Heights, Fort Lee, Stony Point, Albany, Schenectady, Schoharie, Cherry Valley, Wyoming, Oriskany, Oswego, Crown Point, Plattsburgh, and many others, signify in the cause of human opportunity and American nationality.

And it is not all a matter of soldiers by any means. We had in every part of this State, at a very early day, as fine a pioneer farming civilization, as successful manufacturing and commercial accomplishments, as the world has ever seen. We have had as brave and fascinating struggles for the stability of political institutions, as much self-sacrifice for the upbuilding of churches and for their freedom and harmony, as intelligent and generous and abiding a faith in schools, as ever honored the life of any people in the world. It is all in our history, it is expressed in our institutions, and it bears upon our life.

It is our business to see that the children in the New York schools, for their own good and for the country's sake, get their proper share in all this. They are to get the parts of it that they can assimilate, and get it at times and in forms and quantities that will be good for their patriotic health. If they become really concerned about some part of it, they will be about other parts of it. If their love of it begins to grow, it will keep on growing. The generalities, the high points, the speculations, or the philosophy of history, are not of much concern to young people. They want the facts, the action, of it. They want the poetry and the glamour of it. They will come to understand something of the reason and the result of it.

Making American History More Engaging and Relevant

The New York State Education Department, headed by progressive education leader Andrew S. Draper from 1904 to 1913, transformed the teaching of American history in the schools. The changes made it more engaging and exciting for young people, provided for deeper explanations and more conti-

nuity, and introduced the idea that history teachers and their courses could be critical of the past. The new approach also made it clear that historical interpretations could and should change over time. As the 1910 syllabus excerpted below noted, "Patriotism no longer means adhesion to the statement, 'My country, right or wrong, My country,' but a united effort on the part of all its citizens to make the country right." That sentiment dovetailed perfectly with the broader progressive call for reform and change.

∼

FROM *SYLLABUS FOR SECONDARY SCHOOLS* (1910) BY THE STATE EDUCATION DEPARTMENT

The scientific investigations of distinguished [nineteenth century] foreign scholars like DeTocqueville, Von Holst and Bryce have been followed by the creation of a new school of American historians whose work has been to show that the American Constitution was not "struck off at a given time by the brain and purpose of man," but that the history of America, like that of every other country, has been an outgrowth from previous conditions—that America has never occupied an isolated position, but that it has been influenced throughout its development by other nations and that it has in its turn influenced them; that we cannot understand present conditions in our own country without studying how these conditions have come to be; that patriotism no longer means adhesion to the statement, "My country, right or wrong, My country," but a united effort on the part of all its citizens to make the country right.

This new point of view of the historian has been reflected in the textbook written for the schools. This no longer presents in flamboyant style the traditional spectacular events that collectively have been called "the history of the United States," but it treats the history of the country as a natural development. It is no longer a heterogeneous collection of miscellaneous facts chronologically arranged—but it is an orderly presentation of related events. It is not based on rumor, traditions, theories and previously conceived ideas, but on careful investigation of the authorities used. It does not assume that "advanced work in history con sists in reading larger books and more of them," but it adapts both matter and method to the capacities of those who are to use it. The textbook for the elementary and grammar grades presents the picturesque and imaginative side of history in order that the child may have a vivid picture of the conspicuous events of the past. The textbook for the secondary school places emphasis on underlying causes and on the development of great movements in order that the young citizen may appreciate how large is his heritage from the past, how great his obligation to the future.

The new teacher of American history is both a cause and a result of the new textbook. He appreciates the importance of treating American history as a continuous development from European history, not as a disconnected series of special creations. He understands that all society is organic in character and that therefore history cannot be taught as a description of inorganic matter. He knows that the essential in teaching the American Constitution is to teach its underlying principles as they were developed from political conditions, not to teach isolated, unrelated facts. He does not "put the cart before the horse," to use the homely phrase, and attempt to teach civics as a disconnected subject made up of abstractions and constantly fluctuating facts, but he teaches it as an outgrowth of the political conditions of the country. He realizes that it is far more important to know why every state in the Union has its own Constitution and how the functions of the state government resemble or differ from those of the federal government than it is to learn by heart the names of the state officers and the amount of salary attached to each office. He comprehends that in material as well as in spiritual affairs "the things that are seen are temporal, but the things that are unseen are eternal," and he teaches not the boundaries of various assembly and senatorial districts, but what were the historical conditions that gave rise to a representative legislative body and why that body was composed of two houses.

He uses the newspaper, not as a purveyor of transient gossip, but as an intelligent aid in the interpretation of the past by the present. He welcomes pictures in his work, not that of Sir Francis Drake discovering the Pacific, but that of the New England town with its meetinghouse and its school house; not the picture of the battle scene that might be labeled any one of a hundred conflicts, but the plan of a Southern plantation showing the relative location of its numerous buildings; not the photograph of the reigning political boss, but the seal of the federal government and what it signifies. He utilizes outline maps, not to locate the counties in a state, but to show the territories explored by different nationalities and the routes taken by the pioneers in their westward march. He uses a hundred tools in his work where his unskilled predecessor used but one, and the resulting product is not a crude caricature of the past but a faithful, scientific and artistic delineation of the development of America from Europe. The teacher of today who teaches American history appreciates Professor Maitland's apostrophe of the map of England—"that most wonderful of all palimpsests!" He sees in the map of America another most wonderful palimpsest whereon have been written the hopes and aspirations and discouragements, the failures and successes of Spaniard and Frenchman, Swede and Hollander and Englishman of monk and friar, of fur trader and lumberman, of frontiersman and immigrant, of political refugee and religious enthusiast. How indeed, he may say, can he know the real America unless he knows it in its European home? How can he train those who may becalled on to legislate for the Italians in their American home unless they have been taught the failures and successes of that great uprising for independence and unity that culminated in the establishment of the kingdom of Italy—how understand the German of the Northwest without a knowledge of the idealism in politics, art, literature, and music that found expression in the revolutionary uprising of '48 and sent the flower of German youth to our shores—how deal in wisdom and patience with the Hungarians coming to us unless we realize the passionate aspirations for political liberty of the Hungarians in Europe—how assimilate the nearly one million foreigners who come annually to our shores unless we know why they left their native land as well as why they have come to us?

If, then, the new American history strikes its roots deep down into European soil it is because the height and the strength of the tree demands it and because its very life depends on it.

The accompanying outlines of study proposed for the syllabuses in American history and civics have been prepared in accordance with the following recommendations and considerations:

1. That of the full time given to American history and civics, three fifths be devoted to history and two fifths to civics. Corresponding emphasis will be given to these subjects in the examinations.

2. That the work down to 1783 be given as a review summary and that in this review the syllabus be closely followed.

3. That the main emphasis in the teaching of American history be placed on the development of the country under independent government, 1783, to the present time.

4. That American history from 1783 be taught by periods as follows: (a) 1783–1829; (b) 1829–65; (c) 1865 to the present.

5. That under each of these periods five lines of development be presented; viz, political, territorial, commercial, industrial, social; and that in teaching American history, while it may be impossible to cover the entire syllabus a fair balance be preserved between the five fields named.

Lists of required readings to be varied from year to year will be furnished on a separate sheet. One or more questions based on these required readings will be included in each examination. Questions calling for minute details will not be asked.

While history and civics will generally be taught in different recitation periods, it is highly important that the relations between them be made clear as the study of each proceeds and a definite number of recitations, probably not less than 10 per cent, be set aside for topical reviews in which the growth of government as well as its past and present manifestations may be revealed.

History Should Aid Students' Social Development

Many progressives emphasized the need to study history but, as the samples above indicate, views of the appropriate approaches and benefits of studying history varied. John Dewey (1859-1952), a psychologist, philosopher, and educational reformer who taught at Columbia University from 1904 to 1930, went further. He emphasized instead the mission of schools to develop responsible citizens and create a civil society. He believed that the value of history, particularly for young children, was not memorizing facts and dates but rather in coming to understand how people had lived and how civilization had progressed.

He spelled out his views in his book The School and Society, *published in 1915. Education was most meaningful when children could connect what they learned about the past with their own experiences. This would enable them to use history to understand what was happening in their own times and prepare them for the future.*

From *The School and Society* (1915) by John Dewey

The Aim of History in Elementary Education

[History should be] considered as an account of the forces and forms of social life. Social life we have always with us; the distinction of past and present is indifferent to it. Whether it was lived just here or just there is a matter of slight moment. It is life for all that; it shows the motives which draw men together and push them apart, and depicts what is desirable and what is hurtful. Whatever history may be for the scientific historian, for the educator it must be an indirect sociology, a study of society which lays bare its process of becoming and its modes of organization. Existing society is both too complex and too close to the child to be studied. He finds no clues into its labyrinth of detail and mounts no eminence whence to get a perspective of arrangement.

If the aim of historical instruction is to enable the child to appreciate the values of social life, to see in imagination the forces which favor and let men's effective co-operation with one another, to understand the sorts of character that help on and that hold back, the essential thing in its presentation is to make it moving, dynamic. History must be presented, not as an accumulation of results or effects, a mere statement of what happened, but as a forceful, acting thing. The motives—that is, the motors—must stand out. To study history is not to amass information, but to use information in constructing a vivid picture of how and why men did thus and so; achieved their successes and came to their failures.

When history is conceived as dynamic, as moving, its economic and industrial aspects are emphasized. These are but technical terms which express the problem with which humanity is unceasingly engaged; how to live, how to master and use nature so as to make it tributary to the enrichment of human life. The great advances in civilization have come through those manifestations of intelligence which have lifted man from his precarious subjection to nature, and revealed to him how he may make its forces co-operate with his own purposes. The social world in which the child now lives is so rich and full that it is not easy to see how much it cost, how much effort and thought lie back of it.

Man has a tremendous equipment ready at hand. The child may be led to translate these ready-made resources into fluid terms he may be led to see man face to face with nature, without inherited capital, without tools, without manufactured materials. And, step by step, he may follow the processes by which man recognized the needs of his situation, thought out the weapons and instruments that enable him to cope with them; and may learn how these new resources opened new horizons of growth and created new problems. The industrial history of man is not a materialistic or merely utilitarian affair. It is a matter of intelligence. Its record is the record of how man learned to think, to think to some effect, to transform the conditions of life so that life itself became a different thing. It is an ethical record as well; the account of the conditions which men have patiently wrought out to serve their ends.

The question of how human beings live, indeed, represents the dominant interest with which the child approaches historic material. It is this point of view which brings those who worked in the past close to the beings with whom he is daily associated, and confers upon him the gift of sympathetic penetration.

The child who is interested in the way in which men lived, the tools they had to do with, the new inventions they made, the transformations of life that arose from the power and leisure thus gained, is eager to repeat like processes in his own action, to remake utensils, to reproduce processes, to rehandle materials. Since he understands their problems and their successes only by seeing what obstacles and what resources they had from nature, the child is interested in field and forest, ocean and mountain, plant and animal. By building up a conception of the natural environment in which lived the people he is studying, he gets his hold upon their lives. This reproduction he cannot make excepting as he gains acquaintance with the natural forces and forms with which he is himself surrounded. The interest in history gives a more human coloring, a wider significance, to his own study of nature. His knowledge of nature lends point and accuracy to his study of history. This is the natural "correlation" of history and science.

This same end, a deepening appreciation of social life, decides the place of the biographic element in historical instruction. That historical material appeals to the child most completely and vividly when presented in individual form, when summed up in the lives and deeds of some heroic character, there can be no doubt. Yet it is possible to use biographies so that they become a collection of mere stories, interesting, possibly, to the point of sensationalism, but yet bringing the child no nearer to comprehension of social life. This happens when the individual who is the hero of the tale is isolated from his social environment; when the child is not brought to feel the social situations which evoked his acts and the social progress to which his deeds contributed. If biography is presented as a dramatic summary of social needs and achievements, if the child's imagination pictures the social defects and problems that clamored for the man and the ways in which the individual met the emergency, then the biography is an organ of social study.

A New Departure for Higher Education

Institutions of higher learning were impacted by the winds of changing thought during the progressive movement. Several New York colleges and universities moved toward being more open to new ideas, engaged with the problems of the time, and geared to producing graduates who could manage complex modern institutions.

Other leading universities, though, dug in and held to the old ways. In 1919, a group of progressive thinkers, including Columbia University professors John Dewey, James Harvey Robinson, and Charles Beard, joined other progressive educators, including Horace Kallen, whose work was noted in Chapter 6, above, to create a new model of higher education in New York City. They wanted an institution where students could learn from and exchange ideas freely with scholars and artists representing a wide range of intellectual, aesthetic, and political orientations. They wanted a place to nurture a fresh, progressive approach to historical study. They called it The New School for Social Research. It continues today as a division of The New School.

Their initial proposal, reproduced in part below, summarizes their reservations about institutions of higher learning and their vision for a new type of university, fresh and progressive in its outlook and focused on being relevant to the needs of the day. As they noted in the document, "New York is the place" for such a forward-looking educational experiment.

∽

From *A Proposal for an Independent School of Social Science for Men and Women* (1919) by New School for Social Research

The political and social problems forced upon the country by the economic development of the past twenty-five years call for a new type of leadership in every field of American life. These problems have been emphasized and made critical by the great war, and an honest effort toward their solution is the obvious duty of non-combatants at home to the men who are fighting to make a better world. To this end we need teachers who have a first-hand knowledge of the world of actual endeavor and are prepared to apply their several specialties to the current issues of the day.

Our corporations and industrial enterprises are asking for trained workers of scientific insight and generous opinions who can deal with problems of employment and the relations of the employer with labor and the public. These enterprises, through government regulation and the growth of labor organization, have become quasi-public institutions and can no longer be managed by older methods which ignore the social character of the modern world. . . .

The granting of the suffrage to women and the extension of women's interest into new and important spheres of public life will lead them to seek a better equipment [sic] both for power and service.

Our city, state and national governments are undertaking new functions which require for their efficient administration experts in finance, budget-making, education, charities, correction, public safety, public works, industrial services, public employment, purchasing, etc. The growing complexity and significance of international relations—commercial and diplomatic—make necessary a new treatment of these subjects. Newspapers and magazines are calling for writers and editors who can speak competently on the new problems of the day. In all these lines of endeavor scientific methods and independent research must be applied to the changing social order. The ideals, problems and methods of all classes must be studied and interpreted to the whole country.

Our greatly increased knowledge of human nature and of the history and characteristics of man's mind should be freely utilized in the process of reconstruction. How varied and impressive are the recent discoveries in anthropology and psychology, normal and abnormal, few people as yet realize. This type of information should be steadily increased and applied to the solution of social problems. Political Economy and Politics should be thoroughly reconsidered in the light of modern knowledge.

At present critical thought and investigation in the Political and Social sciences is too little organized to be effective; conservative thought, on the other hand, is everywhere fully organized and in a position to defend and perpetuate itself in a way to hamper and to discourage thoroughgoing reform.

While ever increasing attention is given to the Social and Political sciences in our colleges and universities, and much excellent work is being done, the circumstances under which investigation is carried on are by no means so favorable to scientific progress as they should be. The legal control of all our institutions is placed in the hands of bodies of trustees, composed for the most part of men whose views of political, social, religious and moral questions are in no way in advance of those of the average respectable citizen.

Their tendency is therefore rather to defend established thought than to encourage a fundamental reconsideration of long accepted ideals and standards. Our college and university presidents are pathetically responsible to an uncritical public constituency made up of trustees, parents, alumni, prospective donors and casual newspaper reporters and editors. The one consideration that they can always safely neglect is the scientific conscience of the members of their faculties.

Our larger institutions, where the Social and Political sciences receive the most attention, have developed a peculiar obstacle to free investigation as an inevitable result of their great size and complexity and the variety of their aims. The great universities embrace in a single organization undergraduate colleges, graduate departments, scientific, technical and professional schools, all of which have to be held together and conducted by a particular class of officers, who rarely teach or engage in scientific investigation, but who devote a great part of their time and thought to the exigencies of administration. Simplicity, uniformity and routine inevitably appear to them the essentials of university organization, rather than the unaccountable enthusiasm of scientific progress, and the spontaneity and variety of methods which characterize the best teaching. They unwittingly hamper the free expansion of education by their well-meant attempts to standardize it, and they often fruitlessly dissipate the energies of the more original men in the institution.

Our technical and professional schools have won for themselves a fair degree of freedom and autonomy. . . . As yet the Social and Political sciences have not had the benefit of any such emancipation. Their findings are judged from the standpoint of the religious, moral, social and economic standards and conventions, the class and race prejudices which we have received from the past. It is obvious that all scientific research, whatever its field of operation, should be directed not chiefly to the support of accepted ideas, but to the acquisition of new ones, and to the ways in which new knowledge may be applied to remedy existing evils and meet the ever growing needs of mankind. . . .

The Social and Political sciences are treated either as a sort of expansion of the ancient liberal arts in a college or are organized in a separate group of courses attended by *undergraduate* boys and girls as well as by older men and women. This subjects their presentation to all or most of the restraints of convention and propriety imposed quite properly upon undergraduate instruction.

Owing to such circumstances, students receive degrees in economics without ever visiting a factory, or wrestling first hand with any employment problems or attending an open session of a trade union. They are given degrees in finance without being required to walk through a comptroller's office or spend a day in a bond house or a bank. They are made doctors in political science before they have seen either the Board of Aldermen or the Congress of the United States in session. Remote as they are from contemporary life, our universities are not likely to take leadership in the coming days of reconstruction. . . .

The answer is, by establishing an institution free from the ancient embarrassments, where well qualified investigators and thinkers can enjoy the advantage of one another's thought and discoveries, and where they can talk freely upon any theme they judge fit to such grown up and responsible men and women as may wish to seek their instruction. Such a group of teachers and investigators should be emancipated from suspected obligations to donors, trustees and university management in general. They should have before them the exhortation of Lord Bacon to "know their own strength and own weakness both; and take one from the other light of invention, and not fire of contradiction; and esteem of the inquisition of truth as an enterprise, and not as a quality or ornament." They could in a short time build up a new school as powerful in modern life as some of the great universities were in the Middle Ages.

Writing a First Draft of History

Some progressive leaders lived long enough to record their own recollections about what their groups and movements accomplished. These accounts served as something of a first draft of history as well as a source for future historians.

A group of activist women formed the New York Consumers' League in 1891 to secure decreased hours, better pay, and easier working conditions for women in the textile trades and mercantile establishments. They believed that businesses would improve their practices if their customers demanded it. The league focused on women working in textile factories and factory stores. It promulgated a statement of acceptable working conditions and salaries for a "fair house."

As was often the case, New York was a model for the rest of the nation. The National Consumers' League (headquartered in New York City) soon grew out of it as well as leagues in other states and cities.

Social worker and labor activist Maud Nathan (1862–1946) served as president of the New York Consumers' League from 1897 to 1927. Her 1926 book, The Story of an Epochmaking Movement, *traced the origin and development of the league, its strategies and tactics, and its progress. She rather generously (to the point of exaggeration) credited the league with much of that progress. More objectively, she described the league's role in raising public consciousness and demand for change.*

In the book's concluding chapter, "Present-Day Conditions," she focused on progress for women working in department stores.

∼

From *The Story of an Epochmaking Movement* (1926)
by Maud Nathan

[Beginning in 1891,] the Consumers' League was not only educating the purchasing public, its spirit was invading the consciousness of employers as well. No longer were we obliged to plead for much-needed reforms. Merchants began to vie with each other in giving more humane attention to the needs of their employees. In the old days sales women thought of vacations with a sense of dread. They were days without pay. The employers considered a reduction of the force of clerks a necessary economy during the dull season, whilst priding themselves upon granting a vacation to their employees.

Today, no self-respecting merchant juggles with his conscience in this wise. A week's vacation with pay is the rule in all first-class establishments, and two weeks with pay are frequently given. The modern merchant considers the welfare of his employees. A new position has sprung into being: The "Social Secretary" has been ensconced in some of the stores. It is difficult to define her duties; she stands in the relation of "Store Mother" to the girls.

In the old days a working girl could feel no assurance that faithful service and increasing efficiency would receive their due meed [reward] of recognition. As an illustration of this I may well tell of an incident which came to the knowledge of the Consumers' League. A department store, moving into larger and showier quarters, advertised for saleswomen, offering what was then considered a weekly wage beyond that of its competitors. Many girls, tempted by the larger salary, left their assured positions and entered the new establishment. After a few weeks, when the éclat [excitement] incident to the opening of the new store had subsided, these girls were dismissed and cheaper labour employed. This was in the middle of the dull season, when it was difficult to find other employment, and their former positions had been filled by others. Today a young woman entering a mercantile establishment does so with the reasonable confidence that "if she makes good" and desires to make this her life work, she has every opportunity afforded her for advancement. The progressive merchant of to-day appreciates the value of efficiency in his business and is willing to pay for it. He carries this even to the point of a form of cooperation. A few firms throughout the country have established profit-sharing and have inaugurated a policy of self-government. Employees as well as employers are represented on the Board of Directors of such establishments.

Those who, in recent years, have secured positions in any of the large department stores consider themselves fortunate, for they are able, without deduction of salary, to leave the hot, dusty city on a Friday evening to seek the shelter of green trees in near-by country resorts; to get a dip in the cool surf of the ocean, or to nestle under the protecting wing of some mountain. For department stores, as well as all stores claiming the prestige of being considered first class, have been closed during July and August from Friday at 5 p. m. until Monday at 9 a. m. for the last few years. As in former years, the palatial houses and apartments are closed for the summer months, their owners away: over the seas or at seashore or mountain side. Now these vacations have a zest which had been lacking in the old days, for to-day these dwellers in luxurious homes, whose wealth and position spell power, have used this power in order to secure for their less fortunate neighbours the opportunity for refreshment of body and soul.

It requires no vivid imagination to depict the enormous difference this one portentous fact of a week-end vacation during two months of the year makes in the lives of thousands—literally hundreds of thousands—of working girls. Although I have specially stressed the benefit of the *working girls*, it must not be overlooked that, when an industrial establishment closes its doors for a week-end holiday, every employee connected with the business benefits. Today business men realize that the benefit of these week-end holidays accrues not only to the workers, but to their employers, as well; for the employees bring to their work on Monday morning a freshness and zest which make for efficiency and better service. No longer is salesmanship considered "unskilled labour"; there are schools of salesmanship in many of the department stores, and wages, although still low in many stores, considering the rise in the cost of living, yet are considerably higher than the minimum wage demanded by the Consumers' League in its first Standard of a Fair House. Thirty-five years ago it would have been impossible for a society girl to become a shop-girl without feeling that she had lost caste; the conditions of her work were such that she would have been subjected to mortification and humiliation; the physical strain for one gently bred would have been unendurable. Today, young women of good family and high social position are often found taking such "jobs" in order to gain experience. Employers are glad to engage such young women, realizing that their charm, refinement, and family connections attract customers. . . .

No longer is it necessary to drag soap boxes up from a cellar and hide them behind a counter in order to have something to drop upon when overcome with fatigue; now there are seats behind counters, attached to the fixtures so that they cannot be removed. And no longer do floor-walkers consider it "unbusinesslike" to have saleswomen seated until a customer approaches the counter. No longer need a fainting saleswoman be stretched on a concrete floor of a sub-basement. Today, in the leading department stores, the firms show with pride their fine rest rooms (often on the top floor, with open-air loggia on the roof) including rooms where their employees' teeth can be attended to by a good dentist, their feet cared for by a pedicure, a physician's office where they can consult a good physician, and a trained nurse to care for them if they feel tired or slightly ill. In some stores there are basketball, a piano, magazines, papers, and every luxury. Indeed, such rooms might not unfittingly be compared with the lounge of a social club. There is to be found a well-appointed restaurant in charge of a competent woman where, for a trifling sum, a hot or cold luncheon may be procured, or a beverage served with the luncheon brought from home. These luncheons need not be gulped down, standing with anxious eye fixed on a clock, lest the ten or fifteen minutes be exceeded; today there are chairs and tables, and the girls can enjoy their luncheon leisurely, knowing that they have from forty-five minutes to an hour for their meal. . . .

The fundamental idea of the Consumers' League was to arouse a public conscience, with a view to creating a public opinion that would become a dynamic force for good in the community. We started the movement with zeal and enthusiasm to correct certain specific evils which had been brought to our attention. But not one of that small group of women who started the movement dreamed of the enormous power that they were setting in motion.

We educated merchants to see the wisdom of granting vacations. If working girls were to have vacations, where were these vacations to be spent? The vacation houses which have sprung up all over the country, by sea, by lake, by mountain side, are the answer to this question.

We educated merchants to demand efficiency and skill. If efficiency and skill are demanded in industry, where are the workers to obtain the necessary comfort and seclusion which would give them the rest and refreshment for the next day's work? Like magic, working girls' hotels have been founded to meet this new need. In New York, the Association to Promote Proper Housing for Girls has made a special study of this problem, inaugurating community clubs for the girls.

While the Consumers' League has been responsible for pioneer work in many directions, it has always been glad to have other organizations formed for the purpose of carrying on any special piece of work. In this way, an influential group of men and women formed the National Child Labour Association, with branches in several states, in order to concentrate on the abolition of child labour. Another group of men and women organized to promote legislation looking towards the furtherance of better labour conditions, the Association for Labour Legislation. A third group, consisting of well-known captains of industry and labour leaders, cooperated under the name of the Civic Federation, with the view to a better understanding between capital and labour and to further their common interests. We aroused the federations of women's clubs and the woman suffrage organizations to the importance of appointing committees on the industry of women and children, to study local conditions, and to cooperate with the Consumers' League in our work to better these conditions.

It has been left for me to tell the story of the Consumers' League. In looking back over the thirty-six years that have passed since the movement was first started, I am impressed with the entire change of attitude of mind of all the constituents that form the industrial world. I do not claim for the Consumers' League credit for the many remedial agencies organized, or for all the welfare legislation enacted. But I do feel that I am not claiming too much in asserting that to the Consumers' League must be paid the tribute of having aroused a dormant public conscience. It has made clear a sense of personal responsibility in the economic world, and it has created and crystallized a public opinion in the community which makes for high standards. Because of this, I feel justified in calling it an epoch-making movement.

Note

1. "The Present State of Historical Writing in America," American Antiquarian Society, Proceedings (Worcester, MA: American Antiquarian Society, 1910), 18.

Sources

Beard, Charles A., *An Economic Interpretation of the Constitution of the United States* (New York: Macmillan, 1913), 15–18. Available at HathiTrust, https://catalog.hathitrust.org/Record/001141038.

Dewey, John, *The School and Society* (Chicago: University of Chicago Press, 1915), 155–59. Available at Internet Archive, https://archive.org/details/schoolsociety01dewe.

Draper, Andrew S., *No Mummified History in New York Schools* (Syracuse: C. W. Bardeen, Publisher, 1912) 6–8, 21–25, 28–32. Available at HathiTrust, https://catalog.hathitrust.org/Record/006510888.

Hall, Herman Hagaman, *The Hudson-Fulton Celebration, 1909: The Fourth Annual Report of the Hudson-Fulton Celebration Commission to the Legislature* (Albany: J. B. Lyon, 1910), "Introduction," 3–8. Available at HathiTrust, https://catalog.hathitrust.org/Record/001262563.

Nathan, Maud, *The Story of an Epochmaking Movement* (New York: Doubleday, Page & Co., 1926), "Present-Day Conditions," 106–10, 117–18. Available at HathiTrust, https://catalog.hathitrust.org/Record/001106586.

New York State Education Department, "American History," Introduction, *Syllabus for Secondary Schools* (Albany: State Education Department, 1910), 100–103. Available at HathiTrust, https://catalog.hathitrust.org/Record/008641110.

New School for Social Research, *A Proposal for an Independent School of Social Science for Men and Women* (pamphlet, n.p., 1919), 3–10, New School for Social Research, http://newschoolhistories.org/hstrs/the-founding-1919.

Robinson, James Harvey, "The New History," *Proceedings of the American Philosophical Society* 50 (May–August 1911), 179–90. Available at JSTOR, https://www.jstor.org/stable/9840330.

Selected Bibliography

Many articles, books, and reports are available online these days. An excellent place to start is the Online Books Page (https://onlinebooks.library.upenn.edu). It has links to millions of books, periodicals, and other publications that are available online.

Many of the Online Books Page's references are to HathiTrust. (http://www.hathitrust.org), a rich source of digital version of materials and the one I have cited most often in this book.

Google Books (https://books.google.com) and the Internet Archive (https//archive.org) are also very important.

The following books were particularly important:

Argersinger, Joanne. *The Triangle Fire: A Brief History with Documents*. New York: Bedford/St. Marks, 2016.

Arnbinder, Tyler. *City of Dreams: The 400 Year Epic History of Immigrant New York*. New York: Mariner Books, 1917.

Aronson, Amy. *Crystal Eastman: A Revolutionary Life*. New York: Oxford University Press, 2020.

Bailey, Liberty Hyde. *The Country Life Movement in the United States*. New York: Macmillan, 1915.

Baker, Paula. *The Moral Frameworks of Public Life: Gender, Politics, and the State in Rural New York, 1870–1930*. New York: Oxford University Press, 1991.

Berfield, Susan. *The Hour of Fate: Theodore Roosevelt, J. P. Morgan, and the Battle to Transform American Capitalism*. New York: Bloomsbury, 2020.

Blatch, Harriott Stanton, and Alma Lutz. *Challenging Years: The Memoirs of Harriott Stanton Blatch*. New York: G. P. Putman's Sons, 1940.

Catt, Carrie Chapman, and Nettie Rogers Schuler. *Woman Suffrage and Politics: The Inner Story of the Suffrage Movement*. New York: Charles Scribner's Sons, 1926.

Chessman, G. Wallace. *Governor Theodore Roosevelt: The Albany Apprenticeship, 1898–1901.* Cambridge: Harvard University Press, 1965.

Croly, Herbert. *Progressive Democracy.* New York: Macmillan, 1909.

———. *The Promise of American Life.* New York: Macmillan, 1914.

Danelski, Javid J., and Joseph S. Tulchin. *The Autobiographical Notes of Charles Evans Hughes.* Cambridge: Harvard University Press, 1973.

Daniels, Doris Groshen. *Always a Sister: The Feminism of Lillian D. Wald.* New York: The Feminist Press, 1989.

Davis, Allen F. *Spearheads for Reform: The Social Settlements and the Progressive Movement, 1890–1914.* New York: Oxford University Press, 1967.

Dearstyne, Bruce. *The Crucible of Public Policy: New York Courts in the Progressive Era.* Albany: State University of New York Press, 2022.

———. *The Spirit of New York: Defining Events in the Empire State's History.* 2nd ed. Albany: State University of New York Press, 2022.

DeForest, Robert, and Lawrence Veiller, eds. *The Tenement House Problem, Including the Report of the New York State Tenement House Commission of 1900.* 2 vols. New York: Macmillan, 1903.

Downey, Kirstin. *The Woman Behind the New Deal: The Life of FDR's Secretary of Labor and His Moral Conscience.* New York: Doubleday, 2009.

Draper, Andrew S. *American Education.* New York: Houghton, Mifflin Company, 1909.

DuBois, Ellen Carol. *Harriott Stanton Blatch and the Winning of Woman Suffrage.* New Haven: Yale University Press, 1997.

Dye, Nancy Schrom. *As Equals and as Sisters: Feminism, the Labor Movement, and the Women's Trade Union League of New York.* Columbia: University of Missouri Press, 1980.

Eagen, Kathleen Johnson. *The Hudson-Fulton Celebration: New York's River Festival of 1909 and the Making of a Metropolis.* New York: Fordham University Press, 2009.

Eastman, Crystal. *Work Accidents and the Law.* New York: Russell Sage Foundation, 1910.

Eisenstadt, Peter, ed. *The Encyclopedia of New York State.* Syracuse: Syracuse University Press, 2005.

Ellis, David M., James A. Frost, Harold C. Syrett, and Henry J. Carman. *A History of New York State.* Ithaca: Cornell University Press, 1967.

Felt, Jeremy P. *Hostages of Fortune: Child Labor Reform in New York State.* Syracuse: Syracuse University Press, 1965.

Giunta, Edyige, and Mary Anne Trasciatti, eds. *Talking to the Girls: Intimate and Political Essays on the Triangle Shirtwaist Factory Fire.* New York: New Village Press, 2022.

Goldman, Emma. *Living My Life.* New York: Alfred A. Knopf, 1931.

Goldmark, Josephine. *Fatigue and Efficiency: A Study in Industry.* New York: Survey Associates, 1913.

———. *Impatient Crusader: Florence Kelley's Life Story.* Urbana: University of Illinois Press, 1953.
Golway, Terry. *Machine Made: Tammany Hall and the Creation of Modern American Politics.* New York: Liveright, 2014.
Goodier, Susan, and Karen Pastorello. *Women Will Vote.* Ithaca: Cornell University Press, 2017.
Goodwin, Doris Kearns. *The Bully Pulpit: Theodore Roosevelt, William Howard Taft, and the Golden Age of Journalism.* New York: Simon and Schuster, 2013.
Greenwald, Richard. *The Triangle Fire, Protocols of Peace, and Industrial Democracy in Progressive Era New York.* Philadelphia: Temple University Press, 2005.
Hart, Tanya. *Health in the City: Race, Poverty, and the Negotiation of Women's Health in New York City, 1915–1930.* New York: NYU Press, 2015.
Hochschild, Adam. *American Midnight: The Great War, a Violent Peace, and Democracy's Forgotten Crisis.* New York: Mariner Books, 2022.
Hofstadter, Richard. *The Age of Reform: From Bryan to F. D. R.* New York: Vintage, 1955.
Howe, Irving. *World of Our Fathers: The Journey of the East European Jews to America and the Life They Found and Made.* New York: Simon and Schuster, 1976.
Jackson, Kenneth T., ed. *The Encyclopedia of New York City.* 2nd ed. New Haven: Yale University Press, 2010.
Kaplan, Paul. *New York in the Progressive Era: Social Reforms and Cultural Upheaval, 1890–1920.* New York: History Press, 2021.
Kearns, Marguerite. *An Unfinished Revolution: Edna Buckman Kearns and the Struggle for Women's Rights.* Albany: State University of New York Press, 2021.
Kelley, Florence. *Modern Industry: In Relation to the Family, Health, Education, Morality.* New York: Longmans, Green, 1914.
———. *Notes of Sixty Years: The Autobiography of Florence Kelley.* Chicago: C. H. Kerr, 1986.
Kessner, Tomas. *The Golden Door: Italian and Jewish Mobility in New York City, 1880–1915.* New York: Oxford University Press, 1977.
Keyssar, Alexander. *The Right to Vote: The Contested History of Democracy.* New York: Basic Books, 2009.
Klein, Milton M., ed. *The Empire State: A History of New York.* Ithaca: Cornell University Press, 2001.
Kraus, Harry P. *The Settlement House Movement in New York City, 1886–1914.* New York: Arno Press, 1980.
Kroeger, Brooke. *Undaunted: How Women Changed American Journalism.* New York: Alfred A. Knopf, 2023.
Kuhl, Michelle. *The Progressive Era for Whom? African Americans in the Age of Reform, 1890–1920.* New York: Oxford University Press, 2020.
Lears, Jackson. *Rebirth of a Nation: Modern America, 1877–1920.* New York: Harper Collins, 2009.

Lehrer, Susan. *Origins of Protective Labor Legislation for Women 1905–1925.* Albany: State University of New York Press, 1987.

Lemak, Jennifer, and Ashley Hopkins-Benton, *Votes for Women: Celebrating New York's Suffrage Centennial.* Albany: State University of New York Press, 2017.

Lepore, Jill. *These Truths: A History of the United States.* New York: W. W. Norton, 2018.

Lifflander, Matthew L. *The Impeachment of Governor Sulzer: A Story of American Politics.* Albany: State University of New York Press, 2012.

Lippman, Walter. *Drift and Mastery: An Attempt to Diagnose the Current Unrest.* New York: Mitchell Kennerley, 1914.

———. *A Preface to Politics.* New York: Mitchell Kennerley, 1914.

Lubove, Roy. *The Progressives and the Slums: Tenement House Reform in New York City, 1890–1917.* Pittsburgh: University of Pittsburgh Press, 1962.

Mangione, Jerre, and Ben Morreale. *La Storia: Five Centuries of the Italian American Experience.* New York: Harper Collins, 1992.

Meacham, Jon. *The Soul of America: The Battle for Our Better Angels.* New York: Random House, 2018.

McCormick, Richard L. *From Realignment to Reform: Political Change in New York State, 1893–1910.* Ithaca: Cornell University Press, 1981.

McGeer, Michael. *The Decline of Popular Politics: The American North, 1865–1928.* New York: Oxford University Press, 1988.

———. *A Fierce Discontent: The Rise and Fall of the Progressive Movement in America, 1870–1920.* New York: Free Press, 2003.

Moore, Deborah Dash, Jeffrey S. Gurock, Annie Polland, Howard B. Rock, Daniel Soyer, and Diana L. Linden. *Jewish New York: The Remarkable Story of a City and Its People.* New York: New York University Press, 2017.

Morris, Edmund. *Theodore Rex.* New York: Random Books, 2001.

Nokov, Julie. *Constituting Workers, Protecting Women: Gender, Law and Labor in the Progressive Era and the New Deal Years.* Ann Arbor: University of Michigan Press, 2001.

Orleck, Annelise. *Common Sense and a Little Fire: Women and Working-Class Politics in the United States, 1900–1965.* Chapel Hill: University of North Carolina Press, 1995.

Painter, Nell Irvin. *Standing at Armageddon: The United States, 1877–1919.* New York: Norton, 2008.

Pastorello, Karen. *The Progressives: Activism and Reform in American Society, 1883–1917.* New York: Wiley-Blackwell, 2013.

Plunkett, George Washington, and William L. Riordon, *Plunkett of Tammany Hall: A Series of Very Plain Talks on Very Practical Politics. . . . Recorded by William L. Riordon.* New York: McClure, Phillips, 1905.

Polland, Annie, and Daniel Sover. *Emerging Metropolis: New York Jews in the Age of Immigration, 1840–1920.* New York: New York University Press, 2015.

Putnam, Robert D. *The Upswing: How America Came Together a Century Ago and How We Can Do It Again.* New York: Simon and Schuster, 2020.
Rauschenbusch, Walter. *Christianity and the Social Crisis.* New York: Macmillan, 1908.
———. *Christianizing the Social Order.* New York: Macmillan, 1912.
Recchiuti, John Louis. *Civic Engagement: Social Science and Progressive-Era Reform in New York City.* Philadelphia: University of Pennsylvania Press, 2006.
Reitano, Janet. *New York State: Peoples, Places, and Priorities: A Concise History with Sources.* New York: Routledge, 2015.
Riis, Jacob A. *How the Other Half Lives: Studies Among the Tenements of New York.* New York: Charles Scribner's Sons, 1890.
Roosevelt, Theodore. *The Autobiography of Theodore Roosevelt.* New York: Scribner's, 1913.
Sanger, Margaret. *An Autobiography.* New York: Cooper Square Press, 1938.
———. *Woman and the New Race.* New York: Truth Publishing, 1920.
Schurman, Jacob Gould, ed. *Addresses and Papers of Charles Evans Hughes, Governor of New York, 1906-1908.* New York: G. P. Putman's Sons, 1908.
———. *Addresses and Papers of Charles Evans Hughes, 1906-1916.* New York: G. P. Putnam's Sons, 1916.
Smith, Alfred E. *Up to Now: An Autobiography by Alfred E. Smith.* Garden City: Garden City Publishing Company, 1929.
Stein, Leon. *The Triangle Fire.* Ithaca: Cornell University Press, 2011.
Trounstine, Jessica. *Political Monopolies in American Cities: The Rise and Fall of Bosses and Reformers.* New York: Oxford University Press, 2008.
———. *Segregation by Design: Local Politics and Inequality in America.* New York: Oxford University Press, 2016.
Van Kleeck, Mary. *Women in the Bookbinding Trades.* New York: Survey Associates, 1913.
Villard, Oswald Garrison. *Fighting Years: Memoirs of a Fighting Editor.* New York: Harcourt Brace, 1939.
Von Drehle, David. *Triangle: The Fire That Changed America.* New York: Grove Press, 2003.
Wald, Lillian. *The House on Henry Street.* New York: Holt, 1915.
Wallace, Mike. *Greater Gotham: A History of New York City From 1898 to 1919.* New York: Oxford University Press, 2017.
Welch, Richard F. *King of the Bowery: Big Tim Sullivan, Tammany Hall, and New York City from the Gilded Age to the Progressive Era.* Albany: State University of New York Press, 2008.
Wesser, Robert. *Charles Evans Hughes: Politics and Reform in New York, 1905-1910.* Ithaca: Cornell University Press, 1967.
Weyl, Walter. *The New Democracy: An Essay on Certain Political and Economic Tendencies in the United States.* New York: Macmillan, 1912.

———. *A Response to Progressivism: The Democratic Party and New York Politics, 1902–1918*. New York: New York University Press, 1986.

Wiebe, Robert H. *The Search for Order, 1877–1920*. New York: Hill and Wang, 1967.

Woloch, Nancy. *A Class by Herself: Protective Laws for Women Workers, 1890s–1990s*. Princeton: Princeton University Press, 2015.

Wolraich, Michael. *Unreasonable Men: Theodore Roosevelt and the Republican Rebels Who Created Progressive Politics*. New York: Palgrave Macmillan, 2014.

Yellowitz, Irwin. *Labor and the Progressive Movement in New York State, 1897–1916*. Ithaca: Cornell University Press, 1965.

Index

Note: Page numbers followed by *i* indicate illustration.

ACLU, 6, 174
Albany, NY, 7–10, 72–76, 90–95, 118, 163, 73, 259, 264–65, 322, 326
Albany–New York City first flight, 72–76
Allds, Jotham P., 90–92
American Civil Liberties Union (ACLU). *See* ACLU
American Education (Draper), 118
American Federation of Labor, 305–8
An American in the Making . . . (Ravage), 201–5
Anarchist, 3, 48–50, 53, 110–11, 203–4
Anderson, William H., 140–42
Anti-Saloon League, 5, 140–42
Aviation, 72–76

Bailey, Liberty Hyde, 43–48
Bakeshop Law, 13
Ballot reform, 29, 100
Banking, 4, 20, 255, 270–75
Barge Canal, 61–64
Baseball, 69–72
Beard, Charles A., 192, 314–20, 333
Beard, Mary Ritter, 162–66
Biggs, Hermann M., 146–51

Birth control, 48, 143–46, 180–85
Blatch, Harriot Stanton, 9
Blaustein, David, 191–95
Buffalo, NY, 3, 55–64, 128, 210, 268, 295

Cahan, Abraham, 188–91
Canals, New York, 56, 61–64,
Castle Garden, 190, 206
Catt, Carrie Chapman, 169–74
Censorship, 118, 143–47
Chandler, George F., 152–53
Charitable assistance, 30, 128–32
Child labor, advocates for reform, 282–84; compulsory education and, 118–21; Kelley, Florence, 9, 166, 278–84; laws, 106, 158, 282–84; New York Child Labor Committee, 11, 283; social reform and, 210, 279–84; Wald, Lillian, 9, 117, 136–40, 23
Christianity and the Social Crisis (Rauschenbusch), 34–39
The City Workers' World in America (Simkhovitz), 30–34
Civics, 113, 178, 193, 321–30; Americanization and, 320–23

350 | Index

Collective bargaining, 179–80, 278, 301, 305–10
Communist Labor Party, 110–11
Comstock, Anthony, 143–47
Conger, Benn, 90–93
Consumers League, 164
The Country Life Movement in the United States (Bailey), 43–48
The Crisis: A Record of the Darker Races (DuBois), 244–50
Croly, Herbert, 26
Cubist, 40–41
Cultural Pluralism, 214–19
The Curtiss Aviation Book, (Curtiss), 72–76
Curtiss, Glenn Hammond, 56, 72–76, Albany Flyer, 72–76

DeForest, Robert W., 124–28
"Democracy Versus the Melting Pot: A Study of American Nationality" (Kallen), 215
DePew, Chauncey, 93–95
Dewey, John, 330–37
Direct Primary, 7–9, 95–108
Dix, John A., 102–4
Dorr, Rheta Childe, 158–62
Draper, Andrew Sloan and, 118–19, 323–30
Drift and Mastery (Lippmann), 23–26
DuBois, W. E. B., 221i, 228, 244–50
Due process, right of, 13, 264

Eastman, Crystal, 9, 174–78
Eastman, George, 79–81
Eastman Kodak, 56, 79–81
Ebbets Field, 69–72
An Economic Interpretation of the Constitution (Beard), 318–20
Education, 177–78, 237, 244–45, 279–80; civic, 321–30; higher, 333–36; history and, 336–41; New Yorker and 118–21; reform, 330–37; secondary, 327–30
Elections, 95–99, 104, 110; women and, 166–74
Ellis Island, 187i, 187, 198, 202, 206
Enterprises, aviation, 72–76; Barge Canal, 61–64; Grand Central Terminal 76–79; Pan-American Exposition, 55i, 55–61; subway, 64–69
Equal rights for women, 166–78; campaign, 8–9, 157; conventions, 165–66; National Woman Suffrage Association, 172–73. *See also* Suffrage
Erie Canal, 56, 61–64

Fatigue and Efficiency (Goldmark), 298–302
Fifth Avenue, New York City, 19i
Fourteenth Amendment, 13–14
Free speech, 48, 51–52

Glynn, Martin H., 99–102
Goldman, Emma, 48–53
Goldmark, Josephine, 298–302
Gompers, Samuel, 305–8
Governor's Island, 75
Grand Central Terminal, 76–79
Grant, Madison, 211–14

Half a Man: The Status of the Negro in New York (Ovington), 222–26
Half Moon (replica), 313i
Harlem, 67–68, 221–22, 226–38
Harlem: The Cultural Center (Johnson), 230–34
Harriman, Edward H., 94
Hearst, William R., 93, 259
Hedrick, Burton J., 262–66
Henry Street Settlement House, 136–40

Higher education, 333–36
History, study of; celebrations and, 313, 320–23; civics and, 330–33; economics and, 318–20; higher education and, 333–36; interpretation, 318–19; new school of, 336–40; rewriting, 317–18; social development, 323–26, 330–33
The House on Henry Street (Wald), 137–40
How the Other Half Lives (Riis), 122–24
Hudson-Fulton Celebration, 313, 320–23
Hughes, Charles Evans, 253*i*, 5, 7–8, 12; business regulations. 258–61; direct primaries, 95–100; insurance reforms, 253–58; progressive reforms, 87, 102, 205; Public Service Commission, 261–69; workmen's compensation, 295–98

Immigrants, 188–91; assimilation, 191–95; assistance, 195–201; challenges, 205–210; Cultural Pluralism, 214–19; Italian, 195–201; Jewish, 17, 165, 179, 188–95, 199, 201–5
Industrial Code, 278, 286–91
Industrialization, 23–26
International Ladies Garment Workers Union (ILGWU), 178–80, 301–10

Jewish immigrant, 17, 165, 179, 188–95, 199, 201–5
Jeffrey, Hester, 9,
Johnson, James Weldon, 230–34

Kallen, Horace M., 215–19
Kelley, Florence, 83*i*, 9, 166, 278–84
Kellor, Frances, 205–12
Kodak. *See* Eastman Kodak

Labor reform, 99–100; child labor, 282–84; collective bargaining, 305–10; factories, 287–91; industrial codes, 278,0281, 286–91. *See also* unions, women workers' compensation, 295–301
Ladies Garment Workers, 178–80, 301–10
Lippmann, Water, 23–23
Locke, Alain, 226–30

McClure, Samuel S., 87–90
McClure's Magazine, 11, 87–90
McDougald, Elise Douglas, 221*i*, 238–44
McKinley, William, 56–57
"Making of an American" (Outlook) (Blaustein), 191–95
Melting Pot (Kallen), 214–16
Miller, Nathan, 7, 108
Money trust, 269–75
Modern Industry in Relation to the Family, Health, Education Morality (Kelley), 278–82
Morgan, J. P., 94, 269, 270–75
Muckrakers, 11, 20, 87–92, 254, 262
Mulberry Street, 19*i*

NAACP, 6, 9, 222, 230, 234, 244, 278
Nathan, Maud, 237–41
National Progressive Party of New York, 102–8
National Woman Suffrage Association, 172–73
New Democracy (Weyl), 26–30
The New Negro: An Interpretation (Locke), 226–30
New York Canal Improvement Committee, 61–64
New York Central Railroad, 56, 76–78, 93–96

New York Child Labor Committee
(NYCLC), 11, 283
New York City Charity Organization
Society, 128–36
New York City Subway System, 64–69
New York State Board of Health, 1, 8,
12, 146–51; Public Health Council,
146–51
New York State Bureau of Industries
and Immigration, 206–11
New York State Commissioner of
Labor, 210, 289
New York State Constitutional
Convention (1915), 100–1
New York State Court of Appeals,
13–14, 295
New York State Department of
Health, 146–51
New York State Education
Department, 324–30; Draper,
Andrew Sloan and, 118–19
New York State Factory Investigating
Commission (FIC), 277i, 12,
277–78, 287–91
New York State Joint Legislative
Committee Investigating Seditious
Activities, 108–14
New York State Labor Department,
107, 210, 278, 283–85
New York State Police. *See* New York
State Troopers
New York Progressive Party, 102–9
New York State Public Health
Council, 146–51
New York State Public Service
Commission, 261–69
New York State Troopers, 12, 151–54
New York Woman Suffrage Party,
165–69
*No Mummified History in New York
Schools* (Draper), 323–26

Odell, Benjamin, 94, 124
*Official Catalogue and Guide Book to
the Pan-American Exposition*, 56–61
The Old World in the New (Ross),
214–19
Ovington, Mary White, 222–26

Pan-American Exposition, Buffalo,
55i, 55–61
The Passing of the Great Race (Grant),
211–14
Patriotism, 320–33
Perkins, Frances, 164, 288
Phillips, David Graham, 20–23, 93–95
Plunkett of Tammany Hall (Plunkett
and Riordon), 84–88
Plunkett, George W., 84–88
Politics and government, corruption,
89–95; direct primaries, 7–9,
95–108; reform, 83–87, 108–114;
suffrage and, 172–74; Tammany
Hall, 84–90, 99–108, 169–74
Poverty, 10, 27, 31–34, 107; 121–28;
charities and 128–37; women and,
302–5
"Proceedings of the Nineteenth
National Convention of the
Anti-Saloon League of America"
(Anderson), 140–42
Progressivism, 1–5, 14, 19, 118–24;
Christian ethics and, 34–39;
incremental progress, 26–30;
modern trends, 39–43; tenor of the
times, 19–26
Prohibition, 5, 7, 140–42

Racial justice; black women and, 238–
44; DuBois and, 244–50; Harlem
Renaissance, 230–34; New Yorkers
and, 226–26; social equality, 244–
50

Raines, John, 90–91, 141–42
Raines Law, 141–42
Rauschenbusch, Walter, 34–39
Ravage, Marcus Eli, 201–5
Regulations, 7–13; courts and, 11–13, 14, 278; government, 50; insurance companies, 254–59; New York State Public Service Commission, 261–69; Sanitation and, 11–13, 89, 123, 127, 132, 149–50, 208–9, 286–93; trusts, 269–75
Reign of Guilt (Phillips), 20–23
Report of the Commission of Immigration of the State of New York, 205–12
Riis, Jacob, A. 121–24
Riordon, William L., 84–87
The Rise of David Levinsky (Cahan), 188–91
Robinson, James Harvey, 314–18
Rochester, N.Y., 79, 178–80
Roosevelt, Franklin D., 7
Roosevelt, Theodore, art and, 39–43; canal and, 61–64; environment and, 43; Muckraking, 87–88; New York governor and, 3, 5, 11–12, 124; Progressive Party, 102–8
Root, Elihu, 4
Ross, Edward A., 214–19
Rumball, Catherine, 178–81
Rumball, Edwin, 178–81
Rural policing, 151–54

Sanger, Margaret, 157i, 180–85
Sanitation, 11–13, 89, 123, 127, 132, 149–50, 208–9, 286–93
Schneiderman, Rose, 284–86
The School and Society (Dewey), 330–33
Schuler, Nettie Rogers, 170–74
Scott, Miriam Finn, 301–4

Seditious activities, 108–14
Settlement houses, New York City, 9. 33–36; Henry Street Settlement, 136–40. *See also* visiting nurses, Wald, Lillian
Simkhovitz, Mary K., 30–34
Smallpox, 14, 149
Smith, Alfred E., 7–8, 101, 108, 286; government reorganization and, 12–13
Social gospel, 34–36
Socialism, 20, 52, 148, 203
Socialist Labor Party, 7, 28, 110
Society for the Protection of Italian Immigrants, 195–201
"Solving the Immigration Problem" (Speranza), 195–201
Speranza, Gino Carlo, 195–201
"The Spirit of the Girl Strikers" (*Outlook*) (Scott), 301–4
Stevens, Frank W., 266–69
The Story of an Epoch making Movement (Nathan), 237–41
Subway, New York City, 64–69
Suffrage; campaign, 157–60; equality, 158–62; history of woman suffrage movement, 157–60, 165–68; National Woman Suffrage Association, 172–73; New York Woman Suffrage Party, 165–69; voting and, 166–74; working, 178–81; Women's Rights Convention, 165–66. *See also* Women
Sulzer, William, 8, 99–102

Tammany Hall, 84–90, 99–108, 169–74; Glynn, Martin H., 99–102; honest graft, 84–87; Murphy, Charles F., 100–3
The Tenement House Problem (DeForest and Veiller), 124–28

Tenements, 121–28, 129–39, reforms, 124–28, 209–11, 231
"Treason of the Senate..." (Phillips), 93–95
Trusts, money, 269–75
Triangle Shirtwaist Factory Fire, 284–86; consequences of, 286–91

Unions, 33, 111; arbitration, 179–80, 278–81, 309–10; collective bargaining, 305–10; formation, 305–8; strikes, 301–5; working condition and, 9, 277*i*, 277–281
U.S.. Constitution, 348–20
U. S. Supreme Court, 13–14, 298
Utility regulation, 11, 258, 261–71

Van Kleeck, Mary, 291–95
Vanderbilt, Cornelius, 42, 94–95
Veiller, Lawrence, 124–28
Villard, Oswald Garrison, 90, 159
Visiting Nurses, 9, 117, 136–38, 283

Wagner, Robert, 286
Wald, Lillian, 117*i*, 9, 117, 136–40, 283
Weyl, Walter E., 26–30
What I Believe (Goldman), 49–53
White, Walter, 234–38
Whitman, Charles, 142, 151
Woman and the New Race (Sanger), 180–85

Woman's suffrage. *See* Suffrage
Woman Suffrage and Polities: The Inner Story of the Suffrage Movement (Catt and Schuler), 170–74
Women; birth control, 48, 143, 178–85; equality, 157–62; feminist, 174–78; labor movement, 178–80, 301–10 professions, 157–61; workplace safety, 291–95. *See also* New York State Factory Investigating Commission (FIC), Suffrage; working conditions, 83, 178–80, 301–10
Women in the Bookbinding Trade (Van Kleeck), 291–95
Women's Christian Temperance Union, 5, 165
Women's Trade Union League, 162–65, 285–86
Workers, 277–82; *See also* Child Labor; 261–69; conditions and, 9, 277*i*, 277–281
industrial code, 286–91; safety standards, 291–99. *See also* New York State Factory Investigating Commission (FIC), Workmen's compensation,
Workmen's compensation, 295–301
Working condition, 9, 277*i*, 277–281

About the Author

Bruce W. Dearstyne holds a BA in history from Hartwick College and a PhD in history from Syracuse University. He has taught history at SUNY Albany, SUNY Potsdam, and Russell Sage College. Dearstyne has written dozens of articles on history, archives, libraries, and related topics for several publications, including *History News,* AASLH *Technical Leaflets, Public Historian* (guest editor of two special issues), *New York History, New York Archives,* and *New York State Bar Association Journal.*

His books include *The Crucible of Public Policy: New York Courts in the Progressive Era* (State University of New York Press, 2022); *The Spirit of New York: Defining Events in the Empire State's History* (2nd ed., State University of New York Press, 2022), *Leading the Historical Enterprise: Strategic Creativity, Planning, and Advocacy for the Digital Age* (2015); *Managing Historical Records Programs* (2000); *Railroads and Railroad Regulation in New York State, 1903–1913* (1986); and *New York: Yesterday, Today, and Tomorrow* (joint author, 1990).

He served on the staff of the Office of State History and was a program director at the New York State Archives. He was also executive director of the National Association of Government Archives and Records Administrators. Dearstyne was professor at the College of Information Studies, University of Maryland, where he still serves as an adjunct professor. He was interim dean of the college and also directed the university's joint history and library science (HiLS) graduate program.

Dearstyne has written for the *Washington Post*'s Made by History site and the Society for Legal History's *The Docket.* He also writes blog articles for *Gotham Gazette,* New York History (now New York Almanack), and History News Network and opinion essays on history for the "Perspective" section of the Sunday Albany *Times Union.*

www.ingramcontent.com/pod-product-compliance
Lightning Source LLC
Chambersburg PA
CBHW031425230426
43668CB00007B/437